Orthodox Tradition and Human Sexuality

ORTHODOX CHRISTIANITY AND CONTEMPORARY THOUGHT

SERIES EDITORS
Ashley M. Purpura and Aristotle Papanikolaou

This series consists of books that seek to bring Orthodox Christianity into an engagement with contemporary forms of thought. Its goal is to promote (1) historical studies in Orthodox Christianity that are interdisciplinary, employ a variety of methods, and speak to contemporary issues; and (2) constructive theological arguments in conversation with patristic sources and that focus on contemporary questions ranging from the traditional theological and philosophical themes of God and human identity to cultural, political, economic, and ethical concerns. The books in the series explore both the relevancy of Orthodox Christianity to contemporary challenges and the impact of contemporary modes of thought on Orthodox self-understandings.

Orthodox Tradition and Human Sexuality

Thomas Arentzen, Ashley M. Purpura,
and Aristotle Papanikolaou
EDITORS

Foreword by
Metropolitan Ambrosius, Helsinki

FORDHAM UNIVERSITY PRESS
New York • *2022*

Copyright © 2022 Fordham University Press

All rights reserved. No part of this publication may be reproduced, stored in a retrieval system, or transmitted in any form or by any means—electronic, mechanical, photocopy, recording, or any other—except for brief quotations in printed reviews, without the prior permission of the publisher.

Fordham University Press has no responsibility for the persistence or accuracy of URLs for external or third-party Internet websites referred to in this publication and does not guarantee that any content on such websites is, or will remain, accurate or appropriate.

Fordham University Press also publishes its books in a variety of electronic formats. Some content that appears in print may not be available in electronic books.

Visit us online at www.fordhampress.com.

Library of Congress Cataloging-in-Publication Data available online at https://catalog.loc.gov.

Printed in the United States of America

24 23 22   5 4 3 2 1

First edition

Contents

Foreword   *ix*
   Metropolitan Ambrosius, Helsinki

Acknowledgments   *xiii*

Sexuality and Orthodoxy: An Introduction   1
   Thomas Arentzen and Ashley M. Purpura

PART I: THINKING THROUGH TRADITION

1   Relationality, Sexuality, and the Desire for God:
Historical Resources   23
   Susan Ashbrook Harvey

2   Something New under the Sun: Sexualities, Same-Sex
Relationships, and Orthodoxy   46
   Bryce E. Rich

3   Science, Homosexuality, and the Church   66
   Gayle Woloschak

4   Biblical Tradition and Same-Sex Relations:
A Difficult Hermeneutical Path   79
   Ekaterini Tsalampouni

PART II: CULTURAL AND PASTORAL CONTEXTS

5   Civil Marriage and Civil Union from an Ecclesial Perspective:
    The Case of the Orthodox Church of Greece   105
    Pantelis Kalaitzidis

6   Eastern Orthodoxy Identity and "Aggressive Liberalism":
    Nontheological Aspects of the Confrontation   144
    Dmitry Uzlaner

7   Salvation and Same-Sex Relations: An Orthodox Response
    on the Decision by the Lutheran Church of Sweden   154
    Michael Hjälm

8   Homophobia in Orthodox Contexts: Sociopolitical
    Variables and Theological Strategies for Change   172
    Andrii Krawchuk

9   Meeting Michelle: Practical Theological Reflections
    on the Personhood of a Transgender Inmate   192
    Richard René

PART III: THINKING WITH TRADITION

10 A Desire for All Is the Desire for God: "Sexual Orientation"
    in Light of Gregory of Nyssa's Account of Gender, Desire,
    and the Soul's Ascent to God   215
    Spyridoula Athanasopoulou-Kypriou

11 Intersex People: Not Physical Mistakes but God's Image   235
    Kateřina Kočandrle Bauer

12 A Theology of Sex   247
    Aristotle Papanikolaou

13 The Antinomic Eschatological Transfiguration of
    Christian Eros and Sexuality   265
    Haralambos Ventis

14 Sex, Love, and Politics: An (Un)Orthodox
    Theological Approach   281
    Davor Džalto

15 From Adam to Christ: From Male and Female
to Being Human 303
John Behr

List of Contributors *321*

Index *325*

Foreword

Metropolitan Ambrosius, Helsinki

Even though the number of Orthodox Christians in Finland is less than 2 percent, its Orthodox Church has a unique position, being one of two Churches officially recognized by the state. National recognition was granted to our Church over a hundred years ago, respecting the principle of political equality and justice for minorities. When the law on registered partnership for same-sex couples was passed by Parliament in 2002, and then the law on civil marriage in 2017, legal status was granted to the unions of sexual minorities by the state. The Finnish Orthodox Episcopal Synod did not oppose any of this legislation because we understand that it is not within our purview to regulate the diverse models of common life for people who are not Orthodox. As Orthodox Metropolitan of Helsinki, I stated that within the Orthodox Church we would not be able to celebrate the sacrament of marriage for same-sex couples. However, we did perform the ceremony of house-blessing whenever it was requested.

Orthodox Tradition and Human Sexuality offers diverse arguments against black-and-white propagandistic views concerning the diversity of sexuality and how it may be lived in human relationships. I am deeply grateful to the scholars who contributed to this volume for providing us with new information and enlightening perspectives on Christianity and sexuality. It is refreshing to find so many chapters agreeing that *all* committed and faithful sexual partnerships among humankind may show authentic spiritual value. In a loving relationship—whether gay or straight—the presence of God may reside, as several chapters in this volume attest, as long as it opens up to the saving work of *theosis*.

Committed and ethical relationships in a variety of forms are rightly shown to be perpetual journeys toward transfiguration and salvation. Consequently, some chapters emphasize the eschatological future of each person as individuals, members of family, and community. Others point to the problematic aspect of reducing the sacrament of marriage to a one-hour ceremony, and refocus our attention toward marriage as a process of lifelong growth and martyrdom. Marriage is not just a physical union and context for procreation. We may see this clearly whenever we recognize the eschatological depth of all human life and its fundamental purpose. Profound eschatological presence liberates us from the captivity and dilemma of dualism. As some chapters highlight, a heavy stress on masculinity and femininity unilaterally presumes these are ontological components of being human. Yet, Gregory of Nyssa and Maximus the Confessor both argue that sexual differentiation was not God's original intention, and certainly it is not part of the reality of resurrection. As the Gospel of Matthew reminds us, "At the resurrection people will neither marry nor be given in marriage; they will be like the angels in heaven" (Matt. 22:30). From this perspective, all committed relationships where truth, faithfulness, and mutual love are a continuously living reality have spiritual value.

As this emphasis on the spiritual potential of relationships reminds us, carrying one's cross should be a part of everyone's life and interactions with others. In remembering this, we must recognize how much we Orthodox Christians have marginalized homosexuality in history, to the unfortunate extent that oppression and stigma have been almost permanent in Christian tradition. We should not pridefully console ourselves with the sinful thought that such marginalization has functioned to deepen the spiritual lives of those whom the Church has oppressed. It has been a tragic marginalization on our part, and should never have happened to anyone. Many churches tolerate or even practically accept not-registered heterosexual cohabitations and other premarriage sexual relationships based on their potential to lead to sanctifying marital relationships. Yet there appears a double standard when it comes to sexuality, a double standard that penalizes and alienates LGBTQ+ persons by denying the potential and possibility for sanctification in their physical relationships. As a Church, we need to seriously reconsider our views on human sexuality and allow room for change, as was done in history with attitudes toward slavery and the position of women. Tradition does not have to be unchanging to be Orthodox.

In Nordic countries we share fundamental convictions concerning culture and equal opportunities for everyone. We also share many views on how to endorse and support human rights as regards such contemporary issues as sexuality. None of our Orthodox churches *promotes* sexual diversity beyond heterosexual male-female union. However, we must not close our eyes to the reality around and within our churches. The Eastern Orthodox view of humanity, which is bright and optimistic, even idealistic, provides a unique contribution in the ecumenical context. Pseudo-Dionysius the Areopagite says that what is bad will never win over good because it does not have a substance of its own. Friendship, trust, mutual understanding, and support to each other convey God's goodness and love in our hearts. It is all part of the richness of His creation, and this work continues. Keeping this in mind, each Church—from the depth of our faith—should fully respect and make room for the genuine shared life of same-sex and other LGBTQ+ people. This does not mean that we should change the traditional doctrine of Christian marriage between man and woman. The Orthodox sacrament of marriage is reserved for heterosexual unions. Despite this, nothing prevents us from making creative efforts to develop new ceremonies and prayers to bless other authentic forms of spiritual and intimate unions.

Considering this task, we recall and might draw inspiration from the medieval ecclesiastical practices of "friendship union" or "brother-making." There exists a large number of rites where two same-sex persons were joined together by such a ceremony of blessing. Only recently have I discovered the spiritual depth and beauty of the prayers in many of them. For instance, in the eleventh- to twelfth-century Old Church Slavonic *Euchologion*, there is the following prayer: "Bless, Lord, giver of good, lover of mankind, these two servants of thine who love each other with a love of the spirit, and have come . . . to receive thy sanctification and benediction; grant them unabashed faithfulness and sincere love." Is it possible to express more beautifully, more sensitively, such unity and love? Hardly any ritual description rivals these prayers in their articulation of mutual sharing and the giving up of oneself. They call us all to recognize the presence of the Holy Spirit in such a union; they convey eternal hope and love given by Christ, expressing the profound yearning that within the relationship Christ will truly be all in all.

ACKNOWLEDGMENTS

Many constructive, critical, and creative people have contributed to the shaping of this volume and its content. First and foremost the editors would like to thank the Director of The Oslo Coalition on Freedom of Religion or Belief, Lena Larsen; she has passionately championed the "Gender and Sexuality in Orthodox Christianity" project, from which the book emerges. Several of its authors, as well as Stig Simeon Frøyshov, Fr. Cyril Hovorun, and Vera Shevzov, contributed to the challenging but open-minded discussions during the project's workshops at Lysebu, while the participation of many other scholars and church leaders was invaluable to the conversation. The project itself was realized thanks to generous funding from the Norwegian Ministry of Foreign Affairs.

We are deeply grateful, moreover, to Gerald Fitzgerald, Brandon Gallaher, and Gregory Tucker for their collaborative attitude and the permission to include papers from the "Contemporary Eastern Orthodox Identity and the Challenges of Pluralism and Sexual Diversity in a Secular Age" project in the volume. We would also like to thank Will Cerbone and Fred Nachbaur for their support at Fordham University Press. Finally, we extend a particular gratitude to two anonymous readers whose creative comments dared us to rethink and rephrase. Although the topic of the book may be controversial and somewhat challenging, its shaping has come about in a spirit of cooperation.

Orthodox Tradition and Human Sexuality

Sexuality and Orthodoxy

An Introduction

Thomas Arentzen and Ashley M. Purpura

The Orthodox Church blesses marriage between a man and a woman in matrimony praying to God: "Unite them in one mind; wed them into one flesh, granting them the fruit of the body!"[1] While celibacy or virginity is required among monastics, a lush sexual life is clearly expected, and even encouraged, among married people, including priests. Sex, then, is integral to most Christian lives—as uncontroversial and mundane as a family dinner. Or so it would seem. And yet, sex is queer.

Contemporary conceptions of sexuality are diverse. Most theorists would agree that sexuality is not a stable concept sprung directly from anatomical features. In fact, many would question the modern idea of an all-embracing sexuality altogether.[2] Sex, sexuality, sexual acts, and the relationship between sexual difference and gender do not recline in self-evident categories. What counts as sexually acceptable and normative, and what is included in discussions of sex and sexuality, are governed by linguistic structures and systems of power, changing over time and with cultural contexts.[3] Judith Butler has highlighted the socially constructed and performative nature of sexual difference; what renders one legible as male or female, how one's bodily manifestation is interpreted, depends on social expectations of sex.[4] Sexualities—if such do exist—regard not just the shape of bodies but are expressed in desires and rely on self-perception as well as self-identification. Sexual orientations—if they need be categorized—could be spread along a spectrum of varieties and possibilities.[5]

Postmodern theorists may speak of sex in a different vernacular than most Orthodox sources, but ultimately they are discussing the same human experiences. As recent and ancient Christian histories attest, sex is omnipresent, even in Christian sources, in diverse forms and without stable interpretations. In this volume, Orthodox Christian scholars speak explicitly about sexuality—especially homosexuality—as it is experienced in the current historical moment and shaped by recent understandings of sex. The Orthodox Church needs to participate in contemporary conversations about such issues; if it does not, it eventually runs the risk of rendering whole aspects of human lives—human sexualities in diverse forms—outside itself.

Sex from an Orthodox Perspective

Sex is a difficult issue for contemporary Christians.[6] The Church is old, but sexuality is new—or at least concepts like "sexuality," "sexual orientation," and "sexual identity" are relatively recent—and in the past, Orthodox tradition has entertained an ambivalent relationship with change. Modern Orthodox discourse has had its share of "Victorianism," the modern puritanism that is now often cast as "traditionalism." Yet this is not the only strain of Christian modernity. Vasily V. Rozanov (1856–1919), a challenging Russian thinker, made early attempts to marry explicit sexual engagement with religious ponderings. "I grew nipples on [the body of] Christianity," he asserts in one of his less explicit passages. "They were small, childlike, undeveloped. . . . I caressed them . . . pampered them with words. Touched them with my hand. And they became erect."[7] Rozanov summoned traditional religious ideas (as well as the less traditional) and transposed them into an erotic and sexual register. His contemporary, the religious philosopher Vladimir Solovyov (1853–1900), also engaged the topic of eros and love, but in a more ascetic way. He too wished to reappraise the role of sex: "There is only one power which can from within undermine egoism at the root, and really does undermine it, namely love, and chiefly sexual love."[8] Although problematic for the institutional Russian Church, these men unveiled a modern interest in sexuality among Orthodox thinkers.

Modernity, and Orthodox Christianity with it, has gradually (and perhaps problematically?) come to appreciate sexuality as intrinsic to human life, human emotions, and intimate human relations; rather than brief and isolated moments of physical pleasure, it amounts to an aspect of being that cannot be divorced from the personal subject. As friendship and relations are vital to human flourishing, most human beings want to have sexual relations with someone else. The orientation of sexual desire is genetically influenced, as Gayle Woloschak empirically observes in this volume, but a need for intimate relationships is shared across sexualities. Sex is a significant aspect of how humans exist as persons created and called by God to be in relationship with other persons.

During the twentieth century, theologians began to (re)explore the erotic language of the early Church. Byzantine Christianity had spoken in distinctly erotic terms—both figuratively and literally—about Christian life.[9] While the Protestant theologian Anders Nygren famously contrasted the late ancient eros (desirous love) to what he saw as the more Christian agape (charitable love),[10] Orthodox theologians confirmed that eros is a deeply patristic (and thus Christian) term. "The sexual urge is an expression of that natural yearning which is implanted within us by our creator, and leads us toward Him," upheld the late monastic leader and writer George Kapsanis, echoing Church Fathers like Maximus the Confessor.[11]

The influential personalist school of modern Orthodox thought ties sexuality and desire to their fundamental notion of relationships between persons, prioritizing the interactional aspects over physical pleasure and procreation. Among its most outstanding representatives is Christos Yannaras, who draws on both Martin Heidegger and early Christian thinkers. For Yannaras, eros comes to define the way in which persons stretch out toward each other, be they created, like humans, or uncreated, like the persons of the Trinity. Since sexuality, rightly understood and practiced, has to do with relating to other persons, relationality is at the heart of both sexuality and the coming-together of persons that is the Church.[12]

Characteristic of twentieth-century thinkers—whether Orthodox or Freudian—was a rich sense of sexuality as involving the whole person. Thus theologians have sometimes critiqued earlier Christian thought for identifying "the expression of the *sexual* relationship or *sexual* communion between man and woman in a more or less exclusive manner with the act of coition, so that it is regarded as fulfilled in this act . . . early Christian theologians appear to have been incapable of envisaging any aspect of sexuality other than its purely generative and genital expression."[13] An analogous sentiment is expressed by Metropolitan Kallistos Ware, one of the contemporary Orthodox Church's most influential and popular writers, who asks, "Why do we put so great an emphasis upon genital sex? Why do we seek to enquire what adult persons of the same sex are doing in the privacy of their bedrooms? Trying to gaze through the keyhole is never a dignified posture."[14] Similar questions carry through in this book: What are intimate relationships about? Can a holistic anthropology like that of the Church allow such isolation of body parts? Or could, conversely, the modern all-defining sexuality itself be a problem? Relational love is certainly more than the physical union, as Spyridoula Athanasopoulou-Kypriou points out: To what degree should sexual intercourse be allowed to define close relationships and to what degree should their genital aspects stand out as the most essential? And, Davor Džalto asks, is there something inherently *problematic* about sexual intercourse from an Orthodox Christian point of view?

A central argument for reevaluation of sexuality among twentieth-century theologians is that the sexual union of man and woman in marriage mysteriously symbolizes the union between the Church and Christ. Hence the physical, sexual relationship of spouses carries the weight of Christianity's most intimate truth.[15] According to the Epistle to the Ephesians, read during the matrimonial service of the Byzantine rite, "a man will leave his father and mother and be joined to his wife, and the two will become one flesh. *This is a great mystery*, and I am applying it to Christ and the Church" (Ephesians 5:31–32, italics added). The oneness of flesh, the physical union, lends hermeneutical insight into the embrace of salvation, turning a sexless marriage into bad theology. Such an interpretation may undoubtedly serve to elevate sexuality. There is something deeply Christian about the celebration of corporeal intimacy.

At the same time, we should not delude ourselves. The Ephesian argument of a sexual mystery carries with it the unsolved problem of these gritty details. Sex is not always good. Sex is also violence. And sex sometimes defies marriage. The Ephesian argument premises the value of sex upon marriage. The enormous semiotic burden on the sexual marriage risks weighing it down, restricting it to forms that rigorously adhere to prevailing "orthodoxies." While many Christians, of course, consider marital sexuality a blessing, they might also, with Ware, regard it as out of place for clergy to voice opinions about their bedroom details.[16] If a correct interpretation of ecclesiology relies on the correct position of limbs, we may find our walls to be dotted with keyholes.

The last decade of Orthodox theological reflection on sexuality has been vitally important, if certainly limited. Sex never unfolds as neatly and cleanly as theology imagines. Parish priests and spiritual fathers are facing this fact and the challenges of our sexual lives on a daily basis. How does sexuality impact persons' ability to participate in the liturgical and sacramental life of the Church, and how could the Church in its ministry and theology address sexual diversity in the lives of those it recognizes as being created in God's own image? Hardly any Orthodox theologians of the twentieth century have seriously ventured beyond the idealized sexuality of the heterosexual spouses and into the complicated terrain of same-sex attraction or other forms of sexual expressions that only awkwardly fit into the frames of church-sanctioned matrimony.[17] Even Yannaras, whose ontology relies on personal freedom and relationships, ends up describing homosexuality as some sort of crippled eros, as selflove.[18] All the more surprising is such an assertion when one takes into consideration that Yannaras himself, like other Orthodox theologians, tends to model his relational ontology on the relationship between the (hardly "heterosexual") three persons of the Trinity.[19]

It has been argued that the Russian émigré theologian Paul Evdokimov's vision of marriage as a lifelong intimate relationship with the potential to sanctify the couple in discipline and love—rather than an institution for procreation—may work just as well for couples who are not heterosexual. A loving relationship that involves the ascetic struggle of giving oneself up for another can be sanctifying without reflecting the gender binary or including the possibility of offspring. Deep and binding relationships may, regardless of gender or sexuality, bear the stamp of blessing and sacrifice, and can, as John Behr implies herein, be a path toward becoming fully human—human in Christ.[20]

Orthodox books written to address sexuality (and more specifically homosexuality) from a more pastoral perspective are far between, but a few authors have treated the question of homosexuality with pastoral depth and sincerity in recent years, often culminating in a typical "condemn the sin—love the sinner" conclusion. Among the most influential is the American Fr. Thomas Hopko and his *Christian Faith and Same-Sex Attraction* from 2005,[21] thoroughly discussed in Andrii Krawchuk's chapter. The Greek priest and psychologist Vasileios Thermos recently wrote the extensive monograph Ἕλξη και πάθος: Μια διεπιστημονική προσέγγιση της ομοφυλοφιλίας (2016).[22] While relevant scholarship is beginning to emerge, academic reflections about Orthodox theology and sexuality have yet to find substantive impact.

Various Positions in the Orthodox World

Human beings are relational beings. Many find the most profound place for companionship within a monastery. For Orthodox Christians without a monastic calling, marriage may be the framework within which they are able to live loving lives in the service of God. Yet as Susan Ashbrook Harvey highlights in this volume, desire and relationality can enable spiritual advancement in a variety of contexts. Since monastic celibacy and heterosexual marriage are the only options explicitly sanctioned by the ritual life of the Orthodox Church, it is pertinent to ask what one should do if the Church has no blessing for one's relationship (due to the partner's gender or for other reasons) while at the same time one has no monastic calling. Does this mean that the individual is sinful or excluded from the Church, or that the Church wishes the person to live in celibacy? Or, does it mean that the Church has never sufficiently considered the challenges of human sexuality in modernity?

It is now often assumed that the Orthodox Church has always unambiguously promoted the heterosexual nuclear family and just as unambiguously rejected sexual diversity and discouraged any sexual expression before and beyond the heterosexual marriage bed. However, historical sources—the New Testament, the writings of the Church Fathers, and the saints' lives—do not permit such an unequivocal conclusion, partly because the sources offer quite diverse visions of sexuality's role in Christian life, and partly because these sources rarely discuss the topics that we struggle with today.[23] The early Christian world had other sexually related questions. Matthew 19:12 declares that "there are eunuchs who have made themselves eunuchs for the sake of the kingdom of heaven. Let anyone accept this who can." The first canon of the Council of Nicaea (AD 325), on the other hand, clearly discourages the practice of self-mutilation and prohibits access to the priesthood for men who have made themselves eunuchs.[24] Nonetheless, we know that male genital mutilation—although not necessarily voluntarily—remained common in Byzantium, and several patriarchs of Constantinople, including Ignatios the Younger and probably Germanos I, were numbered among the eunuchs.[25] One might see this sort of bodily manipulation (castration) and surgical interference in young men's sexuality as an ancient form of sex reassignment surgery, for it seems that eunuchs were perceived as a third gender—or possibly as part of a more sliding gender scale.[26]

Eunuchism concerned people in the early Christian world. In modern Christian debates, in contrast, it plays a very minor role. It may, however, draw our modern attention to the fact that strictly heterosexual nuclear families have never been the only norm—not even in a predominantly Orthodox culture like the Byzantine. To live with a concubine was not uncommon, but those men who did could not become priests, according to *Justinian's Novels*. Ordained readers could only marry twice, while women who had been married twice could not be ordained to the diaconate.[27] Although an ideal of a monogamous marriage was advocated—especially for clergy—a variety of lifeforms and family constitutions clearly subsisted in Byzantine society.

Similarly, ideas about the body, erotic intimacy, and sex have changed through the centuries—also within Orthodox Christendom. If we take the example of Russia, we may observe that naked bodies never scandalized medieval Russians. The fool St. Basil of Moscow (ca. 1469–1552) famously paraded the streets undressed and was even depicted in the nude on icons. Of course, Basil was an exceptional and provocative figure, but even in common settings where both men and women participated—such as in the bathhouses—Russians thought of nudity as acceptable and normal. Greek clergy was shocked by their naturist neighbors up north.[28] What was true for medieval Russia, however, had partly been true for early Byzantium as well, where nudity in the baths was still not unheard of.[29] In Russia the same bold attitude, which often outraged visitors, continued to flourish well into the modern period.[30] The old Slavs were no libertines, but they tolerated nudity because naked bodies lacked sexual content; nude limbs did not per se carry erotic connotations. A naked body could, in other words, be interpreted in sexual, promiscuous terms in one Orthodox culture in one historical period, while in a different Orthodox culture it was not.

We know little about medieval Russians' sexual ethics, and even less about what intimate activities they actually engaged in.[31] What is striking about medieval Russian clerical texts is that sexual acts are treated as isolated phenomena and seem to lack intrinsic value. If childbearing is a divine gift, conception is ultimately detached from the physical messiness of body fluids.[32] Judging by the sources, the clergy understood sexual acts as strictly corporeal actions, which had no direct relationship with love. The morality of the acts was only partly determined by whom the partner was and the nature of the relationship. For instance, it was worse for a man to engage in anal sex with his wife than to make love to another woman—as long as the latter lay below him, facing him, and did not sit on top of him. Even intimacy with another man was not worse for a man than anal sex with his wife.[33] Clerical manuals regarded anal penetration as a grave sin, whether heterosexual or homosexual. Premarital lesbian sex, on the other hand, seems to have been relatively common and almost accepted, granted that neither was sitting on top of the other. In general, the hierarchs considered expressions of same-sex intimacy, such as kissing, male same-sex "penetration" between the thighs, as well as same-sex mutual masturbation, to belong to a category similar to masturbation alone and other forms of sexual intimacy that were not suited to the marriage bed. Gay and lesbian sex belonged to a relatively vast array of extramarital intimacies that ecclesiastical teaching did not accept, but that were still not singled out or stigmatized as particularly evil. For a man to shave off his beard, however, was a more serious offense in medieval Russia, since it meant turning himself symbolically into a woman.[34]

In our own time, the picture looks very different. As much as 86 percent of Orthodox Russians find homosexual behavior in particular morally wrong, while only 36 percent of the same population judge premarital sex to be unacceptable.[35] To most twenty-first-century Orthodox Russians, then, it seems that it has less to do with the act (of sex outside marriage) and more to do with the gender of the partner. It has shifted from a concern about the purity or correctness of sexual acts to a stigma regarding homosexual acts specifically. We know that medieval Russian clergy had a more tolerant attitude toward homosexual acts than Latin clergy in the West, but they may even have had a more tolerant attitude than modern Russian clergy. In a sermon March 6, 2022, Patriarch Kirill of Moscow insinuated that Pride parades in Ukraine might explain or justify the Russian invasion of the country. This illustrates how extremely contentious the issue is in certain Russian circles today.

In many predominantly Christian countries, young couples now choose to marry simply because they have fallen in love; this has not always been the custom. And, during the last millennium, many heterosexual couples have been wedded through a matrimonial rite in an Orthodox church. This had not happened before. There simply existed no such ceremony in the Byzantine rite prior to the tenth century; nobody got married in church.[36] Presently, in many countries with locally established Orthodox Churches—such as Cyprus, Estonia, Finland, and Greece—same-sex couples live in legally sanctioned monogamous relationships. This is also something that has never happened before.

With the historical rite of *adelphopoiesis*, or "brother-making," on the other hand, there existed, as Susan Ashbrook Harvey points out, a liturgical tradition that sanctioned a kind of same-sex union, even though the rite has fallen into disuse since its emergence in the eighth century. The rite united two laymen in a church to form a blessed kinship. In this way a familial relationship could be shaped and recognized through prayer. The details of physical intimacy within such relationships remain unknown. Although the similarities between adelphopoiesis and present day same-sex marriages may be limited, the ritual evidences a historical tradition of recognizing and blessing relationships in greater diversity than just heterosexual marriage.[37]

Shifts in how Orthodox Christians approach relationships, marriage, and sexuality are not unique to modernity nor to the USA, but have, as Pantelis Kalaitzidis's chapter indicates, occurred throughout Christian history. As always, changes leave priests, parishes, and prayerful people with a series of new questions. In our time, the Church has not prepared sufficient and theologically consistent answers, as Michael Hjälm observes. While in the wider political realm the right-leaning policies of "traditional values" compete with the left-leaning rhetoric of "progress," local Orthodox communities are leading their embodied gendered lives in between or amidst such slogans, trying to understand what is right, and what a genuine Christian existence might mean.

Like anyone else, modern Orthodox Christians are entangled in webs of social values and cultural expectations when they approach the corporeal facets of human existence, and the faithful of this large Christian tradition live in a multiplicity of cultures and social contexts. People's backgrounds shape the way they speak about the hot topic of sex; individuals' culture and religion, as much as gender and ideologies, situate their gaze and determine their position in relation to such issues. Even as Dmitry Uzlaner emphasizes the significance of situating cultural identities in understanding Orthodox responses to sexual diversity, Orthodox people's understandings and social positions are often entwined in theological concerns particular to their Christian tradition.

In theological trajectory the Orthodox Church differs radically from the Protestant denominations that emerged from the Reformation. Whereas the latter are leaning on the foundation of a single biblical corpus, Orthodox theologizing cannot rely on one voice or one library of texts but needs to engage the whole complex heritage of the Church. A living ecclesiastical Tradition, so vital to Orthodox self-understanding, helps Orthodox Christians form their identity and theology, but how believers define the boundaries of this Tradition, envision its dynamism, and understand its relevance, varies considerably. Tradition embraces Scripture and important theological authors like the Byzantine thinkers Maximus the Confessor (c. 580–662) and the fourth-century Cappadocian fathers, but also liturgical practices, canon law, iconography, and hagiography. Expressed in such central sources, the Tradition is understood theologically as the work of the Holy Spirit in the Church[38]—or rather, perhaps, the ears that the Church lends to the whispers of the Spirit. According to the great twentieth-century theologian Vladimir Lossky, Tradition is "the faculty of hearing" granted by the Spirit.[39] It has to do with spiritual discernment, interpreting the signs of the times (Matthew 16:3) in relation to the vast ecclesiastical legacy through which the Holy Spirit moves. Orthodox theology knows no cartesian secure foundation for knowledge but a dynamic cohabitation with the Spirit. Hence, Lossky notes, regarding Tradition and biblical criticism:

> One can say that Tradition represents the critical spirit of the Church. . . . Thus the Church, which will have to correct the inevitable alterations of the sacred texts (that certain "traditionalists" wish to preserve at any price, sometimes attributing a mystical meaning to stupid mistakes of copyists), will be able at the same time to recognize in some late interpolations . . . an authentic expression of the revealed Truth.[40]

Tradition cannot simply embrace the "stupid mistakes" of the past, nor imagine that antiquity trumps novelty. Tradition leaves no easy solutions. Tradition draws no simple maps for the future. Tradition comes with transformation. "The vivifying power of Tradition . . . like all that comes from the Spirit, preserves by a ceaseless renewing," according to Lossky.[41] The present book attempts to participate in the vivifying power of critical hearing.

Even when drawing on a common Tradition, however, the faithful hold radically different attitudes toward sexual diversity and sexuality more broadly, displaying significant variation in how they frame, address, and perceive it. The Holy and Great Council of the Orthodox Church at Crete in 2016 was an important ecclesiastical meeting in modern Orthodox Christendom, gathering church leaders from most local churches. The council took an illiberal stance in sexual matters, as many contributors to this book note. Yet 50 percent of the Orthodox Christians in the host country Greece itself currently believes that society should fully accept homosexuality.[42] More than half of the Orthodox in the USA think gay and lesbian couples should be allowed to marry legally.[43] While many individuals and groups in the Church hold strong opinions about sexual ethics, alas attitudes are not often based on critical reflection. Polarizing positions in these areas emerge without serious theological engagement. Unfortunately, ecclesiastically supported values have sometimes justified or reinforced discrimination, and theological conversations tend to be carried out without the representation of sexual minorities.

How one experiences Church life and sacramental life varies according to background, sexual orientation, and gender. Minorities have sometimes felt marginalized and even betrayed by the Church. A growing distrust between the Church and some of its members on account of gendered and sexual issues does not help those members—nor does it help the Church to be the place of existential healing as it is called to be. Discrimination based on sexual orientation often involves serious consequences for individuals, such as exclusion from the community and personal traumas. How can the Church address its own shortcomings and build a new trust? And how can the Church meaningfully minister to people of sexual minorities? What messages (if any) ought communities to send to their members and the world at large regarding sexual relationships? How does sexual orientation, sexual activity, and even gender identity shape Orthodox encounters with and ministries to another human person? It is precisely this question that Fr. Richard René takes up in his chapter as he reflects on his own prison ministry to an incarcerated non-Orthodox trans woman. What kind of pastoral care can parishes offer to sexual minorities—and how? And what resources—albeit underdeveloped—for dealing with issues of gender and sexuality does the Orthodox Tradition feature?

Recent Engagements

As Michel Foucault has pointed out, the nineteenth and twentieth centuries came with a stricter surveillance of sexual practices in European culture; particularly the "peripheries" were scrutinized and disciplined.[44] Modern sensitivities, moreover, favor simple dichotomies and do not tolerate ambiguities very well.[45] Whereas earlier church history knew of multiple attitudes side by side, of diverse practices that were not in line with ideals, modernity has stimulated an urge to fall down on one side or the other unequivocally. And so far, most Orthodox ecclesiastical authorities have come down on the restrictive side, what we may, with Kallistos Ware's term, call "the keyhole side." Yet the last decade has witnessed a remarkable change in attitudes, a small but significant turn toward openness, and the emergence of various dialogue initiatives. This growing openness is indeed promising for the future of the Church.

On May 12, 2017, the Orthodox Bishops' Conference in Germany issued a letter addressed "to young people concerning love—sexuality—marriage." The letter does not encourage homosexuality but points out that "homosexual men and women were ignored for centuries, and even oppressed and persecuted." The hierarchs promote caution, since "what is certain is that we are largely in ignorance about how homosexuality arises," and they conclude: "All men are made in the image of God. Therefore all people are to be accorded that respect which is in keeping with the existence of this divine image in mankind. This applies also to our parishes, which are requested to show love and respect to *all* men and women" [their italics].[46] *All* human beings are to be treated with respect, irrespective of their sexual orientation. The strength of this statement resides in its lack of entrenchment and its refusal to use the issue of sexuality as a token of pure morality. It clearly promotes tolerance and minority inclusion, without therefore pushing any sort of LGBTQ+ agenda.

This book issues from a number of emerging conversations that have sought to bring the Church out of the trenches. The Finnish Orthodox Church has supported tolerance in sexual issues during recent decades, and in the new millennium, the ecumenical organization Community, as well as the Orthodox Rainbow Society, began working for sexual minorities in Orthodox communities. During the second decade of the new millennium, discourses on sex and the Orthodox tradition started to appear on a more public scene. Faithful from fifteen different countries—theologians and nontheologians, lay and clerical—convened in Helsinki in the fall of 2015 for a conference entitled Orthodox Theological Reflections on LGBT People. One year later, Misha Cherniak, Olga Gerassimenko, and Michael Brinkschröder published the edited volume *"For I Am Wonderfully Made": Texts on Eastern Orthodoxy and LGBT Inclusion*. The first of its kind, this publication offers theological and pastoral resources for rendering Orthodox Christianity more inclusive for sexual minorities.[47]

Almost simultaneously, a new project was launched within the framework of the Oslo Coalition on Freedom of Religion or Belief. It lasted from 2016 to 2018. Under the heading Gender and Sexuality in Orthodox Christianity, scholars from various Orthodox traditions around the world met with hierarchs and people with leading roles in Orthodox communities. Just outside the Norwegian capital, they sat down and discussed how to approach contemporary challenges in new and constructive ways. Included were both those for whom sexual issues had a particularly professional relevance and those whose personal lives had been shaped and affected in a profound way by the same issues. Others were present simply because they experienced the need for dialogue. The project attempted to facilitate interdisciplinary conversations among clergy, historians, theologians, canonists, biblical scholars, political scientists, psychologists, and even therapists with the experience of working with sex- and gender-related issues. It conducted both pastoral and academic conversations aimed at countering religious discrimination based on sexuality. Many of the chapters in the current volume were first presented as papers in Oslo during that three-year period, and the book is a result of the Oslo project, which was organized by Thomas Arentzen, Michael Hjälm, Fr. Cyril Hovorun, Pantelis Kalaitzidis, Aristotle Papanikolaou, and Ashley Purpura.[48]

Similar conversations have taken place elsewhere. In June 2017, the Amsterdam Centre for Orthodox Theology at the Vrije Universiteit Amsterdam hosted a theological symposium on Orthodox pastoral care and sexuality. The meeting led to Andrew Louth's guest-edited double issue of the Orthodox journal *The Wheel* (13/14) in 2018. This special issue, which featured many prominent Orthodox scholars from around the world, raised questions about human sexuality and same-sex love. With kind permission from the journal, we are including a revised version of John Behr's contribution.

The last example we should like to mention is the Exeter University and Fordham University consortium Contemporary Eastern Orthodox Identity and the Challenges of Pluralism and Sexual Diversity in a Secular Age (2018–20). It was part of the British Council's larger Bridging Voices project. Brandon Gallaher and Gregory Tucker edited their interim report *Eastern Orthodoxy & Sexual Diversity: Perspectives on Challenges from the Modern West* (2019) as well as the briefer final report *Orthodox Christianity, Sexual Diversity & Public Policy* (2020). The project hosted a conference in Oxford on sex, gender, and sexuality (August 2019); three of the chapters in the present book were first presented as papers at that conference.

During the past decade, then, a historical process of dialogue has begun. Surely there have been Orthodox pronouncements regarding sexuality before, and there have been meetings that have discussed such issues. What distinguishes these recent events is a wish to listen and enter into conversation. It has not only been meetings *about* individuals with a LGBTQ+ identity, but also meetings *with* and *by* such individuals. People who know firsthand what is at stake have been involved. What happens in those most intimate places of human beings that we call sexuality when they do not confirm to societal expectations? The Oslo project never set out to create an Orthodox "LGBTQ+ manifesto," but it aimed to treat the challenges as *our* challenges. It was not about the sexuality of some *other* people with whom we as Orthodox academics could choose to sympathize or not, to moralize about or not; these issues are *our* issues, issues within Orthodox churches, communities, cultures, and families. Such is also the attitude of this book.

The Present Volume

Born by the conviction that Christianity must and should at all times engage with contemporary challenges, and that such engagement is indeed healthy for the Church and its members, *Orthodox Tradition and Human Sexuality* aims to create an agora for discussing the sexualities that are often thought of as untraditional. It offers a series of academic and pastoral reflections on sex, seeking to open up the conversation about homosexuality and sexual diversity within Orthodox Christianity.

The Orthodox Church has traditionally developed moral conversations in personal encounters between the faithful and their spiritual guides; ethical reflection is carried out not as a molding of eternal principles but as concrete contextual interventions. While this posture has the possible disadvantage of excluding the questions from the public realm, it has the advantage of being contextual and attentive. Without secrecy, this book approaches sexual issues from a listening position, by acknowledging that same-sex orientation is something present in the Church's midst. Offering space for critical considerations of current positions and creative theological and pastoral approaches from within the Orthodox tradition, we attempt to move the discussion beyond simplistic dichotomies and hope to stimulate responsible dialogues about issues that are pressing in modern society but that are insufficiently debated in ecclesiastical and theological arenas.

While all the chapters have theological implications, not all are written by theologians. The authors bring various areas of expertise, personal and pastoral experiences, and cultural perspectives to inform their diverse discussions. Together they provide resources, arguments, and conclusions to improve the theological understanding of and engagement with human sexuality in its diverse forms.

Nearly all the chapters appreciate sexuality as part of the human person called to be transformed in the life of the Christian. Whether it means moving away from objectifying instincts and mere procreative ends on one hand, or it implies the work of sanctifying one's eros in eschatological perfection on the other, the authors propose that sexuality, despite the diverse ways it may be understood, ought to be subject to the newness in Christ. Consequently, persons' identities should not be reduced to their sexuality, and sex cannot be reduced to its simple procreative expressions. Humans are persons created in the divine image, called to be divinized through *theosis*; sexuality is part of the divinizable person.

Beyond this, the chapters present a diversity of thought. The task at hand is not to conclude a discussion, but to begin it. Even though the contributors identify as Orthodox Christians, they come to no uniform conclusion. There is not a singular Orthodox approach to sexuality, nor indeed a singular Orthodox sexuality. Disagreement is reflected in the ways the contributors identify sexual diversity through terminology, acronyms, and even choice of focus. Diversity of attitudes is also expressed in the way each author acknowledges expertise from nonecclesiastical sources to inform Orthodox theological understandings. Yet, as Haralambos Ventis poignantly reminds us, the Church Fathers used the best knowledge and reasoning of their time. The Church today should not do worse.

While the volume does not claim to be in command of ultimate solutions—such solutions are never safe and go against the very grain of tradition—it allows scholars from various Orthodox traditions, with various perspectives, to think deeply about how their tradition *can* or *should* understand sexual diversity and human sexuality. Given the malleability of the topic, we offer ripples and reverberations of consensus alongside differing approaches and conclusions.

The book falls into three parts that consider sexuality within Eastern Orthodox Christianity from different corners: "Thinking through Tradition" includes four chapters, each of which invites the reader to rethink central elements of Orthodox Tradition in relation to sexuality. By providing biblical and historical evidence as well as scientific insights, these chapters reassess fundamental assumptions and revisit central sources. In the five chapters of the second part, "Cultural and Pastoral Contexts," specific cultural-political contexts and pastoral challenges are discussed. These chapters shed light on applications, limitations, and appropriations of theological positions in contemporary life. Indirectly, they pose the question how reflecting on experience of and with sexual diversity can inform theological development. The last part, "Thinking with Tradition," comprises six chapters that keep their eyes on sexuality as they theologize. Thus, they provide modes of thinking about sexuality, desire, and sexual diversity as facets of human life, a life created in God's image. There is, however, a level of constructive porousness between these sections.

If Orthodox leaders and theologians have previously failed to address sexual diversity adequately, we may now have gained enough momentum to act with greater pastoral awareness, compassionate courage, and theological empathy. Such is the hope bound between these covers.

Notes

1. From the priestly prayers during the service of the matrimonial crowning in the Byzantine rite, quoted from John Meyendorff, *Marriage: An Orthodox Perspective* (Crestwood, N.Y.: SVS Press, 1984), 123.

2. See, e.g., Michel Foucault, *The History of Sexuality,* Volume One: *An Introduction*, trans. Robert Hurley (New York: Vintage Books, 1978).

3. Joan Wallach Scott, "Gender: A Useful Category of Historical Analysis," in *Gender and the Politics of History* (New York: Columbia University Press, 1988), 28–50; Luce Irigaray, *An Ethics of Sexual Difference*, trans. Carolyn Burke and Gillian Gill (Ithaca, N.Y.: Cornell University Press, 1993).

4. Judith Butler, *Gender Trouble: Feminism and the Subversion of Identity* (New York: Routledge, 1990), 11.

5. Eve Kosofsky Sedgwick, *Epistemology of the Closet* (Berkeley: University of California Press, 1990), 29; Benjamin Dunning, *Specters of Paul: Sexual Difference in Early Christian Thought* (Philadelphia: University of Pennsylvania Press, 2011), 15.

6. For a collection of sources (not all Eastern Orthodox), see Eugene F. Rogers Jr., ed., *Theology and Sexuality: Classic and Contemporary Readings* (Oxford: Blackwell, 2002).

7. Vasily V. Rozanov, *Sakharna*, quoted in Olga Matich, *Erotic Utopia: The Decadent Imagination in Russia's Fin de Siècle* (Madison: University of Wisconsin Press, 2005), 224. For a treatment of Rozanov's work in the context of Orthodox theology, see Paul Ladouceur, *Modern Orthodox Theology: Behold, I Make All Things New (Rev 21:5)* (London: T&T Clark, 2019), 70–73.

8. Vladimir Solovyov, *The Meaning of Love* (Edinburgh: Floris Books, 1985), 45.

9. Two examples are Dionysius the Areopagite, who speaks of the yearning for God in erotic terms (e.g., *Divine Names* IV.12, 709B) and the great mystic Symeon the New Theologian, who wrote more than fifty hymns on *Divine Eros*, where he, as John McGuckin points out, describes the relationship with God "in terms of erotic passion"; McGuckin, "Symeon the New Theologian's *Hymns of Divine Eros*: A Neglected Masterpiece of the Christian Mystical Tradition," *Spiritus* 5 (2005): 197. For less figurative modes, see, e.g., Susan Ashbrook Harvey, "Holy Impudence, Sacred Desire: The Women of Matthew 1:1–16 in Syriac Tradition," in *Studies on Patristic Texts and Archaeology: If These Stones Could Speak . . . Essays in Honor of Dennis Edward Groh*, ed. George Kalantzis and Thomas F. Martin (Lewiston, N.Y.: Edwin Mellen, 2009), 29–50; Thomas Arentzen, "Sex and the City: Intercourse in Holy Week," *Journal of Early Christian Studies* 28 (2020): 115–47.

10. Anders Nygren, *Agape and Eros:* Part I, *A Study of the Christian Idea of Love.* Part II, *The History of the Christian Idea of Love* (London: Society for Promoting Christian Knowledge, 1982 [first published in Swedish 1930–36]).

11. George Capsanis, *The Eros of Repentance: Four Talks on the Theological Basis of Athonite Monasticism* (Newbury, Mass.: Praxis, 1992), 2–3.

12. See not least Christos Yannaras, *Person and Eros* (Brookline, Mass.: Holy Cross Orthodox Press, 2008 [first published in Greek 1970 under the title *To ontologiko perierkhomeno tis theologikis ennoias tou prosopou*]), but also his *Variations on the Song of Songs* (Brookline, Mass.: Holy Cross Orthodox Press, 2005), and his "Church and Sexuality," *The Wheel* 13/14 (2018): 72–82. An earlier Orthodox personalist of the Russian tradition, Nikolai Berdyaev, also takes an interest in sexuality as spiritual relation.

13. Philip Sherrard, *Christianity and Eros: Essays on the Theme of Sexual Love* (Limni, Greece: Denise Harvey, 1995 [first published in 1976]), 28, italics in the original.

14. Kallistos Ware, foreword to *The Wheel* 13/14 (2018): 9–10.

15. John Chryssavgis's *Love, Sexuality, and the Sacrament of Marriage* (Brookline, Mass.: Holy Cross Orthodox Press, 1996) relies on this argument, as do Philip Sherrard, *Christianity and Eros* (Limni: Denise Harvey, 1995 [first published in 1976]), 4 et passim, and John A. McGuckin, "Foreword: The Mystery of Marriage: An Orthodox Reflection," in *Love, Marriage and Family in Eastern Orthodox Perspective*, ed. Theodore Grey Dedon and Sergey Trostyanskiy (Piscataway, N.J.: Gorgias Press, 2016): xv–xxvi.

16. See Kallistos Ware, foreword to *The Wheel* 13/14 (2018): 9–10.

17. For examples of more recent reflections on Orthodox theology and sexuality, see Philip Abrahamson, "Trends in Eastern Orthodox Theological Anthropology:

Towards a Theology of Sexuality," *Philosophy, Sociology, Psychology and History* 15, no. 2 (2016): 93–102; Brandy Daniels, "Ekstasis as (Beyond?) Jouissance: Sex, Queerness, and Apophaticism in the Eastern Orthodox Tradition," *Theology & Sexuality* 20, no. 2 (2014): 89–107.

18. Christos Yannaras, "Church and Sexuality," *The Wheel* 13/14 (2018): 72–82.

19. See, e.g., Christos Yannaras, *The Freedom of Morality* (Crestwood, N.Y.: SVS Press, 1984), 160–64.

20. Paul Evdokimov, *The Sacrament of Love: The Nuptial Mystery in the Light of the Orthodox Tradition* (Crestwood, N.Y.: SVS Press, 1985); see Eugene F. Rogers Jr., *Sexuality and the Christian Body: Their Way into the Triune God* (Oxford: Blackwell, 1999); idem, "Marriage as an Ascetic Practice," *INTAMS review: The Journal of the International Academy of Marital Spirituality* 11 (2005): 28–36; Michael Plekon, "The Sacrament of Love: Paul Evdokimov's Vision of Marriage, Love and Vocation," in *Love, Marriage and Family in Eastern Orthodox Perspective*, ed. Theodore Grey Dedon and Sergey Trostyanskiy (Piscataway, N.J.: Gorgias Press, 2016): 1–14. The same point may be made regarding the marital theology of William Basil Zion in *Eros and Transformation: Sexuality and Marriage; An Eastern Orthodox Perspective* (Lanham, Md.: University Press of America, 1992) and Christos Yannaras, *The Freedom of Morality* (Crestwood, N.Y.: SVS Press, 1984), 164–69.

21. See also Athanasios Gkikas, Ὁμοφυλοφιλία: Μια σύγχρονη ποιμαντική πρόκληση (Thessaloniki: Μυγδονία, 2016).

22. A shorter English version was published as *Sexual Orientation and Gender Identity: Answers . . . and People* (Athens, Greece: En Plo Editions, 2019). See also his open-minded "The Orthodox Church, Sexual Orientation, and Gender Identity: From Embarrassment to Vocation," *The Wheel* 13/14 (2018): 83–90.

23. See for example the numerous hermeneutical approaches in Ben Dunning, ed., *The Oxford Handbook of New Testament, Gender, and Sexuality* (Oxford: Oxford University Press, 2019), 1–220; for insight to the historical diversity of sex in the ancient world see Mark Masterson, Nancy Sorkin Rabinowitz, and James Robson, eds., *Sex in Antiquity: Exploring Gender and Sexuality in the Ancient World* (New York: Routledge, 2015).

24. Council of Nicaea, canon 1.

25. Shaun Tougher, *The Eunuch in Byzantine History and Society* (London: Routledge, 2008); for the patriarchs, see 70–71.

26. Tougher, *The Eunuch,* 110–11.

27. *Justinian's Novels* 6.5–6.

28. Eve Levin, "Sexual Vocabulary in Medieval Russia," in *Sexuality and the Body in Russian Culture*, ed. Jane T. Costlow, Stephanie Sandler, and Judith Vowles (Stanford, Calif.: Stanford University Press, 1993), 41–52, at 49.

29. Kenneth G. Holum, "The Classical City in the Sixth Century: Survival and Transformation," in *The Cambridge Companion to the Age of Justinian*, ed. Michael Maas (Cambridge: Cambridge University Press, 2005), 103–4.

30. Judith Vowles, "Marriage à la russe," in *Sexuality and the Body in Russian Culture*, ed. Jane T. Costlow, Stephanie Sandler, and Judith Vowles (Stanford, Calif.: Stanford University Press, 1993), 53–72, at 66–72.

31. Our sources primarily consist of penitential manuals, written by clergy who were eager to teach their flock a chaste lifestyle. For us to understand the sexual life of the Eastern Slavs based on these texts is a bit like a twenty-sixth-century person interpreting twentieth-century European cuisine based exclusively on a few dietary tips for weight loss.

32. Eve Levin, "Sexual Vocabulary in Medieval Russia," in *Sexuality and the Body in Russian Culture*, ed. Jane T. Costlow, Stephanie Sandler, and Judith Vowles (Stanford, Calif.: Stanford University Press, 1993), 41–52, at 42.

33. Eve Levin, *Sex and Society in the World of the Orthodox Slavs 900–1700* (Ithaca: Cornell University Press, 2018), 197. For Byzantine perspectives, see Stephen Morris, *"When Brothers Dwell in Unity": Byzantine Christianity and Homosexuality*; Mark Masterson, *Man to Man: Desire, Homosociality, and Authority in Late-Roman Manhood* (Columbus: The Ohio State University Press, 2014); Derek Krueger's BSC papers *"Andromania*: Male Homosexuality and Opprobrium in Tenth-Century Hagiography" (2017) and "The Homophobia of George the Monk" (2019).

34. Eve Levin, *Sex and Society in the World of the Orthodox Slavs 900–1700* (Ithaca, N.Y.: Cornell University Press, 2018), 199–204.

35. Pew Research Center, Nov 8, 2017, "Orthodox Christianity in the 21st Century," 55. It is also worth noting that eighteenth- and nineteenth-century Russia was quite tolerant and saw a much more liberal attitude in sexual affairs (and men without beards). Catholic and Protestant visitors from Western Europe—men as well as women—found themselves stunned by the unrestrained sexuality of Russian women. See, e.g., Jane T. Costlow, Stephanie Sandler, and Judith Vowles, introduction to *Sexuality and the Body in Russian Culture*, ed. Jane T. Costlow, Stephanie Sandler, and Judith Vowles (Stanford, Calif.: Stanford University Press, 1993), 1–38, at 10–11; Vowles, "Marriage à la russe," 66–72.

36. John Meyendorff, "Christian Marriage in Byzantium: The Canonical and Liturgical Tradition," *Dumbarton Oaks Papers* 44 (1990): 99–107.

37. Claudia Rapp, *Brother-Making in Late Antiquity and Byzantium: Monks, Laymen, and Christian Ritual* (Oxford: Oxford University Press, 2016) offers a corrective reading of John Boswell, *Same-Sex Unions in Premodern Europe* (New York: Vintage Books, 1994). For accounts of monks dwelling together in intimate relationships, see also Derek Krueger, "Between Monks: Tales of

Monastic Companionship in Early Byzantium," *Journal of the History of Sexuality* 20, no. 1 (2011): 28–61.

38. For three approaches by three twentieth-century theologians, see Sergius Bulgakov, "The Church as Tradition," in *The Orthodox Church* (St. Vladimir's Seminary Press, 1988), 9–36; Georges Florovsky, *Bible, Church, Tradition: An Eastern Orthodox View*. Collected Works, vol. 2 (Belmont, Mass.: Nordland, 1972), 73–92; Vladimir Lossky, "Tradition and Traditions," in *The Image and Likeness of God* (Crestwood, N.Y.: St. Vladimir's Seminary Press, 1974), 141–68;

39. Lossky, "Tradition and Traditions," 152.

40. Lossky, "Tradition and Traditions," 156.

41. Lossky, "Tradition and Traditions," 160.

42. Pew Research Center, Nov 8, 2017, "Orthodox Christianity in the 21st Century," 52.

43. Pew Research Center, Nov 8, 2017, "Orthodox Christianity in the 21st Century," 53.

44. Foucault, *The History of Sexuality I*, 40.

45. See, e.g., Thomas Bauer, *Die Vereindeutigung der Welt: Über den Verlust an Mehrdeutigkeit und Vielfalt* (Stuttgart: Reclam, 2018).

46. http://www.obkd.de/Texte/Brief%20OBKD%20an%20die%20Jugend-en.pdf. "all men . . . in the image of God" here must mean "all human beings . . . in the image of God."

47. More reflections on personal experiences with homosexuality and Orthodoxy can be found in Justin Cannon, ed., *Homosexuality in the Orthodox Church* (CreateSpace Independent Publishing Platform, 2011).

48. https://www.jus.uio.no/smr/english/about/id/oslocoalition/christianity/index.html.

Part I: Thinking through Tradition

CHAPTER

1

RELATIONALITY, SEXUALITY, AND THE DESIRE FOR GOD

HISTORICAL RESOURCES

Susan Ashbrook Harvey

Recent decades have witnessed a dramatic turn in scholarship regarding sexuality, same-sex relationships, and family identities in Byzantine Christianity. As a result, both the narrative and the evidence by which we consider these issues in the history of Orthodoxy are changing. New paradigms are appearing, relevant to the consideration at hand: how human bodies frame and inform divine-human relation, and how they provide the lived context in which that relationship takes place.

In this essay, I suggest that Byzantine Christianity has left two profound historical legacies bearing upon discussion of Orthodoxy and homosexuality. First is the valuing of relationality as an ascetic resource. Across an array of types of evidence, whether archaeological or textual, we find that close relationships provided fruitful locations for the pursuit of holiness. In Byzantine society, such relationships were familial (parent-child), or cross-sex or same-sex partnerings. They may or may not have involved sexual expressions. But the living patterns of such relationships could require physical as well as emotional intimacy, often sustained over many years of close partnership in religious devotion. Second is a rich attunement to embodiment as an epistemological tool. As John of Damascus argued, bodily experience and sensory engagement provide distinctive means of learning about the divine, and further, distinctive modes of knowing, not possible for the human person by other means.[1] Desire is a fundamental aspect of human embodiment. For the Byzantines, embodied desire could be turned toward a fuller human-divine relationship. Together, I will suggest, the Byzantine legacies of relationality and embodiment can provide transfiguring resources in the quest for a fuller human relationship to God.

Relationality and embodiment are notions with densely textured social histories. Both offer paradigmatic themes for theological exploration, and were engaged in such terms over the course of centuries for premodern Orthodox. I will begin with these social histories before turning to theological issues intrinsically raised for Byzantine Christians, and indeed no less pressing for our present times.

Relationality: Ways of Living with a Body

Though the evidence is not plentiful, yet there is indisputable material witness from earliest Christianity right through the Byzantine era of persons who lived as committed, long-term, same-sex couples. Occasional papyri fragments and lead tablets survive with love charms or spells commissioned for same-sex attraction. There are legal contracts of different kinds, some recognizable in civic terms as tantamount to same-sex marriages. There are wills, inscriptions, and shared burial sites that indicate same-sex relationships of enduring character. Such material and documentary evidence is meager in quantity, though widespread geographically and temporally. It is laconic in nature; we lack narrative content or context to provide stories behind these invariably brief attestations.[2]

Sometimes the evidence is inscrutable. A sixth-century documentary papyrus from Egypt presents a legal contract in which a monk, Aioulios, bequeaths his monastic cell to his cellmate, Eulogios, whether or not Aioulios brings another man into the cell or whether or not he leaves.[3] Other glimpses are more substantial. Several homoerotic love charms survive from the early Christian period, on papyri or lead tablets. One, a lead tablet from Upper Egypt, presents a woman, Sophia, beseeching the attraction of another woman, Gorgonia, through a spell invoking powers to "inflame the heart, the liver, the spirit of Gorgonia, whom Nilogenia bore, with love and affection for Sophia, whom Isara bore."[4] Papyri charms besought the attraction of one woman for another woman, or one man for another man, "now, now; quickly, quickly," "soul and heart."[5] Such evidence does not contain emotional content in forms we might easily recognize, nor does it indicate sexual activity. But it does preserve the names of real men and women in relationships otherwise occluded.

The consistency and continuity of such evidence stands as concrete witness to the historical reality of such relationships. It reminds us that however fierce the condemnation of same-sex physical relationships in ecclesiastical rhetoric, or in civil or canon law, there has been another history at work. That history comprised women and men who found ways to live their lives in same-sex partnerships of their own choosing.

Over the course of late antiquity, Christian developments brought new social patterns that bore upon possibilities for same-sex relationships. The emergence of asceticism in institutionalized forms during the late third and fourth centuries offered alternative means of social organization to the traditional biological family. Ascetic households or monasteries could fulfill many of the social, economic, and even political functions of biological families. They organized people into highly effective living units, providing ways and means for lodging, food, and health care; economic interaction with others; education; and sophisticated legal structures.[6] Ascetic households established socially acceptable and culturally viable long-term, single-sex or unmarried cross-sex living arrangements. At the same time, they unleashed socially fraught sexual anxieties. When the great Saint Antony undertook the solitary testing that prefigured the monastic communities of the Egyptian desert, he was tempted by demons in the guise of both women and young boys.[7] The earliest extant monastic legislation addressed both hetero- and homosexual possibilities, temptations, and infractions in blunt terms.[8] So, too, did sermons, letters, and treatises addressed to celibates living in nonmonastic arrangements (clergy, consecrated virgins, widows). John Chrysostom called the practice "a third way" of cohabitation, neither marriage nor prostitution. He denounced it as "a violent and tyrannical pleasure," even if it did not involve sexual activity, because of the psychological dangers he claimed it posed.[9]

From the very beginnings of monasticism, considerable variation in monastic living patterns has been evident. From the start (and still), persons choosing the ascetic life sometimes opted to do so in very small groups—two or sometimes three individuals, living apart from society whether monastic or secular, and choosing to follow a shared lifestyle of disciplined commitment in pursuit of holiness. The historical record is littered with monastic pairs, differently comprised: two ascetics, usually but not always of the same gender; sometimes a parent and child, or other biological relation; sometimes two companions. Their living arrangements also varied: from ascetic seclusion in a cave or hut in desert or wilderness, to a shared cell within a larger monastic community, to a life of continual pilgrimage, to ascetic withdrawal in a civic household. Derek Krueger and Claudia Rapp have drawn attention to the occasional material or documentary evidence attesting such couples, in addition to the more abundant literary evidence in hagiography and related ascetical literature, including letters.[10]

Different literary conventions frame and articulate the literary attestations of monastic couples. Sometimes, the pairs or groups were familial. In Cappadocia, Macrina at age twelve declared herself a widow when her fiancé died, and vowed "never to be separated for a moment from her mother."[11] Macrina subsequently transformed the household into a famed double-monastery of both men and women, including family members, where she and her mother remained constant companions until their deaths. "For this they had asked from God all through their life, that after death their bodies should be together and that in death they should not be deprived of the comradeship they had had in their lifetime."[12] The widow Euphemia and her daughter Maria lived a rigorous prayer life together, serving the poor and needy in the city of Amida for decades.[13] In Scetis, Abba Carion received his son Zacharias into harsh ascetic partnership.[14] Families decided to enter monasticism collectively, the wife taking the daughters and the husband taking the sons to different monastic communities, as did Thomas the Armenian and his wife, Maria.[15] The ascetic Abraham of Qidun raised his orphaned niece Mary in strict isolation;[16] a widowed father might take monastic vows accompanied by his daughter in monastic disguise, such as in the story of St. Marina/Marinos.[17] In such cases, the devotion of one ascetic to another was articulated in terms that combined familial piety with reference to the pedagogical model of intimate teacher-disciple relationship: the faithful adult and lovingly loyal child, also cast as wise elder and devoted follower.

Not only family couples, but peer couples also lived in conjoined ascetic commitment, sometimes cross-sex and sometimes same-sex. Heterosexual couples might live together in celibate marriages that provided an acceptable social veneer of normative marital arrangements while allowing them freedom for shared ascetic prayer life. Sometimes the couple took vows of celibacy but continued to live together for many years, until one died or they decided to separate into established monastic communities. Amoun of Nitria converted his wife, his "saintly companion," to the ascetic life on their wedding night. For eighteen years they shared a house but lived separately in their shared ascetic practice, until she decided they should take up separate lives.[18] These accounts often indicate deep and poignant devotion to one another, enacted through ascetic discipline that expressed a partnership like that idealized for marriage by Tertullian some centuries earlier.[19] Even after his move to Nitria, Amoun continued to visit his "blessed companion" twice each year until his death.[20] John and Sosianna, a married couple in the service of the patrician widow Caesaria, lived more than thirty years in a secret ascetic partnership, "in purity, never holding carnal intercourse with one another . . . occupying themselves in fasting and prayer, and genuflexion and recitation of service and watching by night, while hair mats were laid down for them each apart."[21]

But how different were such heteronormative accounts from those of same-sex monastic pairs, male or female, who lived together over many years? The two noblewomen Marana and Cyra had been living together in a small enclosure for forty-two years, while directing a small convent nearby, when Theodoret of Cyrrhos reported their work.[22] Sophronios of Jerusalem and John Moschos lived and traveled together, in shared ascetic pursuit, for more than forty years.[23] Accounts of such monastic couples often contained warm praise from witnesses for their many years together. The relationship was valued as a vehicle for the life of holiness, better enabled and enacted through a pair than in complete isolation. After their many years of shared ascetic labor, bishop Paul of Qentos, approaching death, comforted his companion the priest John of Edessa that in the afterlife, "in the company of our Lord we will forever rejoice with one another."[24] Such stories lauded the fidelity of these relationships, precisely as vehicles of shared devotion to God.

Monastic pairs, whether cross-sex or same-sex, might live together in highly intimate proximity, over many years. Their relationship may have involved sexual intimacy, or not. There is no means for us to know. But such a closely bound lifestyle—a partnership deliberately sharing ascetic, disciplined, prayer life—by its very nature was a relationship of intense closeness and familiarity, in physical as well as devotional terms, even if not explicitly sexual. The early seventeenth-century Ethiopian nun Walatta Petros and her companion the nun Eheta Khristos labored through their long shared career "together in mutual love, like soul and body."[25] Such partnership *served* holy devotion, rather than detracting from it.

Claudia Rapp has argued that these varieties of monastic partnerships provided the likely context in which the practice of *adelphopoiesis*, "brother-making," emerged in Byzantine society. Adelphopoiesis was a ritual blessing that established a relationship between two men, not biologically related, for the rest of their lives: the ritual affirmation of a same-sex friendship. The ritual is attested in more than sixty liturgical manuscripts, beginning in the eighth century.[26] Sometimes adelphopoiesis functioned like adoption, as a means for extending kinship ties with their attendant duties, obligations, and responsibilities. Sometimes it marked particularly significant friendships, whether between the imperial family and others outside, or between a monk and a layman, or between monks. It carried substantial social and sometimes financial obligations.

Adelphopoiesis was a ritual that functioned to allow a same-sex relationship special legal recognition as well as ecclesiastical blessing. The prayers in different variations called for God to "Bless your servants NN and NN, who are not bound by nature, but by faith. Grant them to love one another, and that their brotherhood remain without hatred [*amisêton*] and free from offense [*askandaliston*] all the days of their lives, through the power of your Holy Spirit, the intercession of the All-Holy [Mother of God] . . . and of holy John the Forerunner."[27] Repeatedly, one sees the phrase "Grant them faith without shame [*pistin akataischynton*], love without suspicion [*agapên anhypokriton*]."[28] If not an affirmation of same-sex "marriage" as John Boswell wanted to argue, adelphopoiesis nonetheless offered striking affirmation of same-sex friendship as a relationship potent in its spiritual implications.[29]

Such a historical record of monastic and ritual bonds suggests a fundamental recognition that close, committed, long-term relationships provided fruitful context for pursuing a life of holiness. Those relationships were historically both cross-sex and same-sex. And they were affirmed as worthy vehicles for holy devotion in hagiographical and ascetic literature, as well as in the concrete liturgical practice of adelphopoiesis. Despite an ascetic ideal of solitude, the vast bulk of monastic history attests communal living. In the Byzantine era, that communal context was often small: two people, pursuing a life of prayer together. Such a life comprised a shared ascetic discipline in which physical and emotional proximity and intimacy contributed to the goal of religious observance. What made that life effective was the nature of the relationship itself, each partner strengthening the other's devotion to God.

Embodiment and Desire: Rhetorics of the Body

How do we know that the living conditions for such couples were intense in their intimacy? The texts take us there, and indeed, their authors seem to enjoy doing so. In hagiography, holy persons present their bodies in various states of dress or undress.[30] In holiness, the body might seduce toward salvation rather than sin. The body of Mary of Egypt first appeared to the priest monk Zosimas scorched, phantasmal, and levitating, her nakedness evoking wonder rather than temptation.[31] Abba Stephan the Cappadocian in church one Holy Thursday suddenly realized that two anchorites entering together "were naked, yet not another of the fathers perceived that they were naked, except me.... [B]efore my very eyes they went onto the water of the Red Sea on foot and departed across it."[32] Just so, the monk Paphnutios encountered remote hermits clothed only in their hair, or perhaps a few leaves, whose nakedness resembled the perfection of Adam before the fall, free from shame and without sin.[33] In these stories, the sight of nakedness edified the monk.[34] Still, the proximity of bodies, little or partly clothed, might trouble a monk. "A brother, being tempted by a demon, went to a hermit and said, 'Those two monks over there who live together live sinfully.' But the hermit knew that a demon was deceiving him." For edification, the hermit summoned the two brothers and in the evening provided them a single mat and blanket for their rest, saying, "They are sons of God, and holy persons." But the "slandering brother" who had accused them, the hermit ordered to be shut away, for "suffering from the passion of which he accuses them."[35]

Such texts could trouble the reader or listener, as well. For the text held the image of the naked body before the mind of the audience; the text lingered upon it. As both Derek Krueger and Virginia Burrus have discussed,[36] such textual play recurred in hagiographical texts with perhaps surprising frequency, and did so in both hetero- and homoerotic terms. When Mary of Egypt recounted the story of her former debauchery to the chaste Zosimas, for example, her reminiscence allowed the reader or listener to pause on its details at length. She did not mince her words:

> I first destroyed my own virginity ... I then threw myself entirely and insatiably into the lust of sexual intercourse.... I had an insatiable passion and uncontrollable lust to wallow in filth.... There is no kind of licentiousness, speakable or unspeakable, that I did not teach those miserable men.[37]

The hagiographical text or ascetic memoir could offer paradoxical temptations to its audience, whether monastic or lay.

To what extent might textual nudity mirror aspects of late ancient social reality? The twenty-first-century West presents a society filled with a hypersexualized visual culture in which advertising, films, television, social media, and the internet are awash in virtual nudity displayed with erotic intention. The ancient Mediterranean, too, displayed nudity in frankly material terms. Nudity was commonplace in this ancient social world that valued public baths, athletic games, and theatrical entertainment—activities much loved by civic populations and routinely castigated by late antique and early Byzantine preachers.[38] Nudity was also intrinsic to the power dynamics of a slave society, where the display, handling, bathing, and dressing of nude bodies by and in the presence of slaves was not morally problematic, for Christians or anyone else.[39]

The theologically didactic mirror to such a social background might be seen in the early Christian practice of nude baptism for adult converts (the vast majority of baptisms until at least the sixth century). Baptismal nudity underscored significant theological teachings on baptism as a new birth and return to a prelapsarian human condition signified by nakedness without shame.[40] Generally performed at night, baptism was framed by the scrupulous assistance of male and female deacons to assist the priest with anointing and clothing the naked neophytes with propriety.[41]

Yet the nudity of baptism could be problematic. The Cilician priest Conon was troubled in his baptismal duties until a vision of John the Baptist "stripped him of his clothes and three times made the sign of the cross beneath his navel," enabling him thereafter to anoint and baptize "without suffering any physical disturbance and with no awareness of women's femininity."[42] Or, baptismal nudity could be instructively employed. When the Najran martyr Mahya was stripped naked in the public stadium prior to her martyrdom, she taunted the king and her executioners by shouting, "It is to your shame . . . that you have done this. . . . I have been naked in the presence of men and women without feeling ashamed, for I am a woman—such as was created by God."[43]

There was a concrete physicality to embodiment for late ancient and Byzantine Christians, which later Byzantines—or modern Church leaders—have tended to mitigate. The liturgical stichera and apostika now in use for the Sunday of Mary of Egypt, for example, in contrast to her sixth-century hagiography, enumerate nothing of her debauched past. Instead, they dwell on Mary's penitential asceticism.⁴⁴ Although her feast day is commemorated three times during the liturgical year, her troparion omits the lascivious remembrances of her hagiographical account:

> In thee, O Mother, was preserved unimpaired that which is according to God's image, for thou hast taken up the Cross and followed Christ. By thine actions thou hast taught us to despise the flesh, for it passes away, but to care for the soul, which is a thing immortal; and so thy spirit, Holy Mary, rejoices with the angels.⁴⁵

In contrast to present liturgical remembrances, the living patterns of ancient Christians enabled intimate relationships both cross- and same-sex in character. So, too, did the rhetorical habits of ancient Christian authors enhance the emotional and sensory qualities of such relationships, adding further texture to embodiment as the location and condition in which relationality played out. Such rhetoric not only highlighted embodiment, it enhanced the significance of its physicality.

Intimate Christian partnerships, ascetic or otherwise, were presented through inherited rhetorical conventions of friendship, or of master-disciple relationships, both deeply rooted in classical and Hellenistic philosophical traditions. Here the rhetoric could be frankly homoerotic, often in terms that echoed the dialogues of Plato, particularly the *Symposium*.⁴⁶ Gregory of Nazianzos lauded his friendship with Basil of Caesarea just so, in his funeral oration at Basil's death.⁴⁷ Amidst metaphors of burning, longing, fervor, and joy, Gregory recalled their days together as students in Athens:

> We were everything to each other, roommates, messmates, soulmates in contemplation of the One, forever strengthening and intensifying each other's desire. . . . It was as if one soul carried the bodies of us both . . . we were in each other and next to each other.⁴⁸

Similar rhetoric adorned Gregory's early letters to Basil, in which he lamented their separations and longed for their shared retreats: "Rather would I breathe you than the air, and I live only in that which I am with you, in your presence, or in your absence by your image."⁴⁹

The homoeroticism of such rhetoric carried multiple valences from its philosophical roots. Inherent in this notion of friendship was shared commitment to a philosophical life. That life required a physically disciplined and intellectually focused pursuit of truth, conducted through probing dialogue with (same-sex) friends of like mind, and enacted in living arrangements that contributed to this pursuit. Gregory and Basil had shared such a life in Athens and also in Cappadocia at Basil's family estate in Annesi. Augustine of Hippo had lived in Cassiciacum for several years in similar retreat with his closest friends, prior to his consecration as bishop.[50] At times, male monastic pairs were literally presented in terms that presume a rhetoric such as that intentionally employed by Gregory for Basil.

For example, Symeon the Fool and his monastic partner John lived together in ascetic retreat for twenty-nine long years, before the latter decided he must return to society and tend to the salvation of others. Symeon's hagiography presents a separation of wrenching pain. After lengthy argument, John agreed to let Symeon depart:

> And after they had prayed for many hours and kissed each other's breast and drenched them with their tears, John let go of Symeon and traveled together with him a long distance. For his soul would not let him be separated from him, but whenever Abba Symeon said to him, "Turn back, brother," he heard the word as if a knife separated him from his body, and again he asked if he could accompany him a little further. Therefore, when Abba Symeon forced him, he turned back to his cell drenching the earth with tears.[51]

Occasionally, such rhetoric also characterized the shared bonds between nuns. In the "Life of Febronia,"[52] for example, the young pagan widow Hieria was converted to Christianity by Febronia, whom Hieria calls "my sister, my lady, my teacher." The two women sat through the night together, as Febronia read aloud from the Bible and offered instruction, while Hieria listened, wept, and sighed with longing. When Febronia fell ill, Hieria would not leave her side. At the news of Febronia's arrest by pagan authorities, Hieria ran to the stadium, weeping and lamenting bitterly. During Febronia's grim public torture and execution, Hieria shouted encouragement and devotion, attempting to join her at her end. Following Febronia's death, Hieria took her place at the convent. The entire hagiography presents the convent as a place of devoted friendships, rich intellectual activity, and fervently enacted ascetic discipline. Yet the friendship between Febronia and Hieria is set apart for narrative focus. The intensity of its emotional quality is textually valued; as in the case of other monastic pairs, it is offered to the reader as instructive precisely for its concentrated strength.

Another example would be the decades-long partnership between the seventeenth-century Ethiopian Orthodox nuns Walatta Petros and Eheta Khristos. The hagiography describes their first encounter as initiation into a bond of incandescent devotion:

> As soon as our holy mother Walatta Petros and Eheta Khristos saw each other from afar, love was infused into both their hearts, love for one another, and [approaching], they exchanged the kiss of greeting. . . . There was no fear or mistrust between them. They were like people who had known each other beforehand because the Holy Spirit united them.[53]

But hagiography and ascetical literature were not the only sources for an erotically articulated holy desire. Rhetorics of desire, longing, and relationality in the quest for God also found expression in the abundant liturgical poetry of Byzantium, cast in both homo- and heterosexual terms. Here, the context was one of communal worship, wherein ritual participation formed and shaped Christian subjectivity. Liturgy provided a school for the Christian body, as its component parts set the senses into high relief. It demanded attention to bodily sensation, even as its verbal content instructed the worshipper how to experience and grasp its religious significations. Among these was the sense of desire, articulated in patterns of musical exchange between chanters, choirs, congregation, and clergy.

Romanos the Melodist (d. circa 556), for example, used the kontakion form to explore the human-divine relation through stories of biblical figures cast in the form of sung dramas. The chanter sang in vivid first-person terms, searching his own heart and also the hearts and minds of different biblical characters, set in dialogue with one another. The congregation joined the refrain, entering the subjectivity of each different character in turn.[54]

In Romanos's kontakion on the baptism of Christ, for example, the chanter invites the congregation to join him in recalling the story:

> Therefore let us all, Adam's naked children,
> Put [Christ] on that we may be kept warm;
> For as a covering for the naked and a light for the darkened
> You [Lord] have come, you have appeared,
>   (refrain) *The unapproachable Light.*[55]

In strophe 3, the Savior calls out in the voice of the singer to the congregation who stand in the place of Adam:

> In my mercy, I [Christ] was overcome by my compassion and came to my creature [Adam],
> Stretching out my hands to embrace you.
> So do not be ashamed in front of me; for your sake, naked as you are, I am stripped naked and baptized.[56]

Here, then, Romanos sings in imagery whereby a fully incarnate Lord embraces Adam in the naked moment of baptism. In that nakedness, the garment of shame can be exchanged for the garment of glory, as the faithful one "puts on" the body of Christ. Sung in the night vigil in a small Constantinopolitan church, the hymn echoed through voices monastic and lay, male and female. Whose voice was Adam's, whose was that of Christ? Who met Christ in naked embrace?

In his hymn on the Apostle Thomas, again, Romanos sings the encounter between the doubting disciple and his risen Lord. While Thomas trembles before the sacred body he cannot escape, erotic tension slowly burns in the poet's voice. The stichera turn to the moment of touch. The chanter lingers as Christ draws the hand of Thomas into his side: "Oh the wonder, the patience, the infinite gentleness! / The intangible is handled, is grasped by a slave." The congregation replies with Thomas, singing the refrain, "You are our Lord and our God." The poet proceeds in Thomas' voice:

> Stay gentle, that I may take my delight in you, Lord.
> Satisfy me, who am yours. You were patient with strangers;
> be patient too with your own and show me your wounds,
> that, like springs, I may draw from them and drink.
> Do not burn me up, O Saviour, for you are fire by nature,
> But, by your will, you are the body which you became.
> Hide yourself, then, just a little, I beg.
> Accept me, my Saviour, like the woman with the issue of blood.
> It is not the hem of your garment that I grasp, but you I touch, saying,
>
> (refrain) *You are our Lord and our God.*[57]

These two kontakia hymned the exquisitely physical encounter between Jesus and his male devotees, in the context of a civic congregation where men and women both were present. The celibate faith of ascetic clergy and urban monks mingled with the singing voices of the (heterosexually) married, in the flickering candles of the night vigil, amidst incense, perfumed lamp oil, and antiphonal voices. Whose bodies took gentle, patient pleasure in the song of contemplation? The hymnist gave no generic human-divine encounter, no abstraction of lofty ideas with the collective human reality. Rather, Romanos's verses sang of concrete, physical encounter: body to body; one to one.[58]

Then again, the poet might "queer" his voice. In his kontakion on the Sinful Woman, Romanos took his congregation with measured deliberation into the mind of the harlot: "I would like to search the mind of the wise woman [the Harlot] / and to know how Jesus came to shine in her; / he the loveliest and the creator of what is lovely, / whose form the harlot longed for before she saw him."[59] As he did for Thomas (and indeed, for Adam), Romanos sang the Woman's encounter by imagining her own voice:

> I am going to him, because it is for me he has come.
> I am leaving those who were once mine, because now I long greatly for him.
> And as the One who loves me, I anoint him and caress him;
> I weep and I groan and I urge him fittingly to long for me.
> I am changed to the longing of the One who is longed for,
> And, as he wishes to be kissed, so I kiss my lover.
> I grieve and bow myself down, for this is what he wishes.
> I keep silent and withdrawn, for in these he delights.
> I break with past lovers, that I may please my new love.
> In short, by blowing on it, I renounce
>   (refrain) *the filth of my deeds.*[60]

Male voice sang of female desire. Heteronormative in articulation (perhaps voicing what men thought women desired), yet the performance was homoerotically gendered. And the congregation? Each individual, male and female, was called to enter the song's voices; to join the refrain that voiced the singer's (male) subject (Romanos), the (female) object of contemplation (the Harlot), the (female) subject's quest for the (male) body of Christ; to contemplate the handling of body with, by, and through body. Each singing voice, male and female, entered the rhetorically crafted subjectivities of the kontakion's performance. Each participant was called to pay attention and to learn.

The Sinful Woman was one of the most liturgically important biblical characters for Byzantine Christians (as for Orthodox now). Her brief biblical story (Luke 7: 36–50) received lavish attention in hymns and sermons. On the one hand, the story's nature provided sharply defined, heteronormative sexual articulation, which Byzantine liturgical poets, such as Romanos, did not hesitate to explore with graphic detail.[61] On the other, liturgical performance destabilized heterosexual ownership of the story's content. Male preachers and chanters voiced the Woman's longing, singing the physicality of her encounter with Jesus' body. Male and female congregants—monastic or lay—voiced their participation in the story as they sang the refrain.

The kontakia of Romanos were performed in an urban context of mixed monastic, clerical, and lay congregations. But liturgy was also fundamental to monastic life, in same-sex communities of any size. Ascetic discipline required bodily engagement, sensory awareness, and bodily attention as tools through which the monastic (male or female) trained the self anew: to seek God, to know God, to live wholly toward God, and to experience divine encounter. Again, such profound bodily attunement did not deny desire as a fundamental quality of bodily experience.

This is nowhere clearer than in the writings of Symeon the New Theologian (949–1022), where keenly homoerotic imagery drew the monk to contemplation of his own body, in and through contemplation of the wholly incarnate and wholly divine body of Christ.

> We are made members of Christ, and Christ becomes our members
>   (I Cor. 6.16)
> And Christ becomes the hand and the foot of all-wretched me,
> And wretched I become the hand of Christ and the foot of Christ.
> . . .
> And thus every member of each one of us
> Shall become a member of Christ, and Christ our members,
> And He shall make all shameful things decent (I Cor. 12.23–24)
> By the beauty of His divinity and by His glory He shall adorn them. . . .
> And thus so you well know that both my finger and my penis
>   are Christ,
> Do you tremble or feel ashamed?
> But God was not afraid to become like you,
> Yet you are ashamed to become like Him.[62]

Extolling the transcendent state of his spiritual father, Symeon the Studite, Symeon continued the meditation:

> [Symeon] was not ashamed about the members of any person,
> neither to see any naked people nor to be seen naked;
> . . .
> and he remained unmoved, innocent, and dispassionate,
> since he . . . saw
> all the baptized, who have put on the whole Christ as Christ.[63]

Elsewhere, in a parable patterned on the Prodigal Son (Luke 15:11–32), Symeon depicted a penitent rebel reunited with his forgiving emperor: "day and night [the emperor] rejoices and is glad with him, embracing him and kissing his mouth with his own. So much does he love him exceedingly that he is not separated from him even in sleep, but lies together with him embracing him on his bed, and he covers him all about with his own cloak, and places his face upon all his members."[64] As Derek Krueger has demonstrated, Symeon's writings cannot be turned to other meanings. For this monk, embodied desire was woven deeply into his mystical devotion, and that desire was frankly homoerotic in concrete as well as imagistic articulation.[65]

The eroticism of Christian mystical writings has a long history well-known to theologians and historians alike.[66] What must be remembered—and indeed, instructively considered—is that the mystic's body was not necessarily a heterosexual one. In the imagery of mystical contemplation such as Symeon the New Theologian's, we encounter a rhetoric that shares much with the erotic rhetoric of friendship, and with the eroticism of sacred story liturgically sung. What emerges time and again in these habits of shared rhetorical artistry is the efficacy—indeed, the expedience—of employing affective, erotic imagery, performed through gendered expressions both hetero- and homosexual. Desire is as basic to human, bodily epistemology as any other bodily experience. As with relationality, embodied desire could enable effective human-divine relationship.

In Sum: Basic Theological Reflections

With a phrase that recurs now and again in Byzantine monastic stories, John Moschos tells of two monks who "had sworn an oath to each other that they would never be separated from each other, either in life or in death."[67] In time, one brother held true to their vocation and one fell; yet the oath held. Staying together despite their tribulations, the sinner came to repent. Together they returned to their shared monastic practice, arriving at their deaths each in the peace of the Lord. Because of their devotion to one another, their devotion to God prevailed.

What does the model of faithful monastic relationships teach us? Byzantine history offers striking witness to relationality as an instrument in the human advancement toward God, and to embodied desire as an ontological aspect of that effort. Moreover, this history attests to both cross-sex and same-sex contexts for these fundamental themes, with both homo- and heterosexual expressions. There are important ramifications here for the consideration of Orthodoxy and homosexuality. First, the historical record cannot be reduced to one of consistent opposition. Second, we must ask how these inherited patterns of relationality and embodied desire might inform theological discussion of humanity, sexuality, and the desire for God. The practice of celibate, ascetic cross-sex couples does not, in the eyes of Christian tradition, invalidate nor diminish heterosexual marriage, including sexual intimacy, as a vehicle for religious devotion. Nor should the record of celibate same-sex monastic couples deny the religious devotion lived in and through those homosexual relationships where shared devotion to one another includes shared devotion to God. Rather, this history demonstrates that we should take seriously the very real strengths that committed relationships, illuminated with embodied desire, offer for leading a life of faith. Those strengths are apparent in the texts I have discussed here regardless of the sexual orientation involved.

I suggest that relationality matters theologically because it stands at the very heart of Christianity. The Trinity itself is intrinsically and indivisibly relational: three Persons coexisting in perfect, harmonious union. The incarnation was an irreducibly relational event, uniting divine and human. Jesus held the Beloved Disciple in intimate embrace (John 13:23–25). Relation is how the divine operates, how the human and divine meet, and how the divine works with and within us. But what draws us, the human part of that relation, to want relation with God, to want God's own self to be known within our own very selves? That is where desire must be paired with relationality.[68]

Desire, of course, cannot be reduced to sexual desire, any more than the human person can be reduced to sexual activity. But that human persons experience sexuality as intrinsic to their embodiment, and that desire—of multiple valences—is equally fundamental, are basic human truths. Throughout Byzantine history—in social history no less than literary forms, in living patterns no less than liturgical traditions—we see erotic desire fruitfully engaged for purposes of religious devotion and religious knowledge. We see, in fact, the promise that embodied desire might be conjoined to relationships of shared devotion to God.

The body is where we experience and know; it is where we express what we know.[69] We are commanded to relationship: to love one another, even as we love God. In relationship we articulate and express that which God calls us to do and to be. God calls us to long for relationship, to recognize and respond to it, to seek its fulfillment. We can only do so as we are: in our bodies, through and with our embodied humanity. Yet these same bodies, relational and desiring, can yield faithful, transfigured, and transfiguring lives, blessed in the presence of God.

Notes

1. E.g., the oft-cited passage from John of Damascus, *Apology* 1.11, trans. Andrew Louth, *St. John of Damascus, Three Treatises on the Divine Images* (Crestwood, N.Y.: St. Vladimir's Seminary Press, 2003), 26.

2. A wide range of evidence is collected and critically analyzed in, e.g., John Boswell, *Christianity, Social Tolerance, and Homosexuality: Gay People in Western Europe from the Beginning of the Christian Era to the Fourteenth Century* (Chicago: University of Chicago Press, 1980); John Boswell, *Same-Sex Unions in Premodern Europe* (New York: Villard, 1994); Bernadette Brooten, *Love between Women: Early Christian Responses to Female Homoeroticism* (Chicago: University of Chicago Press, 1996); Derek Krueger, "Between Monks: Tales of Monastic Companionship in Early Byzantium," *Journal of the History of Sexuality* 20, no. 1 (2011): 28–61; Claudia Rapp, *Brother-Making in Late Antiquity and Byzantium: Monks, Laymen, and Christian Ritual* (Oxford: Oxford University Press, 2016); Stephen Morris, *"When Brothers Dwell in Unity": Byzantine Christianity and Homosexuality* (Jefferson, N.C.: McFarland and Co. Inc., 2016); Roland Betancourt, *Byzantine Intersectionality: Sexuality, Gender and Race in the Middle Ages* (Princeton: Princeton University Press, 2020).

3. Trinity College Dublin Pap. D 5; edition and commentary in Brian C. McGing, "Melitian Monks at Labla," *Tyche: Beitrage zur alten Geschichte, Papyrologie, und Epigraphik* 5 (1990): 67–94, a group of three papyri representing a complicated legal tangle between Aiouios, Eulogios, and others.

4. Supplementum Magicum 1.42, analyzed in Brooten, *Love between Women*, 81–90.

5. Papyri Graecae Magicae 32 and 32a, analyzed in Brooten, *Love between Women*, 77–81; see 73–113 for the full discussion of Greek erotic spells in various media.

6. There is abundant scholarship. On variations in social arrangements, see, e.g., Susanna Elm, *Virgins of God: The Making of Asceticism in Late Antiquity* (New York: Oxford University Press, 1994); Rebecca Krawiec, *Shenoute and the Women of the White Monastery: Egyptian Monasticism in Late Antiquity* (New York: Oxford University Press, 2002); Caroline Schroeder, *Monastic Bodies: Discipline and Salvation in Shenoute of Atripe* (Philadelphia: University of Pennsylvania Press, 2007); S. A. Harvey, *Asceticism and Society in Crisis: John of Ephesus and the Lives of the Eastern Saints* (Berkeley: University of California Press, 1990).

7. Athanasius, *The Life of Antony*, sec. 4–5, trans. Robert Gregg, in *Athanasius: The Life of Antony and the Letter to Marcellinus* (New York: Paulist Press, 1980), 34–35.

8. E.g., Morris, "When Brothers Dwell in Unity," 17–41, 197–99; Terry Wilfong, "Friendship and Physical Desire: The Discourse of Female Homoeroticism in Fifth-Century CE Egypt," in *Among Women: From Homosocial to the Homoerotic in the Ancient World*, ed. Nancy Sorkin Rabinowitz and Lisa Auanger (Austin: University of Texas Press, 2002), 304–30. For contextualization, see David Brakke, *Demons and the Making of the Monk: Spiritual Combat in Early Christianity* (Cambridge, Mass.: Harvard University Press, 2006), esp. 97–124, 157–81.

9. John Chrysostom, "Instruction and Refutation Directed against Men Cohabiting with Virgins," here quoted from sec. 1, trans. in Elizabeth A. Clark, *Jerome, Chrysostom, and Friends: Essays and Translations* (New York: Elwin Mellen Press, 1979), 164–205, at 164–65. There is a consistency of themes in these instances and with monastic and ascetic literature, in terms of constant admonition against sexual misconduct. Typical examples would be: Aphrahat the Persian Sage, Demonstration 6, "On Covenanters," trans. in Adam Lehto, *The Demonstrations of Aphrahat, the Persian Sage* (Piscataway, N.J.: 2010), 169–98; John Chrysostom, "On the Necessity of Guarding Virginity," trans. Clark, in *Jerome, Chrysostom, and Friends*, 209–48.

10. Krueger, "Between Monks"; Rapp, *Brother-Making*, esp. 88–179.

11. Gregory of Nyssa, "The Life of St. Macrina," trans. Virginia Woods Callahan, in *Saint Gregory of Nyssa, Ascetical Works* (Washington, DC: The Catholic University of America Press, 1967), 163–91, at 166.

12. "Life of St. Macrina," 188.

13. John of Ephesus, *Lives of the Eastern Saints*, ch. 12; "Euphemia and Maria," trans. in S. P. Brock and S. A. Harvey, *Holy Women of the Syrian Orient* (Berkeley: University of California Press, 1987, 1998), 124–33; see S. A. Harvey, "Sacred

Bonding: Mothers and Daughters in Early Syriac Hagiography," *Journal of Early Christian Studies* 4, no. 1 (1996): 27–56.

14. Abba Carion and Zacharias, in *The Sayings of the Desert Fathers: The Alphabetical Collection*, trans. Benedicta Ward (rev. ed. Kalamazoo, Mich.: Cistercian Publications, 1984), 116–18. See the important discussion in Caroline Schroeder, "Queer Eye for the Ascetic Guy: Homoeroticism, Children, and the Making of Monks in Late Antique Egypt," *Journal of the American Academy of Religion* 77 (2009): 333–47.

15. John of Ephesus, *Lives of the Eastern Saints*, ed. and trans. E. W. Brooks, *Patrologia Orientalis* 17 (1923): 283–98 (ch. 21, Thomas the Armenian); also 18 (1924): 576–85 (ch. 31, Elijah and Theodore).

16. "Mary the Niece of Abraham of Qidun," in Brock and Harvey, *Holy Women of the Syrian Orient*, 27–39.

17. E.g., "The Life of St. Mary/Marinos," trans. Nicholas Constas, in *Holy Women of Byzantium*, ed. Alice-Mary Talbot (Washington, DC: Dumbarton Oaks, 1996), 1–12. See the important discussion in Caroline Schroeder, *Children and Family in Late Antique Egyptian Monasticism* (Cambridge: Cambridge University Press, 2021).

18. E.g.: Elizabeth A. Clark, *The Life of Melania the Younger* (New York: Edwin Mellen Press, 1984); Palladius, *The Lausiac History*, ch. 8 (Amoun of Nitria), trans. R. T. Meyer, Ancient Christian Writers 34 (New York: Newman Press, 1964), 41–43.

19. Tertullian, "To His Wife," 2.8, trans. William P. Le Saint, in *Tertullian: Treatises on Marriage and Remarriage*, Ancient Christian Writers 13 (Westminster, Md.: Newman Press, 1951), at 35.

20. Palladius, *Lausiac History*, ch. 8.

21. John of Ephesus, *Lives of the Eastern Saints*, ch. 55, *Patrologia Orientalis* 19 (1926): 191–96.

22. Theodoret of Cyrrhus, *History of the Monks of Syria*, ch. 29, trans. R. M. Price (Kalamazoo, Mich.: Cistercian Publications, 1985), 183–85.

23. Krueger, "Between Monks." See the discussion of Symeon the Fool and his companion John, below.

24. *The History of the Great Deeds of Bishop Paul of Qentos and Priest John of Edessa*, ed. and trans. Hans Arneson, Emanuel Fiano, Christine Luckritz, and Kyle Smith (Piscataway, N.J.: Gorgias Press, 2010), at 78 (sec. 44).

25. Galawdewos, *The Life and Struggles of Our Mother Walatta Petros: A Seventeenth-Century African Biography of an Ethiopian Woman*, trans. and ed. Wendy Laura Belcher and Michael Kleiner (Princeton: Princeton University Press, 2015), 116 (ch. 13). See Wendy Laura Belcher, "Same-Sex Intimacies in the Early African Text *Gädlä Wälättä Petros* (1672): Queer Reading an Ethiopian Woman Saint," *Research in African Literatures* 47, no. 2 (2016): 20–45.

26. Boswell, *Same-Sex Unions*, 372–74, identified sixty-two manuscripts between the eighth and sixteenth centuries that contained prayers for the adelphopoiesis ritual, but see Rapp's comments, *Brother-Making*, 263. Rapp widened the pool to include euchologia not known to Boswell, but also limited herself to the eighth through fifteenth centuries (prior to the printing press): sixty-six Greek and two non-Greek manuscripts. See Rapp, *Brother-Making*, at 55, and Appendix 1, 263–81, for the Table of Manuscripts. Appendix 3, 293–301, includes translations of sixteen prayers from the adelphopoiesis services preserved in Byzantine euchologia.

27. Rapp, *Brother-Making*, Prayer A, at 293.

28. Rapp. *Brother-Making*, Prayer B, 294; Prayer E, 296; Prayer G, 197; see also Prayer O, 301.

29. Rapp, *Brother-Making*; Boswell, *Same-Sex Unions*.

30. Lynda Coon, *Sacred Fictions: Holy Women and Hagiography in Late Antiquity* (Philadelphia: University of Pennsylvania Press, 1997).

31. "The Life of St. Mary of Egypt," sec. 10–16, trans. Maria Kouli, in Talbot, *Holy Women of Byzantium*, 65–94.

32. John Moschos, *The Spiritual Meadow*, ch. 122, trans. John Wortley (Kalamazoo, Mich.: Cistercian Publications, 1992), 99–100.

33. Paphnutius, *The Life of Onnophrius*, chs. 3, 10, trans. Tim Vivian, in *Histories of the Monks of Upper Egypt and the Life of Onnuphrius* (Kalamazoo, Mich.: Cistercian Publications, 1993), 146 (ch. 3, Timothy the Hermit), 151 (ch. 10, Paphnutius meets Onnophrius). See further Kristi Upson-Saia, "Hairiness and Holiness in the Early Christian Desert," in *Dressing Judeans and Christians in Antiquity*, ed. Kristi Upson-Saia, Carly Daniel-Hughes, and Alicia J. Batten (London: Routledge, 2014), 155–72.

34. Similarly, the naked female body could sometimes be textually displayed in heroic terms, without causing harm or shame. Stavroula Constantinou, *Female Corporeal Performances: Reading the Body in Byzantine Passions and Lives of Holy Women* (Uppsala, Sweden: Uppsala University Press, 2005), 19–89.

35. "On Lust," sec. 23, trans. Benedicta Ward, *The Desert Fathers: Sayings of the Early Christian Monks* (London: Penguin, 2003), 43. See also Krueger, "Between Monks," 39–40.

36. Virginia Burrus, *The Sex Lives of Saints: An Erotics of Ancient Hagiography* (Philadelphia: University of Pennsylvania Press, 2004); Krueger, "Between Monks."

37. "Mary of Egypt," secs. 18–21, trans. Kouli, 80–81.

38. E.g., Ruth Webb, *Demons and Dancers: Performance in Late Antiquity* (Cambridge, Mass.: Harvard University Press, 2008); Blake Leyerle, *Theatrical Shows and Ascetic Lives: John Chrysostom's Attack on Spiritual Marriage* (Berkeley: University of California Press, 2001). Baths were a particular problem.

39. A point emphasized in Peter Brown, "Late Antiquity," in *A History of Private Life: from Pagan Rome to Byzantium*, ed. Paul Veyne, trans. Arthur Goldhammer (Cambridge, Mass.: Belknap Press of Harvard University Press, 1987), at 241–46.

40. Cyril of Jerusalem, Mystagogical Catechesis 2.2–3, trans. Maxwell E. Johnson, in *Lectures on the Christian Sacraments: The Procatechesis and the Five Mystagogical Catecheses Ascribed to St. Cyril of Jerusalem* (Yonkers, N.Y.: St. Vladimir's Seminary Press, 2017).

41. Anointing the bodies of female initiates was one of the ministries of the female diaconate in the early church: see Valerie Karras, "Female Deacons in the Byzantine Church," *Church History* 73, no. 2 (2004): 272–316.

42. E.g., John Moschos, *Spiritual Meadow*, ch. 3, trans. Wortley, 5–6.

43. Brock and Harvey, *Holy Women of the Syrian Orient*, at 110.

44. The services are translated in *The Lenten Triodion*, trans. Mother Mary and Archimandrite Kallistos Ware (London: Faber and Faber, 1977), 445–63.

45. *Lenten Triodion*, 449–50. In the Byzantine calendar, Mary of Egypt is commemorated on April 1, the fifth Sunday of Lent, and Great and Holy Thursday.

46. David Konstan, *Friendship in the Classical World* (Cambridge: Cambridge University Press, 1997), is a useful guide.

47. Gregory of Nazianzus, Oration 43, "On St. Basil the Great," trans. R. J. Deferrari, in *St. Gregory Nazianzen and St. Ambrose, Funeral Orations*, trans. L. McCauley, J. J. Sullivan, M. R. P. McGuire, and R. J. Deferrari, Fathers of the Church 22 (New York: Newman Press, 1953), 27–99. See the important discussion in Jostein Børtnes, "Eros Transformed: Same-Sex Love and Divine Desire," in *Greek Biography and Panegyric in Late Antiquity*, ed. Tomas Hägg and Philip Rousseau (Berkeley: University of California Press, 2000), 180–93.

48. I follow Børtnes' translation, at 184 and 188.

49. Gregory of Nazianzus, Letter 6, trans. NPNF2, vol. 7.

50. P. L. R. Brown, *Augustine of Hippo: A Biography* (rev. ed. Berkeley: University of California Press, 2000), 50–53, 108–20.

51. Trans. Derek Krueger, "The Life of Symeon the Holy Fool," sec. 3, in Krueger, *Symeon the Holy Fool: Leontius's "Life" and the Late Antique City* (Berkeley: University of California Press, 1996), at 148–50. Compare *The History of the Great Deeds of Bishop Paul of Qentos and Priest John of Edessa*.

52. "Febronia," Brock and Harvey, *Holy Women of the Syrian Orient*, 150–76.

53. *Gadla Walatta Petros*, ch. 12, trans. Belcher and Kleiner, 115.

54. Crucial here is the work of Derek Krueger, *Liturgical Subjects: Christian Ritual, Biblical Narrative, and the Formation of the Self in Byzantium* (Philadelphia: University of Pennsylvania Press, 2014), 29–65. See also Georgia Frank, "Romanos and the Night Vigil in the Sixth Century," in *A People's History of Christianity*,

vol. 3: *Byzantine Christianity*, ed. D. Krueger (Minneapolis: Fortress, 2006), 59–78.

55. Romanos the Melodist, "On the Holy Theophany," str. 1, trans. Ephrem Lash, *St. Romanos the Melodist, On the Life of Christ: Kontakia* (San Francisco: Harper Collins, 1995), 39. For the Greek text, see Paul Maas and C. A. Trypanis, *Sancti Romani Melodi Canatica: Cantica Genuina* (Oxford: Clarendon Press, 1963), 34–41.

56. Romanos the Melodist, "On the Holy Theophany," str. 3, Lash, *St. Romanos*, 40.

57. Romanos the Melodist, "On the Apostle Thomas," str. 13, 14; Lash, *St. Romanos*, 188–89; Greek text in Maas and Trypanis, *Sancti Romani Melodi*, 234–41. On the Doubting Thomas as a scene of homoerotic treatment in Byzantine art and literature, see further Betancourt, *Byzantine Intersectionality*, 121–60.

58. For Romanos' engagement with heterosexual eroticism, see Thomas Arentzen, *The Virgin in Song: Mary and the Poetry of Romanos the Melodist* (Philadelphia: University of Pennsylvania Press, 2017), 46–86.

59. Romanos the Melodist, "On the Harlot," str. 4; Lash, *St. Romanos*, 78; Greek text in Maas and Trypanis, *Sancti Romani Melodi*, 73–80.

60. Romanos the Melodist, "On the Harlot," str. 5, Lash, *St. Romanos*, 79.

61. Another powerful example would be Jacob of Sarug's homily on the Sinful Woman, trans. Scott Fitzgerald Johnson, *Jacob of Sarug's Homily on the Sinful Woman* (Piscataway, N.J.: Gorgias Press, 2013).

62. Hymn 15, 141–63, trans. Daniel K. Griggs, *Divine Eros: Hymns of St. Symeon the New Theologian* (Crestwood, N.Y.: St. Vladimir's Seminary Press, 2010), 81–91, at 87.

63. Hymn 15, 207–14, Griggs, *St. Symeon*, 89.

64. Symeon the New Theologian, "Tenth Ethical Discourse," trans. Alexander Golitzin, *St. Symeon the New Theologian, On the Mystical Life: The Ethical Discourses*, vol. 1: *The Church and the Last Things* (Crestwood, N.Y.: St. Vladimir's Seminary Press, 1995), 142–70, at 150–51.

65. Derek Krueger, "Homoerotic Spectacle and the Monastic Body in Symeon the New Theologian," in *Toward a Theology of Eros: Transfiguring Passion at the Limits of Discipline,* ed. Virginia Burrus and Catherine Keller (New York: Fordham University Press, 2006), 99–118.

66. One thinks of Origen's and Gregory of Nyssa's commentaries on the Song of Songs, but unlike Western medieval theologians, Orthodox tradition has more often drawn on the image of Christ as Heavenly Bridegroom from the New Testament parables in Lk 14: 7–14, Mt 22: 1–14, Mt 25: 1–13.

67. John Moschos, *Spiritual Meadow*, 97; Wortley, 78–79.

68. On the connection between relationality, desire (including homosexual desire), and holiness, I am much helped by Sarah Coakley, *The New Asceticism: Sexuality, Gender, and the Quest for God* (London: Bloomsbury, 2015), and Sarah Coakley, *God, Sexuality, and the Self: An Essay "On the Trinity"* (Cambridge: Cambridge University Press, 2013).

69. S. A. Harvey, "Embodiment in Time and Eternity: A Syriac Perspective," *St. Vladimir's Theological Quarterly* 43 (1999): 105–30, repr. in *Theology and Sexuality: Classic and Contemporary Readings,* ed. Eugene F. Rogers Jr. (Oxford: Blackwell Publishers, 2002), 3–22.

CHAPTER

2

Something New under the Sun

Sexualities, Same-Sex Relationships, and Orthodoxy

Bryce E. Rich

Questions of sexuality and the possibility of recognizing same-sex relationships have only recently begun to emerge within intra-Orthodox conversations. These topics, often associated with secularization and the culture wars, have proven difficult to discuss. However, the consequences of this lack of engagement threaten Orthodoxy's ability to speak to modern questions and, closer to home, they create a culture in which lesbian, gay, and bisexual Orthodox, their families, and their friends find worship and spiritual growth difficult and, sometimes, impossible. Some stay and experience further hurt and pain, while others choose to leave their parishes. Some reject Christianity entirely.

Using insights from contemporary queer theory, the first half of the essay explores the concept of *sexualities* with particular attention to same-sex orientation. Some queer theorists suggest that, far from a single, unified concept, sexualities are constructions of particular, historically contingent discourses. Modern homosexuality, rather than replacing previous models, exists in addition to these various figures from the past. To understand our current predicament, it is important to grasp the various facets of these historical figures that both compete with and contribute to our understandings of contemporary gays and lesbians. Much of the territory covered in this essay has been a part of conversations in other Christian traditions about sexualities and same-sex relationships for over fifty years. However, for an Orthodox audience, much of this information is likely new. The second half of the essay briefly frames a set of current impediments to the full acceptance of loving, covenanted, same-sex erotic relationships within the Orthodox Church. These include, among others, traditional interpretations of scripture, legal-canonical prohibitions, and anthropological models that inform traditional Orthodox theological reflection. I offer the survey presented in the first part of the paper as a first step toward addressing some of the impediments outlined in the second.

The Rise of Sexualities

While same-sex erotic activity[1] has existed for at least as long as written records, the idea of *sexuality* is of much more recent origin. Indeed, *homosexuality* as a concept in the social sciences came into existence in 1868 and entered the English language some twenty-four years later. The language of *sexual orientation* is part of a broader set of discourses that constitute the idea of sexuality, which began in this same period in the medical and psychiatric disciplines.

In a well-known, oft-quoted, and frequently misunderstood passage from *The History of Sexuality*, volume I, Michel Foucault writes:

> As defined by the ancient civil or canonical codes, sodomy was a category of forbidden acts; their perpetrator was nothing more than the juridical subject of them. The nineteenth-century homosexual became a personage, a past, a case history, and a childhood, in addition to being a type of life, a life form, and a morphology, with an indiscreet anatomy and possibly a mysterious physiology. Nothing that went into his total composition was unaffected by his sexuality. It was everywhere present in him: at the root of all his actions because it was their insidious and indefinitely active principle; written immodestly on his face and body because it was a secret that always gave itself away. It was consubstantial with him, less as a habitual sin than as a singular nature.[2]

The homosexual of nineteenth-century medical and psychoanalytic discourses that Foucault goes on to describe is based on the idea of gender inversion. In this model, an individual's biological sex is seen as either male or female. If he is male, then a heterosexual orientation would call for affective attraction to (and, by extension, sexual relations with) a female. A heterosexual female is attracted to males. But with gender inversion, the desires and gender roles of the homosexual male lead to typically feminine desires and behaviors.[3] Likewise, according to this model, the homosexual female exhibits typically masculine desires and behaviors.

However, few of us, when we refer to "sexual orientation" today, have in mind the homosexual of nineteenth-century discourse. To be sure, this figure still lurks in the shadows, sometimes surfacing in schoolyard taunts that question a boy's masculinity. But what do *we* mean today? Queer theorist David Halperin makes casual reference to the "straight-acting and -appearing gay male" who is "distinct from other men in absolutely no other respect besides that of his 'sexuality'" as the typical understanding of homosexuality in our own time.[4] And yet, this is also an idealization. While there are many gay men who "pass" as straight in our day-to-day life, certainly not all do.

In critiquing both Foucault and Halperin, gender and queer theorist Eve Kosofsky Sedgwick notes that there is no one model for homosexuality "as we understand [it] today."[5] Rather, there are a variety of competing tropes that continue to circulate simultaneously in an unrationalized coexistence. To understand what Sedgwick means, it will be helpful for us to first examine a variety of precursors to the modern concept of sexuality.

We begin our survey with examples drawn from the Hebrew scriptures. Chief among these are the accounts of the destruction of Sodom and Gomorrah in Genesis 19 and a parallel passage in Judges 19 that takes place in Gibeah in the territory of the Benjaminites. The two accounts have a parallel structure, and it appears that one is dependent on the other. While their details vary, key to both episodes is the demand of the citizens of the respective towns that visitors be sent out to them that they may "know them."[6] In both instances, counteroffers are made to send women out from the respective houses—Lot's virgin daughters in Genesis and the Levite's concubine in Judges—to assuage the mobs.

From ancient times, commentators have offered various interpretations for these accounts.[7] At issue in both instances is the sacred duty of showing hospitality to strangers. Christ's own words in the gospel accounts suggest that the sin of Sodom is not only inhospitality to strangers, but also rejecting emissaries.[8] In the context of Hellenization, writers of the pseudepigrapha, apocrypha, and first-century Jewish commentators such as Josephus and Philo connect the sin of Sodom with pederasty. These texts influence the authors of 1 Peter and Jude, and the view then appears in further patristic writings and beyond.[9] But at least one other conclusion can be drawn: It is better to offer up one's own daughters or one's wife to gang rape than to allow the same fate to befall a man.[10] This interpretation gathers further support when we remember that Saul, having fallen in battle, commands his armorbearer to kill him rather than face the fate of being captured and "abused" by the Philistines.[11] Each of these accounts refer to sexual assault.

In Leviticus, we find two prohibitions against a man lying with a male as with women, the second of which, in its received form, calls for the death penalty.[12] Both passages lie within the Holiness Code, a geographically contingent covenant within the larger work, concerned with cultic purity. In both passages, male same-sex intercourse is characterized as *tôʿēbâ*, normally translated as "abomination," which refers to ritual impurity. Verses 18:3 and 24–30 frame the first set of prohibitions as Canaanite practices that defiled both the land and its inhabitants. Thus, the land vomited them out, just as it would the Israelites if they were to engage in the same acts.

While the literary setting of the Holiness Code is the time of Moses and the Israelites traveling in the desert between Egypt and Canaan, the dating of the received redaction appears to be the Babylonian exile, a time when the Israelites were attempting to maintain a distinct cultural identity in a foreign country.[13] Their solution is found in reinforcing an ethnic and religious identity over and against the cultic practices of neighboring peoples. As such, the Levitical proscriptions should be read as attributing sexual acts between two males—specifically anal intercourse—to those who worship other gods. While it would be easy to think of proscriptions against male homosexuality as part of a comprehensive sexual ethic, the prohibition against sacrificing one's children to Molech draws the focus back to cultic practices.[14]

We break here from biblical sources to turn to Greco-Roman models of same-sex erotic activity that inform the writers of the New Testament and early patristic authors. Common to both Greek and Roman cultures is a sensibility that modern readers would interpret as bisexuality. Desire was commonly associated with a particular aesthetic of beauty. More precisely, a smooth youth (*ephēbos*), a pubescent girl, and a woman were all considered proper sexual objects.[15] Sexual relations in both cultures were rigidly hierarchical. Irrespective of his partner's identity, the citizen male was expected to act as penetrative partner, whether vaginally or anally.[16]

There are several terms used in Greco-Roman culture to describe those who participate in same-sex erotic activity. Among these are the effeminate *malakos* and the gender-variant *androgynos*, the scare figure of the *kinaidos*, the gender-variant female *tribas*, and the *erastēs* and *eromenos* of Greek pederasty. Let us briefly examine each one in turn.

The *malthakos* or *malakos* (literally "soft" and often translated as "fainthearted," "cowardly," or "effeminate"; the Latin equivalent is *mollis*) was a figure much derided for his lack of self-control. Like other males, he might seek out sexual encounters with both women and boys. However, the *malakos* was mocked for giving himself over to his desires. In his attempt to appear more youthful for his pursuit of sexual partners, he wore expensive clothing, used cosmetics and perfumes, and removed his body hair.[17] While some measure of self-care in an effort to appear more appealing was certainly within the norm, the *malakos* was ridiculed for his excesses, which were viewed as a betrayal of self-control and his masculine nature.

Likewise, the *androgynos* was a figure derided for his feminine character. His aberration was one of gender rather than sexual partners, who, like those of the *malakos*, might be either male or female.[18] Descriptions of the *androgynos* tend to focus on his effeminate gait, posture, and manner of speech.[19] In later periods, his physical description is shared by the *kinaidos*.[20]

Within the Ancient Greek context, the *kinaidos* (Latin *cinaedus*) serves as a warning to male citizens.[21] He combines both the excesses of the *malakos* and the effeminacy of the *androgynos*. In pursuit of sexual pleasures, he allows himself to be penetrated as the receptive partner in anal intercourse, resulting in the utter loss of his masculine status through assuming the sexual role of a woman. However, the *kinaidos* is not the equivalent of a passive homosexual. Unlike the modern character, he may still engage in an active (i.e., insertive) role with both men and women.[22] Over time, the *cinaedus* is also associated with prostitution.

Though drawing much less attention, ancient Greeks also spoke of the *tribas* (same in Latin), a woman who rubbed her genitals against another woman. The *tribas* was a liminal figure not because of her attraction to other women, but because of her transgression of gender roles in assuming the dominant role reserved for men.[23]

It is critical to note that the sexual partners of both the *tribas* and the *kinaidos* were not painted with the same brush of shame or depravity. A woman penetrated by a *tribas* was still acting within expected gender roles, while the man who penetrated a *kinaidos* was also still on top of the pecking order.[24] Roman sexual questions tend to revolve around both who is penetrated and who is penetrating, as well as via what orifice. Far more descriptive than the Greeks, Latin uses a separate verb for assuming the active or passive position with respect to anal, vaginal, and oral sex.[25] Further, a man who practiced cunnilingus could receive more intense abuse than a fellator. However, if a man practiced one, it was generally assumed that he would enjoy the other.[26] These Roman sensibilities do not readily translate to our own culture.

Finally, we come to the ancient Greek practice of pederasty. Within this arrangement, freeborn youths would enter into patronage relationships with older male citizens. The older partner, known as the *erastēs* or "lover," would provide favors, counsel, and mentorship. The younger partner was known as the *eromenos* ("beloved") or *pais* ("boy"). The role of *erastēs* was adopted by young men, generally in their twenties, while the *eromenos* tended to be between the ages of the onset of puberty and the appearance of his beard.[27] Sexual contact between the two partners consisted of anal or interfemoral intercourse with the *erastēs* acting as insertive partner. The hair growth associated with secondary male sex characteristics was considered aesthetically unpleasing and marked the transition into adulthood. Pederastic relationships generally ended by the time the youth reached the age of his *dokimasia*, a form of vetting used to determine a man's worthiness of citizenship.[28] However, being penetrated at any age was risky business for ancient Greek males. One significant difference between the *eromenos* and the older *kinaidos* was the idea that, while the younger might choose to "gratify" (*kharizesthai*) his *erastēs* out of gratitude or esteem (or even opportunistically to curry favor in the pursuit of the older man's wealth), he could never be seen as enjoying his passive role.[29]

In the Roman context, citizen males were strictly forbidden from assuming the passive role in a same-sex erotic encounter. Any freeborn man who allowed himself to be penetrated was punished through the confiscation of half his property and a declaration of *infamia*, stripping him of his citizen privileges such as the right to give testimony or participate in legal proceedings.[30] However, unlike the Greek context in which future citizens entered same-sex relationships as *eromenoi*, the use of a freeborn boy as a sexual partner was forbidden under the laws concerning *stuprum*, or illicit sexual activity, and carried severe penalties. As such, the use of boys as sexual objects was limited to slaves, both within one's own household and those forced into brothels.[31]

In further contrast with the Greeks, licit same-sex eroticism in the Roman context was not limited by the expectations that a male play a particular role dependent on his age. Roman citizen males engaged in same-sex erotic acts not only with youths, but also with both bearded slaves and male prostitutes who had passed the bloom of youth. The latter, known as an *exoletus* (literally "grown" or "outgrown" as distinct from the *adolescens* or "growing up"),[32] not only served as an object of penetration, but clients were also known to pay to be penetrated by him. In the fourth and sixth centuries, emperors Theodosius the Great and Justinian respectively passed legislation under which *exoleti* were characterized as a contagion that brought moral decay to the empire. Theodosius called for the public burning of *exoleti* and the men who hired their services—the former for throwing away their male sex to become women and the latter for their shameful sensuality that damned the *exoleti* to the passive role of women.[33] Justinian blamed the *exoleti* for a series of earthquakes, floods, pestilence, and plague throughout the empire that he saw as signs of divine wrath. While he made allowance for repentance, repeat offenders were to be executed.[34] We've already seen the claim that homosexual activity brings divine wrath in the form of natural disasters and punishment of an entire people in Leviticus. And the claim remains popular even today in various Christian traditions.

It is in this environment of sexual exploitation and abuse that we find the intertestamental Jewish polemic of *geneseōs enallagē* (literally "changing of kind") in the Wisdom of Solomon that serves as the model for the speech presented by the Apostle Paul in Romans 1.[35] In both instances, same-sex erotic behavior is characterized as a pagan practice, a result of a clouding of the mind due to idolatry. Of the New Testament passages associated with homosexual activity, the diatribe in Romans 1 is probably the most frequently cited. However, recent scholarship opens questions about this carefully crafted rhetorical trap.[36] Does Paul agree with the view presented in Romans 1:18–32? A strong moral case can certainly be made based on our knowledge of Roman practices of forcing slaves into sexual service.[37] But the presence of many slaves in the Roman church who, subject to their masters' whims, do not enjoy full bodily autonomy and cannot help being forced into same-sex sexual acts complicates blanket condemnations. In this context, what is Paul's good news for those who have no control over their own fates?[38] Here again we speak not of loving, committed relationships, but of exploitation and rape.

Pagan practices are also the context of the vice lists offered in 1 Corinthians and 1 Timothy that include the neologism *arsenokoitēs* and the already familiar *malakos*. The term *arsenokoitēs* appears to have been coined by Paul and is repeated only much later and without commentary in Christian vice lists. While twentieth-century English translations have rendered these words variously as "effeminate," "sexual perverts," "male prostitutes," "sodomites," and "homosexuals," the meaning of *arsenokoitēs* in the original passage is unclear.³⁹ *Malakos* appears only in the first vice list. While rendered as "homosexuals" by the Living Bible and NKJV, and as "male prostitutes" by the NIV and the NRSV, the more traditional translation is "effeminate." Contemporary translators have sometimes paired the two terms as active and passive male same-sex partners. However, as we have already seen, according to the cultural values of the day, a penetrated male was definitely *malakos*, but not every *malakos* is penetrated.⁴⁰ Turning to *arsenokoitēs*, the source appears to be the LXX translation of Leviticus 20:13, where the words *arsenos koitēn* ("male" and "bed") appear together in the prohibition. Some scholars have argued that if Paul was indeed drawing language from the Holiness Code, then how he understood the Levitical passage determines the meaning of the new word (i.e., allowing etymology to determine not only the word's history, but also its meaning). Other scholars have argued that the word includes connotations of economic exploitation and sex trafficking.⁴¹ In another short (but important) essay, William Petersen questions the translation of *arsenokoitēs* as "homosexual." Petersen explores the coining of the term *homosexual* to specifically describe a person's desire, orientation, or affect. He then follows the line of argument that distinguishes between desires and acts. Due to the lack of equivalence between the two words, the use of the word *homosexual* does not include (1) celibate people of a same-sex orientation or (2) heterosexuals engaged in same-sex erotic acts, but does include (3) lesbians, who are not included under the original term.⁴² Again we find a lack of meaningful equivalence between diachronic categories.

Within Orthodox canon law, the term *arsenokoitia* comes to denote a series of illicit sexual practices analogous to medieval understandings of sodomy. While mutual masturbation is not considered full *arsenokoitia*, the category includes both interfemoral and anal intercourse between males and anal intercourse between a man and his wife. Various penances for each of these acts are found in a list interpolated in the canons of John the Faster. The penance imposed in each case was eighty days for mutual masturbation, four years for acts between unmarried males, and eight years for the married couple. In the Latin West, same-sex erotic behaviors (as well as nonprocreative sexual acts between opposite-sex partners) are eventually labeled *sodomy*, a term whose pedigree includes a dual movement of condensation and expansion of meaning that would be unrecognizable to earlier readers of the scriptures.[43]

Finally, as we approach more contemporary conversations, we must add two more figures. The *pedophile* is an adolescent or adult whose primary or exclusive sexual attraction is oriented to prepubescent children, while the *ephebophile* has a primary attraction to mid-to-late adolescents.[44] Both pedophiles and ephebophiles can be attracted to females, males, or both sexes. The primary criterion for both classifications is the physical stage of development of the object of sexual interest, designated roughly by physical age. In much discussion among Orthodox today, there is a conflation between pedophilia and homosexuality, suggesting that adults who engage in same-sex erotic activity are also a threat to children. Some people do not actually realize that pedophilia and homosexuality are two separate phenomena. However, in some cases, this conflation is a rhetorical move executed in bad faith.

Though this whirlwind survey of categories and descriptors for same-sex erotic activity is necessarily short, I hope it shows that *orientation* is a slippery term—a term of relatively recent origin that coexists with a variety of other older ideas. I will also add that it is a disputed term in both ecclesiastical and academic circles. Within gender theory, sexuality is said to exist in a triad along with gender roles and biological sex. Further, some theorists characterize all three (gender, biological sex, and orientation) as contingent descriptors that vary through time and across cultural contexts. Foucault's initial genealogy of sexualities was specifically intended to draw into question the psychoanalytic paradigm in which an individual's identity is defined by his or her desires. Further projects in the social sciences continue to question the validity of sexualities as stable, universal categories as opposed to culturally situated constructs. As examples, recent scholarship suggests a greater flexibility in women's desire than the ideas of homo- and heterosexuality allow.[45] Likewise, recent work suggests straight, white men may also engage in a variety of homoerotic sexual practices without taking on the label homosexual by virtue of the intersection of their other privileged identities.[46] Thus, even within the social sciences, the idea of fixed orientation is complicated beyond earlier categories.

Here we find a possible point of agreement between some modern discourses and traditional Orthodox thought. Traditional Orthodox anthropology views desires as a function of the passions. The passions in and of themselves are good gifts from God. When misdirected, they can drag a person away from God, resulting in perdition. But when correctly oriented, they drive the human person toward divine-human communion (*theosis*). When we cease to view everything through the lens of modern sexual orientations, a different dynamic becomes evident in Athanasius's accounts of the temptations faced by Antony while he was in the desert. Within the *vita*, Antony is tempted first by a woman. But when this proves unacceptable, he is tempted again by a dark boy (*melas . . . pais*, a word that we previously saw associated with the younger partner in a pederastic relationship) who identifies himself as the spirit of fornication (*pneuma porneias*).[47] With what we now know of ancient aesthetics, it is not the sex of the partner offered to Antony that is key, but rather understanding that both a woman and a boy were considered appropriate objects for sexual gratification in the broader culture, a culture that Antony renounced when he fled to the desert.

Returning to Sedgwick's observation, we recall that newer paradigms such as the gender-inverted homosexual or the straight-acting, straight-looking gay man do not *supersede* older paradigms. Rather, the various paradigms tend to coexist simultaneously in an unrationalized manner. Thus, as I have described various earlier figures that deviate from the ideal of the modern heterosexual—*malakoi, androgynoi, kinaidoi, tribades, erastai, eromenoi, exoleti*, pedophiles, ephebophiles, and inverts—chances are that moments in each of these descriptions have touched on characteristics commonly associated with the contemporary concept of gays and, to a lesser extent, lesbians. Yet because these various tropes have never been fully reconciled with one another, the range of gendered, physical, and psychological characteristics results in a contradictory and imprecise idea of exactly what we are talking about. While such slippage may prove rhetorically convenient in a culture-wars debate, it does little to constructively address the lives of lesbian, gay, and bisexual people within the Orthodox Church. It is to these people and their relationships that I now wish to turn.

Current Impediments to Recognizing Same-Sex Erotic Relationships

I would like to explore a proposition—that a loving, covenanted, same-sex erotic relationship can serve as a vehicle for moving its participants toward *theosis* in a way analogous to an Orthodox sacramental marriage. There are several impediments within current Orthodox discussions of this proposal that I believe we Orthodox must address to clarify both what we are talking about and what is at stake.

Having gone to great lengths above to name and explore a variety of relevant historical models of same-sex erotic activity, I want to suggest that what we are dealing with in terms of a loving, covenanted, same-sex relationship with a licit erotic expression is, indeed, something new under the sun.[48] Let us exclude rape, coercion, and exploitation as nonstarters. Likewise, we are not in the realm of ancient Near Eastern or Greco-Roman pagan cultic practice. While it is true that some same-sex erotic activities, like their opposite-sex counterparts, are predicated on a dissipated desire to experience ever more and newer sexual pleasures through prostitution, this is also not our current focus. Rather, I wish to focus specifically on those same-sex relationships that, within their commitments to fidelity and longevity of relationship, have at least the potential to serve as expressions of self-sacrificial love and offer venues to foster the development of the fruits of the spirit that characterize analogous opposite-sex relationships.[49] But before such a discussion can take place, there are still further hurdles to clear within the Orthodox context.

First, we must offer a reasonable account of the ways in which the living Holy Tradition responds to the presence of new information and new questions. Contemporary Orthodoxy throughout the world is experiencing a rise in what Vasilios Makrides has labeled "rigorism," a phenomenon analogous to "fundamentalism" associated with contemporary Protestantism and "integrism" associated with the parallel phenomenon in Catholicism.[50] While the twentieth century witnessed a productive period of engagement with modern philosophy and Western Christianity, the current temptation for Orthodox is to retreat into an idealized version of the past and parrot the words of the fathers. However, study of the Tradition that includes the cultural and historical contexts in which Orthodoxy developed reveals a multitude of instances in which patristic authors have drawn from classical education, the scientific understandings of their day, and their own cultural contexts in the attempt to articulate their theological vision in ways that were true to their understandings of how the world works. While the message of the gospel handed down in the Tradition remains the same, it is the task of every generation to articulate it in understandable ways.[51]

Once we have opened a way for reexamining our teachings in light of new information, we must address the biblical proscriptions against homosexual activity. Orthodox have, especially in our interactions with the Western Christian tradition, received a common set of interpretations for the passages explored above. However, since the mid-twentieth century, theologians and biblical scholars have been applying historical-critical methods to scripture as they explore authorship, dating, provenance, and issues addressed within the text. This essay provides many references in its footnotes to the better exegetical work that has already been produced. Orthodox need neither to reinvent the wheel nor to adopt this research in full. There is much to be learned through an open, critical engagement with these sources.

Related to this careful exegesis of biblical texts commonly understood to address homosexual acts, we must also address related questions of gender subordination. Familiar interpretations of the Pauline corpus promote a series of hierarchical relationship within the family based on gender roles. But same-sex relationships problematize headship arguments that suggest an iconic parallel between Christ and the Church and the husband and wife in an opposite-sex marriage[52] In order to maintain commonly accepted hierarchical relations within the couple, a woman must serve as head of a female couple, while a man would occupy the subordinate position in a male couple. Here also much exegetical and theological reflection has already been carried out in broader Christian circles from which Orthodox may draw in considering new realities.

In addition to biblical questions, Orthodox must consider additional guidance provided by canon law. Canon prohibitions often address ad hoc instances within a localized context. The same is true of their prohibitions against same-sex erotic acts. As mentioned above, *arsenokoitia*, much like the Western theological concept of *sodomy*, has a variety of meanings that do not always coincide with the acts and relationships we are concerned with here. The preceding survey of the many varied understandings of same-sex eroticism and sexual violence predating contemporary discourses of sexuality provide some context for church canons. This knowledge should also make us more cautious about lumping canon laws together under a general category of "homosexuality" as, for example, modern translations of canonical collections are wont to do. As with scripture, context is key.

Among the arguments imported into Orthodoxy from other Christian traditions, we must address claims that same-sex relationships are prohibited on the basis of nongenerativity. The Orthodox wedding service is replete with petitions regarding the procreation of biological offspring. Regardless of the ages of the bride and groom, their actual desire for children, or knowledge of their individual reproductive capacity, the service uses the same liturgical language for all couples entering marriage. Like their opposite-sex counterparts, same-sex couples may also form families that include children from previous relationships. They may also choose to adopt. On a related note, Orthodox teachings on erotic relations within the marriage relationship are inconsistent across the history of the tradition and even in the advice offered from priest to priest. While some insist that all sexual activity be open to the possibility of procreation, others are more accepting of a variety of practices including oral sex and contraception. Further theological reflection, while sometimes uncomfortable, is nonetheless required if Orthodox are to answer well a variety of questions being asked today both within the Church and in the broader world.

In addition to questions of generativity, we must address claims of gender essentialism that have entered Orthodox conversations. While it has become something of a commonplace to hear arguments about specific personality traits, roles, and charisms based on the gender (and by this, speakers generally mean biological sex) of individuals, such conceptions are challenged in patristic anthropology and can be traced to the introduction of a combination of ideas from Jewish and German mysticism and German Romanticism into Russian religious philosophy and subsequent Orthodox theological reflection. For example, the works of Vladimir Solovyov, Sergei Bulgakov, Nikolai Berdyaev, and Paul Evdokimov are influenced by various combinations of the classical trope of the androgyne, the Kabbalistic idea of the union between male and female as the necessary precondition of revealing the image of God stamped on humanity, and the idea that spiritual charisms are bestowed according to sexual distinctions.[53] I am not suggesting, as would the rigorist position, that these conversations are alien to Orthodoxy and should thus be excluded as legitimate resources for theological reflection. Rather, I suggest that they must be carefully weighed by the same standards applied to all other discourses. We must avoid the temptation to incorporate them unreflectively out of a desire either to bring discussion to an end or to substantiate preexisting biases. The same discernment must be applied to contemporary gender theory and sexual ethics. We must weigh all these subjects with a view to the gospel of Christ.

Conclusion

With these tasks in mind, I bring this essay to a close. I hope to have shown that our current popular models of sexual orientation are not synonymous with the historical paradigms familiar to the cultures that produced the Bible and the patristic corpus. Nor are our contemporary understandings uncontested in our own time. However, we can say that the covenanted same-sex erotic relationships found among many people in our broader society (including among members of various Christian traditions) are, indeed, without recognized historical precedent within Orthodoxy. To judge them solely by the tradition is to subsume them into ill-fitting categories that obscure the potential for loving self-sacrifice and mutual support in the journey toward *theosis*. With attention to the impediments noted above, coupled with listening to the experiences of actual same-sex couples, it is my hope that Orthodox can articulate a nuanced and faithful teaching. We can condemn rape, exploitation, and objectification. And, at the same time, we can encourage covenanted same-sex erotic relationships that foster intimacy and growth for their members. It is my hope that with a spirit of openness to the movement of the Holy Spirit in the lives of our lesbian, gay, and bisexual siblings in Christ, we can come to a theological account that blesses and celebrates these relationships. This would genuinely be something new under the sun.

Notes

1. As we begin, a note on language. The word *homosexuality* is freighted, as we shall see below, with many contradictory meanings in its common usage. I have chosen the language of *same-sex eroticism* to signal two aspects of the issues under discussion. The first, *same-sex*, seems clear enough. However, I acknowledge the ambiguities associated with human bodies that do not fall clearly into either the *male* or *female* category of the sex binary. In this essay, I am referring to the medically assigned designation without respect to intersex conditions or personal subjectivities that may be at odds with an individual's legal status. Secondly, by using the word *erotic* I am signaling that the activities and affective desires under consideration have a sexual component that is coupled with attraction. I exclude same-sex rape (which also appears in the discussion below) from this category as belonging to the category of violence.

2. Michel Foucault, *The History of Sexuality*, trans. Robert Hurley (New York: Vintage Books, 1980), I:43. Note that far more attention is given to male

homosexuality than its female counterpart. This has historically been the case and is driven primarily by cultural reactions to men who transgress gender boundaries (as we shall see below). Historically, female same-sex erotic behavior is either of no concern, or, when it is addressed, draws much less attention.

Foucault's characterization of the Sodomite as a subject of civil and canonical codes has left many readers with the impression that sodomy boils down to specific acts, while the newly constituted homosexual is a full-fledged subjective identity. We will address the problems with this argument below.

3. In Foucault's words: "The psychological, psychiatric, medical category of homosexuality was constituted from the moment it was characterized . . . less by a type of sexual relations than by a certain quality of sexual sensibility, a certain way of inverting the masculine and the feminine in oneself. Homosexuality appeared as one of the forms of sexuality when it was transposed from the practice of sodomy onto a kind of interior androgyny, a hermaphrodism of the soul. The sodomite had been a temporary aberration; the homosexual was now a species." See Foucault, *The History of Sexuality*, 1:43.

4. See David M. Halperin, *One Hundred Years of Homosexuality: And Other Essays on Greek Love*, The New Ancient World (New York: Routledge, 1990), 9.

5. Quoted material is Halperin's formulation, which Sedgwick critiques. See Eve Kosofsky Sedgwick, *Epistemology of the Closet*, 2nd ed. (Berkeley: University of California Press, 2008), 44–48, especially 46.

6. Gen. 19:5; Judg. 19:22.

7. Within both the Jewish and Christian traditions, much more commentary has been written on the Sodom account. Nissinen, citing Harrington, notes that early commentators did not comment on the link between the two accounts until Pseudo-Philo in the first century BCE. See Martti Nissinen, *Homoeroticism in the Biblical World: A Historical Perspective* (Minneapolis: Fortress Press, 1998), 50; Daniel J. Harrington, "Pseudo-Philo," in *The Old Testament Pseudepigrapha*, ed. James H. Charlesworth (Garden City, N.Y.: Doubleday, 1983), 359. However, Bailey notes that neither Josephus nor Pseudo-Philo interprets the demands of the Gibeahites to include seeking sex with the Levite. See Derrick Sherwin Bailey, *Homosexuality and the Western Christian Tradition* (London: Longmans, Green and Company, Ltd., 1955), 55n4.

8. See Matt. 10:15, 11:24; Mark 6:11, and Luke 10:12.

9. See Bailey, *Homosexuality*, 9–28.

10. Here I follow the insight offered in Phyllis Bird, "The Bible in Christian Ethical Deliberation concerning Homosexuality: Old Testament Contributions," in *Homosexuality, Science, and the "Plain Sense" of Scripture*, ed. David L. Balch (Grand Rapids, Mich.: William B. Eerdmans Publishing Company, 2000), 147–48.

11. See 1 Sam. 31:4 (1 Kingdoms 31:4); 1 Chron. 10:4 (1 Paraleipomenon 10:4), and Judg. 19:25. The word *abuse* (Greek *empaixōsi* and *enepaizon* respectively, both from *empaizō*) appears in both passages. LSJ notes that the occurrence in Judges is euphemistic. See Henry George Liddell et al., *A Greek-English Lexicon*, 9th ed. (Oxford: Oxford University Press, 1996), 543.

12. Lev. 18:22, 20:13. Three contemporary scholars who deal with the texts are Saul M. Olyan, "'And with a Male You Shall Not Lie the Lying Down of a Woman': On the Meaning and Significance of Leviticus 18:22 and 20:13," *Journal of the History of Sexuality* 5, no. 2 (1994); Nissinen, *Homoeroticism*, 37–44; Bird, "The Bible in Christian Ethical Deliberation," 149–54.

13. For dating of the Holiness Code, see Jeffrey Stackert, "Holiness Code and Writings," in *The Oxford Encyclopedia of the Bible and Law*, ed. Brent A. Strawn (New York: Oxford University Press, 2015), 394. See also "Political Allegory in the Priestly Source: The Destruction of Jerusalem, the Exile and Their Alternatives," in *The Fall of Jerusalem and the Rise of the Torah*, ed. Peter Dubovsky, Dominik Markl, and Jean-Pierre Sonnet (Tübingen: Mohr Siebeck, 2016), 223.

14. See Lev. 18:21, 20:2–5.

15. A vanquished enemy might also serve as a sexual object as evidenced by the famous Eurymedon vase, an Attic red-figure wine jug that portrays a Greek warrior holding his erection, approaching a bent-over, defeated Persian archer from behind. This illustration of Greco-Persian sexual domination is congruent with the story in 1 Sam. (1 Kingdoms) 31 referenced above. However, as mentioned previously, I am drawing a distinction between same-sex erotic acts and rape.

16. It should be noted that fellatio was considered suspect in both cultures. In his *Oneirokritika* ("Dream Analysis"), Artemidoros of Daldis categorizes oral-genital contact with another as "unconventional" and self-fellatio as "unnatural." Both practices were met with "great horror." See John J. Winkler, *The Constraints of Desire: The Anthropology of Sex and Gender in Ancient Greece* (New York: Routledge, 1990), 37, 38, 43. Romans ridiculed males who were orally penetrated in fellatio and cunnilingus and characterized these activities as "shameful." See Craig A. Williams, *Roman Homosexuality*, 2nd ed. (Oxford: Oxford University Press, 2010), 179, 86.

17. Williams notes: "Other signifiers of effeminacy in Latin texts include walking delicately, talking in a womanish way, wearing loose, colorful, feminine clothing (including the *mitra* or Eastern-style turban), overindulging in perfume, curling one's hair, and above all depilation, particularly of the chest and legs. If a man does these things, he is not only making himself look more like an idealized woman but he is also displaying an excessive concern for his appearance, a self-absorption stereotypically associated with women." See Williams, *Roman*

Homosexuality, 141. For a more in-depth discussion of depilation, see 141–42. For more on how the *mollis* attracts women, see 163–65.

18. Gleason addresses Clement of Alexandria's invective against the *androgynos*: "What is deviant in the behavior of these *androgynoi* and *cinaedi* is not the gender of their sexual object choice (a preoccupation of contemporary North Americans and Northern Europeans), but the style of their erotic pursuit. A man who actively penetrates and dominates others, whether male or female, is still a man. A man who aims to please—anyone, male or female—in his erotic encounters is ipso facto effeminate." (Note that Clement lumps the *androgynos* and the *kinaidos* together under one category of gender deviance. Polemicizing against certain women of Alexandria, he writes: "[These women] delight in intercourse with *androgynoi*, and crowds of *cinaedi* flow in, with mouths that will not shut. Contaminated in body and speech, they are men enough for obscene service, ministers of adultery . . . by lewdness of word and gesture endeavoring to please" [*Paidagogos* 3.29.2–3]. See Maud W. Gleason, *Making Men: Sophists and Self-Presentation in Ancient Rome* [Princeton: Princeton University Press, 1995], 64–65).

19. Gleason provides the following translation of Marcus Antonius Polemon of Laodicea (c. 90–144 CE), a famous sophist and physiognomist: "You may recognize him [the *androgynos*] by his provocatively melting glance and by the rapid movement of his intensely staring eyes. His brow is furrowed while his eyebrows and cheeks are in constant motion. His head is tilted to the side, his loins do not hold still, and his slack limbs never stay in one position. He minces along with little jumping steps; his knees knock together. He carries his hands with palms turned upward. He has a shifting gaze, and his voice is thin, weepy, shrill, and drawling." See Gleason, *Making Men*, 63. The translation is a composite of sources, cited in note 37.

20. Philo uses *androgynos* in his description of the penetrated sexual partner in a same-sex erotic relationship. See Nissinen, *Homoeroticism*, 95. Polemon discusses all men who "deck themselves out to please other men and women" in one group. He continues: "Some men pursue boys with these techniques. Others, such as pathics (*cinaedi*), who have a woman's sexual desire, use these techniques to catch men the way prostitutes do." *De physiognomonia* 49, 1.256–58F as quoted in Gleason, *Making Men*, 79.

21. Winkler suggests that the *kinaidos* of ancient Greece was a "scare-image" that warned male citizens of the dangers of allowing themselves to be used sexually by another man. Key to the concept are three components: promiscuity, payment, and passivity. See Winkler, *Constraints of Desire*, 46. Halperin further develops Winkler's view: "The *kinaidos*, on this view, is not someone who has a different sexual orientation from other men or who belongs to some autonomous sexual species. Rather, he is someone who represents what *every* man would be

like if he were so shameless as to sacrifice his dignity and masculine gender status for the sake of gratifying the most odious and disgraceful, though no doubt voluptuous, bodily appetites." See David M. Halperin, *How to Do the History of Homosexuality* (Chicago: University of Chicago Press, 2002), 33–34.

22. See Williams, *Roman Homosexuality*, 197.

23. Williams recounts a fable by Phaedrus, a first-century CE Roman fabulist, in which Prometheus is interrupted during his work of creating some humans by an invitation to dinner. Returning home drunk, he continues his work, mistakenly attaching penises to some women and vaginas to some men. The fable provides an etiology for *tribades* and *molles*. See Williams, *Roman Homosexuality*, 233–34.

24. Williams, *Roman Homosexuality*, 234.

25. Williams, *Roman Homosexuality*, 178.

26. Williams, *Roman Homosexuality*, 218–24.

27. In ancient Greece, men who continued to pursue youths for pederastic relationships beyond a certain age were viewed with derision. In a court speech written by Lysias sometime after 394 BC, an unnamed defendant answers charges of wounding with the intent to kill brought against him by a man named Simon. The two men had brawled over a Plataean youth named Theodotus. Simon claims in the case that he had previously entered a contract with Theodotus for the latter's sexual favors. In the speech, Lysias addresses an elephant in the room: the defendant is of an age considered too old to be chasing after boys. The defendant repeatedly expresses embarrassment about airing his conflict with Simon in the council of the Aereopagus, but suggests that in his liability to desire, he had sought to bear his affliction in an orderly manner. *Lysias* 3.3–4. For a translation see Lysias, *Lysias*, ed. W. R. M. Lamb, Loeb Classical Library (London: W. Heinemann, 1930), 73–74.

28. See Winkler, *Constraints of Desire*, 54–63.

29. See Halperin, *How to Do the History of Homosexuality*, 72.

30. This is especially true of the imperial period. See Kyle Harper, *From Shame to Sin: The Christian Transformation of Sexual Morality in Late Antiquity* (Cambridge, Mass.: Harvard University Press, 2013), 150–53.

31. Boys within the brothels were referred to as both *pueri meritorii* ("professional boys") and *pueri lenonii* ("pimps' boys"). See Harper, *From Shame to Sin*, 90.

32. The Greeks referred to a youth or man who had grown past the acceptable age to be considered a proper object of sexual desire as *eksōros* ("past the prime"). However, this was an aesthetic judgment rather than a class of grown men deemed appropriate sexual partners as in the Roman custom. See Williams, *Roman Homosexuality*, 92.

33. *Collatio legum mosaicarum et romanarum* 5.1.3.1–2. For an English translation, see Robert M. Frakes, *Compiling the Collatio Legum Mosaicarum et Romanarum in Late Antiquity*, Oxford Studies in Roman Society and Law (Oxford: Oxford University Press, 2011), 213.

34. See Bailey, *Homosexuality*, 73–77.

35. Wisdom of Solomon 12:22 ff. The referenced phrase is in v. 26, rendered as "sexual perversion" in the NRSV. For commentary, see Bailey, *Homosexuality*, 45–48; Nissinen, *Homoeroticism*, 90–91.

36. Douglas Campbell suggests that the first five chapters of Romans, which have been reread since the Reformation to support the doctrine of justification, are not Paul's own words, but prosopopoeia, a rhetorical device that lays out an argument in the voice of another. See Douglas A. Campbell, *The Deliverance of God: An Apocalyptic Rereading of Justification in Paul* (Grand Rapids, Mich.: William B. Eerdmans Publishing Company, 2009).

37. See Sarah Ruden, *Paul among the People: The Apostle Reinterpreted and Reimagined in His Own Time* (New York: Pantheon Books, 2010), 45–71.

38. See Thomas Hanks, "Romans," in *The Queer Bible Commentary*, ed. Deryn Guest (London: SCM, 2006), 582–605.

39. 1 Cor. 6:9–10; 1 Tm 1:9–10.

40. See Fredrik Ivarsson, "Vice Lists and Deviant Masculinity: The Rhetorical Function of 1 Corinthians 5:10–11 and 6:9–10," in *Mapping Gender in Ancient Religious Discourses*, ed. Todd Penner and Caroline Vander Stichele, Biblical Interpretation Series (Leiden: Brill, 2007), 180.

41. For a critique of the linguistic argument, as well as a detailed list of citations of various viewpoints, see Dale B. Martin, "*Arsenokoitês* and *Malakos*: Meanings and Consequences," in *Biblical Ethics & Homosexuality: Listening to Scripture* (Louisville, Ky.: Westminster John Knox Press, 1996).

42. See William Lawrence Petersen, "Can *Arsenokoitai* Be Translated by 'Homosexuals' (1 Cor. 6:9, 1 Tim. 1:10)," *Vigiliae christianae* 40, no. 2 (1986): 189.

43. See Mark D. Jordan, *The Invention of Sodomy in Christian Theology* (Chicago: University of Chicago Press, 1997).

44. In the technical definition, the adolescent pedophile is at least five years older than the children that are the objects of his or her desire. For adult pedophiles, the cutoff age for children as the object of desire is thirteen. Ephebophiles are generally attracted to adolescents in the age range of fifteen to nineteen.

45. See Lisa M. Diamond, *Sexual Fluidity: Understanding Women's Love and Desire* (Cambridge, Mass.: Harvard University Press, 2008).

46. See Elizabeth Jane Ward, *Not Gay: Sex between Straight White Men*, Sexual Cultures (New York: New York University Press, 2015).

47. See *Vita Antonii* 5.5; 6.1; 11.2.

48. See Eccles. 1:9.

49. For fruits of the spirit, see Gal. 5:22–23.

50. See Vasilios N. Makrides to *Public Orthodoxy* (blog), September 16, 2016, https://publicorthodoxy.org/2016/09/06/orthodox-christian-rigorism-a-multifaceted-phenomenon/.

51. See John Anthony McGuckin, *The Orthodox Church: An Introduction to Its History, Doctrine, and Spiritual Culture* (Malden, Mass.: Wiley-Blackwell, 2008), 116.

52. Verna Harrison has critiqued this line of reason, which she traces back to an argument found in a doctoral dissertation by David Ford. Harrison claims that Ford's argument is at least in part based on Protestant exegesis that he labels as "holy Tradition." See Verna E. F. Harrison, "Orthodox Arguments against the Ordination of Women as Priests," *Sobornost (incorporating Eastern Churches Review)* 14, no. 1 (1992): 10, 12.

53. See chapter four of Bryce E. Rich, "Beyond Male and Female: Gender Essentialism and Orthodoxy" (PhD diss., University of Chicago, 2017). I will provide a closer examination of these Russian thinkers and the texts that inspired them in a forthcoming edited volume by Fordham University Press.

CHAPTER

3

SCIENCE, HOMOSEXUALITY, AND THE CHURCH

Gayle Woloschak

For many in the academic spheres of life, the gaps between our daily praxis of dealing with students and the questions that are faced in the Orthodox Church have become wider and more difficult to navigate. On most large campuses in the US it is illegal to discriminate against students based on sexual preference or personal lifestyle, and showing biases or even disfavor is inappropriate and could have legal ramifications. In particular, on most campuses there is no one who is not affected by LGBTQ individuals; attitudes that are inclusive and open to LGBTQ students are expected, and those staff and faculty that are especially supportive of such students are called "allies." The student body itself is not only supportive of the LGBTQ community but has special clubs and organizations for LGBTQ students and their supporters that are funded at least in part by the university. Many faculty attend LGBTQ training to learn how to properly interact with LGBTQ individuals. In the academic world, most scholars feel the importance of these attitudes, especially to young people and students; a condemning perspective is not understood and even not tolerated.

This environment is very opposed to what many experience in the Orthodox Church, where priests have been known to condemn young women in their parishes for not being married, and have offered to "match them up," and where gay persons are tolerated only if they enter with the understanding that it is totally a "don't ask don't tell" approach in the parish with regard to their sexuality, and that they will certainly hear condemnation of homosexuality from the altar if not also from the parishioners. This is not compatible with today's world and with today's youth. Many (especially among the youth) have left and continue to leave the Church on this one issue alone. This is a daily experience, and it has become more significant today even than it was five years ago.

Now, honestly, the Church should stand up for what is right, but on this issue with so many people abandoning or never turning to the Church, the Church should be darn sure it is right in its decisions on this issue. Many people are not so sure, and they hope in discussions with broad audiences not afraid to express all perspectives that some explanation of the Church position on homosexuality (and indeed many similar issues) can be found.

It should be pointed out that the Orthodox Church is generally not opposed to scientific knowledge and scientific endeavors. In fact, many of the early theologians of the Church (St. Basil, Sts. Cosmas and Damian, etc.) considered themselves to be scientists exploring nature and using nature's pharmaceuticals to treat disease. When the Orthodox Church finds itself opposing science, it should take a clear look at this and be certain again that the stands it is taking are correct. This is not to say that science dictates theology, but more that theology is influenced by all things in the world, including nature and how it is described. I must also note that scientists are influenced by their culture, prejudices of the time, and false understandings. In the not-so-distant past, scientists agreed that since women had smaller brains than men, they should not be allowed the same education and that education must in some way adversely affect their reproductive abilities.[1]

With all of this, then, this paper will begin at least a cursory examination of scientific thinking about homosexuality and its perspectives. I have not dealt with perspectives on heterosexuality (including biology, evolution, etc.) because these issues have been explored extensively in the biological literature and in textbooks.[2]

Genetics

The nature vs. nurture argument has been raging in biology for centuries. In today's world that means trying to define the exact role of genetics vs. environment in most situations. This has certainly been the case in most complex situations, particularly with reference to behaviors and responses to the environment. Sexuality is among the most difficult to discern, clearly showing a complex behavior pattern with likely genetic and environmental components.³ As such, then, the true mechanisms responsible for the occurrence of homosexuality may be difficult to ascertain. As Patricia Greenspan[4] has noted, during the formative years when personality and values are established, nature and nurture are certainly beyond the control of the child. Just as this applies to personality—which colors all of one's human interactions—so it applies to sexuality, which will mold the person's intimate relationships, regardless of the gender of their chosen partner. The discussion below will examine genetic relationships first.

In general, many people have assumed that if homosexuality could be found to have a genetic basis, then this would affect all religious thinking. In other words, for these believers, genes associated with homosexual behavior would mean that sexuality is somehow part of creation and therefore heterosexual and homosexual behaviors must be equally accepted. A *Boston Globe* editorial noted: "A discovery that male homosexuality may be caused in part by a certain gene or cluster of genetic material raises hopes that the debate over sexual orientation may soon move into more rational, factual and appropriate sphere. . . . If proven . . . [the evidence would] go far toward undermining the narrowly gauged argument that homosexual behavior is misconduct."[5] While I understand the logic behind this editorial, I do not necessarily subscribe to it myself. There are many spheres of human behavior that have a genetic component; for example, personal survival is hard-wired into each living being, yet we know of many examples of human and animal behavior that must be recognized as altruistic. It is of course valuable to explore the genetic base of sexuality, but I do believe that understanding the basis of homosexuality will help us to clarify much of how we think about the gay population and gay individuals. I will also note that even if there is shown to be an inherited component, from a genetic perspective, there is often extreme variability of effect in inherited genetic traits.

In the 1990s, two different groups published evidence of genetic inheritance of homosexuality. Bailey and Pillard[6] did this using a twin study, but more prominent in the news was the genetic study done by Hamer et al.[7] that received significant media attention for having identified a putative gay gene.[8] Despite all of the focus and attention and continued reference to the work, the work that Hamer did in identifying the "gay gene" has not been repeated by the scientific community and remains one of the persistent controversies in the field of the genetics of homosexuality.[9] Despite the concerns about the Hamer findings that pointed to a single gene locus or gene cluster that was associated with male homosexuality, there have been numerous reports since that have pointed to multiple genetic components to the behavior. Here are some conclusions that have come from the literature that continue to influence our understanding of this topic:

- Bailey and Bell (1993)[10] determined that homosexuality is influenced by genetic and/or shared environmental factors, but family study methodology is not likely to resolve these issues much further; they have published several reports suggesting that genetics is at least as important if not more important than shared environment, but methodological impediments prevent a definitive study.[11]
- Several candidate genes have been shown to have no association with male homosexuality, including the gene for the androgen receptor and the gene for aromatase cytochrome P450.[12]
- A genome-wide screening study was done by the Hamer group that suggested chromosomal region 7q36 (part of chromosome 7, its larger arm called q region 36) correlating with homosexuality. Because this is one of the autosomal chromosomes (unlike chromosomes X and Y that determine sex), contributions to the "genetic trait" would be equally maternal and paternal.[13] It should be noted however that while correlation with 7q36 was noted, no specific gene (although many are present in that chromosomal region) was pinned down at the time to this location.
- Wang et al (2012) found an association between the gene region associated with what is referred to as the Sonic Hedgehog polymorphism (called rs9333613) in the chromosome 7q36 area. What does the Shh (Sonic Hedgehog) gene do? It is associated with the patterning of the embryo, defining the arrangement of neuronal cells in the neural tube. This could suggest that the same gene may at the same time have a role for early embryo neuronal development and homosexuality. Such genes—so-called pleiotropic genes with multiple functions in different cell types and at different stages of development—are numerous.[14] Nevertheless, it would be premature to draw extensive conclusions about the Shh gene at this point.
- Roper (2016)[15] put forth the hypothesis that there is a relationship between genes involved in microprolactinoma production and male homosexuality. A microprolactinoma is a benign tumor of the

pituitary gland that often secretes the hormone prolactin. The model proposed by Roper is that production of prolactin during fetal development prevents masculinization of the male brain, resulting in homosexuality. It should be noted that this work of Roper's, while it has gained some interest in the popular arena, is predominantly a hypothesis with no support data.

Twin studies support the idea that inheritance of male homosexuality is more likely through the matriline than through the patriline.[16]

The summary of the various different genetics data are that twin and other inheritance studies provide evidence to support an association of genetics with homosexuality. It is likely to be a complex genetic trait, and while a few potential genes and/or gene clusters have been identified, these have not been associated in a causal way with the behavior. Identifying all of the genes involved is likely to be not only complicated but challenging, even in light of the vast wealth of genomics data that is available today.

Recognizing that sexual behaviors in general and homosexual behavior specifically are not associated with the same genes is additionally complicating the situation. It is however worth pointing out that while we do know a lot about sexual reproduction, we still have limited knowledge (and devote limited resources) to exploration of the genetic basis of heterosexual behavior, for example.

The possibility of a genetic association with homosexuality has caused a great deal of concern within the gay community. Possibilities of screening the population and using it for hiring has been an issue that raised great discussion. Similarly, with IVF it is now possible to screen for and against certain traits, so the idea that screening against gay children could be done if genes were identified was also voiced as a concern. More recently with the use of CRISPR for gene editing, it is in theory possible to edit any gene, so this too could be done with male homosexuality genes if they exist. In another venue, I discussed possible genetic manipulation of complex genetic trails[17] and declared that use of CRISPR technology for fine genetic manipulation of multiple genes would be difficult if not impossible to achieve with today's technology; homosexuality appears to fit into this category, being a complex behavior with both multigenic and environmental components.

Some of these fears were brought closer to reality with the publication at the end of August 2019 of a paper in *Science* by Ganna et al.[18] describing work done as part of a genome-wide association study (GWAS) of 477,522 individuals who had biobanked their DNA either in the UK or the US and given permission for this study. Of these individuals, 2–5 percent in the UK (and a larger sample from the US that had used 23andMe) reported at least one same-sex encounter, and were labeled as "nonheterosexuals" in the study (although the authors note that this is a problematic nomenclature). The purpose of the study then was to determine genetic variants associated with same-sex sexual behavior and to probe the biology and complexity of the trait.

It should be noted that GWAS was an observational study done to determine if any particular variant in genes is associated with a particular trait. The GWAS project investigated the entire genome as opposed to some studies that examine one or a few genes. While the GWA studies can determine if there is a genetic association with particular traits, they cannot determine exactly which genes might be involved because they use gene fragments rather than entire genes.[19]

What did this study show? There were several key findings that influence how we consider same-sex sexual behavior: (1) This study confirmed the work of familial and twin studies documenting that genetics plays a role in determination of same-sex sexual behavior; there are clearly other factors that are likely to be important in such an environment, but this study could not test for that. (2) Same-sex sexual behavior is influenced by not one or even a few but many genes. The underlying genetic architecture of the trait is highly complex. (3) The data support the model that many different genetic loci contribute to individual differences in predisposition to same-sex sexual behavior. (4) Many of the loci with small effects are overlapping in male and female same-sex behavior and may contribute additively to the behavior. (5) It is impossible from these results to either predict a particular behavior from one's genetic make-up or to identify specific genes that might be associated with the behavior. (6) In general, the work did not support the idea that the more someone is attracted to the same sex, the less they are attracted to the opposite sex, as had been suggested by Kinsey. They suggest the need for the development of new tools for the evaluation of sexual orientation.

While specific genes could not be identified using these technique, five genetic variations were found to reach a very high significance. These are associated with genes related to male-pattern baldness and another set with olfaction. They both suggest a possible role for sex hormones in the process since both sets of genes are hormonally influenced.

The authors have very clearly demarcated limitations from their work and are careful to point out potential pitfalls in interpreting the study. As noted above, absolutely no predictions can be made about a person's sexual orientation based on genetics, both because there are likely to be unknown nongenetic factors involved in the behavior and also because the genetic patterns are complex and multigenic. It can also be stated only that there is a genetic component to the behavior, not the relative contribution of the genetics (or environment) to the trait. These genetic features have not been shown to cause the behavior, they merely are associated with it and may play a role in its expression. As the authors note, much more work is needed in this field.

At the end of the day, this work confirms previous studies documenting genetic patterns associated with same-sex sexual behavior, perhaps adding to the literature a level of complexity that was not clear previously.

Environment

Research on the role of nurture in homosexuality is more in the realm of psychology than of biology, so I will limit myself here to the biological aspects. Biologists note that there is certainly an environmental (familial or otherwise) component to sexual as well as all other behaviors. As noted above, there are several twin studies (monozygotic compared to dizygotic, for example) that have demonstrated a familial association of homosexuality, suggesting a role for both nature and nurture in the behavior. Indeed, in one of the largest studies of familial homosexuality,[20] it was suggested that homosexuality per se is familial but it did not support the idea that male and female homosexuality run in different families. This suggests that the familial determinants of male and female homosexuality may be the same.

While most scientists involved in these studies support the idea of an environmental role for homosexual behavior, the actual degree to which the cause of the behavior should be attributed to environment vs. genetics is unclear and is likely to remain unclear for some time. For example, there is evidence from older literature that birth order appears to affect homosexuality; male homosexuality is positively correlated with the number of older brothers but not the number of older sisters.[21] These results again suggest that the social environment experienced by younger brothers may be important, although there are certainly other potential explanations.

From a psychological perspective, probably the most important milestone for thinking about homosexuality was the declassification of the behavior as a disorder by removing it from the official *Diagnostic and Statistical Manual of Mental Disorders* (DSM) in 1973.[22] This was based in part on Kinsey et al.'s earlier studies demonstrating that sexual behavior in the male is not binary (either strictly homosexual or strictly heterosexual) but on a spectrum.[23] Another significant work done by Evelyn Hooker compared the test results from thirty nonpatient homosexual men with those of thirty nonpatient heterosexual men; this study found that experienced psychologists could not distinguish between the two groups. This of course challenged the now-rejected paradigm that homosexuality was always associated with some psychopathology.[24]

In most psychological circles today, homosexuality is not treated as a disorder, and "conversion" therapy (converting a homosexual to a heterosexual) is considered inappropriate, unwarranted, and even harmful.

Homosexuality and Evolution

Evolution is driven by changes in genes—these can be changes in copy number, changes in the content of the gene, or deletions of genes or portions of them. In short, virtually any change of sequence of a gene that leads to a mutation. Evolution involves natural selection where there is a selection for those individuals in a population that are best suited for survival in particular conditions. Let me make this clear: Sexual reproduction occurs in humans because evolution selected for it as the most efficient reproductive mechanism for human beings. Evolution is driven only by sexual reproduction (to which sexual behavior only contributes) and selection of the reproductively fit offspring (for which parenting is important and sexual behavior is likely of little relevance). Populations evolve; individuals do not evolve. Individuals who do not reproduce do not contribute their genes to evolution. In the same vein, individuals who are beyond their reproductive years can no longer contribute genes for evolution. Does this mean that none of the individuals who are without generations of offspring did not contribute to evolution? Some people have hypothesized, for example, that grandparents contribute to the health of the offspring and so there is a selection for longevity beyond reproductive years in humans; nevertheless, there are others who argue that humans died during their reproductive years (aged 30–35) throughout most of human evolution and that it is only modern inventions (antibiotics, for example) that have allowed for survival beyond these years and thus there is no benefit from longevity to evolution per se.

When one considers all of this, the dilemma concerning a genetic cause (or even genetic association) of homosexuality becomes apparent. What could allow for the continued existence of homosexuality in the human population when the birth rates among homosexuals are at least five times lower[25] than what one finds in the general population? In other words, is there any selection for having homosexual individuals in the human population despite the low birth rates in this population? This has been a very challenging question to address, and several models have been put forth to help explain it. As Ciani et al. have noted, "In spite of its relatively low frequency, the stable permanence in all human populations of this apparently [evolutionarily] detrimental trait constitutes a puzzling 'Darwinian paradox.'"[26]

> One hypothesis has posited that there is a selection for homosexuality in the human population because somehow human beings are able to compete better as a species with a subpopulation of homosexuals in our number. Exactly what homosexual behavior contributes to the population is unclear, and it is very difficult to speculate without over-generalizing about differences between heterosexuals and homosexuals. This argument would suggest that somehow humanity is better with both heterosexual and homosexual members of the population. This may be even more important when one considers the lengthy period that humans spend dependent upon their parents in their early years, time during which support from nonimmediate family members would be of especial value.
>
> Ciani et al. in the work referenced above developed mathematical models to predict how inheritance under such conditions would be possible. Working under a given set of assumptions, they predicted that the basic evolutionary dynamics of male homosexuality could be based on a model where genes associated with homosexuality could also increase female fitness while decreasing male fitness. These models were totally hypothetical.

Another group of mathematical models was provided by Gavrilets and Rice[27] but they argued that these models are all dependent on testing in an experimental situation.

The question of "Darwin's paradox" for homosexuality remains even with some of the more plausible models available for further study. Many have argued that new whole genome sequencing will permit determination of the validity of such models. Realizing the complexity of homosexuality as a behavior, some have even speculated that all of the models (and more) may be accurate, each one valid in a particular situation.

We Are More Than Our Biology

From the perspective of the Church, human beings are more than a package of genes and chemical reactions that occur; we are more than our reproductive capacity and evolution. We do carry out these processes—DNA synthesis, replication of our genes, passing our genes on to offspring through sexual reproduction. As part of our species, we have evolved and continue to evolve; in fact, "those that evolve" is one of the definitions of life on Earth. Nevertheless, human beings contemplate, create culture, pray, build cities, and do so much more that partly depends on our biology but goes beyond it as well. In addition, we should not forget that intimate relationships involve couples—the effect that one person's sexuality has on their counterpart is an important subtext for their sexual behavior. If we insist that homosexuals should ignore their inclinations, how good will they be as spouses? Can we expect them to be loving parents to their forcefully produced children to the same degree as they would be loving to their nieces and nephews?

In my opinion (and this is strictly my opinion) an emphasis on biology that "hard-wires" it to behavior (and we do seem to correlate reproductive capacity with sexual behavior in this instance) is making us less than human and not more so. It puts the Church into the mindset of those who would blame an infertile person for his or her infertility. Being a 100 percent biologically productive human animal is not sufficient for being true to our humanity. (I am not discussing here the asexual life of the monastic.)

To claim that sexual reproduction and the contribution to evolution are more important than the relationship to God, interactions with other human beings, caring for others, and other spiritual dimensions in defining the communing Orthodox Christian is too limiting. In fact, we are not making the claim for all of our biology, just for one biological function. We are placing too much emphasis on reproduction and evolution and not enough on relationship. For a Church that values sex for relationship's sake (and not only for reproduction), condemnation of homosexuality is confusing and difficult to justify. Finally, we need to consider new questions that we have not discussed as a Church until only recently: How far should we go in expecting people to ignore genetic inclinations? Are human beings just about evolution (reproduction is the only real driver of evolution) or are we also about relationship and communion? Have we articulated a theology to deal with same-sex behaviors? There is much work to be done.

Notes

1. R. Hubbard and E. Wald, *Exploding the Gene Myth* (Boston: Beacon Press, 1993). This issue is also well-explored in D. L. Gabard, "Homosexuality and the Human Genome Project: Private and Public Choices," *Journal of Homosexuality* 37, no. 1 (1999): 25–51.

2. R. D. Martin, "The Evolution of Human Reproduction: A Primatological Perspective," *Yearbook of Physical Anthropology* 50 (2007): 59–84. This article provides a good review with five pages of reference resources. Another good source is the book by R. Martin, *How We Do It: The Evolution and Future of Human Reproduction* (Chicago: University of Chicago Press, 2013).

3. This is discussed as a controversy in sexual medicine in E. A. Jannini, R. Blanchard, A. Camperio-Ciani, and J. Bancroft, "Male Homosexuality: Nature or Culture?" *Journal of Sexual Medicine* 7 (2010): 3245–53.

4. P. S. Greenspan, "Free Will and the Genome Project," *Philosophy and Public Affairs* 22, no. 1 (1992): 31–43.

5. *Boston Globe*, July 20, 1993, quoted in P. Conrad and S. Markens, "Constructing the 'Gay Gene' in the News: Optimism and Skepticism in the US and British Press," *Health* 5, no. 3 (2001): 373–40.

6. J. M. Bailey and R. Pillard, "A Genetic Study of Male Sexual Orientation," *Archives of General Psychiatry* 48, no. 12 (1991): 1089–96, was the first study done with male twins. The second study done with female twins was two years later: J. M. Bailey and D. S. Benishay, "Familial Aggregation of Female Sexual Orientation," *Archives of General Psychiatry* 150, no. 2 (1993): 272–77.

7. D. H. Hamer, S. Hus, V. L. Magnuson, N. Hu, and A. M. L. Pattatucci, "A Linkage between DNA Markers on the X Chromosome and Male Sexual Orientation," *Science* 261 (1993): 321–27. This original paper was followed by a book: D. Hamer and P. Copeland, *The Science of Desire: The Search for the Gay Gene and the Biology of Behavior* (New York: Simon and Schuster, 1994).

8. Conrad and Markens, "Constructing the 'Gay Gene' in the News." In this article there is a good description of the different understandings of the media in the US vs. Britain toward the studies of the "gay gene." The media at the time and shortly after the publication of these reexamined the question several times.

9. K. O'Riordan, "The Life of the Gay Gene: From Hypothetical Genetic Marker to Social Reality," *Journal of Sexual Research* 49 (2012): 362–68. As early as 1995 the "gay gene" model was being questioned in the scientific community. See for example E. Marshall, "Discovery of 'Gay Gene' Questioned," *Science* 268, no. 5219 (1995): 1841.

10. J. M. Bailey and A. P. Bell, "Familiality of Female and Male Homosexuality," *Behavior Genetics* 23, no. 4 (1993): 313–23. Table IV in this text lists several references that have examined this issue.

11. See Bailey and Pillard, 1992, as well as F. L. Whitam, M. Diamond, and J. Martin, "Homosexual Orientation in Twins: A Report on 62 Pairs and Three Triplet Sets," *Archives of Sexual Behavior* 22, no. 3 (1993): 197–20.

12. J. P. Macke, N. Hu, S. Hu, M. Bailey, V. L. King, T. Brown, D. Hamer, and J. Nathans, "Sequence Variation in the Androgen Receptor Gene Is Not a Common Determinant of Male Sexual Orientation," *American Journal of Human Genetics* 53 (1993): 844–52; M. G. DupPree, B. S. Mustanski, S. Bocklandt, C. Nievergelt, and D. H. Hamer, "A Candidate Gene Study of CYP19 (aromatase) and Male Sexual Orientation," *Behavior Genetics* 34, no. 3 (2004): 243–50.

13. B. S. Mustanski, M. G. Dupree, C. M. Nievergelt, S. Bocklandt, N. J. Scholrk, and D. H. Hamer, "A Genomewide Scan of Male Sexual Orientation," *Human Genetics* 116, no. 4 (2005): 272–78.

14. For example, protein alpha A crystallin is a chaperone that is at the same time necessary for eyesight and for normal kidney function (https://www.proteinatlas.org/ENSG00000160202-CRYAA/tissue). Because of this dual role, the gene is active in species that do not have eyesight. Therefore, this gene is often used to document evolution of pleiotropic genes—in blind mole rats this gene is not accumulating mutations at the same rate as other "not-needed" genetic regions. W. Hendriks, J. Leunissen, E. Nevo, H. Bloemendal, W. W. de Jong, "The Lens Protein Alpha A-crystallin of the Blind Mole Rat, Spalax ehrenbergi: Evolutionary Change and Functional Constraints," *Proceedings of the National Academy of Sciences of the United States of America* 84, no. 15 (Aug. 1987): 5320–24.

15. W. G. Roper, "The Interrelationship between Genes, Microprolactinoma and Male Sexuality," *Medical Hypotheses* 94 (2016): 55–56.

16. R. C. Pillard, J. Poumadere, and R. A. Carretta, "Is Homosexuality Familial? A Review, Some Data, and a Suggestion," *Archives of Sexual Behavior*

10 (1981): 465–75; R. C. Pillard, J. Poumadere, and R. A. Carretta, "A Family Study of Sexual Orientation," *Archives of Sexual Behavior* 11 (1982): 511–20.

17. G. E. Woloschak, "Can We Genetically Engineer Virtue and Deification?," *Theology and Science* 16, no. 3 (August 2018): 300–307.

18. A. Ganna, K. J. H. Verweij, M. G. Nivard, R. Mainer, R. Wedoe, A. S. Busch, A. Abdellaoui, S. Guo, J. F. Sathirapongsauti, 23andMe Research Team, P. Lichtenstein, S. Lundstrom, N. Langstrom, A. Auton, K. M. Harris, G. W. Beecham, E. R. Martin, A. R. Sanders, J. r. B. Perry, B. M. Neale, and B. P. Zietsch, "Large-scale GWAS Reveals Insights into the Genetic Architecture of Same-Sex Sexual Behavior," *Science* 365 (2019): 882, eaat7693.

19. "Genome-Wide Association Study," Wikipedia, https://en.wikipedia.org/wiki/Genome-wide_association_study (accessed November 11, 2019).

20. Bailey and Bell, "Familiality."

21. R. Blanchard and A. F. Bogaert, "Homosexuality in Men and the Number of Older Brothers," *American Journal of Psychiatry* 153 (1996): 27–31; R. Blanchard, "Quantitative and Theoretical Analysis of the Relation between Older Brothers and Homosexuality in Men," *Journal of Theoretical Biology* 230: 173–87.

22. *Diagnostic and Statistical Manual of Mental Disorders* (Arlington, Va.: American Psychiatric Association, 1973).

23. A. C. Kinsey, W. B. Pomery, and C. E. Martin, *Sexual Behavior in the Human Male* (Philadelphia: Saunders, 1948).

24. E. Hooker, "The Adjustment of the Male Overt Homosexual," *Journal of Projective Techniques* 21 (1957): 18–31.

25. G. Chaladze, "Heterosexual Male Carriers Could Explain Persistence of Homosexuality in Men: Individual-Based Simulations of an X-Linked Model," *Archives of Sexual Behavior* 45 (2016): 1705–11.

26. A. C. Ciani, P. Cermelli, and G. Zanzotto, "Sexually Antagonistic Selection in Human Male Homosexuality," *PloS One* 3, no. 6 (2008): e2282.

27. S. Gavrilets and W. R. Rice, "Genetic Models of Homosexuality: Generating Testable Predictions," *Proceedings of the Royal Society* B 273 (2008): 3031–38.

CHAPTER

4

BIBLICAL TRADITION AND SAME-SEX RELATIONS

A Difficult Hermeneutical Path

Ekaterini Tsalampouni

Homosexual relations and same-sex marriage are among those topics that have been hotly debated by members of various Churches during the last decades. Although in the earlier stages this discussion seemed to have been restricted to the Western part of Christianity, the Orthodox Churches have also gotten involved in similar discussions since the beginning of the twenty-first century. The reasons for this development seem to have been, first, the public and visible place that homosexuality has gradually taken up not only in Western societies but also in those of the so-called Orthodox countries and, second, as a result, the decision of many governments in these countries to introduce common laws that sanction the union and marriage of homosexual couples. On the one hand, the official position of the Orthodox Churches is sometimes a particularly passionate "no" to all these innovations that are discarded as symptoms of dangerous globalization and deviation from the traditional understanding of sexual identities.[1] On the other hand, many Orthodox voices urge for a reconsideration of the Orthodox position or at least for entering into a discussion about the possibilities, presuppositions, and limits of such a reconsideration. So far, the focus has primarily been on the pastoral challenges that homosexuality poses to Christian communities.[2] What is, however, missing is a thorough and critical theological reflection that would address the issue from the perspective of Christian anthropology, soteriology, and eschatology. It is, moreover, necessary to reflect upon the tension between previous tradition and the current situation, and to develop useful hermeneutical lenses that could help keep the balance and produce a meaningful and constructive discourse and practice. In other words, the whole discussion has to revolve around two interconnected questions: namely, first, how to deal with the previous Church tradition and its stance toward homosexual identities and desires (for example, the Bible, Church Fathers, and the canons), and, second, how to respond to the contemporary challenge of same-sex relations and to the ever-growing demand that the Churches should reconsider or at least discuss their current position that is informed by this traditional stance. This tension between past and present is directly related to the important question about the nature and function of tradition in the Orthodox Churches[3] and the distinction between tradition as the "self-identity of the Church"[4] and traditions as temporally, locally and also culturally conditioned practices and customs.[5]

One particular aspect of this written tradition, the Scripture and its views on homoeroticism, will be discussed in the present paper. Scripture, undoubtedly, plays an essential role in the life of all Churches. Consequently, its few utterances against same-sex relations and practices are often evoked against contemporary homosexuality in various documents and studies dealing with the issue. It is, therefore, necessary to examine the biblical texts, to assess their normative character, and to explore the possibilities and limitations of this particular part of Christian tradition. In the Orthodox Church, the Holy Scripture is regarded as an integral and vital part of her tradition and not as an independent and self-sufficient authority distinct from the rest of Church tradition.[6] Thus, a critical discussion of the scriptural position on same-sex relations could be of paradigmatic significance in the discussion about Christian tradition as a whole and its possible normative character in contemporary situations.

In the first part of the essay, a short review of previous scholarly stances toward biblical texts dealing with homoerotic relations will be offered and critically discussed. Undoubtedly, some of these studies belong to the early stages of scholarly research. They all also come from non-Orthodox contexts and reflect the discussion of other Christian traditions. They are, however, included for the following reasons. They are a useful point of departure because they represent the beginning of a long and ongoing discussion among biblical scholars about homosexuality and the Bible and highlight most of the exegetical and theological challenges in this context that are also of relevance for Orthodox biblical scholarship. Unfortunately, this pioneer work remains unacknowledged by most Orthodox biblical scholars.[7] It is, however, useful to listen to these voices, reflect upon their testimony, and get critically engaged in a discussion with them regarding methodological lenses and hermeneutical presuppositions. Such an encounter could enrich current Orthodox discussions about homosexuality and their quest for answers in early Christian tradition. Some of these insights will be implemented in the second part of this essay, where presumable biblical evidence on the issue will be presented. Finally, in the third part, some critical thoughts regarding the use of the Bible in the discussion of same-sex unions and marriages in the Orthodox context will be expressed.

The Bible and Homosexuality: A Review of the Previous Research

According to Louis Menéndez-Antuña's typology, previous scholarly discussion of the biblical evidence on the issue of same-sex relations could be schematically divided into two main trends that act as the two opposite poles in a wide spectrum of varied opinions and interpretations of the biblical text.

On the one end of this spectrum, one can find those scholars who advocate some form of continuity between the circumstances of the communities of the past that biblical texts originally addressed and these of contemporary Christian communities. Most representatives of "continuism" claim that the biblical text can be applied to modern challenges and that, therefore, all homosexual relations and behavior should accordingly be condemned.[8] Those who adopt this stance are usually very critical toward homosexuality and often fail to distinguish between homosexual acts and identity. They usually moralize and detach homosexuality from social or cultural systems.[9] In its moderate manifestations, though, this tendency exhibits a certain compassion for the identity of homosexual persons but condemns homosexual acts and relations.[10] It should be noted, though, that the idea of continuity between the past and present is also adopted by some scholars who are sympathetic or even positive toward homosexuality.[11]

The other end of the spectrum is the so-called "alterism"—namely, the position that biblical writers did not know anything about stable homoerotic relationships between adults and had a very narrow perception of homosexuality shaped by their cultural background. Moreover, even if some similarities between now and then could be traced, the cultural presuppositions and the concept of normal differ.[12] The numerous studies published since the previous century (especially from the 1980s onwards) should be placed somewhere on this spectrum, each proposing its solution to the very difficult puzzle that biblical texts provide to their readers. It remains, however, open to debate whether and in which ways sexual practices and relations were homogeneous in antiquity and today.[13]

In his 1980 seminal study on the history of homosexuality, John Boswell, a medieval historian at Yale University, argued that ancient Christianity had not always been hostile toward homosexuality and that the negative stance adopted since the twelfth century also relied on a misinterpretation of the biblical texts and early Christian tradition.[14] According to Boswell, nothing in the Scripture or the earlier stages of this tradition betrayed an explicit rejection of homoeroticism.[15] His work was received with mixed feelings; the gay community was very critical toward it and many scholars expressed their concern about the brilliant yet one-sided discussion of the evidence.[16] More particularly, Boswell was criticized for a tendentious reading of certain biblical texts.[17] According to him, for example, in Romans 1:24–28 Paul did not condemn homosexual but rather heterosexual men who engaged themselves in same-sex intercourse.[18] It is, however, rather improbable that Paul as a Jew could have made such a distinction.[19] Despite being criticized as anachronistic or oversimplifying, Boswell's study remains a point of reference, especially by those who adopt a more sympathetic attitude toward same-sex relations among Christians.

Robin Scroggs's study that appeared in 1983 similarly attempted to exonerate early Christianity, and more particularly the New Testament, from any homophobic views.[20] Scroggs claimed that the New Testament, and most prominently Paul, was critical only toward pederasty, a particular kind of homosexual relations in antiquity. Scroggs was criticized because in his analysis of ancient data he suppressed important evidence of other types of ancient homoeroticism that Paul or the other New Testament authors could have known and implied in their texts.[21] Despite this criticism, his main position was adopted by many scholars, and it is often repeated in biblical commentaries.[22]

Scroggs's most important contribution is the threefold hermeneutical model that he applied in the interpretation of biblical texts addressing same-sex practices: (1) using the established exegetical tools to understand its meaning, (2) comparing this meaning to the major theological and ethical themes of the Bible, and (3) determining whether the cultural background of the text is similar to modern contexts.[23] Scroggs's model is built upon historical criticism, a system of exegetical methods that aims at understanding the world "behind the text," at reconstructing, namely, the original historical context of the text, its author, and early communities.[24]

This is also the point of departure in William Loader's work. In a series of studies on ancient Jewish and Christian views on sexuality Loader stressed the importance of focusing on the text and its religious and cultural context.[25] His meticulous historical-critical analysis led him to the conclusion that Paul's comments in Romans and 1 Corinthians indicate that Paul shared the Jewish view that same-sex acts were associated with idolatry and were, therefore, manifestations of sin. Engaging, however, the biblical text in the current discussion on homosexuality—either to defend or condemn it—could be anachronistic and misleading. Loader is aware of the shortcomings of the historical-critical method and proposes a careful hermeneutical treatment of biblical texts. In his own words, such a hermeneutical approach should "include acknowledging distance as well as embracing proximity" to the biblical text.[26]

Loader's proposal indicates the necessity to move beyond the alienation of the text through a historical-critical reading and make evident its significance for contemporary faith communities. Undoubtedly, the focus of historical criticism is not on the reader(s) of the text through the ages or its reception history. Furthermore, its point of departure is not that of the Bible as the authoritative Scripture of a religious community but rather of the Bible as a historical source that needs to be situated in its historical context to be properly appreciated. Like any other method, historical criticism has its limits and despite its claim of being objective and neutral, it also reflects the presuppositions of individual interpreters. This is evident in the case of those biblical texts that refer to same-sex relations; quite often the historical reconstructions proposed are informed by the ideological presuppositions or the norms of sexual behavior of the cultural and social system that the interpreter belongs to.[27] This is evident, for example, in the case of Scroggs's proposal of pederasty as the cultural background of the New Testament hostility toward homoerotic acts. Ancient sources presuppose a much more complex situation that cannot easily correspond to the contemporary pederasty understanding. Nevertheless, historical-critical readings are essential and can certainly prevent anachronistic identifications; the texts of the Bible were created within temporally and culturally defined contexts, and the reconstruction of these contexts is a useful contribution to the analysis of our texts. Such an approach, though, usually fails to create bridges with the present situation or contribute to the appropriation of the biblical text by the Church community in a constructive way.[28] This is evident, for example, in current discussions not only of homosexuality but also of environmental ethics or social issues whenever the members of the Christian communities turn to Scripture for answers. In these cases, historical criticism points to the dead ends and limits of the biblical text but fails to provide a way out of the biblical impasse or to propose ways of bringing together the horizons of the biblical texts and of faith communities that acknowledge these texts as their own. The main questions about the nature of scriptural authority and inspiration or the distinction between the text's letter and spirit remain unanswered. The hermeneutical challenge that interpreters have to face is certainly difficult since various issues are interwoven in the process of interpretation: questions of historical accuracy and objectivity when reconstructing the setting of the text, of text transparency when dealing with the world of the text itself and of authority (either of the text or its interpreters) when turning to the world in front of the text. It seems, therefore, necessary to move beyond the narrow scope of historical criticism and to develop hermeneutical lenses that will balance between a "decontextualization" and a "recontextualization" of the text and produce meaning that will be of relevance to current Christian communities.[29]

Biblical Evidence

Interestingly, there are only a few texts in the Bible directly addressing the issue of same-sex practices. In the Old Testament, for example, three texts are often used when arguing against contemporary homosexuality: (1) Genesis 19:1–12 (the story of Sodom and Gomorrah),[30] (2) Leviticus 18:22 and 20:13 (a series of prohibitions against same-sex relations between two men), and (3) Wisdom 14:26 (a description of sinful life and practices of the Gentile nations).

It is usually disputed, however, whether in the story of Sodom the focus is on homosexuality per se. Contemporary studies claim that the main motif in this narrative is, in fact, the humiliating treatment of Lot's guests by the Sodomites who violated the hospitality laws.[31] Their aggressive sexual behavior actually assigned to these male foreigners a female sexual role, an insult usually reserved for war prisoners in the ancient Levant.[32] As Derrick

Sherwin Bailey has demonstrated, Sodom's sin was identified with same-sex practices in Jewish texts after the first century BCE.[33] Indeed, in many biblical passages Sodom comes up as an example of inhospitality (most prominently in Ezekiel 16:48–50 but also in Wisdom 19:13–17 and Luke 10:12),[34] arrogance and pride (Sirach 16:8; 3 Maccabees 2:4–5), idolatry (Deuteronomy 29:23; 32:32)[35] and unbelief (Matthew 10:14–15; 11:23–24) or God's awe-inspiring punishment (Romans 9:29; 2 Peter 2:6). Although a connection to sexual sins is already attested in 2 Peter 2:6 and Jude 7, there is no reference to homoerotic practices[36] as it is the case in part of the ancient Jewish tradition and mainly in ancient Christian literature.[37]

While the story of Sodom is not a clear case against same-sex practices, the Leviticus prohibitions (18:22; 20:13) are the opposite. These proscriptions against homoerotic relations between men, under threat of the death penalty, belong to the so-called Holiness Code, a set of texts that emphasize Israel's duty to keep herself clean among the Gentile nations.[38] In ancient Israel's cultural environment, homosexual activities were closely related to cults and cultic prostitution.[39] The Leviticus texts, however, do not seem to refer to cultic but to moral purity.[40] There is also no allusion to the creation story, and this makes it difficult to relate them to procreation and family relations.[41] The rationale, therefore, behind these prohibitions is still debated among scholars. Their immediate context, though, probably indicates that they should be seen as a means of setting Israel apart from her Gentile neighbors (the command of holiness) while the submotif of male honor can be traced here as well.[42]

The association of same-sex practices with idolatry also seems to be evident in the Wisdom of Solomon, where these practices are described as an "interchange of sex roles" (γενέσεως παραλλαγή, 14:26)[43] in a list of various transgressions that demonstrate the decadence of those who venerate the idols (14:25–26).[44] This text is of particular significance since it is claimed to have influenced Paul's discussion of the issue in Romans 1.[45] Some scholars, though, point to the phrase γάμων ἀταξίαι that follows and claim that γενέσεως παραλλαγή does not refer to same-sex practices but is rather an allusion to the story of Genesis about the unnatural relations between humans and angels (Genesis 6:4).[46] This association is supported by other Jewish texts as well.[47] It seems that even if there is a reference to homosexuality in this passage, this is rather vague and part of a broader discussion of idolatry as the basis of depraved relations with God and people.

The issue of homosexuality is more often dealt with in nonbiblical Jewish texts of the same period that mainly come from the diaspora milieu. In them, homoerotic acts are perceived as against the divine order and as a particular feature of the pagan people among whom the Jewish diaspora communities lived.[48] At the same time, Jewish authors like Philo reproduced the cultural stereotypes of their environment regarding same-sex relations: They were disgraceful, especially for those taking up a passive role, since this was assigned to women and slaves. Moreover, these acts were often identified with pederasty.[49] The fact that these texts come mainly from the diaspora seems also to reflect the identity crisis that the diaspora Judaism faced in its encounter with Hellenism as well as its effort to use sexuality as an identity marker.

This connection of same-sex relations to Gentile identities is also evident in the New Testament. All references can be found in the *Corpus Paulinum*: Romans 1:24–27, 1 Corinthians 6:9, and 1 Timothy 1:10. These three texts, though, are not read in the same way by all scholars. Those who assume continuity between Paul's situation and contemporary homosexuality regard them as a clear condemnation of homosexual behavior, although some of them are very careful to note that Paul is critical toward behaviors and acts and not toward inclinations, attitudes, or even genetics.[50] It remains, however, open to discussion whether Paul or his contemporaries were able to make this differentiation, which probably reflects later developments in the discussion of sexual identities.[51] On the other side of the spectrum, the advocates of discontinuity claim that Paul refers to certain forms of homosexuality—like pederasty[52] or paid male prostitution[53]—or to heterosexuals committing homosexual acts[54] or legitimate desires expressed through illegitimate freedoms.[55] A critical exegetical approach and a balanced evaluation of the arguments of both sides lead to the conclusion that these texts are not so straightforward as it is often claimed.

It is beyond the scope of this paper to provide a detailed exegesis of these three texts. Some aspects of them, though, that demonstrate the complexity of their exegesis will be briefly discussed.

Romans 1:26b-27 is part of a broader unit of Paul's letter (1:18–3:30) in which Paul explains how both Jews and Gentiles are bound to sin and both need God's saving righteousness that is now revealed in Christ (3:9). More particularly, in 1:18–32 Paul describes the sinful path that mankind chose: Their turning away from God led them to idolatry, moral degradation, and improper conduct. In this context, and as a sign of their depravity, Paul briefly mentions homoerotic relations between men and probably women. Although Paul's focus here is on the Gentiles, he does not explicitly mention them.[56] He prefers the ambiguous "humans" (ἄνθρωποι, 1:18) as the subject of all the immoral acts listed in this passage. This ambiguity probably serves Paul's theological purposes better; his emphasis is on the guilt of all humanity and thus on the universal significance of God's salvation.[57] This universal character is further supported by his allusion to the story of creation.[58] Paul undoubtedly thinks like a Jew and reproduces some of the anti-Gentile topoi found in Jewish literature.[59] However, his intention does not seem to be the condemnation of idolatry or certain acts committed by the Gentiles.[60] These are rather signs of humanity's distancing from God and instances of their perverted state of mind. In this respect, same-sex relations are treated as a symptom and not as the cause per se of mankind's sinful past.[61]

The theological but nonmoralizing purpose of Paul's argumentation is further supported by the literary context of the passage. Paul does not mention these homoerotic acts in the paraenetic part of his letter but treats them in the broader context of his theological discourse about mankind's fall before the manifestation of God's righteousness. Therefore, the implications of these verses are theological and not ethical.[62] Paul's extensive negative reference in 1:18–32 is used as a rhetorical tool for the transition to 2:1–3:29 where he also demonstrates a similar failure of the Jews. In Paul's thought, therefore, all humans are in the same boat because they all have sinned (3:9). Such a reading certainly does not eliminate Paul's negative attitude toward same-sex relations. Paul seems to reaffirm the Old Testament statements on this issue. Furthermore, he seems to be aware of various forms of such relations and is very critical toward them because as a true Jew he thinks that the only blessed bond would be between man and woman for procreation.[63] The literary context and the character of his arguments, however, place Paul's discussion of the issue in the broader theological context of idolatry and universal sin, which makes his treatment less poignant. Moreover, reading his position in the context of his cultural background—namely, that of a diaspora Jew of the first century CE—raises the important question of whether it is legitimate to treat his words as transcultural and ahistorical and apply them noncritically in contemporary situations.

The exegetical difficulty is also evident in the case of v. 26b. In it, Paul provides the first of two exempla to support his general statement that humans were delivered by God to their disgraceful passions: Women exchanged "the natural use for the unnatural." The majority of scholars think that this is a reference to female homoeroticism.[64] They point to the parallelism between verses 26 and 27 that is established through the appearance of the terms "natural use" (φυσικὴ χρῆσις) and "female" (θήλεια) in both verses and the adverb "likewise" (ὁμοίως) that connects v. 27 to v. 26.[65] Paul, thus, describes two different kinds of conduct against or beyond natural law (παρὰ φύσιν),[66] the first by females and the second by males.

This parallelism, though, is not so smooth as it is usually supposed. Paul provides a detailed description of the unnatural acts of males in v. 27 but he is rather elliptic when dealing with those of females in v. 26. He adds the genitive objective τῆς θηλείας ("of the females") to the noun φυσικὴ χρῆσις ("natural use") in v. 27, thus elaborating what the object of male use should be, but he leaves out the object of the female use in the previous verse.[67] In the ancient literary sources the verb χρῶμαι and its noun χρῆσις are often used to denote intercourse but not in the context of female homoeroticism. This raises the question of what Paul meant when he referred to unnatural female sexual activity.[68] Female homoeroticism was certainly known in the ancient world and we could safely assume that Paul also knew about it. Surprisingly, though, female same-sex relations are not often mentioned in the ancient sources and even the Old Testament is silent about them.[69] The sexual behavior of women did not attract much attention probably because the sphere of female activities was that of the private rooms of the ancient house.[70] However, this limited evidence confirms that female homoeroticism was frowned upon because it failed to meet the purpose of procreation and also enabled females to take up the role of the penetrator, which was exclusively male.[71] Paul probably assumes this fixed sexual hierarchy, which is also confirmed by his Jewish background. For him, the natural order of creation presupposes a distinction between male and female and the subordination of the latter to the former. The phrase παρὰ φύσιν could, therefore, refer to same-sex relations. Nevertheless, the ancient literary sources indicate that this phrase could have a variety of meanings;[72] in a sexual context, it could denote male homoeroticism or nonprocreative intercourse between male and female.[73] This seems to leave open the possibility that v. 26b might not condemn same-sex practices among women but other forms of intercourse that did not conform to the norms of the Graeco-Roman society and were perceived as unnatural.

The main argument for reading v. 26b as a reference to female homoerotic acts is its connection to v. 27 through the adverb ὁμοίως ("similarly"). However, as Jamie Banister has demonstrated, sentences introduced with this adverb do not define the meaning of the antecedent sentence, but their meaning is dependent on that of the previous sentence.[74] This, admittedly, does not eliminate the possibility of Paul referring to female same-sex relations in v. 26; however, it questions the tendency to use v. 27 to limit the meaning of v. 26 and creates space for different interpretations.[75]

Interestingly, Paul uses παρὰ φύσιν again in 11:24. In that verse, though, the term bears a positive meaning because it describes God's unexpected love for the Gentiles that is parallel to his love for Israel. God's action to accept the Gentiles in his people defies the established distinction between Jews and Gentiles and creates a paradox that is also stressed by the image of the wild branches grafted onto the domestic olive tree of Israel.[76] Paul's deployment of this initially negative term in order to describe God's saving act deconstructs the stereotype used in Romans 1 and in retrospect makes his description there subtly ironic.[77]

A certain form of ambiguity is also evident in the interpretation of the other two New Testament texts that are usually evoked against homosexuality: 1 Corinthians 6:9 and 1 Timothy 1:10. In both texts, the term ἀρσενοκοῖται, which is usually understood as referring to those who have intercourse with other men, appears in vice lists that include various sins, like those of sexual transgressions, violence, injustice, and economic exploitation. The interpretation of the term, however, is debated. It is a compound noun of ἄρσεν ("male") and κοίτη ("bed") that appears in the New Testament for the first time[78] without any further explanation.[79] It is, therefore, difficult to decide what the exact meaning of the word is.[80] Scholars usually assume that it is a Pauline neologism deriving from the prohibitions of Leviticus against the intercourse between males.[81] It remains, however, open to debate whether it refers generally to homosexual acts or pederasty or paid male prostitution as it has often been proposed.[82] In the case of 1 Corinthians 6:9, the term is usually connected with μαλακός that follows in the list. It is assumed that they refer to the penetrator (ἀρσενοκοίτης) and the penetrated (μαλακός) in a male same-sex relation. However, as Dale Martin and others have demonstrated, μαλακός should not necessarily be understood in the context of same-sex relations; its meaning ranges from softness and delicacy to laziness, decadence, and all forms of femininity.[83] Despite this, the word's sexual connotation in 1 Corinthians cannot be contested. The term appears together with two more sexual transgressions (ἀρσενοκοῖται and μοιχοί), probably as explications of the more generic terms of prostitution and idolatry that are mentioned at the beginning of the list.[84] In this list, Paul uses classic topoi about pagans found in Jewish writings of this period as an additional argument against the practice of the Corinthians to bring their cases in pagan courts.[85] However, it is not quite clear whether these vices are specific for the situation in Corinth nor whether any of them is more important in Paul's argumentation.[86] Therefore, the context cannot assist in the quest of the exact meaning of ἀρσενοκοίτης and μαλακός. It has to be asked then whether it is exegetically legitimate to use these particular verses as a solid argument against contemporary homosexuality.

It seems that the biblical evidence usually quoted in current discussions against homosexuality is not as conclusive as it is usually claimed. The literary and cultural context should be taken into consideration and each of these passages should be treated individually. As it has already been claimed, a careful exegesis of these texts often demonstrates the openness of their interpretation or at least the uncertainty about the exact meaning of certain terms. Furthermore, the cultural setting of these texts—namely, that of Hellenistic-Jewish tradition enhanced by Graeco-Roman perceptions of female and male bodies, power, or honor—influence the way biblical authors like Paul approach gender and sexuality issues. The stance of some texts like those of Leviticus or 1 Corinthians is undoubtedly negative and dismissive. The advocates of discontinuity usually argue that the ancient perception of homosexuality differs from ours. Indeed, Greeks and Romans seem not to have made a distinction between homosexual identities and acts. Humans were simply sexual, and they could express their sexuality in many different ways, with their own sex or the opposite or, perhaps more commonly, with both. There is certainly a diversity of sexual practices but sex was used to confirm social hierarchy; sexual hierarchy was identified with social hierarchy and was accepted as the natural order.[87] In this respect, it cannot be claimed that Jewish writers, like Paul, were not aware of the multiform sexual activities of their contemporaries. Paul's position is informed by the prevalent social paradigm, but at the same time, sexuality is used as an identity marker and as an element of separation from the pagan world in line with the Old Testament tradition.[88] Furthermore, same-sex practices are linked to his perception of salvation history.[89] This is evident, for example, in Romans 1:26–26 or 1 Corinthians 6:9. At the same time, though, the discontinuity between antiquity and modernity is not that sharp; both seem to endorse a similar attitude toward sexuality—namely, diversity and fluidity. Their main point of difference cannot be (in)equality in the way sexual relations are structured. It seems that there is a "partial connection" between past and present in matters of sexuality that makes any attempt to use the Bible as conclusive argument for or against contemporary homosexuality futile and anachronistic.[90]

How to Deal with Our Texts?

Dealing with the biblical text when discussing issues like homosexuality is certainly not an easy task. The paths of the biblical texts are certainly difficult to follow for many reasons, most prominently because they reflect particular worldviews very different from our own. This realization—a fruit of wisdom from the tree of historical criticism—certainly steals from us any naïveté regarding the transparency of the text. Closely related to it are the character of the biblical text and its role in the lives of those who read it. Undoubtedly, texts like Romans 1 cannot be easily ignored. Nevertheless, due to the already mentioned historical and cultural limitations of the text itself, the question about the normativity of such texts needs to be posed. Is the biblical text an absolute, ahistorical, and unchangeable transcendent authority? Or is it to be understood as a foundational text of the Christian tradition, normative but within its historical and cultural limits? The Orthodox perception of the Bible being part of the Church tradition, important but still just part of it, seems to point to a positive answer to this last question. If this is the case, what are the criteria that one should apply in order to decide what belongs to the everlasting normative character of the text? More concretely, in the case of Romans 1, how can it be claimed that its condemning reference to homosexuality cannot be relevant for contemporary cultures whereas what Paul says in the same context regarding universal sin and the opportunity to be saved, or the anthropological implications of his argumentation, can still be valid today? What or who decides the relevance?

I would dare to say that the one who decides is the Church herself, not in her institutional form but as the community of members who react to the challenges of their time and interpret accordingly the event of God's salvation through Christ, thus, enriching and developing the Church's tradition—namely, their experience of life under the inspiration of the Holy

Spirit. It is the same Spirit that brings up new members in the Church, thus contributing to her unending renewal and enrichment.[91] This might sound rather abstract, especially from the perspective of our contemporary institutionalized understanding of the Church. However, this would not be the first time that biblical statements are relativized because of the change of the cultural paradigm. The cases of the biblical assertions to slavery or female subordination are clear examples of this. In those cases, particular sets of criteria and solid methodological procedures were applied. Although such endeavors are difficult and sometimes debated, they demonstrate that the Bible is an "inconvenient text" full of "grey" texts whose existence has first to be acknowledged.[92] Furthermore, more holistic approaches of reading the biblical text have to be adopted. As Paul Ricoeur has suggested, texts always have a "surplus of meaning" that goes beyond what our objective methods can bring to the surface.[93] This certainly affirms the potential that texts and more particularly the Bible can have for its readers. The biblical text remains normative, but through its appropriation by its interpretive community.[94]

This is the case, for example, when discussing biblical statements against homosexuality. It is important then to decide whether the prevalent interpretation of such texts could provide the necessary pastoral guidance or, more important, whether they meet the need of contemporary Christians to experience in their everyday lives God's salvation. This is certainly a difficult decision that exceeds the mere hermeneutical proposals of a biblical scholar. At the same time, though, biblical interpretation can provide some useful clues out of the maze of the ambiguities or certainties of our texts. As it has already been stated, it is also necessary to enhance the solutions provided by historical criticism. In the case of homosexuality, historical criticism provides useful clues about the meaning of the text and its place in the broader context of the Graeco-Roman world. In its more tolerant form, it would perhaps leave some room for homosexual orientations (but perhaps not for homosexual acts) but will never consider the existence and the needs of the queer.[95] On the other hand, approaches like those of postcolonialism or queer criticism could certainly help us trace in the biblical text many significant manifestations of the queer and their significance as expressions of resistance in structures of domination and social subordination: for example, Paul's insistence on celibacy as an authentic Christian way of life, Jesus's praise of the eunuchs who will enter God's Kingdom, Paul's feminine self-descriptions, or even Jesus's queer family relations.

These, among others, provide different approaches to an issue that can surpass same-sex relations. It can offer challenges but also possibilities to read texts from different perspectives. It could, finally, bring into the discussion not only those negative texts but also texts where gender discriminations and social conventions are challenged, like for example Galatians 3:28, which, although it does not abolish these kinds of categorizations, certainly questions them under the light of the eschatological new creation of God.

Notes

1. See, for example, the press release of October 17, 2013, of the Holy Synod of Greece that clearly describes homosexual families as symptoms of the de-Christianization of modern societies: http://www.ecclesia.gr/greek/holysynod/holysynod.asp?id=1711&what_sub=d_typou (accessed June 15, 2018). Article 10 of the document on "The Sacrament of Marriage and Its Impediments" of the Holy and Great Council of the Orthodox Church also rejected same-sex unions and stated that "The Church exerts all possible pastoral efforts to help her members who enter into such unions understand the true meaning of repentance and love as blessed by the Church." A similar critical stance is implied in article 14 of the document titled "The Mission of the Orthodox Church in the Contemporary World."

2. For such pastoral approaches to same-sex desires and relations, see, for example, Thomas Hopko, *Christian Faith and Same-Sex Attraction: Eastern Orthodox Reflections* (Ben Lomond, Calif: Conciliar Press, 2006) and most recently, Athanasios Gkikas, *Ομοφυλοφιλία: Μία Σύγχρονη Ποιμαντική Πρόκληση* (Thessaloniki: Mygdonia, 2016).

3. The main dilemma in this respect is whether tradition should be understood as the fixed, timeless, revealed Truth of the Church or rather as the "unique mode of receiving" this Truth, the ability of the Church to understand and interpret it in the light of the Holy Spirit. See Vladimir Lossky, "Tradition and Traditions," in *In the Image and Likeness of God*, ed. Vladimir Lossky, trans. T. E. Bird (Crestwood, N.Y.: St. Vladimir's Seminary Press, 1974), 152–54. In Gregory Tucker's metaphor, the contrast is, in fact, between perceiving tradition as a fully prepared loaf of bread or as the yeast that produces a variety of breads. Gregory Tucker, "A Preliminary Response to Dr. Ford's Open Letter on Homosexuality," *The Wheel* (February 28, 2018): https://www.wheeljournal.com/blog/2018/2/28/gregory-tucker-a-preliminary-response-to-dr-fords-open-letter-on-homosexuality (accessed August 14, 2018).

4. John Meyendorff, *Living Tradition: Orthodox Witness in the Contemporary World* (Crestwood, N.Y.: St. Vladimir's Seminary Press, 1978), 21.1.

5. Thomas Hopko, *The Orthodox Faith*. Volume 1: *Doctrine and Scripture*, Revised edition (Crestwood, N.Y.: St. Vladimir's Seminary Press, 2016), 12.

6. John Breck, *Scripture in Tradition: The Bible and Its Interpretation in the Orthodox Church* (Crestwood, N.Y.: St. Vladimir's Seminary Press, 2001), 3. The foundational role of Scripture in Church tradition should, however, not be downplayed; Scripture contains the history of God's revelation and as such is itself divine revelation. Georges Florovsky, *Bible, Church, Tradition: An Eastern Orthodox View*, vol. 1, *The Collected Works of Georges Florovsky* (Vaduz: Bücher-Vertriebs Anstalt, 1987), 20–21.

7. There are also exceptions like the recent study of Vasileios Thermos, Έλξη και πάθος: Μία διεπιστημονική προσέγγιση της ομοφυλοφιλίας (Athens, Greece: En Plo, 2016).

8. Luis Menéndez-Antuña, "Is There a Room for Queer Desires in the House of Biblical Scholarship?," *Biblical Interpretation* 23, no. 3 (June 2015): 402.

9. Menéndez-Antuña, "Is There a Room?," 404.

10. See, for example, Douglas J. Moo, *Romans: The NIV Application Commentary: From Biblical Text to Contemporary Life* (Grand Rapids, Mich.: Zondervan Academic, 2000), 62.

11. Bernadette Brooten, for example, in her influential work, *Love between Women: Early Christian Responses to Female Homoeroticism*, The Chicago Series on Sexuality, History, and Society (Chicago: University of Chicago Press, 1998), maintains that both past and present share the same predominant patriarchal features that dictate a particular attitude toward women and their relations. However, she proposes a change of this attitude on ethical grounds and especially on those of equality and justice. For a similar position, see Lilly Nortjé-Meyer, "Critical Principles for a Homosexual Reading of Biblical Texts: An Introduction," *Scriptura* 88 (2005): 174–82.

12. Menéndez-Antuña, "Is There a Room?," 402.

13. Menéndez-Antuña, "Is There a Room?," 421–23.

14. Boswell seems to have been inspired by the study of Derrick Sherwin Bailey, *Homosexuality and the Western Christian Tradition* (London: Longmans Green, 1955). However, Bailey maintained that the misreading of the Scripture had already started in the very first centuries of Christian tradition.

15. John Boswell, *Christianity, Social Tolerance, and Homosexuality: Gay People in Western Europe from the Beginning of the Christian Era to the Fourteenth Century* (Chicago: Chicago University Press, 1980).

16. For an overview of the reactions to Boswell's study, see Matthew Kuefler, "The Boswell Thesis," in *The Boswell Thesis: Essays on Christianity, Social Tolerance, and Homosexuality*, ed. Matthew Kuefler (Chicago: University of Chicago Press, 2006), 6–13.

17. Lynne C. Boughton, "Biblical Texts and Homosexuality: A Response to John Boswell," *Irish Theological Quarterly* 58, no. 2 (1992): 141–53.

18. Boswell, *Christianity, Social Tolerance, and Homosexuality*, 111–14.

19. William Loader, "Same-Sex Relationships: A 1st Century Perspective," *Hervormde Teologiese Studies* 70, no. 1 (2014): 4: http://dx.doi.org/10.4102/hts.v70i1.2114.

20. Robin Scroggs, *The New Testament and Homosexuality: Contextual Background for Contemporary Debate* (Philadelphia: Fortress Press, 1983).

21. Mark D. Smith, "Ancient Bisexuality and the Interpretation of Romans 1:26–27," *Journal of the American Academy of Religion* 64, no. 2 (1996): 226–27. For the diversity of homoerotic relations known to the ancient world, see Thomas K. Hubbard, *Homosexuality in Greece and Rome: A Sourcebook of Basic Documents* (Berkeley: University of California Press, 2003), 4–5.

22. Hermann C. Waetjen, "Same-Sex Relations in Antiquity and Sexuality and Sexual Identity in Contemporary American Society," in *Biblical Ethics and Homosexuality: Listening to Scripture*, ed. Robert L. Brawley (Louisville, Ky.: Westminster John Knox Press, 1996), 103–16; C. E. B. Cranfield, *A Critical and Exegetical Commentary on the Epistle to the Romans*, ICC (London: T & T Clark International, 2004), 127.

23. Scroggs, *The New Testament and Homosexuality*, 123.

24. Paul Ricoeur, "Time and Narrative: Threefold Mimesis," in *Time and Narrative*, trans. Kathleen McLaughlin and David Pellauer, vol. 1 (Chicago: University of Chicago Press, 1984), 52–87, introduced the concept of the three worlds of the text: the world *behind* the text, the world *of* the text, and the world *in front of* the text.

25. See, for example, his studies: William Loader, *The Septuagint, Sexuality, and the New Testament: Case Studies on the Impact of the LXX in Philo and the New Testament* (Grand Rapids, Mich.: Eerdmans, 2004); *Enoch, Levi, and Jubilees on Sexuality: Attitudes towards Sexuality in the Early Enoch Literature, the Aramaic Levi Document, and the Book of Jubilees* (Grand Rapids, Mich.: Eerdmans, 2007); *The Dead Sea Scrolls on Sexuality: Attitudes towards Sexuality in Sectarian and Related Literature at Qumran* (Grand Rapids, Mich.: Eerdmans, 2009); *Sexuality in the New Testament: Understanding the Key Texts* (Louisville, Ky.: Westminster John Knox Press, 2010); *The Pseudepigrapha on Sexuality: Attitudes towards Sexuality in Apocalypses, Testaments, Legends, Wisdom, and Related Literature* (Grand Rapids, Mich.: Eerdmans, 2011); *Philo, Josephus, and the Testaments on Sexuality: Attitudes towards Sexuality in the Writings of Philo, Josephus, and in the Testaments of the Twelve Patriarchs* (Grand Rapids, Mich.: Eerdmans, 2011); *The New Testament on Sexuality* (Grand Rapids, Mich.: Eerdmans, 2012).

26. William Loader, "Same-Sex Relationships," 8.

27. Richard S. Briggs, "What Does Hermeneutics Have to Do with Biblical Interpretation," *Heythrop Journal* 47, no. 1 (2006): 69–70.

28. See, however, the remark of Paul Ricoeur, *From Text to Action: Essays in Hermeneutics*, trans. Kathleen Blamey and John B. Thompson, vol. 2 (Evanston, Ill.: Northeastern University Press, 1991), 83–84, that written texts have a meaning that goes beyond the meaning intended by its author and the limits of its original setting.

29. Ricoeur, *From Text to Action*, 83. See also his remark in *Interpretation Theory: Discourse and the Surplus of Meaning* (Fort Worth: Texas Christian University Press, 1976), 44, that "Interpretation, philosophically understood, is nothing else than an attempt to make estrangement and distanciation productive."

30. This story is often associated to a similar narrative of an incident in Gibeah (Judges 19).

31. Martin Stowasser, "Homosexualität und Bibel: Exegetische und hermeneutische Überlegungen zu einem schwierigen Thema," *New Testament Studies* 43, no. 4 (1997): 504; Weston W. Fields, *Sodom and Gomorrah: History and Motif in Biblical Narrative*, JSOT Supp 231 (Sheffield, U.K.: Sheffield Academic Press, 1997), 28–53.

32. G. J. Wenham, "The Old Testament Attitude to Homosexuality," *The Expository Times* 102, no. 12 (1991): 361.

33. Although the sexual character of Sodom's sin appears in various texts of ancient Judaism, like, for example, *Jubilees* 16:5–6; 20:5–6 and *Testament of Benjamin* 9:1–3, its identification with homosexual acts can probably be first traced in the *Testament Naphtali* 3:4 (however, a connection to idolatry also seems probable—see Philip Francis Esler, "The Sodom Tradition in Romans 1:18–32," *Biblical Theology Bulletin* 34, no. 1 [2004]: 8) and more clearly in Philo's *On the Life of Abraham* 26, 134–36 and *2 Enoch* 10:2 (see also *Testimony of Levi* 17.11). For this, see Bailey, *Homosexuality and the Western Christian Tradition*, 21–22.

34. Similarly, Sodom is connected with inhospitality, injustice, arrogance, and ingratitude toward God in Josephus, *Jewish Antiquities* 1.194–95. For a detailed discussion of the passage, see Michael Carden, *Sodomy: A History of a Christian Biblical Myth*, BibleWorld (London: Equinox, 2004), 72–74.

35. Interestingly, Sodom is also used as the prototype of Babylon that is described as idolatrous in Isaiah 13:19–20 and Jeremiah 27:33–40.

36. In the *Testimony of Levi* 14.6–7, though, Sodom's sin is equated to marriage of Israelites to Gentile women.

37. This identification appears in texts of the fourth century CE, like, for example, the *Apostolic Constitutions* 6.18 or the *Apocalypse of Paul* 40. A detailed presentation of ancient Christian interpretations of the story of Sodom is in Carden, *Sodomy*, 128–54.

38. Stowasser, "Homosexualität und Bibel," 504. The contrast between Israel's contact and that of her Gentile neighbors is also made clear by the context of these prohibitions (Leviticus 18:1–5. 24–30).

39. Stowasser, "Homosexualität und Bibel," 504–5.

40. Jay Sklar, "The Prohibitions against Homosexual Sex in Leviticus 18:22 and 20:13: Are They Relevant Today?," *Biblical Interpretation* 28, no. 2 (2018): 174–81. See, however, William Loader's careful remark about the close relation between cultic and moral purity. William Loader, "'Not as the Gentiles': Sexual Issues at the Interface between Judaism and Its Greco-Roman World," *Religions* 9, no. 258 (2018): 2.

41. For a different view, see Jacob Milgrom, *Leviticus 17–22: A New Translation with Introduction and Commentary*, Anchor Yale Biblical Commentary 3A (New Haven: Yale University Press, 2008), 1568–69 and Sklar, "The Prohibitions against Homosexual Sex in Leviticus," 189–92.

42. See, for example, the connection of all sexual offences to Egypt and Canaan (Leviticus 18:2) and to Moloch (Leviticus 18:21).

43. It remains, however, unclear why the author does not use the word γένος (sex) here that would fit better in this context. For some explanations, see Stowasser, "Homosexualität und Bibel," 508n32.

44. Verses 22 and 27 seem to point to idolatry as the background of all transgressions in vv. 23–26.

45. Brooten, *Love between Women*, 294–98; Loader, *The Pseudepigrapha on Sexuality*, 419–22.

46. Stowasser, "Homosexualität und Bibel," 508.

47. In the *Testimony of Naphtali* 3.1.4–5, for example, the phrase "ἐνήλλαξεν τάξιν φύσεως" (change of the order of nature) describes both the behavior of the Sodomites and the Watchers with no clear reference to homosexuality. For a similar context, see Jude 6–7. Likewise, in Philo's *Cherubim* 93.1 the phrase "φύσεως ἔργων ἐναλλαγή" does not necessarily refer to sexual relations but could generally describe a perverted way of mentality and life. See also *Acts of Peter* 38.18 for a similar use.

48. E.g., *Letter of Aristeas* 152; *Sibylline Oracles* 4:33–34; 5:166–68; *Ps.-Phocylides* 190–92; Philo, *On the Contemplative Life* 50.

49. *On the Special Laws* 2.50; 3.37.40–41; *On the Contemplative Life* 50; *On the Embassy to Gaius* 14.

50. Ben Witherington and Darlene Hyatt, *Paul's Letter to the Romans: A Socio-Rhetorical Commentary* (Grand Rapids, Mich.: Eerdmans, 2004), 69–71; Frank J. Matera, *Romans* (Grand Rapids, Mich.: Baker Academic, 2010), 54–56.

51. Moreover, such a distinction presupposes that acts have a moral value independent of cultural and social systems; see Menéndez-Antuña, "Is There a Room?," 404.

52. Scroggs, *The New Testament and Homosexuality*, 109–18; Waetjen, "Same-Sex Relations in Antiquity," 110–12.

53. Wolfgang Stegemann, "Paul and the Sexual Mentality of His World," *Biblical Theology Bulletin* 23 (1993): 164. For a connection to slavery, see Robert Jewett, *Romans: A Commentary*, Hermeneia (Minneapolis: Fortress Press, 2006), 181.

54. Boswell, *Christianity, Social Tolerance, and Homosexuality*, 108–9.

55. Dale B. Martin, "Heterosexism and the Interpretation of Romans 1:18–32," *Biblical Interpretation* 3, no. 3 (1995): 344.

56. Stanley K. Stowers, *A Rereading of Romans: Justice, Jews, and Gentiles* (New Haven: Yale University Press, 1994), 93–95.

57. Leon Morris, *The Epistle to the Romans*, PNTC (Grand Rapids, Mich.: Eerdmans/InterVarsity, 1988), 74. One should also note the contrast between "God's wrath" in 1:18 to "God's righteousness" in 2:21–22 as God's unexpected response to human failure.

58. Paul prefers the terms "male" (ἄρσεν) and "female" (θῆλυ) instead of "man" (ἀνήρ) or "woman" (γυνή), thus clearly alluding to the Genesis story of creation. See, furthermore, his clear reference to God as the Creator in 1:25.

59. See, for example, the affinity to Wisdom 14:26 or *T.Naph.* 3:3–5. However, as Douglas A. Campbell, *The Deliverance of God: An Apocalyptic Rereading of Justification in Paul* (Grand Rapids, Mich.: Eerdmans, 2009), 360, rightly observes, Paul's stereotypical description of the Gentiles here probably presupposes a broader cluster of relevant Jewish texts.

60. For a different view, see Martin, "Heterosexism," 333.

61. See also the remark of Jeremy Punt, "Sin as Sex or Sex as Sin? Rom 1:18–32 as First Century CE Theological Argument," *Neotestamentica*, 42, no. 1 (2008): 73–92, here 78 and 85, that homoerotic acts do not appear in the vice list in Romans 1:29–31.

62. Michael Theobald, *Der Römerbrief* (Darmstadt: WBG, 2000), 144; Reidar Hvalvik, "The Present Context in the Light of the New Testament and Its Background: The Case of Homosexuality," *European Journal of Theology* 24, no. 2 (2015): 150.

63. William Loader, "Reading Romans 1 on Homosexuality in the Light of Biblical/Jewish and Greco-Roman Perspectives of Its Time," *Zeitschrift für die neutestamentliche Wissenschaft*, 108, no. 1 (2017): 119–49, here 137–38.

64. Jewett, *Romans*, 174–76; Joseph A. Fitzmyer, *Romans: A New Translation with Introduction and Commentary*, vol. 33, Anchor Yale Biblical Commentary (London: Yale University Press, 2008), 285.

65. Cranfield, *Romans*, 125.

66. For this alternative translation see Michael P. Wilson, "Should We Translate St. Paul's Παρα Φυσιν as Contrary to Nature? Text versus Received

Dogma in the Translation of St. Paul," *Theology & Sexuality* 20, no. 2 (2014): 129–50.

67. See, though, the addition of the genitive τῆς θηλείας by Didymus the Blind, *Commentary of Zechariah* 2.208 and 4.52 in his citation of Romans 1:26 that blurs even more the meaning of the Pauline text. David J. Murphy, "More Evidence Pertaining to 'Their Females' in Romans 1:26," *Journal of Biblical Literature*, 138, no. 1 (2019): 221–40, here 225–26.

68. For a summary of these views, see Loader, "Reading Romans 1 on Homosexuality," 142.

69. Later Jewish authors, like *Ps-Phocylides* 190–192, probably applied the Leviticus prohibitions to female homoeroticism. Brooten, *Love between Women*, 64.

70. There were certainly exceptions to this general rule but for the upper social layers. For a discussion of this evidence, see Roy Bowen Ward, "Why Unnatural? The Tradition behind Romans 1:26–27," *Harvard Theological Review*, 90, no. 3 (1997): 263–84, here 279–82.

71. Johannes N. Vorster, "The Making of Male Same-Sex in the Graeco-Roman World and Its Implications for the Interpretation of Biblical Discourse," *Scriptura* 93 (2006): 432–54, here 436–39.

72. For a discussion of the various meanings of παρά + accusative, see Daniel B. Wallace, *Greek Grammar beyond the Basics* (Grand Rapids, Mich.: Zondervan, 1996), 378, and F. Blass and A. Debrunner, *Greek Grammar of the New Testament and Other Early Christian Literature*, trans. Robert W. Funk, rev. ed. (Chicago: University of Chicago Press, 1961), 123–24.

73. E.g., Plutarch, *Amatorius* 751c-d; Josephus, *Contra Apionem* 2.199; Artemidorus, *Onirocritica* 1.79–80. For further discussion, see Murphy, "More Evidence," 223–25. 230.

74. J. A. Banister, "Use of Parallelism in Romans 1:26–27," *Journal of Biblical Studies* 128, no. 3 (2009): 569–90.

75. This exegetical ambiguity is also evident in the ancient Christian interpretation of the verse; the interpretation—namely, of v. 26b as a reference to female homoeroticism—is first attested in the fourth century; see Murphy, "More Evidence," 231–35.

76. For a detailed discussion, see Eugene F. Rogers, "Romans and the Gender of the Gentiles," *Soundings* 94, no. 3–4 (2011): 359–74, who refers to the comments on Romans 1 and 11 by Stowers, *A Rereading of Romans* and Campbell, *The Deliverance of God*.

77. In the sense that Romans 11:24 leads to a meaning reversal of the description of the Gentiles in Romans 1:26. For this type of literary irony, see Eleni Kapogianni, "Differences in Use and Function of Verbal Irony between Real

and Fictional Discourse: (Mis)Interpretation and Irony Blindness," *Humor* 27, no. 4 (2014): 597–618.

78. All other early references (besides those quoting the New Testament verses) are dated after Paul. In the vice lists of the *Sibylline Oracles* 2.70–77; *Acts of John* 36; Theophilus, *Ad Autolycum* 1.2.25; Aristides, *Apology* 12.9.5, the word is listed among other sins of economic injustice and exploitation. Dale Martin, "Arsenokoitês and Malakos: Meanings and Consequences," in *Biblical Ethics and Homosexuality: Listening to Scripture*, ed. Robert L. Brawley (Louisville, Ky.: Westminster John Knox Press, 1993), 120–22. However, in Hippolytus, *Refutation of All Heresies,* 23 ἀρσενοκοιτία is identified with pederasty, and in some other early Christian writers, like Origen, the word is related to sexual acts "against nature" with no further elaboration.

79. Ἄρσεν is probably the object and not the subject of the verb deriving from the second compound; see Hvalvik, "The Present Context," 152.

80. For the difficult task of translating both ἀρσενοκοῖται and μαλακοί in 1 Corinthians 6:9 see Linda L. Belleville, "The Challenge of Translating ἀρσενοκοῖται and μαλακοί in 1 Corinthians 6:9: A Reassessment in Light of Koine Greek and First Century Cultural *Mores*," *Bible Translator* 62, no. 1 (2011): 22–29.

81. Scroggs, *The New Testament and Homosexuality*, 107–8, however, suggests a rabbinic provenance of the term.

82. For a discussion of the various interpretations of the term see Simon Hedlund, "Who Are the Ἀρσενοκοῖται, and Why Does Paul Condemn Them (1 Cor 6:9)?," *Svensk Exegetisk Årsbok* 82 (2017): 116–53, here 121–25.

83. Martin, "Arsenokoitês and Malakos," 124–26; Peter Arzt-Grabner et al., *1. Korinther*, Papyrologische Kommentare zum Neuen Testament 2 (Göttingen: Vandenhoeck & Ruprecht, 2006), 230–31.

84. Interestingly, all three terms and the preceding εἰδωλολάτραι are *hapax legomena* in the Pauline letters.

85. For a discussion of this and the other vice lists in 1 Corinthians, see Anthony C. Thiselton, *The First Epistle to the Corinthians : A Commentary on the Greek Text*, NIGTC (Grand Rapids, Mich.: Eerdmans, 2000), 440–44.

86. Raymond Collins, *Sacra Pagina: First Corinthians* (Collegeville, Minn.: Liturgical Press, 1999), 229–31.

87. For a discussion of this and further literature, see Vorster, "The Making of Male Same-Sex," 436–41.

88. Anthony C. Thiselton, "Can Hermeneutics Ease the Deadlock? Some Biblical Exegesis and Hermeneutical Models," in *The Way Forward?: Christian Voices on Homosexuality and the Church*, ed. Timothy Bradshaw, 2nd ed. (Grand Rapids, Mich.: Eerdmans, 2004), 164–65.

89. Dale B. Martin, *Sex and the Single Savior: Gender and Sexuality in Biblical Interpretation* (Louisville, Ky.: Westminster John Knox Press, 2006), 54–55.

90. Menéndez-Antuña, "Is There a Room?," 420–23.

91. For a similar ecclesiological view in the liberal Anglican tradition, see Deirdre J. Good et al., "The Liberal Response," *Anglican Theological Review* 93, no. 1 (2011): 102–10 and especially 104–5.

92. I borrow here the term "grey texts" from Norman Habel, *An Inconvenient Text: Is a Green Reading of the Bible Possible?* (Adelaide, Australia: ATF Press, 2012), 2.

93. Ricoeur, *Interpretation Theory*, 45–46, 55.

94. For the role of the interpretive community in determining the meaning of the text, see Stanley Fish, *Is There a Text in This Class? The Authority of the Interpretive Communities* (Cambridge, Mass.: Harvard University Press, 1980), 14–15.

95. For a similar criticism, see Menéndez-Antuña, "Is There a Room?," 414–15.

Part II: Cultural and Pastoral Contexts

CHAPTER

5

CIVIL MARRIAGE AND CIVIL UNION FROM AN ECCLESIAL PERSPECTIVE

THE CASE OF THE ORTHODOX CHURCH OF GREECE

Pantelis Kalaitzidis

A Story to Start

In the issues of July and August of 1979, *Ecclesia*, the official monthly bulletin of the Holy Synod of the Church of Greece, published or republished the articles of three significant Greek ecclesiastical, theological, and juridical figures, that were all against the implementation of civil marriage in Greece. The authors provided theoretical and theological as well as legal support for the then-applicable statutory and universal character of the so-called "religious marriage" for all Greek citizens formally belonging to the "Orthodox" religion.[1] This publication appeared five years after the fall of the far-right dictatorial regime (with whom the institutional Church, as well as a significant number of priests and lay theologians, have collaborated), and in a period during which Greek society was experiencing an accelerating secularization process.

A few years later, in 1982, the Greek government—at that time socialist—attempted for the first time to proceed to a radical change in the family law by introducing civil marriage as the only type of marriage recognized by the state. The government finally retreated in the face of the strong

---

It goes without saying that possible mistakes and shortcomings are mine, and that ideas and views expressed in the present paper are my own responsibility and do not engage the theological institution I am in charge of.

reactions (meetings, rallies, newspapers articles, parliamentary interventions, etc.) of the Orthodox Church of Greece and other religious organizations, and ended up initiating civil marriage as an equal type of marriage alongside the religious one. By this move, it put an end to a situation where the religious freedom of nonbelievers was constantly violated while ecclesial sacraments were often ridiculed and mocked.

It is worth noticing that it was not the institutional Church that took the initiative to end this very problematic situation—from both the religious freedom perspective but also from the ecclesiological perspective, and that of the canon law and the ecclesial self-consciousness.[2] Since then, the initial strict, and even excessive reaction and controversy of the institutional Church concerning those who had contracted civil marriage was followed in recent years by a clearly more cautious attitude that recognizes the complexity of the matter and the existence of other, for instance, practical reasons for the alleged "denial" of the holy sacraments of the Church and the choice to proceed to a civil marriage. The excessive reaction of the Church of Greece ranged from the denial of ecclesiastical burial for people who performed civil marriage, along with the refusal to accept them as godparents, to the refusal in some very extreme cases by some bishops or priests to baptize children born into a civil marriage—a refusal based on the view that those Orthodox Christians had, with their choice, denied in practice the sacraments of the Church and therefore were cut off from the Church body and the community of believers. Sixteen years after the establishment of civil marriage in Greece—in other words, in October 1998, at the beginning of the new era inaugurated by the late Archbishop Christodoulos—the Holy Synod of the Hierarchy of the Church of Greece, following a suggestion by His Eminence the Metropolitan of Messinia Chrysostomos that those who engaged only in civil marriage were "neither cut off (from the Church) nor de-Christianized," issued a statement that the Holy Synod finally accepted the following proposition: "The Hierarchy of the Church of Greece continues to accept the Decisions of the Hierarchy of 1982 and 1984 concerning civil marriage, and from today onwards it assigns it to the pastoral discernment of each Hierarch to individually evaluate the cases of those who did and still insist on the civil marriage, based on the criterion of philanthropy and the ecclesiastical economy according to Christ, whenever he deals with the funerals of those people."[3] This change of attitude on behalf of the Orthodox Church of Greece regarding its reactions against the faithful who participated in civil marriage was confirmed by a new decision taken by the Holy Synod in 2002. According to this latter decision, civil marriage was implicitly recognized as valid (ἔγκυρος), since its performance is counted among the valid (ἔγκυροι) marriages when it comes to grand blessing and permission for a third ecclesiastical marriage.[4]

In all its severe reactions against the implementation of civil marriage in Greece, the Orthodox Church never took into account the fact that in other countries or contexts, the Orthodox had to perform compulsory civil marriage before the ecclesiastical one, and that for almost ten centuries in Byzantium, marriage was mainly, if not exclusively, civil (I will come back to this point later), without any similar type of reactions against these realities or accusation for betrayal or abandon of the Orthodox faith.

The Civil Unions for Heterosexual and Homosexual Couples

In March 2008, in relation to the bill (then under discussion and now, since November 2008, official state law) on the civil unions (contracts of cohabitation) applicable only to heterosexual couples, the Standing Holy Synod of the Church of Greece took the following decision:

> a. The Church of Greece, through the Standing Holy Synod, proclaims the absolute respect and the appropriate honor to the Church's sacred sacrament of marriage, whose purpose is the mutual spiritual complementarity of the spouses in order to achieve salvation in Jesus Christ, and whose fruit is the birth of children. Thus, the Church accepts and blesses the recognized wedding ceremony according to the Orthodox rite and considers as fornication any other "marital" cohabitation outside the Orthodox marriage.
>
> b. The Church of Greece calls the congregation of its faithful children to make sure that the Church, which has always defended the sanctity of the sacred sacrament of marriage, endeavors to apply the teachings of the Lord Jesus Christ in order to keep the principles of the holy Gospel in all areas of life and to maintain the respect for the holy canons regarding life and behavior of the children of the Church.
>
> c. On the basis of these principles and with a deep sense of responsibility toward the sacred clergy and the pious people, it states that it is absolutely impossible to consent to the drafting bill on "Civil Union," the application of which supports and legitimizes serious moral sins and will be a devastating bomb to the foundations of the

Christian family and the whole of Greek society. The Standing Holy Synod expresses the hope and wish that this bill will not become a State Law.[5]

In 2012, five years after the initial strong statement, the Holy Synod slightly reviewed its position on the matter, avoiding the use of sharp expressions and the move to moral condemnations, and ended its new statement by saying that the Church ought to pastorally evaluate and to address the new alternative forms of private life.[6]

We could then easily imagine what was the official synodal reaction of the Orthodox Church of Greece (still considered to be a moderate one in comparison to some ultraconservative bishops or religious organizations) when in December 2015, the radical left Greek government expanded the law on civil unions to homosexual couples as well. The Standing Holy Synod of the Church of Greece issued the following statement on the gay civil registered partnerships:

> Regarding the forthcoming submission to the House of Law to extend the registered civil union to same-sex couples, the Standing Holy Synod recalls that it adheres to the decision of the Session of the Holy Synod of Hierarchy of the Church of Greece of October 17, 2013, when it dealt with the family institution in the context of the modern crisis, which decision was updated by the Standing Holy Synod at its session of June 19, 2015. The decision at that time emphasized, inter alia:
> The Session of the Standing Synod, at today's session, persists and updates the decision of the session of the Holy Synod of Hierarchy of October 17, 2013, in which it was noted that:
> "modern forms of organization of people's private lives—alternative forms of family—for the Church and its theology of marriage and the family constitute 'aberrations' of the family institution as it has been shaped and operated for centuries in the life of the ecclesial body."
> "Marriage and the family, an ecclesiastical and social institution par excellence, of fundamental importance, are increasingly becoming an individual affair within the realm of privacy."
> "Phenomena-'deviations' extremely relevant to the Greek reality are civil marriage, single parenthood, civil union and the so-called gay marriage."

The above decision of the Holy Synod of the Hierarchy shall be deemed firm and irrevocable.

It is clarified that the starting point of the Church's position on the above issue is respect for the value of humankind, which is central to Orthodox Theology, but also a fundamental principle in the Greek Constitution. Respect for human value results in the rejection of any substitute institution such as civil union, which seeks to reduce family life to the level of civil transactions, which is sufficient to overthrow a simple change of opinion of the parties.[7]

Previous to this synodical decision, the Archbishop of Athens and all Greece, Hieronymus, addressed in June 2015 an official letter to the Greek Minister of Justice, expressing in a moderate way his and the Church's opposition to the whole idea of civil union, and particularly to the extension of the registered partnerships to gay couples, while in a personal statement dated in the same period declared that "The union of two persons through marriage is a great sacrament for our Church. Everything outside this sacrament is alien to Church life."[8]

The reactions were clearly stronger and more aggressive at the nonofficial level than at that of individual bishops, theologians, religious organizations, grassroots faithful, or religious blogs. Thus, Metropolitan Ambrosius, at that time bishop of Egion and Kalavryta (he resigned on August 2019), as he did on other occasions too, issued a strong antigay statement saying: "Homosexuality is a deviation from the laws of nature! It's a social crime! It's a sin! So those who either experience it or support it are not normal people! They are scum of society. . . . Don't hesitate, then! When and wherever you meet them, spit on them!"[9] Metropolitan Ambrosius was condemned for the above statement in January 2019 by the Greek justice for "public incitement to violence or hatred" and "abuse of ecclesiastical office."[10] This same hierarch, in order to dramatize and to make more theatrical his reaction against the vote of the Greek Parliament, decided to mournfully ring the bells in the temples of his diocese as a protest against the gay civil unions bill.

Metropolitan Seraphim of Piraeus, from his side, repeatedly publicly intervened on this issue. According to him, homosexuality and, consequently, the gay civil unions run counter to our cultural identity, which is grounded in the sacred institution of the family that has long been regarded as a bond between man and woman. This type of civil union changes also our legal culture, which considers by the Article 347 of the Criminal Code the practice of homosexuality to be criminal. He argued also that it legislates a reversal of human ontology and physiology, while creating legally a new kind of human being that had never existed before: a bisexual person. Following Metropolitan Seraphim's argument, gay civil union allows the young people to use their body as they wish, which leads to terrifying diseases at the expense of the psycho-physical health of human beings. The crucial question that arises, always according to Metropolitan Seraphim, is why does Mr. Soros's "Open Society" Foundation fund the "activist" actions of homosexuals in Greece and in Europe?[11] Two other Greek Metropolitans (Seraphim of Kythira and Ieremias of Gortyna), along with Metropolitan Seraphim of Piraeus, appealed to the Council of State, one of the two highest juridical institutions in Greece, in order to invalidate the law voted by the Greek Parliament regulating the gay civil union, and to cancel its implementation.[12]

Statements or communiqués of analogous content or style were issued also by Metropolitan Kosmas of Etolia and Akarnania,[13] Metropolitan Nikolaos of Mesogaia and Lavreotiki,[14] Metropolitan Seraphim of Kythira,[15] the Clergy Conference of the Metropolis of Florina (in northern Greece),[16] and even the Holy Monastic Community of Mount Athos, which in its official letter to the Greek Minister of Justice maintains, among others, that "As Orthodox Christians, we deeply respect the personal preferences of each individual, and his or her right to be a member or not of the Church, because we strongly believe that no one has the right to compromise the divine gift of freedom. However," continues the letter from Mount Athos, "it is clearly against the morals of our people and particularly challenging for the Greek society, to suggest that the 'same-sex couples' can be deemed to be a family, bestowed with all the legal and social advantages, as the adoption of children etc."[17] Previously, in August 2014, at the eve of the voting by the Greek Parliament on the antiracist bill, Metropolitan Nikolaos of Mesogaia and Lavreotiki (a graduate of Harvard and MIT, who worked also for NASA), issued a statement in which he equated homosexuality with genocide in the following terms:

> The societies, however, that prohibit the stigmatization and control of the various psychosocial perversions, such as genocide and homosexuality, but also racism, these societies are neither societies nor democracies. Let us ask the advocates of the law (sc. against racism,

and hatred discourse) to explain why antiracism should be protected and "homophobia" should be banned by the law. After all, the problem is not "homophobia" itself, which we have just learned as a word, as much as the homomania we experience in our daily lives.[18]

Strong antigay statements and communiqués were also issued by the ultraconservative Pan-Hellenic Union of Theologians (PETh),[19] the League of Cretan Theologians,[20] the Orthodox Christian Brotherhoods, and the associations of the city of Larissa (in central Greece).[21] This aggressive antigay discourse was prepared and reinforced by popular religious publications such as the editorial on October 2013 in the religious journal *O Sotir* (The Savior) by the theological brotherhood of the same name, titled "A Beastly Abominable Passion" ("Πάθος κτηνῶδες βδελυρό"), and in which an appeal was made to the Holy Synod of the Orthodox Church of Greece "to raise a strong condemnatory voice, stigmatizing the shameless homosexuality and defending the rational (λογικό) flock of Christ's Church," reminding that "the road was already opened by the Moldovan Orthodox hierarchy."[22]

Civil Union, Concubinage (Παλλακεία), and Civil Marriage in Byzantium: A Dynamic Interpretation

However, to come back to the wording that has marked and made more widely known the aforementioned decision by the Standing Holy Synod of March 2008 that asserted that "the Church . . . regards as fornication any other 'marital' relationship outside the Orthodox marriage." This wording defines as fornication any form of permanent cohabitation, even the one legally or notarially institutionalized, but also civil marriage. In addition it gives at first glance the impression that it includes also under the same term marriages celebrated according to the rites of other religions, or even according to the rite of other Christian confessions, something that would contradict the practice of mixed (inter-Christian) marriages that the Orthodox Church has blessed and committed on a global scale for more than a century. The identification of the permanent registered cohabitation (concubinage) with fornication seems also to contradict the steady views of both Byzantine law and the interpreters of the holy canons regarding the relation of fornication and concubinage (the equivalent of today's free or civil unions), and even of numerous Church Fathers who, against the current dominant ecclesiastical discourse, underlined *expressis verbis*, the difference and distinction between concubinage and fornication.

Free cohabitation between man and woman (what in the ancient, Byzantine, and post-Byzantine time was called concubinage [παλλακεία]) was for the Church a problem that existed long before its historical establishment, a problem with which it dealt in a timely and bold way. In this context, the Church defined those free cohabitations on the basis of its evangelical, moral, and social criteria, while it demanded the concubinage, once contracted, to be maintained, strictly monogamous, and even lifelong, ascribing to it a clear consciousness of *affectio maritalis*. It is clear then that the Church, obviously, accepted this kind of cohabitation/partnership but at the same time it wanted by this understanding to express a mutual respect for the two sexes. The acceptance of this cohabitation was based on a clear and bold condition: the lifelong monogamous life of the spouses, understood through the lens of a marriage and a family formation (see for instance Chapter 15 of *The Apostolic Tradition* of St. Hippolytus from the second to the third century AD, which refers to the case of a slave woman in a free cohabitation with a non-Christian, and who was accepted for catechesis and baptism, under the sole condition to be, at least from her side, in a monogamous relationship[23]). It is clear, then, that the Church, with good judgment and discernment, has preceded the state on the issue of upgrading the value of the cohabitations/partnerships.[24]

As for the clear distinction between concubinage and fornication adopted by numerous Church Fathers, Byzantine law and the interpreters of the holy canons, St. Hippolytus, for instance, calls "loving God" (φιλόθεο) a woman named Markia, the concubine of the Roman emperor Komodos, while he allows any concubine that respects monogamy to take the holy communion.[25] According to the Greek theologian Rev. Konstantinos Papadopoulos, this provision "is respected by the ancient Church as a whole: The faithful concubine of a pagan man has been accepted, while she is devoted to him, and obeys the commandments concerning herself. A faithful man is not allowed to have a concubine, but is required to have a spouse. And this is because at that time it was possible for a man to marry because he was considered as strong, but this was not the case with a woman who was considered as weak."[26] This analysis provided by canon law and theology has been confirmed also by historians such as the distinguished scholar of Byzantine studies and professor at Harvard University Angeliki E. Laiou, when she states that "Concubinage, which was recognized as a form of 'legal cohabitation without marriage' by Justinian's legislation, as well as by the *Nomocanon* in fourteen titles, among others, was a stable sexual relationship. It differed from fornication in that it was a relationship that was in principle monogamous and lasting."[27] The fact that concubinage (παλλακεία) was formally abolished by *Novella* (Νεαρά or "new laws") 91 of Leo VI does not negate the importance of this institution for the subject under discussion in this study, an institution that did not disappear with the issue of the *novella* by Emperor Leo (d. 912) but that continued to exist until the end of the Byzantine period and even beyond, into the Ottoman period. Thus, the well-known Byzantine canonist Balsamon (twelfth century), interpreting canon 26 of St. Basil the Great and its canonical sanctions for this type of sexual relationship, writes: "There is a difference between a concubine and a prostitute. And that's because the former, i.e., the concubine, is subject to the law even though she sins with only one man. On the contrary, the latter (i.e., the prostitute), when she sins with various men, although she is not subject to the law, she is however being prosecuted from the prostitute housing."[28] A respective treatment is also evident in the decisions and opinions of Demetrios Chomatinos, an Archbishop of Ohrid from 1216 to 1236 with jurisdiction from the island of Corfu in the Ionian Sea to the region of Drama in eastern Macedonia: According to them, assets are granted to concubine women after the dissolution of the cohabitation or the death of the man, in order to be able to ensure her and her children maintenance. If the cases judged by Chomatinos revealed that in some cases concubinage (and the relevant terms παλλακεία, παλλακή) was also covering nonmonogamous or even adulterous and promiscuous relationships, it is not without interest to notice that among those who contracted such a union (concubinage) were clerics (at least a priest and a deacon).[29] This treatment of the concubine and of her children echoes the older legal provisions of Emperors Anastasios I and Justinian (*Novella* 89), giving them some kind of recognition and inheritance rights.[30] In the *Exabiblos* of Armenopoulos (IV, 9, 35), a fourteenth-century jurist in Byzantine Thessaloniki, the monogamous concubinage is indirectly recognized, since children born out of this type of relationship are considered as legal, and thus financial security is provided to their mother. St. Nikodemos the Hagiorite also writes in the *Rudder*: "The prostitute differs from the concubine, as she sins with several persons, while the concubine with one," while conveying and adopting the view from the text of St. Photius called "Nomicon," according to which "The concubine . . . is a modest woman, whom the man she lives with, makes clear testimony of her cohabitation, showing to the people around him that she is his wife;"[31] the same St. Photius in his *Nomocanon* maintains that "the concubine is a woman that cohabitates legally with somebody in his house without a wedding."[32] More generally, however, we should observe that in Byzantine law, concubinage was not labeled as fornication, nor was it treated as adultery, although it was forbidden or legally rejected by some Byzantine emperors. Although the Church disagreed with and disapproved of some legal (according to the state) forms of nonmarital cohabitation (such as the concubinage), it, however, tolerated them due to its loyalty to the law and by applying the ecclesiastical principle of economy.[33] This meets the general remark made by Angeliki E. Laiou according to which the attitude of the Church as regards the institution of concubinage was not unequivocal.[34] This bold statement is further confirmed by two examples of concubinage judged by Chomatinos as they are commented by Nikolaos Pantazopoulos: Following Pantazopoulos's analysis, what is surprising and worth noticing is that Archbishop Chomatinos did not ask to stop the concubinage union, while he made decisions in order to regulate the financial relations of the couple of concubines and the rights of the children born out of these relations (theoretically disapproved by the Church), and did not exert any pressure (e.g., by invoking excommunication or other canonical sanctions) in order to get the promise for the celebration of the sacrament of marriage.[35] This ambivalence as regards the attitude of the Church toward concubinage could be explained through the pastoral concerns, and the application of the canonical principle of οἰκονομία,[36] since even contemporary theologians of promonastic milieus speak about the "the simultaneous focus [περιστροφή] of the pastoral treatment of the concubinage [παλλακεία] around the axes of ἀκρίβεια and οἰκονομία, an attitude which . . . should also inspire the contemporary pastoral approach to the problem."[37] In the contemporary context, this dynamic and modern way to address the well-known phenomenon of concubinage (παλλακεία) from the history of the Church considers the civil union as the present version of the ancient or Byzantine institution, and one should stress that this quite bold statement comes from representatives of the conservative side such as the Greek professor of canon law at the Faculty of Theology of the University of Athens Panayiotis I. Boumis, who points out that "The civil union relates the androgynous couple to the status of concubinage [παλλακείας]."[38]

Therefore, and especially with regard to the sensitivity of conservative Orthodox clergy and faithful, the way the Fathers and canon law dealt with concubinage (παλλακεία) in that remote time, could help and inspire (and not restrict) the pastoral discernment of the Church in dealing with the new or the alternative forms of cohabitation and civil unions.[39]

The key to interpret this patristic and canonical principle of the Byzantine and even post-Byzantine era, and to further apply it to the contemporary issues of civil marriage and civil unions, seems to lie, in addition to the monogamous or polygamous character of the relations under discussion, in the distinction also between the permanent and stable cohabitation on the one hand, and the precarious or temporary one on the other. Following the analysis of Boumis, based on the writings and the canons of St. Basil as well as on those of Ecumenical Councils, and the interpretations of Byzantine canonists such as Zonaras (end of eleventh to the beginning of twelfth centuries) and Balsamon (twelfth century), what decisively defines the character of the relationship between a man and a woman is permanence (μονιμότητα) and duration in the case of concubinage, precariousness and uncertainty in the case of fornication. Following this principle, Boumis goes so far as to maintain:

> Thus, the more certain, permanent and stable a kind of cohabitation is, the closer it is to the concept of marriage, and therefore it is justifiable to be defined as marriage. On the contrary, the more temporary and unstable or uncertain a type of cohabitation is, the more it departs from the idea of marriage and the closer it is to the concept of fornication. In addition, and to conclude this observation, we could add: Anything that contributes to the permanence and stability of this cohabitation builds on the concept and institution of marriage; otherwise it is an integral part of marriage, it enhances marriage. In contrast, whatever contributes to the temporary character and the destabilization, to the uncertainty of this cohabitation, it drives it away from the idea of marriage and directs it to the fornication.[40]

The same Greek canonist dared to ask also a series of crucial and difficult questions as regards civil marriage, and the use of the term "fornication" in speaking on sexual intercourse outside Orthodox wedding, questions that challenge the stereotypes of the ecclesiastical establishment, and of the usual churchgoers:

Many—especially ecclesiastical officials—argue that civil marriage, since it is not celebrated by the Church, equals fornication. In this light, the following question arises: Can we so roughly, indiscriminately and unambiguously argue, without any deeper consideration of the facts, that civil marriage can be generally considered as a fornication, for the sole reason, that it is not celebrated by the Church? A further question: If we assume that civil marriage was always considered as fornication, then would St. Paul allow in his Epistles the Christian husband to cohabit with his non-Christian wife (and vice versa), since they had not had a Christian marriage? . . . And if it was fornication, would the canon 72 of the Quinisext (in Trullo) Ecumenical Council describe the marriage between two non-Christians as a "legal marriage"? The answer then to our question must be negative: By no means, we can accept and say so generally and unequivocally that every marriage based on the civil law, is fornication.[41]

Contrary to what the conservative Orthodox claim, historians, canonists, and professors of law agree that in the first ten centuries of the history of Christianity, marriage and its legislation were the sole responsibility of the state (what we use to call today "civil marriage").[42] "Notwithstanding the theoretically sacramental character of marriage in the early Christian centuries, in practice marriage had only political and civil significance. Christians were obliged to marry according to the provision of Roman Law and it seems that the Church accepted the sacredness of marriage even though it may not have been blessed by a bishop or a priest. There is no evidence that the Church remarried her members. It seems that for several centuries the blessing of a marriage by the Church was not required."[43] It is not by accident that ancient Christian writers, when referring to marriage, imply a marriage performed according the civil law (i.e., the civil marriage of their time).[44] As it is pointed out, the indisputable conclusion remains that "the Church of the Ecumenical Councils, accepted the civil form of marriage during the Byzantine period or at least did not regard it as prostitution, nor did it reject it."[45]

It is well known, however, that St. Ignatius of Antioch (ca. 100 AD) exhorted those of both sexes who were going to get married to unite with the knowledge and the blessing of the bishop, so that marriage may be according to the Lord, and not by human desire.[46] According to the Serbian liturgical scholar Nenad S. Milošević—who dedicated his doctoral dissertation and other scholarly papers (based on research done in manuscript and printed liturgical editions) to the relationship of the sacraments to the Eucharist—the right interpretation of this suggestion is not of an administrative or "political" (in the sense of the Church interfering in the political realm) nature, but of an ecclesiological and Eucharistic one, since it is established that initially the sacrament of marriage was linked with the Eucharist, and was celebrated within it.[47] As noticed by the prominent Orthodox historian and theologian Fr. John Meyendorff, commenting on the way in which Christian marriage was celebrated in the early Church, and specifically in the relevant quotation of the bishop-martyr St. Ignatius of Antioch,

> Early Christian writers—the same ones who otherwise give full recognition to the legal validity of civil marriage "according to laws"—also affirm that it is the Eucharist which gives to marriage its specifically Christian meaning. . . . Every Christian couple desirous of marriage went through the formalities of civil registration, which gave it validity in secular society; and then through their joint participation in the regular Sunday liturgy, in the presence of the entire local Christian community, they received the Bishop's blessing. It was then that their civil agreement became also "sacrament," with eternal value, transcending their earthly lives because it was also "inscribed in heaven," and not only in a secular "registry." It became an eternal union in Christ.[48]

As the Eucharist was the only true seal of marriage, a non-Christian couple admitted into the Church through Baptism, Chrismation, and Communion was—according to the canonical tradition and the practice of the Church during the first centuries—not "remarried"; their joint reception of the Eucharist was the Christian fulfillment of a "natural" (or civil) marriage concluded outside the Church.[49]

It should be noticed that this narrative of Christian marriage, and the consequent implicit or explicit ecclesial recognition of civil marriage, is not an isolated case in the history of the Church, but characterizes the practice of the Church at least in the East. According to the brief historical overview by Fr. John Meyendorff,[50] until the tenth century there was no autonomous ecclesial rite of marriage, separate from the Eucharistic Liturgy, although various aspects of its subsequent development, like a specific solemnization of the sacrament and the rite of "crowning," were already part of the Eucharist since the fourth century. This crowning was very early substantiated by prayers as is evident in various liturgical texts of the time. This rite of crowning did not find a general application to the believers, the "crowning" never became a legal obligation, as it is clear from the legal collection *Epanagoge* (XVI, 1) (describing in detail the relations between Church and state, and whose author is most probably the great patriarch Photius, 857–67, 877–86 AD), which offers to Christians three alternatives for concluding marriage: "by a blessing, or by a crowning, or by an agreement."[51] Previously to this, at the time of Byzantine emperor Justinian, and particularly in December 537 AD, according to the *Novella* 74, chapter 4, three categories of subjects were defined, to which three types of marriage corresponded: the glorious (for the *personae illustrae*), the middle (for the state dignitaries, the merchants, etc.), and the vile (for the soldiers, the farmers, etc.). The former established their marriage by contract; those of the second category declared their decision to cohabitate in the presence of the ἔκδικος (a kind of legal advisor of the Church) and three or four clergy, the presence of whom in the marriage of this category of subjects did not have a sacramental or even ritualistic tone, but it served to testify the event; and as for the third category, the vile or the poor, no specific process was required.[52]

Going back to Meyendorff's analysis we see that the rite of crowning, however, never became a legal obligation.[53] This was the case until the tenth century, when a decisive step took place and the rite of crowning was separated from the Eucharist for free citizens (though not for slaves). This development was a result of the imperial *Novella* 89 of the Byzantine Emperor Leo VI, which states that the two legal acts of adoption of a child and of marriage—as long as they involve free citizens, and not slaves—will henceforth be sanctioned by a Church ceremony, and that a marriage not blessed by the Church will not be considered as marriage, "but as an illegitimate concubinage." The most important implication of the decree was that the Church was invested with the responsibility of giving *legal status* to marriage, something quite unusual in the previous centuries.[54] The change was indeed striking, since before Leo VI a citizen could enter (with the respective canonical consequences) a marriage disapproved by the Church (second or third marriage, mixed marriage, etc.), and do so legally and in good standing before the law, while now, and specifically after the *novella* of Leo VI, the Church had to determine the legal status of all marriages, even those that contradicted Christian norms. The new situation, in principle, gave the Church an upper hand over the morals of all citizens, but the Church had to pay a high price for the new social responsibility that it had received. One serious consequence of this development was the obliteration of the distinction between the "secular" and the "sacred," between the fallen human society and the Kingdom of God, and in our case between the so-called marriage as contract or civil marriage of the time and marriage as sacrament, since the Church was obliged not only to bless marriages that it did not approve, but even to "dissolve" them (i.e., give "divorces"). This was a preliminary case of secularization in the life of the Church since the latter was obliged to secularize its pastoral care toward marriage and to be compromised in several cases as soon as marriage became legally obligatory. In the words of Fr. Meyendorff himself,

> Was it possible, for example, to refuse Church blessing to a remarried widower when this refusal implied deprivation of civil rights for one or two years? As soon as the sacrament of marriage—received in the Church—became legally obligatory, compromises of all sorts became unavoidable; and, simultaneously, the idea that marriage was a unique and eternal bond—reflecting the union of Christ and the Church—was obliterated in the pastoral practice of the Church and in the conscience of the faithful. Emperor Leo VI himself, the author of the *novella*, forced upon the Church his own fourth marriage with Zoe Carbonopsina in 906.[55]

In order, however, to preserve the so-to-say purity of the Eucharist from the various compromises in marriage, the Church had to separate the latter from the former by establishing a separate rite, since it could not, for example, give communion to a non-Orthodox, or to a couple entering a second marriage. The change was made more acceptable by the fact that the obvious connection between the Church marriage and the Eucharist was lost altogether as soon as Church marriage became a legal requirement. However, even the *novella* of Leo VI failed to suppress entirely the possibility for a particular category of Church members to marry sacramentally, through the Eucharist, without a separate—and often expensive—"crowning." The slaves—i.e., more than half of the Empire's population—were not touched by the new law. This discrepancy between marriage law for slaves and for free citizens was suppressed by Emperor Alexius I Komnenos (1081–1118), who issued another *novella* making "crowning" a legal obligation for slaves as well.[56] According to Panos Nikolopoulos, "even after the establishment of the wedding ceremony (ἱερολογία) as a constituent element of marriage . . . , civil marriage is preferred by the Orthodox that wish to get married with heretics, as can be concluded from the *Nomocanon* of St. Photius (see chapter II, 13). Moreover, in the Constitution of Matthaios Blastaris (thirteenth century), the marriage is recognized as 'marriage, either by blessing, or by crowning, or by contract.'"[57] Even during the Ottoman period, according to Nikolopoulos's analysis, largely based on the insights of Professor Nikolaos Pantazopoulos, professor of the history of Greek law at the University of Thessaloniki:

> Forms of constitution of civil marriage can be found in various collections of canon law, in codes or in nomocanons, forms which are opposed to the religious one. In the Nomocanon of Manuel Malaxos (1574), as in the Nomicon of Theophilus, Bishop of Campania (1788) in Central Macedonia, a marriage is foreseen to be contracted by virtue of the redaction of simple accords without a wedding ceremony (ἱερολογία), while there are corresponding regulations in the Metropolitan Code of Kastoria (early sixteenth century), and the Vlacho-Hungarian Code (of 1818), and it is argued that the type of marriage provided by the above provisions is called Kepinion, i.e., the oral agreement of the prospective married couples following the civil provisory marriage, which is confirmed in written form by the non-Christian, Muslim judge (Kadi).[58]

Especially regarding *Kepinion* (the "civil marriage" of the Ottoman period), it is interesting and insightful to know, as Nikolaos Pantazopoulos has demonstrated in a set of his studies, that during the Ottoman period, the kind of "civil marriage" represented by *Kepinion* was applied not only to mixed marriages between Christians and Muslims, but also—due to sociological and financial reasons as well as for reasons related to the canonical impediments—to marriages between Christians.[59] As regards the reaction of the Church to this kind of marriage, it should be noticed that, as in other cases too, its initial strong reaction and rejection came to the point, in some cases, of implicit or explicit acceptance by virtue of the principle of οἰκονομία.[60] Moreover, throughout the history and canon law of the Church, we know cases in which the latter tolerated some marriages that did not have its blessing.[61]

Marriage as Sacrament and as Civil Agreement

As it has been argued in the previous section of this paper, as long as marriage was regulated under the exclusive jurisdiction of the state authority, its ecclesiastical blessing had almost no ritual content, and the spouses were married during the Eucharistic gathering, as we read for example in the writings of St. Ignatius, Bishop of Antioch (ca. 100 AD). In addition, the *Didache of the Apostles*, the *Apostolic Tradition*, the *Apostolic Instructions*, the *Covenant of the Lord*, and the *Euchologion of Serapion of Thmuis* contain prayers for Baptism, Chrismation, Eucharist, ordinations, anointing of the sick, birth, funeral, etc., but surprisingly enough, one cannot find the slightest reference to any service or sacrament of marriage.[62] It is not meaningless to point out that in the *Corpus Areopagiticum*, written as it is well-known at the end of the fifth or the beginning of the sixth century, and that had a tremendous influence on the formation of the ecclesiastical and theological tradition both in the East and in the West, thanks to its writing disguise, in this *Corpus* the Baptism, the synaxis or the communion, the ordination, the "monastic perfection" (i.e., the tonsure), and the ceremony "for those rested sacredly in peace" (the funerals) are recognized as sacraments, and a full description of the corresponding ecclesiastical rites is given for them; at the same time there is no reference to any sacrament of marriage in this *Corpus*. In the eighth century John of Damascus names baptism and communion as sacraments, while a century later Theodore of the Studion repeats also what Ps.-Dionysius was saying, without any reference to or presentation of marriage. In fact, "for several centuries there was no unanimity among Church Fathers as to the exact number of Church mysteries or whether marriage was included among them. Justin the Martyr and Philosopher mentions only two; St. Cyprian five; Tertullian six; St. Cyril of Jerusalem three; St. Ambrose of Milan three; Theodore of Mopsuestia three; Pseudo-Dionysios the Areopagite six."[63] It is probably not by chance that the rite for the sacrament of marriage included in the oldest manuscripts (end of the eighth to the beginning of the ninth century) is extremely short, and that a longer and richer service starts to appear only after the tenth century.[64]

As it follows from the previous analysis, marriage did not function in any way as the sacrament of entrance to the ecclesial life; it was not the one that marked the entrance to or the exit from the ecclesial community, it by no means determined the Christian identity and status. This role has been assigned to the faithful by the sacraments par excellence—namely, the baptism/confirmation and the divine Eucharist. Therefore, with regard to this, as maintained by Panayiotis Boumis, it is not by accident that "there is no testimony that it [sc. the Church] considered nonecclesiastical matrimony liable to canonical pursuits, such as forbidding the participation in the Holy Communion, as is the case today."[65] The same conservative Greek professor firmly opposes the often-dominant idea in many traditional or traditionalistic Orthodox milieus, especially in countries of Orthodox tradition or majority, that civil marriage, due to the lack of a separate ecclesiastical ritual, is equivalent to fornication. Boumis, without accepting the sacredness of civil marriage, refuses nonetheless to accept this equation and the radical rejection of the nonecclesiastical marriage for the sole reason of the lack of a ritual, by appealing again to the distinction between permanent and precarious relationship (see above), and to the canon law and Church history, in which we see that in some cases the Church tolerates, and even silently recognizes, some types of marriage without its blessing.[66] In addition, he associates civil marriage with engagement (μνηστεία), referring, in support of his interpretation, to biblical stories and quotations, to patristic evidence, and to canonical regulations, the engagement (μνηστεία) with blessing being understood, even by St. Nikodemos of Mount Athos and his *Rudder*, as "no less than a perfect marriage."[67]

When, however, starting from the tenth century, the Church acquired legal or secular jurisdiction over marriage, many things began to change. The ecclesiological and sacramental character of marriage was significantly diminished, if not completely marginalized, and its legal dimension prevailed. In turn this development highlighted social conformism and a perception of marriage as a religious legitimation of the sexual relationship. It was then that the Church gave in to the imposed social conventions, and the cultural conditions that dominated in each place or time led to the adoption and acceptance of prohibitions and limitations that we now tend to report and to identify with the core and the very essence of Christian faith. In addition, this retreat of the original ecclesiological/sacramental understanding of marriage coincides with the parallel tendencies of the depreciation of corporeality, of woman, and of the material world, and the stripping of sexuality from its spiritual dimension.

As stated characteristically by Christos Yannaras in the first Greek edition (1970) of his now-classic *The Freedom of Morality*,

In the mystery of marriage, the Church comes to redefine love with its fullness, to reveal to love the path of the knowledge of God [θεογνωσία], to reveal the image of the Trinitarian Prototype in the androgynous oneness of human nature. And in this mystery, as in every mystery, the human being brings his natural life to the Church, in order to graft it into the transformed creation of the Church, and this entrance becomes the event of an encounter of his freedom with the innovative energy of the grace of the Holy Spirit. Every sacrament is an inclusion in the body of the Church, a personal activation of the participation in the divine–human nature, making imperishable the perishable temporality in "duration" of personal communion. Thus marriage is not a "legalization" of a love affair or a "ceremonial blessing" of the natural conjugal bond of the spouses, but a mystery— that is, a way of salvation and knowledge of God [θεογνωσία], the manifestation of the Church as the truth of God's incarnation and the human being's deification. . . . Not a mere blessing or a legal recognition of erotic life, but the realization of the Church, the manifestation of God, the existential transformation of the human being [ὑπαρκτικὴ μεταμόρφωση τοῦ ἀνθρώπου].[68]

But whoever speaks of a sacrament in a theological perspective is aware of the intimate and primordial link between sacraments and the sacrament par excellence of the Church—i.e., the Eucharist, the sacrament that makes the Church what really is: namely, the gathering of the scattered people of God and the participation in the eschatological dinner, image of the Trinitarian communion within History. The same applies to the sacrament of marriage. To refer again to the authority of Fr. John Meyendorff:

> For Orthodox Christians, . . . the Eucharist, or "Divine Liturgy," is the moment and the place when and where a Christian should realize what he truly is. In the Eucharist, the Kingdom of God—whose citizen he is by baptism—becomes available directly to his spiritual senses. . . . In the Liturgy, the Church, being concretely a gathering of people, ceases to be a human organization and becomes truly the "Church of God." Then Christ Himself leads the assembly, and the assembly is transformed into His Body. Then all partitions between concrete historical happenings and eternity are broken. The true meaning of marriage as a sacrament becomes understandable in the framework of the Eucharistic Divine Liturgy.[69]

In our contemporary practice, as we know, the connection of marriage with the Eucharist is lost, while, since the tenth century, the Church is invested with the responsibility of giving legal status to marriage, a practice that in numerous countries of Orthodox tradition survived secularization and sociocultural changes. Marriage appears to us primarily as a ritual, as a personal or a family affair, and of course as the legalization of sexual intercourse. These gradual displacements associated with the process of legalization and the state institutionalization of ecclesiastical marriage, as it is evident from the above findings and critical remarks, are not unrelated to the overall capitulation on the part of the institutional Church to the Empire and the gradual retreat of the primitive Christian eschatological vision. Since it was believed that the Empire realizes the Kingdom of God on earth, and that the given social order of the Empire comprises an image and reflection of the Kingdom of heaven, it was not difficult to make the next step and to consider that the institutions of the Empire were terrestrial manifestations and expressions of the celestial or eternal life. In this context, the ecclesiological and sacramental understanding of marriage was declined, while, as in other traditional societies, marriage was proclaimed as self-esteemed value and an end, a telos in itself, while the eschatologically originated distance from any kind of physical or natural bond (such as language, customs, culture, marriage, family, homeland, nation, law, etc.) was forgotten. Things were even more complicated when, after the fall of Byzantium in 1453, the Church was forced to undertake, within the framework of its particular political role assigned by the Ottoman millet system (ethnarchy), secular responsibilities and roles strange to its own mission, and indeed largely judicial and statute-like functions. In this regard, the local bishop or the patriarch was the one who was charged with dealing with issues of family law, but also more widely was responsible for the political representation of the enslaved Christians before the Muslim conqueror and ruler. From that period onwards, the Church, at least in the Greek-speaking world, but also more widely in the Balkans and Southeastern Europe (and to some extent also in Russia), has a tremendous difficulty in separating these civil status responsibilities, and in general is unable to discern for itself, in today's pluralistic secularized world, another mission distinct from what it has been inherited from its ethnarchic past. Unfortunately, we have not yet sufficiently studied the addictions and trappings that the ethnarchical period has bequeathed to us, which, apart from a period of glory and heroism for the Church, is also a period of largely forgetting the authentic ecclesiological and theological criteria. With regard to our discussion, the Orthodox Church has inherited from this period a continuous vacillation and ambivalence between the national or popular Church in which we participate as Greeks, Russians, Romanians, and so on, due to our birth and our ancestral heritage (cultural Orthodoxy), and to the Church of the "little leaven," the "little lemma," and "interference" (παρεμβολή) (with the biblical meaning of the terms), in which we participate by personal choice and decision, regardless of national, ethnic, or cultural origin and ancestral heritage. All the theological renewal that Orthodoxy experienced in the twentieth century mostly refers to the latter, while the dominant ecclesiastical discourse in Orthodoxy, except the diaspora, mainly refers to the former!

In the light of the above remarks, and to the degree that in the Christian perspective the aim and primary mission of the Church are not marriage itself and family, but the salvation of the world and of humankind (and the primary purpose of marriage itself is the deep personal communion and union of the spouses, and not the procreation), I believe that the legal regulation on behalf of the state of free partnerships by the establishment of civil unions resolves some serious problems, and may possibly work "in a charitable way" for those whom conservative Christians usually consider as "sinners" or completely lost: i.e., heterosexual couples who freely cohabit, and homosexuals. There are serious legal, social, and human problems arising from these cohabitations, which a responsible state, exercising its rights and prerogatives in the domain of its own jurisdiction, while at the same time respecting religious diversity and freedom as well as the personal choices of its citizens, cannot ignore. With regard to these same problems, a pastorally sensitive Church cannot hypocritically shut the eyes and issue only condemning and absurd statements. In this regard, the thoughtful and timely reflections that Fr. John Jillions offered as an Orthodox response to the recognition of same-sex marriage by the US Supreme Court, could clear the ground, and help mature the theological, and not just the sociological or legal, arguments.[70] As noticed by Fr. Jillions himself, while his article concerns the US context, "Orthodox Christians in other parts of the world will recognize their own analogous situations.... While it is just one court decision in one country, I believe that Obergefell v. Hodges reflects the rapidly changing and widely accepted social conditions [as for example regarding same-sex marriage] in which Orthodox Christians are being called to witness and serve in many parts of the world.

It raises essential questions about how we live in our societies not only as faithful Christians but as citizens, how we contribute to the common good, how we exercise and defend our rights to the free expression of our religious faith, how we defend the rights of others and speak out against abuse, and how we treat members of the LGBT community and their families whose new civil rights conflict with the teachings and discipline of the Orthodox Church."

Moreover, it would be wrong for the Church to deny that even in these supposed "sinful" relationships (such as, for example, the new forms of partnership, either heterosexual or homosexual), there is not a complete lack of love: "For that which totally lacks a share in the Good has neither being nor a place in existence," reminds us Pseudo-Dionysius the Areopagite.[71]

With the law about the civil unions, the State comes to legally regulate a reality that everyone, except the very conservatives, recognizes. It would be necessary, of course, that the State should take steps to strengthen the marriage and family institution and not to promote this form of cohabitation as a model.

The Church for its part should avoid easy assertions and cheap (and hypocritical) moral condemnations. Its task does not consist in interfering continuously on issues that lie within State's jurisdiction or to rush to substitute God's judgment. It is rather called to remind in our "fluid" postmodern era that promotes as its model the "liquid love"—the precariousness and the wider fluidity of human bonds, the "man-tourist," the "pleasure-seeker" and the "pleasure-collector," to recall Zygmunt Bauman,[72] the one that walks in and out of relationships and of life, and who is unable to love truly, and to stand to the value of fidelity, duration, and reciprocity/interconnection—to remind the spiritual dimension of marriage and sexuality (according to the model of the reciprocal interconnected relationship between Christ and the Church in Eph. 5:21); to remind the cross-centered, sacrificial, and ascetic ethos of love and of overcoming the ego as the only true antidote to the relationship breakdown and to uncertainty that threatens to destroy the social fabric and social cohesion. In this perspective, and given that fidelity and loyalty seem to be the most difficult and demanding achievements, I believe that if Christian marriage remains the ideal and perfect model of the androgynous relationship, civil marriage and civil unions, either heterosexual or homosexual, could, in turn, from an ecclesial point of view, be considered as an alternative or maybe an elliptic and incomplete form of cohabitation that should not be discredited or rejected altogether. As maintained by the Greek theologian Athanasios Koliofoutis with regard to the civil union / partnership bill for heterosexual couples voted in 2008,

> Modern pastors are expected to seek out couples who choose the form of the free or legally regulated cohabitation rather than embody pastoral practices that will convey the message of exclusion from the Church to its intended recipients. Instead, modern pastors have to address an invitation of encounter with all these people in order to communicate and to dialogue. . . . By boldly highlighting the dominant pastoral principle that no one is excluded from God's love, such a move will positively contribute to accepting this invitation. Therefore, pastors should not adopt a contemptuous attitude towards these couples; rather it needs to invite them to an encounter, which is the first step towards a comprehensive pastoral intervention.[73]

Civil marriage and civil unions, either heterosexual or homosexual, should not be discredited or rejected altogether as they involve and imply the principle of mutual commitment, fidelity, and loyalty, which is increasingly scarce. This was also, if I am not mistaken, the meaning and the purpose of the tolerant attitude of the ancient Church toward the phenomena of concubinage and civil marriage during the first Christian centuries,[74] and that was one of the core arguments advanced by His Eminence Metropolitan Kallistos Ware in his recent written intervention on the difficult issue of homosexuality. In his own words,

> A second anomaly is to be found in the way homosexuals are commonly treated in the sacrament of confession. All of us recognize that there is an important distinction to be made between those homosexuals who engage in casual encounters, seeking out in some "gay" bar a partner for a single night; and on the other hand, those homosexuals who are committed to a permanent relationship, faithful and monogamous, in which deep love is involved. . . .
>
> There is a third question which we have to ask ourselves. The Orthodox tradition teaches clearly that sexual acts between persons of the same sex are not permitted. Yet at the same time, most of us recognize authentic spiritual value in deep friendships between such persons, even passionate friendships such as that formed by Father

Pavel Florensky (see Giacomo Sanfilippo's contribution to this issue). Why do we put so great an emphasis upon genital sex? Why do we seek to enquire what adult persons of the same sex are doing in the privacy of their bedrooms? Trying to gaze through the keyhole is never a dignified posture. What harm are they doing to others? . . . I am not suggesting here that we should bluntly set aside the traditional Orthodox teaching, but we do need to enquire more rigorously into the reasons that lie behind it.[75]

However, the Church's adoption of a constructive attitude in the issues under discussion cannot occur without the following conditions: (a) The Church should accept that the legal and notarial matters relating to marriage and cohabitation lay in the exclusive competence of the state, holding for itself the mystical, sacramental, and spiritual dimension; it should also overcome the "infant disease," and the naïve, overoptimistic idea that makes it think it may be a "Bride of Christ" and a "mystagogue of salvation," and at the same time a state registrar!; (b) The Church should recover the whole variety of attitudes and views that characterized the ancient Church to similar problems, and on the basis of which we can maintain that Christian morality is neither universal nor diachronic;[76] (c) It should recognize also that the sacrament of marriage begins from the encounter itself of a man and a woman (and not just with the wedding ceremony [ἱερολογία]),[77] and reconsider in a theological perspective the issue of sexuality, by reapproaching in a more positive and constructive way the challenge of a theology of pleasure, tenderness, and affection, away from the unilateralism of viewing marriage solely in the light of procreation;[78] (d) to reconnect the sacrament of marriage with the divine liturgy, and to take all the necessary steps in order to remove the causes that initially led to their separation. As pointed out by Nenad Milošević, "marriage needs to become a state responsibility, meaning that the civil marriage needs to precede the ecclesiastical one. A second key point is the necessary combination of the wedding festivities with the civil marriage rather than with the ecclesial one;"[79] and (e) finally to deal seriously with the catechism and the elementary theological training of its members, while recognizing the reality of open society and overcoming its imperial or ethnocentric chimaeras and its anachronistic and reactionary attachment to the past, leading it to an illusion and a tragic misconception that the boundaries of society continue to be identical to the limits of the Church.

By Way of Conclusion

In the light of the above theological remarks, historical analysis, and examples, especially the ones related to the centuries-old attitude of the Orthodox Church in matters of sexual morality as witnessed by its tolerant and flexible way of handling the cases of civil marriage, and the monogamous concubinage, an attitude that bears the marks of the diachronic application of the canonical principle of *oikonomia*, I would propose, in concluding the present study, to pay attention to a reflection offered by the French Orthodox priest Fr. Michel Evdokimov on the reality of the free partnership that, in my opinion, could apply both to heterosexual and homosexual couples. If the Church, thanks to its strong pastoral sense, was able to give solutions to the challenging situations of couples married outside the Church or living with people of other faiths or in a concubine partnership, why not imagine the Church exercising and contextualizing its pastoral care to the today's needs and expectations?

Especially for the pastoral care of gay couples, it would be increasingly difficult for the Church to maintain its traditional teaching, since according to it, homosexuality is understood in terms of a "passion" or a perversion against nature and natural law, as anomaly and insanity, a passion like avarice, greed, lecherousness, gluttony, anger, blame, and so on. This teaching does not correspond to the new scientific data and findings on the matter or to the awareness acquired by the practice of the physicians, the psychologists, and the psychoanalysts. In most cases, the contemporary Orthodox refuse to accept the reality of a homosexual orientation and think of homosexuality in terms of personal choice initiated by a "passion." As noted by Metropolitan Kallistos Ware, "until recent times, Orthodox thinkers did not make use of the concept of sexual orientation, as this is understood in contemporary psychology. More precisely, they assumed that there is only one orientation, and that is heterosexual. They considered that persons of homosexual inclination were such because of personal choice and were therefore willfully wicked."[80] Therefore, homosexuals are called to fight against their "passion" and to overcome it through repentance and spiritual struggle including fasting, prayer, and genuflections, or to be helped in order to return to a "normal" sexual life by conversion therapies. If conversion therapy fails, then the homosexual is called to follow a life of celibacy and permanent sexual abstinence. In the words of Fr. Vasileios Thermos, "homosexuals are called to lead a celibate life, whether or not they feel a vocation for this."[81]

The quotation below by Fr. Michel Evdokimov, written many years ago, and for a different context, could perhaps provide some criteria for how the Church should face these new challenges in a way faithful to its faith and tradition, and pastorally sensitive and open minded:

> The Church does not exist to judge or condemn, but to help the sinner to do the will of God in his life. Should we offer or deny the grace of the mysteries, this "medicine of immortality" according to the Fathers, to those who live outside the moral rules of the Church? The question is a delicate one and the answer varies according to the degree of spiritual maturity and most notably according to their attachment to the marriage, to the extent that only marriage completes this union. To use the Law as a threat against the young people who are not prepared to follow it, will lead them away from the mystery of marriage, losing thus the opportunity to know and approach the source of pure love. Do those who live in faithfulness and self-sacrifice not participate in the offering of God's love? Has not the God, the only source of love for people, meet them at the very moment of their first rendezvous, where they might have ignored Him? What is worse? Is it better for someone to cohabit out of wedlock and stay loyal to the relationship or be married and commit infidelity? How many spouses have broken their vows and no one has ever bothered them? Certainly, those who cohabit, regardless of their age, remain in a state of sin. But this sinful and weak human nature, which has the tendency to yield to anything that desires, has been assumed by the Son of God to restore it, magnify its presence, strengthen it with His power: "Go and sin no more." God loves our children, even though they are quite different from their parents' generation. However, not all the children are different, because many of them live happily in a state of real engagement. Have the morals changed? So let us be careful not to accept them all, but to discern the positive signs in an emerging and inevitably different world, in order to eliminate the challenge of this widespread alienation by our confidence, hope, and love.[82]

It seems that the Orthodox Churches all around the world are not ignoring the above sociocultural data, and come more and more to face the new challenges. The Orthodox Church of Greece also, at different moments after the end of the dictatorship, had to respond to major changes happening in the country, especially in the domain of family life, and sexual morality, as well as in the understanding of human being, and human sexuality, changes closely associated with the wider phenomena of postmodernity, globalization, multiculturalism, the revolution of biotechnology, and the information technology. Especially regarding issues related to the performance of civil marriage (without any sort of a ritual that would follow) by Orthodox Christians, the Holy Synod issued at different moments circulars in order to face this challenge, and to take accordingly canonical measures against these faithful. As it is recognized even by conservative theologians, it more or less failed![83]

There are, however, signs of hope, pointing to the direction of a more relevant and theologically (and not only canonically) founded answer of the Orthodox Church—even at the official or institutional level—to the challenges of our time, regarding issues of marriage, love, and sexuality, such as the recent Pastoral Letter, issued in December 2017, by the Conference of the Orthodox Bishops in Germany. This letter was addressed to the Orthodox youth of the country and attempted to cope with the sensitive issues of love, sexuality, and marriage. The importance and novelty of this letter, issued in German, English, and different other languages (Greek, Arabic, Russian, Romanian, and Bulgarian) spoken by the Orthodox people living in Germany, resides in the fact that it is the first official Orthodox document that does not condemn homosexuality, approaching it in a mere pastoral way, but rather it seems to be open to responsible premarital sexual relations.[84] Similar concerns can be found in the very recent document "For the Life of the World: Toward a Social Ethos of the Orthodox Church," composed by a special commission of Orthodox scholars appointed by Ecumenical Patriarch Bartholomew and blessed for publication by the Holy and Sacred Synod of the Ecumenical Patriarchate. This highly significant document is not without controversy since "it addresses contemporary social issues in a sustained manner that is unusual for the Orthodox Church, including poverty, racism, human rights, reproductive technology, and the environment." In other words, along with its social sensitivity, and its concern for social justice and inclusion, this document seems to be more open to modern issues like human rights, Western democratic values, or issues like new forms of marital and family life.[85] Even more surprising is the interview given to the Serbian television by the recently elected patriarch of the Serbian Orthodox Church—a Church well known for its social and moral conservatism, as well as for its recent turn to and support of the agenda of the Russian Orthodox Church. In that interview the new elected patriarch expressed the view that he himself is not against the recognition by the civil authorities of the same-sex legal unions, while he goes as far as to express his sympathy regarding the challenges the LGBT community is facing. However, he would not call these unions a "marriage," since this term, evident already in the Old Testament, has been reserved for the union of man and woman.[86]

The Orthodox Church and theology have just started to openly (and institutionally in some cases) discuss the difficult issues related to human sexuality and to different (or new) forms of family and partnership. It is hoped that while it will take into account the experience and the lessons of the past and of history, it would also be open to eschatology, which introduces an element of active expectation accompanied by the dimension of the future and the renewing breeze of the Spirit, dimensions so definitive for the life and theology of the Church and yet so lacking today. For in response to the challenges of globalization, cosmopolitanism, postmodernity, and multiculturalism, today the wind of traditionalism and fundamentalism is once again blowing violently through the life and theology of the Church. Eschatology is an active and demanding expectation of the coming Kingdom of God, the new world that we await; as such, it feeds into a dynamic commitment to the present, an affirmation and opening to the future of the Kingdom in which the fullness and identity of the Church is to be found.

Notes

This paper was first presented in Greek, at a Conference titled "Holy Canons of the Church and State Laws," jointly organized in Volos, Greece, February 13–15, 2015, by the Volos Academy for Theological Studies, the Ecclesiastical and Canon Law Association, and the Volos Bar Association. The English version was initially prepared for the International Symposium on "Orthodox Pastoral Care and Sexuality," held in Amsterdam, on June 7–9, 2017, and organized by the Center of Orthodox Theology at the Free University Amsterdam. It was since then enriched and further elaborated thanks to the series of workshops on "Gender and Sexuality in Orthodox Christianity: Same-sex Relations and Orientation"; "Gender in Orthodox Christianity"; and "New Directions in Orthodox Ministry," which took place in the framework of the three-year seminar (Lysebu, Oslo, December 2016 to 2018) titled "New Directions in

Orthodox Thought and Practice," initiated by the Oslo Coalition on Freedom of Religion or Belief, and the Norwegian Center for Human Rights of the University of Oslo, to which I have the privilege to serve as member of the International Planning Group. I am grateful to the Norwegian institutions and colleagues for generously hosting in Lysebu this seminar, and for the opportunity for encounter and exchange. I would also like to extend warm thanks to my colleague and friend Dr. Nikolaos Asproulis, deputy director of the Volos Academy for Theological Studies, for his gracious help in translating quotations from Greek into English, and in editing the English of the present paper.

1. See the articles by the late Archbishop of Athens Chrysosotomos Papadopoulos (1923–38), former professor at the Faculty of Theology of Athens University; the Archimandrite Christodoulos Paraskevaïdis, secretary of the Holy Synod of the Church of Greece, and later (after 1974) Metropolitan of Demetrias, and Archbishop of Athens (1998–2008); and Christos I. Kathareios, at that time Honorary Member of Areopagus, one of the two highest juridic instances in Greece, all three published in Ἐκκλησία [Ecclesia] (the official monthly bulletin of the Holy Synod of the Church of Greece)13/14 (July 1–15, 1979): 291–303; and 15/16 (August 1–15, 1979): 328–42.

2. The Greek theologian Athanasios N. Papathanasiou, editor-in-chief of the Greek theological journal *Synaxi*, maintains that the Orthodox Church in Greece had never, by its own initiative, given up its "privileges" (such as the religious ceremony of wedding as the only state-sanctioned type of marriage until 1982) in order not to lose its social hegemony. See Athanasios N. Papathanasiou, Ἡ ρήξη μὲ τὸ μηδέν: Σφηνάκια πολιτικῆς θεολογίας [The Clash with the Null: Some Shots of Political Theology] (Athens: Armos, 2015), 52–53.

3. See Ἐκκλησιαστικὴ Ἀλήθεια [Ecclesiastical Truth], 16–10–1998, quoted in Panayiotis Boumis, Ὁ Κανονικὸς γάμος. Ἀντιθέσεις καὶ συνθέσεις [Canonical Marriage: Oppositions and Syntheses] (Athens: Symmetria Publications, 1998), 61.

4. Grigorios Papathomas, "An Open Ecclesial Communitarism: Dispar-Mixed Marriages and Adult Conversions," *Folia canonica*, 8 (2005): 157. In the same paper, its author, an Orthodox priest and distinguished scholar of Canon Law, professor at the Faculty of Theology of Athens University, and at St. Sergius Institute of Orthodox Theology in Paris, explains how the Orthodox Church came to the point of not celebrating mixed religious marriages, and criticizes its persistent refusal on this decision, while the initial socio-cultural context (after the fall of Byzantium in 1453), which decisively influenced this decision, has completely changed in Europe and the Americas.

5. See the press release of March 17, 2008 (in the original Greek) of the Standing Holy Synod of the Church of Greece in its official website: http://

www.ecclesia.gr/greek/holysynod/holysynod.asp?id=996&what_sub=d_typou/ (last accessed September 21, 2019). A critical note from a Christian perspective on this statement of the Standing Holy Synod of the Church of Greece was published by Dr. Panos Nikolopoulos, a research and teaching associate (and now an assistant professor) at the School of Law of Athens University in the weekly newspaper Ἡ Χριστιανική [I Christianiki], 7/24/2008. See also my newspaper articles: "Τὸ Σύμφωνο γιὰ τὴν ἐλεύθερη συμβίωση καὶ ἡ Ἐκκλησία" [Civil Unions and the Church], Ἡ Θεσσαλία [Thessalia], 3/23/2008, and "Συμβίωση καὶ Ἐκκλησία" [Free Partnership and the Church], Ἡ Καθημερινὴ [Kathimerini], 3/25/2008.

6. See http://www.dogma.gr/default.php?pname=Article&art_id=4770&catid=3/.

7. See the press release of December 9, 2015 (in the original Greek) of the Standing Holy Synod of the Church of Greece in its official website: http://www.ecclesia.gr/greek/holysynod/holysynod.asp?id=2067&what_sub=d_typou/ (last accessed September 21, 2019).

8. See https://www.tideon.org/oikogeneia/2012-05-07-21-01-51/2012-02-16-20-47-49/6389-2015-06-16-18-10-50/; and https://www.tideon.org/oikogeneia/2012-05-07-21-01-51/2012-02-16-20-47-49/6359-2015-06-12-18-05-26/.

9. See https://www.iefimerida.gr/news/239971/apisteyto-paralirima-amvrosioy-kata-ton-omofylofilon-opoy-toys-synantate-ftyste-toys/.

10. See https://www.efsyn.gr/ellada/dikaiosyni/181073_enohos-gia-ftyste-toys-o-ambrosios/.

11. See his own and his diocese communiqués, statements, official letters, and interviews at https://www.tideon.org/oikogeneia/2012-05-07-21-01-51/2012-02-16-20-47-49/7166-2015-12-21-22-06-00/; https://www.tideon.org/oikogeneia/2012-05-07-21-01-51/2012-02-16-20-47-49/7177-mega/; https://www.tideon.org/oikogeneia/2012-05-07-21-01-51/2012-02-16-20-47-49/7140-2015-12-16-21-59-15; https://www.tideon.org/oikogeneia/2012-05-07-21-01-51/2012-02-16-20-47-49/6938-2015-11-11-13-55-25/; https://www.tideon.org/oikogeneia/2012-05-07-21-01-51/2012-02-16-20-47-49/6360-2015-06-12-18-17-05/; https://www.tideon.org/oikogeneia/2012-02-11-19-15-55/4537-2013-11-27-22-25-52/.

12. See http://ikivotos.gr/post/6013/treis-ierarxes-sto-ste-gia-to-symfwno-symbiwshs/.

13. See https://www.tideon.org/oikogeneia/2012-05-07-21-01-51/2012-02-16-20-47-49/7168-2015-12-21-23-10-03/. See also the statement of Metropolitan Kosmas and of the Assembly of the priests of his diocese: https://www.tideon.org/oikogeneia/2012-05-07-21-01-51/2012-02-16-20-47-49/6426-2015-06-25-18-04-02/.

14. See https://www.tideon.org/oikogeneia/2012-05-07-21-01-51/2012-02-16-20-47-49/7148-2015-12-18-22-51-44/.

15. See https://www.tideon.org/oikogeneia/2012-05-07-21-01-51/2012-02-16-20-47-49/6523-2015-07-24-18-59-35/.
16. https://www.tideon.org/oikogeneia/2012-05-07-21-01-51/2012-02-16-20-47-49/7045-2015-12-04-21-04-07/.
17. See https://www.tovima.gr/2015/12/22/politics/trixotomimeni-i-nd-dixotomimenoi-oi-anel-sto-nomosxedio-gia-to-symfwno-symbiwsis-poioi-psifisan-yper-kai-poioi-kata/; https://www.tideon.org/oikogeneia/2012-05-07-21-01-51/2012-02-16-20-47-49/7171-2015-12-22-15-19-18/.
18. See https://tvxs.gr/news/ellada/o-mitropolitis-mesogaias-yper-toy-stigmatismoy-ton-omofylofilon&dr=tvxsmrstvxs/.
19. See https://www.tideon.org/oikogeneia/2012-05-07-21-01-51/2012-02-16-20-47-49/6969-2015-11-17-21-36-21/.
20. See https://www.tideon.org/oikogeneia/2012-05-07-21-01-51/2012-02-16-20-47-49/7208-2015-12-26-11-40-05/.
21. See https://www.tideon.org/oikogeneia/2012-05-07-21-01-51/2012-02-16-20-47-49/6957-2015-11-15-19-05-39/.
22. See https://www.tideon.org/oikogeneia/2012-05-07-21-01-51/2012-02-16-20-47-49/4788-2014-03-21-22-05-51/. For more statements and communiqués on the same issue, see https://www.tideon.org/oikogeneia/2012-05-07-21-01-51/2012-02-16-20-47-49/6935-2015-11-09-22-33-14/.
23. Dom Bernard Botte, *La Tradition apostolique de Saint Hippolyte. Essai de reconstitution* (Münster: Aschendorffsche Verlagsbuchhandlung, 1989), 5.
24. Georgios St. Vagianos, "Ἀνδροκρατικὴ μονογαμία καὶ πολυγαμία στὸν Ἀρχαῖο Ἰσραήλ" [Androcratic Monogamy and Polygamy in Ancient Israel], in *Ἀγάπη καὶ Μαρτυρία: Ἀναζητήσεις λόγου καὶ ἤθους στὸ ἔργο τοῦ Ἠλία Βουλγαράκη. Ἀφιέρωμα ἀπὸ τοὺς μαθητές του* [Love and Witness: In Search of *Logos* and *Ethos* in the Work of Elias Voulgarakis: A Tribute from his Disciples], ed. Evi Voulgaraki-Pissinas (Athens: Akritas Publications, 2001), 95–98. See Vagianos, "Ποιὰ στάση τήρησε ἡ Ἐκκλησία ἀπέναντι στὶς ἐλεύθερες συμβιώσεις *(Ρώμη-Βυζάντιο)*" [The Church's Attitude Facing Free Unions (Rome-Byzantium)] (Athens, 1991). Fr. Michel Evdokimov attempts from his side to theologically reflect and to pastorally deal with the challenge of free unions, significantly increased after the May '68 politico-cultural upheaval, in a paper entitled "Νόημα καὶ πραγματικότητα τοῦ ἀνθρώπινου ἔρωτα στὸ σημερινὸ κόσμο" [Meaning and Reality of Human Love in Today's World], and published in Greek translation by Giorgos Filias in the journal *Synaxi*, issue 32 (1989): 65–72. For a more systematic approach to the phenomenon of concubinage in the late antiquity and Byzantium, see the study by Vaggelis Karabelias, *Γάμος καὶ Παλλακεία στὴν Ὕστερη Ἀρχαιότητα: Ρωμαϊκὲς Καταβολὲς καὶ Βυζαντινὲς Θεσμικὲς Προεκτάσεις* [Marriage and Concubinage in Late Antiquity: Roman Origins and Byzantine Institutional Extensions] (Athens: Ant. N. Sakkoulas

Publications, 1988). See also Jos. Zhishman, *Τὸ δίκαιον τοῦ γάμου τῆς Ἀνατολικῆς Ὀρθοδόξου Ἐκκλησίας* [The Law on Marriage of the Eastern Orthodox Church], transl. from German into Greek with additions and corrections by Meletios Apostolopoulos, vol. 1 (Athens, 1912), 316–23. For the post-Byzantine / Ottoman period, rich information is provided by Nikolaos Pantazopoulos, "Κεπήνιον. Συμβολὴ εἰς τὴν ἔρευναν τοῦ πολιτικοῦ γάμου ἐπὶ Τουρκοκρατίας" [Contribution to the Research of Civil Marriage during the Turkish Occupation], *Ἐπιστημονικὴ Ἐπετηρὶς Σχολῆς Νομικῶν καὶ Οἰκονομικῶν Ἐπιστημῶν ΑΠΘ* [Scientific Yearbook of the Faculty of Law and Economics of the Aristotle University of Thessaloniki], *Τιμητικὸς Τόμος Νικολάου Πανταζοπούλου* [Festschrift to Nikolaos Pantazopoulos], vol. 19, no. 3 (1986): 489–520.

25. See Bernard Botte, *La Tradition apostolique de Saint Hippolyte*, SC 11b (Paris: Cerf, 1968), 74; Botte, "Refutatio Omnium Haeresium," 9, 12, ed. P. Wendland (Leipzig, 1916), reproduced in the ΒΕΠΕΣ edition, vol. 5 (Athens, 1955), 352, 36 ff.; see Konstantinos Papadopoulos, "Γύρω ἀπὸ τὴν ἱστορία τῆς ἱερολογίας τοῦ γάμου" [On the History of the Rite of Marriage], *Synaxi* 32 (1989): 58; Panos Nikolopoulos, "Κανονικὴ παράδοση περὶ γάμου καὶ σύγχρονες μορφὲς συμβίωσης" [Canonical Tradition on Marriage and Contemporary Forms of Cohabitation], in *Κανόνες τῆς Ἐκκλησίας καὶ σύγχρονες προκλήσεις* [Canons of the Church and Contemporary Challenges], ed. Grigorios Papathomas, Nikolaos Asproulis, and Pantelis Kalaitzidis, Papers of the 2014 Volos International Conference (Volos, Greece: Acadimia Demetriados Publications [under publication]).

26. Papadopoulos, "Γύρω ἀπὸ τὴν ἱστορία τῆς ἱερολογίας τοῦ γάμου," 58.

27. Angeliki E. Laiou, "Contribution à l'étude de l'institution familiale en Epire au XIIIème siècle," *Fontes Minores* 6 (1984), 284.

28. G. A. Rallis and M. Potlis, eds., *Σύνταγμα των θείων καὶ ἱερῶν κανόνων* [Syntagma of Holy and Sacred Canons], vol. 4 (Athens, 1854), 160; Νικόλαος Πανταζόπουλος, "'Άγραφος γάμος-παλλακεία" [Customary Marriage-Concubinage], *Ἐπιστημονικὴ Ἐπετηρὶς Σχολῆς Νομικῶν καὶ Οἰκονομικῶν Ἐπιστημῶν ΑΠΘ* [Scientific Yearbook of the Faculty of Law and Economics of the Aristotle University of Thessaloniki], *Τιμητικὸς Τόμος Νικολάου Πανταζοπούλου* [Festschrift of Nikolaos Pantazopoulos], vol. 19, no. 2 (1983), 45. Nikolopoulos, "Κανονικὴ παράδοση"; Panayiotis I. Skaltsis, *Γάμος καὶ θεία Λειτουργία. Συμβολὴ στὴν ἱστορία καὶ τὴ θεολογία τῆς λατρείας* [Marriage and Divine Liturgy: Contributing to the History and Theology of Worship] (Thessaloniki: Pournaras, 1998), 159–60.

29. Laiou, "Contribution à l'étude de l'institution familiale," 285–90, where a classification of the cases of concubinage is also provided. Moreover, Laiou in her paper (290–96) proceeds further to a detailed study of some cases and of the popular perception of this institution.

30. Antonios Kalligeris, *Γάμος: Ἀπὸ τὸ μυστήριο στὸν θεσμό* [Marriage: From Sacrament to the Institution] (Athens: Maïstros, 2008), 106. See Nikolopoulos, "Κανονικὴ παράδοση."

31. *Πηδάλιον* [Rudder], canons 17 and 18, fifth edition (Athens: Astir Publications, 1990), 18–20.

32. Nikolopoulos, "Κανονικὴ παράδοση."

33. Karabelias, *Γάμος καὶ Παλλακεία στὴν Ὕστερη Ἀρχαιότητα*, 46–47, quoted in Nikolopoulos, "Κανονικὴ παράδοση"; See Skaltsis, *Γάμος καὶ θεία Λειτουργία*, 160.

34. Laiou, "Contribution à l'étude de l'institution familiale," 298.

35. Nikolaos Pantazopoulos, "Ὁ ἐσωτερικὸς ἀνταγωνισμὸς τοῦ ἑλληνικοῦ δικαίου ὡς ἐπίπτωσις τῆς Λατινοκρατίας" [The Internal Tension of the Greek Law as a Result of the Latin Occupation Period], *Ἐπιστημονικὴ Ἐπετηρὶς Σχολῆς Νομικῶν καὶ Οἰκονομικῶν Ἐπιστημῶν ΑΠΘ* [Scientific Yearbook of the Faculty of Law and Economics of the Aristotle University of Thessaloniki], *Τιμητικὸς Τόμος Νικολάου Πανταζοπούλου* [Festschrift of Nikolaos Pantazopoulos], vol. 19, no. 2 (1983): 153–54.

36. *Oikonomia* is a concept, and practice, in Eastern Orthodox Canon Law, often presented together with *akribeia* (precision, strictness). It is used to denote an exception (mainly for pastoral reasons) from the strict rule of the canons that is usually called *akribeia*.

37. Athanasios Koliofoutis, "Ἡ πατερικὴ στάση ἀπέναντι στὸ θεσμὸ τῆς παλλακείας" [The Patristic Attitude towards the Institution of Concubinage (Παλλακεί)], published in the electronic magazine *Πεμπτουσία* [Pemptousia], and accessible via https://www.pemptousia.gr/2015/08/i-pateriki-stasi-apenanti-sto-thesmo-tis-pallakias/.

38. Panayiotis I. Boumis, "Θεώρηση του Συμφώνου Ελεύθερης Συμβίωσης" [On the Civil Union], *Ἐκκλησία* [Ecclesia] 6 (2008): 440.

39. Athanasios Koliofoutis, "Σύγκριση τοῦ Συμφώνου Συμβίωσης μὲ τὴ βυζαντινὴ παλλακεία" [A Comparison of the Civil Union with Byzantine Concubinage], published in the electronic magazine *Πεμπτουσία* [Pemptousia], and accessible via https://www.pemptousia.gr/2015/07/102540/.

40. Panayiots I. Boumis, *Θεώρηση καὶ προβλήματα τοῦ πολιτικοῦ γάμου* [On the Concept and the Problems of Civil Marriage] (Athens, 1985), 14.

41. Boumis, *Θεώρηση καὶ προβλήματα τοῦ πολιτικοῦ γάμου*, 19. See Boumis, *Ὁ Κανονικὸς γάμος*, 24–25.

42. From a very rich bibliography on this specific topic we refer to the following works: Zhishman, *Τὸ δίκαιον τοῦ γάμου τῆς Ἀνατολικῆς Ὀρθοδόξου Ἐκκλησίας* vol. I, 178–81, 229–31, 294; 298 ff.; Phédon Koukoulès, *Vie et civilization byzantines*, t. IV, Collection de l'Institut français d'Athènes no 73 (Athens 1951), 93; Vasileios Stephanidis, *Ἐκκλησιαστικὴ Ἱστορία* [Ecclesiastical History],

third edition (Athens: Astir, 1970), 454; Demetrios J. Constantelos, *Marriage, Sexuality & Celibacy: A Greek Orthodox Perspective* (Minneapolis, Minn.: Light and Life Publishing Co, 1975), 44–53; John Meyendorff, *Marriage: An Orthodox Perspective*, 3rd rev. ed. (New York: St. Vladimir's Seminary Press, 1984), 24–29; Meyendorff, "Christian Marriage in Byzantium: The Canonical and Liturgical Tradition," *Dumbarton Oaks Papers*, 44 (1990), 99–107; Pantazopoulos, "Κεπήνιον," 489–520; Papadopoulos, "Γύρω ἀπὸ τὴν ἱστορία τῆς ἱερολογίας τοῦ γάμου," 57–62; Skaltsis, *Γάμος καὶ θεία Λειτουργία*, 132–61; Nenad S. Milošević, *Ἡ θεία Εὐχαριστία ὡς κέντρον τῆς θείας Λατρείας. Ἡ σύνδεσις τῶν μυστηρίων μετὰ τῆς θείας Εὐχαριστίας* [The Divine Eucharist as the Center of Divine Worship: The Connection of the Sacraments to the Holy Eucharist] (Thessaloniki: Pournaras, 2001), 188–217; Milošević, "Ἡ εὐχαριστιακὴ συγκρότηση τῶν μυστηρίων" [The Eucharistic Constitution of the Sacraments], *Theologia* 80, no. 4 (2009): 123–36, particularly 131–35; Antonios Kalligeris, *Γάμος: Ἀπὸ τὸ μυστήριο στὸν θεσμό*, 101–33.

43. Constantelos, *Marriage, Sexuality & Celibacy*, 44.

44. For example, *Epistle to Diognetus*, V, 6; Athenagoras, Πρεσβεία περὶ χριστιανῶν, 33, ed. Edgar Goodspeed, *Die ältesten Apologeten* (Göttigen, 1914), reproduced in the ΒΕΠΕΣ edition, v. 4 (Athens, 1955), 308, 10–12. See Papadopoulos, "Γύρω ἀπό την ιστορία της ιερολογίας τοῦ γάμου," 61n19.

45. Panayiotis I. Boumis, Θεώρηση καὶ προβλήματα τοῦ πολιτικοῦ γάμου, 37.

46. Ignatius, *Lettre à Polycarpe*, 5:2, SC 10, 150. See John Meyendorff, *Marriage: An Orthodox Perspective*, 22; Constantellos, *Marriage, Sexuality & Celibacy*, 44–45; Skaltsis, *Γάμος καὶ θεία Λειτουργία*, 132–34; Milošević, *Ἡ θεία Εὐχαριστία ὡς κέντρον τῆς θείας Λατρείας*, 142 ff.; Milošević, "Ἡ εὐχαριστιακὴ συγκρότηση τῶν μυστηρίων," 133–34; Papadopoulos, "Γύρω ἀπό την ιστορία της ιερολογίας του γάμου," 58; Kalligeris, *Γάμος: Ἀπὸ τὸ μυστήριο στὸν θεσμό*, 125.

47. Milošević, *Ἡ θεία Εὐχαριστία ὡς κέντρον τῆς θείας Λατρείας*, 142–46; Milošević, "Ἡ εὐχαριστιακὴ συγκρότηση τῶν μυστηρίων," 133–34.

48. Meyendorff, *Marriage: An Orthodox Perspective*, 21–22.

49. Meyendorff, *Marriage: An Orthodox Perspective*, 29. Grigorios Papathomas ("An Open Ecclesial Communitarism," 239) also highlights from his side the fact that the ancient Church did not remarry the non-Christian couples received in the Christian community, meaning that it implicitly recognized as "marriage-sacrament of love" the one preformed even in the pagan religious community!

50. For what follows, see Meyendorff, *Marriage: An Orthodox Perspective*, 24–29. See Constantelos, *Marriage, Sexuality & Celibacy*, 44–53; Papadopoulos, "Γύρω ἀπὸ τὴν ἱστορία τῆς ἱερολογίας τοῦ γάμου," 57–62; Skaltsis, *Γάμος καὶ θεία Λειτουργία*, 132–61; Milošević, *Ἡ θεία Εὐχαριστία ὡς κέντρον τῆς θείας Λατρείας*, 188–217; idem, "Ἡ εὐχαριστιακὴ συγκρότηση τῶν μυστηρίων,"

123–36, particularly 131–35; Kalligeris, Γάμος: Ἀπὸ τὸ μυστήριο στὸν θεσμό, 101–33.

51. From another source (the *Ekloge* II, 8, of the Emperors Leo and Constantine the Isavroi, ed. Zeppos, *Jus GraecoRomanum-JGR*, v. 2, 23), we learn that still during the centuries following Justinian, marriage was contracted either by written agreement or by oral common consent by the wedding ceremony (ἱερολογία). See Skaltis, Γάμος καὶ θεία Λειτουργία, 157n671.

52. Zhishman, Τὸ δίκαιον τοῦ γάμου τῆς Ἀνατολικῆς Ὀρθοδόξου Ἐκκλησίας, vol. I, 254–56; Skaltsis, Γάμος καὶ θεία Λειτουργία, 156–57.

53. For what follows see Meyendorff, *Marriage: An Orthodox Perspective*, 25 ff.

54. Zhishman, Τὸ δίκαιον τοῦ γάμου τῆς Ἀνατολικῆς Ὀρθοδόξου Ἐκκλησίας, vol. I, 298 ff.; Skaltsis, Γάμος καὶ θεία Λειτουργία, 158.

55. Meyendorff, *Marriage: An Orthodox Perspective*, 27.

56. Meyendorff, *Marriage: An Orthodox Perspective*, 27–28.

57. G. A. Rallis and M. Potlis, eds., Σύνταγμα των θείων καὶ ἱερῶν κανόνων [Syntagma of Holy and Sacred Canons], vol. 6 (Athens, 1859), 153–54. See Boumis, Θεώρηση καὶ προβλήματα τοῦ πολιτικοῦ γάμου, 22.

58. Nikolopoulos, "Κανονικὴ παράδοση." See Kyrillos Katérelos, *La dissociation des esprits comme motif de divorce en Grèce pendant la période ottomane. La contribution des facteurs sociologiques à l'évolution du droit canonique et à la pratique de l'Église* (Thessaloniki: Publications "The Palimpsest," n.d.), 27; G. Arabatzoglou, "Ὁ διὰ καπηνίου ἢ κεπηνίου γάμος," Ὀρθοδοξία (1929), 162–64; 24 (1949), 310–11, quoted in Katérelos, *La dissociation des esprits*, 27n38.

59. Pantazopoulos, "Κεπήνιον"; Pantazopoulos, "Ἐκκλησία καὶ Δίκαιον εἰς τὴν χερσόνησον τοῦ Αἴμου ἐπὶ Τουρκοκρατίας" [Church and Law in the Peninsula of Aimos during the Turkish Occupation], Ἐπιστημονικὴ Ἐπετηρὶς Σχολῆς Νομικῶν καὶ Οἰκονομικῶν Ἐπιστημῶν ΑΠΘ [Scientific Yearbook of the Faculty of Law and Economics of the Aristotle University of Thessaloniki], Τιμητικὸς Τόμος Νικολάου Πανταζοπούλου [Festschrift of Nikolaos Pantazopoulos], vol. 19, no. 3 (1986), 218–24; Pantazopoulos, "Ἄγραφος γάμος-παλλακεία," 4.

60. See for example Pantazopoulos, "Κεπήνιο," 497–99, 506–58.

61. Zhishman, Τὸ δίκαιον τοῦ γάμου τῆς Ἀνατολικῆς Ὀρθοδόξου Ἐκκλησίας, vol. I, 290–91. See Boumis, Θεώρηση καὶ προβλήματα τοῦ πολιτικοῦ γάμου, 19–21.

62. Papadopoulos, "Γύρω ἀπὸ τὴν ἱστορία τῆς ἱερολογίας τοῦ γάμου," 59.

63. Constantelos, *Marriage, Sexuality & Celibacy*, 49–50. See Zhishman, Τὸ δίκαιον τοῦ γάμου τῆς Ἀνατολικῆς Ὀρθοδόξου Ἐκκλησίας, vol. I, 229–31.

64. Panayiotis N. Trembelas, Μικρὸν Εὐχολόγιον [Minor Eychologion], v. I, Athens, 1950, 9–11.

65. Constantelos, *Marriage, Sexuality & Celibacy*, 49.

66. Boumis, *Θεώρηση καὶ προβλήματα τοῦ πολιτικοῦ γάμου*, 19–21.

67. St. Nikodemos of Mount Athos, *Τὸ Πηδάλιον*, 18n1 (Apostolic canon 17) and 308–9 (canon 98 of Quinixt Ecumenical Council in Trullo, 691 AD) respectively; see Boumis, *Θεώρηση καὶ προβλήματα τοῦ πολιτικοῦ γάμου*, 23–27.

68. Christos Yannaras, *Ἡ ἐλευθερία τοῦ ἤθους. Δοκιμὲς γιὰ μιὰ ὀρθόδοξη θεώρηση τῆς Ἠθικῆς* [The Freedom of Morality: Essays for an Orthodox Understanding of Ethics], Series "Synoro" #2 (Athens: Athena Publications, 1970), 118–19. This book was supposed to be first published in a shorter version into French, as an Orthodox contribution to the ecumenical collective volume *La loi de la liberté: Évangile et morale*, which finally appeared in Paris, by Mame Publishing House, in 1972.

69. Meyendorff, *Marriage: An Orthodox Perspective*, 10.

70. John Jillions, "Obergefell v. Hodges: Questions for Orthodox Christians," *The Wheel* 13/14 (Spring-Summer 2018): 117–28, mainly 117, 128.

71. "Τὸ γὰρ πάντη ἄμοιρον τοῦ ἀγαθοῦ οὔτε ὂν οὔτε ἐν τοῖς οὖσι," Dionysius the Pseudo-Areopagite, DN, IV, 20, PG 3, 720D, ed. Beate Regina Suchla, 167, English text from the volume *Pseudo-Dionysius: The Complete Works*, trans. by Colm Luibheid, foreword, notes, and translation collaboration by Paul Rorem, preface by René Roques, introduction by Jaroslav Pelican, Jean Leclercq, and Karlfried Froehlich, The Classics of Western Spirituality (New York: Paulist Press, 1987), 87.

72. See for example Zygmunt Bauman, *Liquid Love: On the Frailty of Human Bonds* (Cambridge: Polity Press, 2003). For the wider liquid condition of postmodern humans, see also Bauman, *Postmodernity and Its Discontents* (Cambridge: Polity Press, 1997); Bauman, *Globalization: The Human Consequences* (New York: Columbia University Press, 1998); Bauman, *Liquid Life* (Cambridge: Polity Press, 2005); Bauman, *Liquid Times: Living in an Age of Uncertainty* (Cambridge: Polity Press, 2007); Bauman, *Liquid Modernity* (Cambridge: Polity Press, 2012); Zygmunt Bauman and Thomas Leoncini, *Born Liquid: Transformations in the Third Millennium* (Cambridge: Polity Press, 2019).

73. Athanasios Koliofoutis, "Ἡ πατερικὴ στάση ἀπέναντι στὸ θεσμὸ τῆς παλλακείας," published in the electronic magazine *Πεμπτουσία* [Pemptousia], accessible via https://www.pemptousia.gr/2015/08/i-pateriki-stasi-apenanti-sto-thesmo-tis-pallakias/.

74. See analogous arguments and analyses based on the permanent, lasting and stable character of a relationship provided by the Greek canonist Panayiotis I. Boumis in previous sections of the present study.

75. Kallistos Ware, Metropolitan of Diokleia, foreword to *The Wheel* 13/14 (Spring-Summer 2018): 9–10. See Aristotle Papanikolaou, "Sex, Marriage, and

Theosis," *The Wheel* 13/14 (Spring-Summer 2018): 91–97; Marjorie Corbman, Steven Payne, and Gregory Tucker, "Jesus Christ and Same-Sex Marriage," *The Wheel* 13/14 (Spring-Summer 2018): mainly 115–16; Anastasios Kallis, "I Wish I Knew That," in *"For I Am Wonderfully Made": Texts on Eastern Orthodoxy and LGBT Inclusion*, ed. Misha Cherniak, Olga Gerassimenko, and Michael Brinkschröder (Amsterdam: The European Forum of Lesbian, Gay, Bisexual and Transgender Christian Groups, 2016), 110–18, mainly 118. See also Eugene F. Rogers Jr., *Sexuality and the Christian Body: Their Way into the Triune God* (Oxford: Blackwell, 1999), 67–86; Rogers, "Marriage as an Ascetic Practice," *Intams Review* 11 (2005): 28–36. Rogers, among others, claims to find in Zizioulas significant elements in favor of a positive theological assessment of homosexuality (personal conversation with Rogers at Princeton, fall semester of 2012–13). See, for example, Rogers, *Sexuality and the Christian Body*, 73n11, 211n74, 256n21; and Rogers, "Sanctification, Homosexuality, and God's Triune Life," in *Theology and Sexuality: Classic and Contemporary Readings*, ed. Eugene F. Rogers Jr. (Oxford: Blackwell, 2002), 217–46 and 243n17; and in other works of Eastern Orthodox theologians (especially in Evdokimov's *The Sacrament of Love: The Nuptial Mystery in the Light of the Orthodox Tradition* [Crestwood, N.Y.: St. Vladimir's Seminary Press, 1985], which is probably the most cited theological work in support of Rogers's argument).

76. See the profound and well-documented analysis provided by Georgios Skaltsis in his study, "Τὸ ἄφυλο τοῦ θεοῦ καὶ ἡ ἀνθρώπινη σεξουαλικότητα. Ἱστορικὴ μελέτη στὴ θεολογικὴ σκέψη τῶν πρώτων χριστιανικῶν αἰώνων" [The Genderless of God and Human Sexuality: Historical Study on the Theological Thought of the First Christian Centuries], in Pantelis Kalaitzidis and Nikos Ntontos (ed.), *Φύλο καὶ Θρησκεία—Ἡ θέση τῆς γυναίκας στὴν Ἐκκλησία* [Gender and Religion—The Place of Woman in the Church] (Athens: Indiktos Publications, 2004), 87–141.

77. As the Serbian liturgical scholar Nenad S. Milošević (*Ἡ θεία Εὐχαριστία ὡς κέντρον τῆς θείας Λατρείας*, 133), puts it: "Formal ecclesiastical marriage or civil marriage are solely intended to legalize either before God or the society an already accomplished (τετελειωμένης) relationship in love." In this perspective, the famous quotation by St. Paul in Ephes. 5:32: "τὸ μυστήριον τοῦτο μέγα ἐστίν· ἐγὼ δὲ λέγω εἰς Χριστὸν καὶ εἰς τὴν ἐκκλησίαν" (This is a great mystery, and I am applying it to Christ and the church, NRSV) should or could be read in ecclesiological and not in moral perspective, meaning that the accomplished sexual relationship is presented to the Church for sanctification and transformation. In the same way, avoiding prostitution in Pauline letters is merely ecclesiological and less moral imperative: "Do you not know that your bodies are members of Christ?" says the sixth chapter of 1 Corinthians, to continue below: "Should I

therefore take the members of Christ and make them members of a prostitute? Never! Do you not know that whoever is united to a prostitute becomes one body with her? For it is said, 'The two shall be one flesh.'" (1 Cor. 15–16).

78. See, for example, Evdokimov, *The Sacrament of Love*; Philip Sherrard, *Christianity and Eros: Essays on the Theme of Sexual Love* (Limni, Evia, Greece: Denise Harvey Publisher, 1995); Olivier Clément, en collaboration avec Stanislas Rougier, *La révolte de l'Esprit: Repères pour la situation spirituelle d'aujourd'hui* (Paris: Stock, 1979): 367–406; Clément, *On Human Being: A Spiritual Anthropology*, trans. from French by Jeremy Hummerstone (London: New City Press, 2000), 69–90; Anastasios Kallis, "I Wish I Knew That."

79. Milošević, *Ἡ θεία Εὐχαριστία ὡς κέντρον τῆς θείας Λατρείας*, 134.

80. Kallistos Ware, Metropolitan of Diokleia, foreword to *The Wheel* 13/14 (Spring-Summer 2018): 8.

81. Vasileios Thermos, "The Orthodox Church, Sexual Orientation, and Gender Identity: From Embarrassment to Calling," *The Wheel* 13–14 (Spring-Summer 2018): 86. See in the same issue, Kallistos Ware, foreword, 9. See also Vasileios Thermos, *Ἕλξη καὶ Πάθος: Μιὰ διεπιστημονικὴ προσέγγιση τῆς ὁμοφυλοφιλίας* [*Attraction and Passion: An Interdisciplinary Approach of Homosexuality*] (Athens: En plo, 2016). For the discussion on the new scientific data and the traditional Orthodox teaching on homosexuality, see Pantelis Kalaitzidis, "The Ambiguous Relationship between Orthodoxy and Science as Part of the Pending Discussion between Orthodoxy and Modernity: From the Polemic against the Enlightenment to the Debate over Homosexuality," in *Orthodox Christianity and Modern Science: Tensions, Ambiguities, Potential*, ed. Vasilios N. Makrides and Gayle E. Woloschak (Tournhout, Belgium: Brepols, 2019), 46–66, mainly 57–66.

82. Michel Evdokimov, "Νόημα καὶ πραγματικότητα τοῦ ἀνθρώπινου ἔρωτα στὸ σημερινὸ κόσμο" [Meaning and Reality of Human Love in Today's World], and published in Greek translation by Giorgos Filias in the journal *Synaxi* 32 (1989): 71–72.

83. Athanasios Koliofoutis, "Κανονικὸ Δίκαιο καὶ οἰκογενειακοὶ θεσμοί: Εἰσαγωγικά" [Canon Law and Family Institutions: Introductory Notes], published in the electronic magazine *Πεμπτουσία* [Pemptousia], and accessible via https://www.pemptousia.gr/2015/02/89927/.

84. See the English version of the text: "A Letter from the Bishops of the Orthodox Church in Germany to Young People concerning Love—Sexuality—Marriage," posted at the website of the Orthodox Bishops' Conference in Germany: http://www.obkd.de/Texte/Brief%20OBKD%20an%20die%20Jugend-en.pdf.

85. https://www.goarch.org/el/social-ethos?p_p_id=56_INSTANCE _km0Xa4sy69OV&p_p_lifecycle=0&p_p_state=normal&p_p_mode=view&p

_p_col_id=column-1&p_p_col_count=1&_56_INSTANCE_km0Xa4sy69OV_languageId=en_US/ (§18–29). Made public during the Great Lent of 2020, this document appeared in fifteen languages (Korean, Serbian, English, Finnish, Italian, French, German, Russian, Ukrainian, Romanian, Greek, Georgian, Portuguese, Spanish, Arabic).

86. https://www.bbc.com/serbian/cyr/srbija-56266813/.

CHAPTER

6

Eastern Orthodoxy Identity and "Aggressive Liberalism"

Nontheological Aspects of the Confrontation

Dmitry Uzlaner

In the discourse of contemporary Eastern Orthodoxy (Russian), one of the most important topics in recent years has been the struggle with what is called in this rhetoric "aggressive liberalism" or "aggressive secularism."[1] Aggressive liberalism is a multidimensional concept, but the most threatening part, often mentioned as evidence of why liberalism is dangerous, is sexual diversity—in particular, nontraditional sexual relations, same-sex marriages, feminism, and so on.[2] It seems that the Church's vision of itself is structured around this confrontation, around this feeling of being attacked by an aggressive ideological enemy imposing upon it some alien values and practices.[3] I would like to structure my contribution around six consecutive points that clarify different aspects of this struggle and reveal what stands behind this harsh opposition to sexual diversity.

My first point is that this confrontation is theologically motivated only to a very limited degree. It is possible, of course, to find theological arguments in support of this confrontation with sexual diversity. In particular, some of these arguments were outlined in the corresponding official document of the Russian Orthodox Church: "The Russian Orthodox Church's Basic Teaching on Human Dignity, Freedom and Rights" (2008).[4] However, this opposition does not seem to be driven by theology. I would even say that there is a huge resistance to the very idea of making "sexual diversity" a legitimate part of theological reflection—the argument often given here is that of an "Overton window": We discuss it and therefore automatically start to legitimize it.⁵ So I would say that in order for the issues of sexual diversity to receive an adequate theological solution, they must first *become* theological—i.e., be accepted as a legitimate part of theological debate. But this has yet to happen.

So, the sources of Eastern Orthodox opposition to sexual diversity should be looked elsewhere. Somewhere beyond theology, in nontheological factors that nourish this confrontation. What do I mean by nontheological factors? These are the factors that are determined not by theological arguments, but rather by political, ideological, and other influences.

My second point is that opposition to sexual diversity is one of the key (perhaps *the* key) axes around which contemporary Orthodox identity is structured. Sex and gender issues are the cornerstone of contemporary Orthodox identity. Through this opposition to sexual diversity the construction of a "we"-identity happens as opposed to "them." Moreover, "we" are not only different from "them" (in the Russian case, "they" refers to the post-Christian liberal West), but "we" are morally superior to "them"—"we" are moral, "they" are immoral; "we" are spiritual, "they" are material.⁶ This logic was perfectly illustrated by one of the speakers at the conference "Contemporary Eastern Orthodox Identity and the Challenges of Pluralism and Sexual Diversity in a Secular Age" that took place in Oxford, August, 2019,⁷ and that became one of the first attempts to start a discussion on these issues among Orthodox intellectuals. This speaker organized his presentation around the opposition between moral Christians and immoral "new pagans"—this, by the way, proved that the case of Russian Orthodoxy is not an exception.

This aspect of Russian Orthodoxy was analyzed by Alexander Agadjanian,⁸ who showed how contemporary Orthodox identity is increasingly structured around rejection of what he calls "the imagined 'western liberal ethos.'"⁹ This immoral liberal ethos is contrasted with a set of moral Orthodox principles including emphasis on family values, inequality of gender roles, responsibilities rather than rights, intracollective social control and solidarity, the priority of the "spiritual" over the "material," sexual (self) restraint, homophobia, and the subjugation of individual interests and expressions to the collective good.¹⁰

There are a number of burning questions that require answers. What does it mean to be an Orthodox Christian today (as opposed to being an atheist or non-Orthodox Christian)? What distinguishes a true believer from a nonbeliever? Where are the signs of apostasy? What makes Orthodox

Christians "the salt of the earth"? Where is the proof that Christians have not dissolved into the everyday reality of contemporary secular societies? Opposition to "sexual diversity" has become an answer these questions. This opposition has become a line that allows to differentiate "us" and "them," to establish a stable identity and a stable system of coordinates in the rapidly changing reality of contemporary fluid societies.[11]

So, to repeat: Opposition to "sexual diversity" is the axis, the cornerstone on which contemporary Orthodox identity is constructed. Opposition to same-sex marriage is becoming in the Russian Orthodox context a kind of "shibboleth" that allows "true" believers to quickly differentiate who they are dealing with: Is he one of "us," Christians, or is he one of "them"—immoral liberal, pseudo-Christian, and so forth?[12] Opposition to "sexual diversity" is not a theologically justified position; it is a mechanism for constructing contemporary Orthodox identity.

My third point is that this Orthodox identity is always portrayed as if it is under attack—the enemy is not just liberalism or secularism, but *aggressive* liberalism and *aggressive* secularism. Orthodox identity is always persecuted and has to defend itself. Even the title of the above-mentioned conference has the traces of this logic: "Eastern Orthodox identity and the *challenges* of pluralism and diversity." You can't just have identity and that's all. This identity must be perceived as constantly challenged and, consequently, defended.

The narrative that illustrates this logic is very simple. One can come across it in many Church documents: There is a good Church that unites "millions of people in prayer, good deeds, care for the future of the people," and so on, and there is secularism and liberalism, adopted by alien anti-Christian forces, which tries to ruin this benign existence.[13] Of course, we are dealing with a standard ideological trick here.[14] The Orthodox identity constructed through the opposition to "sexual diversity" is highly unstable in itself for the simple reason that all identities are unstable. There are internal tensions in this identity, internal antagonisms. These internal tensions are externalized, are placed outside and embodied in the figures of "antichurch" and "anti-Christian forces."[15]

Challenges of "sexual diversity" that are positioned as external threats to the Orthodox identity are eating away this identity from inside. Not nontraditional sexual relationships and the Church, not feminism and the Church, not the crisis of traditional family and the Church—but nontraditional sexual relationships inside the Church,[16] feminism inside the

Church (I mean the problem of the place of women inside the Church), the crisis of the traditional family inside the Church (i.e., the crisis of priests' families, domestic violence in Orthodox families),[17] and so forth. All these problems, which concern not only contemporary secular society but also the Church itself, receive a simple ideological solution—they are externalized and portrayed as external forces threatening Orthodox identity from the outside.

There is a burning undecidedness around issues of "sexual diversity" that is eating Orthodox identity—be it individual or collective—alive. Externalizing this undecidedness is a strategy to cope with it. This is a defense mechanism—in the Freudian sense—against something that is too painful and that cannot be approached directly yet.[18]

Another way of overcoming this tension inside Orthodox identity is, of course, the "scapegoating" so masterfully described by Rene Girard.[19] Internal antagonism is embodied in the figure of the scapegoat who is blamed for destabilizing the community and causing chaos in it. Then this embodied antagonism is thrown out of the community and the internal piece restores itself. Something like this happens when LGBTQ+ people are being kicked out of parishes after coming out.

My fourth point is that there is a parallel story that nourishes Russian Orthodox opposition to "sexual diversity." Though this story is connected to the one mentioned above, this is the story of demographic anxiety (and nationalism, which is connected to demographic anxiety). The anxiety that "we" will disappear and "they"—Muslims or Chinese who are more vital, who have more children etc.—will come and take all our resources and territories.[20] This anxiety is behind opposition to "sexual diversity" and not just the position of Church fathers. What is interesting is that this anxiety results not in attempts to achieve a realistic scientific understanding of the demographic situation and to find ways to improve it. This anxiety results in paranoia, à la the conspiracy theory narratives about gay or feminist or liberal elites trying to destroy Russia, to subvert its demography, to destroy traditional families (for example, through propaganda of nontraditional sexual relations—that's why you need a special law that prevents this propaganda from harming children![21]), and so on.[22]

My fifth point is that this undecidedness is burning, that opposition to "sexual diversity" is saturated with anxiety about the future of Orthodoxy. As a result, this confrontation becomes overinvested (in the psychoanalytic sense) and, consequently, closed to any meaningful discussion. It is just not possible to debate the issues of sexual relations and family in a rational way; these topics are explosive. I will give just one example: Some time ago a well-known and quite respected priest gave an interview where he said that families with a lot of children sometimes face burnout as it could be quite hard to live in poverty. This provoked such a huge storm that the interview was retracted, and a refutation was published—basically saying that discussion of these issues in such a way is unacceptable.[23] I don't want even to touch the question of same-sex relations, because here the degree of overinvestment is so high that it becomes a question of life and death, of physical survival for those who dare to address this anxiety and undecidedness.

This means that rational theological discussion of issues of sexual diversity is almost impossible in the current situation. These issues must first become disinvested, and only then theological discussion could become possible. But could it be that as soon as this disinvestment happens—and I am sure that it will happen one day—this discussion would no longer be interesting to anyone?

My sixth point: I am not saying that all Orthodox believers construct their identity around the axis of "sexual diversity." This is the way this identity is constructed in the discourse of official and nonofficial but very influential Church speakers. Not only in Russia. To question this identity-building and to search for an alternative is a very easy way to become "an enemy of the Church."[24]

The most obvious objection to what I've said is the objection that opposition to "sexual diversity" could not be the cornerstone of Orthodox identity as the cornerstone of Orthodox identity is Jesus Christ. To this I can answer: First of all, I speak not as a theologian, I speak as an external observer who describes not what ought to be ideally, but what I see. Second, negative identity (identity against somebody or something) is stronger than positive identity (identity in favor of something or someone). But third—and this answer seems to me the most convincing—because a huge number of Orthodox believers (out of 260 million[25]) do not believe in Jesus Christ at all (in his Incarnation, Resurrection, etc.). In Russia, one third of Orthodox Christian believers do not believe in God,[26] one in ten (of self-proclaimed Orthodox Christians) is not baptized,[27] and so on.[28] Faith in Christ cannot be the basis of Christian identity when belonging to Christianity is just a marker of national and cultural belonging. Faith in Christ may well be the cornerstone of Orthodox identity—but only for those few percent for whom their faith as faith makes any sense. For others opposition to sexual diversity as the foundation of their religious identity seems like a logical option.

I am not a theologian and I am not going to argue as a theologian. But I will dare to finish by asking a theological question. Constructing identity through opposing moral "us" to immoral "them," ideological concealment of internal antagonisms, scapegoating, anxiety over the future and search for whom to blame—these are typical, almost universal features of any human community, of any human identity (pagan, atheist, etc.). Does it mean that Christian community, Christian identity is in no way different from other communities (be it pagan or atheist ones)? Or is it different? And if it is different, then where does one search for this difference? And by search I don't mean some theological explanation of what a Christian community *ought* to be in some ideal world. I mean, where does one look in order to *see* the difference?

Notes

1. One can come across multiple cases of this in the speeches of key representatives of the Russian Orthodox Church (ROC), as well as in official documents. See, for example: Mitropolit Volokolamskij Ilarion, "Sovremennye vyzovy global'nogo mira: sekuljarizm i religioznoe mirovozzrenie" [Contemporary challenges of the modern world: Secularism and religious worldview], *Official Site of the Moscow Patriarchate* (2010): http://www.patriarchia.ru/db/text/1178278.html (accessed February 12, 2020); Russian Orthodox Church, "Sostojalas' vstrecha Svjatejshego Patriarha Kirilla s General'nym sekretarem Organizacii Ob'edinennyh Nacij" [A meeting took place between His Holiness Patriarch Kirill and General Secretary of the United Nations], *Official Site of the Moscow Patriarchate* (2018): http://www.patriarchia.ru/db/text/5225036.html (accessed February 12, 2020).

2. In one of the documents, anti-Church forces are described in the following way: "Those who promote the false values of aggressive liberalism, for the Church is adamant in its position against such anti-Christian phenomena as the recognition of same-sex unions, freedom of expression of all desires, irrepressible consumerism, propaganda of permissiveness and fornication" (Russian Orthodox Church, "Obrashhenie Vysshego Cerkovnogo Soveta Russkoj Pravoslavnoj Cerkvi" [Address of the Highest Council of the Russian Orthodox Church], *Official Site of the Moscow Patriarchate* [2012]: http://www.patriarchia.ru/db/text/2135736.html [accessed February 12, 2020]). This was a document published

after and as a reaction to the famous "punk-prayer" of the Pussy Riot group in 2012. See also Dmitry Uzlaner, "The Pussy Riot Case and the Peculiarities of Russian Post-Secularism," *State, Religion and Church* 1, no. 1 (2014): 23–58: http://www.srch.ranepa.ru/node/443 (accessed February 12, 2020); Dmitry Uzlaner and Kristina Stoeckl, "From Pussy Riot's 'Punk Prayer' to Matilda: Orthodox Believers, Critique, and Religious Freedom in Russia," *Journal of Contemporary Religion* 34, no. 3 (2019): 427–45: DOI: 10.1080/13537903.2019.1658432.

3. Russian Orthodoxy is not an exception here. One can find similar logic elsewhere. See, for example, Rod Dreher, *The Benedict Option: A Strategy for Christians in a Post-Christian Nation* (New York: Sentinel, 2018).

4. Russian Orthodox Church, "The Russian Orthodox Church's Basic Teaching on Human Dignity, Freedom and Rights," Department for External Church Relations (2008): https://mospat.ru/en/documents/dignity-freedom-rights/ (accessed February 12, 2020).

5. On the way this concept is used in Russia, see Vladimir Ruvinskij, "Rozhdenie teorii zagovora. Kto prorubil 'okno Overtona' v Rossiju" [The birth of the conspiracy theory: Who opened the "Overton window" in Russia], *Republic* (7/2/2018): https://republic.ru/posts/89363 (accessed February 12, 2020).

6. On the concept of traditional morality and its key role in elaborating new Orthodox identity, see Alexander Agadjanian, "Tradition, Morality and Community: Elaborating Orthodox Identity in Putin's Russia," *Religion, State and Society* 45, no. 1 (2017): 39–60: DOI: 10.1080/09637494.2016.1272893; Gulnaz Sharafutdinova, "Managing National Ressentiment: Morality Politics in Putin's Russia," in *Vocabularies of International Relations after the Crisis in Ukraine*, Post-Soviet Politics, ed. Andrey Makarychev (New York: Routledge, 2016).

7. See more on this conference: https://www.fordham.edu/info/28289/bridging_voices/11036/press_release_2019_oxford_conference.

8. Agadjanian, "Tradition, Morality and Community."

9. Agadjanian, "Tradition, Morality and Community," 4.

10. Agadjanian, "Tradition, Morality and Community," 5–6. Agadjanian shows continuity between the contemporary moral identity of Russian Orthodoxy and what he calls the "late Soviet conservative ethos" (3). This late Soviet ethos is sacralized by the ROC today.

Moreover, opposition to "sexual diversity," and especially homophobia, is relevant far beyond the Russian Orthodox context: One can say that this is also one of the key axes around which contemporary Russian political regime is structured. This can be illustrated by two antigay political ads that were produced as a way of mobilizing Russian citizens to participate first in presidential elections in 2018 (see https://www.youtube.com/watch?v=OfRIwR6ya6U [accessed 20,

2020]), and then in a referendum about the new Russian constitution in 2020 (see Nathan Hodge and Mary Ilyushina, "Anti-gay viral video stirs outrage ahead of Russian referendum," *BBC* [June 3, 2020]: https://edition.cnn.com/2020/06/03/europe/anti-lgbtq-video-russia-referendum-intl/index.html [accessed June 20, 2020]). Both are structured around the nightmarish image of a future Russia in which homosexuals are allowed to adopt children and each Russian family is obliged to include a homosexual person. Participation in elections is presented as a way to prevent this vision from become true—as one ad finishes: "Is this the Russia you want?"

11. This process is not limited only to Eastern Orthodoxy; for example, on evangelicals, see Mark Vasey-Saunders, *The Scandal of Evangelicals and Homosexuality: English Evangelical Texts, 1960–2010* (London: Routledge, 2015).

12. Recognition of same-sex marriages is interpreted as an "apocalyptic symptom" and as a step on the "path of self-destruction." See Kirill, patriarch of ROC: "My dolzhny delat' vse dlia togo, chtoby na prostranstvakh Sviatoi Rusi grekh nikogda ne utverzhdalsia zakonom gosudarstva" [We must do our best to ensure that sin never be established by state law on the territory of Holy Rus'], *Official Site of the Moscow Patriarchate* (7/21/2013): http://www.patriarchia.ru/db/text/ (accessed February 12, 2020).

13. Russian Orthodox Church, "Obrashhenie Vysshego Cerkovnogo Soveta Russkoj Pravoslavnoj Cerkvi" [Address of the Highest Council of the Russian Orthodox Church], *Official Site of the Moscow Patriarchate* (2012): http://www.patriarchia.ru/db/text/2135736.html (accessed February 12, 2020). This rhetoric became widespread during the Pussy Riot case; see Ilya Yablokov, "Pussy Riot as Agent Provocateur: Conspiracy Theories and the Media Construction of Nation in Putin's Russia," *Natl. pap.* 42, no. 4 (2014): 622–36, DOI: 10.1080/00905992.2014.923390.

14. Slavoj Žižek, *The Sublime Object of Ideology* (London: Verso, 2008), 139–44.

15. See also Dmitry Uzlaner, "Perverse Conservatism: A Lacanian Interpretation of Russia's Turn to Traditional Values," *Psychoanal Cult Soc* 22, no. 2 (2017): 173–92: DOI: 10.1057/s41282-016-0036-6; Dmitry Uzlaner, "The Logic of Scapegoating in Contemporary Russian Moral Conservatism," in *Contemporary Russian Conservatism: Problems, Paradoxes, and Perspectives*, ed. Mikhail Suslov and Dmitry Uzlaner, *Eurasian Studies Library: History, Societies and Cultures in Eurasia*, vol. 13 (Leiden: Brill, 2019).

16. There is a very impressive book by Frédéric Martel about the Catholic Church that deals with problems that also exist in the Orthodox context. See Frédéric Martel, *In the Closet of the Vatican. Power, Homosexuality, Hypocrisy* (London: Bloomsbury Continuum, 2019).

17. Many cases of this are documented on the independent Orthodox media *Ahilla* (http://ahilla.ru/).

18. For more on this, see Uzlaner, "Perverse Conservatism."

19. René Girard, *The Scapegoat* (Baltimore: Johns Hopkins University Press, 1986).

20. This was a constant lamentation in the speeches by the head of the Moscow Patriarchal Commission on Family Matters, Father Dimitry Smirnov (1951–2020). See, for example, Protoierej Dimitry Smirnov, "Rossijane zakonchatsja k 2050 godu" [Archpriest Dimitry Smirnov: "Russians will be over by 2050"], *Znak* (4/3/2019): https://www.znak.com/2019-03-04/protoierey_dimitriy_smirnov_rossiyane_zakonchatsya_k_2050_godu (accessed February 12, 2020).

21. On this law, see C. Wilkinson, "Putting 'Traditional Values' into Practice: The Rise and Contestation of Anti-Homopropaganda Laws in Russia," *Journal of Human Rights* 13, no. 3 (2014): 363–79.

22. For more on this, see Dmitry Uzlaner, "The Logic of Scapegoating in Contemporary Russian Moral Conservatism," in *Contemporary Russian Conservatism: Problems, Paradoxes, and Perspectives*, ed. Mikhail Suslov and Dmitry Uzlaner, vol. 13 of *Eurasian Studies Library: History, Societies and Cultures in Eurasia* (Leiden: Brill, 2019). On conspiracy theories thriving in today's Russia, see Ilya Yablokov, *Fortress Russia. Conspiracy Theories in Post-Soviet Russia* (Cambridge: Polity Press, 2018).

23. Nikolaj Emel'janov, "O 'pechati mnogodetnosti': Neskol'ko slov ob interv'ju o. Pavla Velikanova" [On the "burden of possessing many children": A few words on the interview by Father Pavel Velikanov], *Miloserdie.ru* (11/29/2016): https://www.miloserdie.ru/article/o-pechati-mnogodetnosti/ (accessed February 12, 2020).

24. The notions of "enemy of the Church" as well as of "betrayers in cassocks" became quite a significant aspect of contemporary Russian Orthodox rhetoric. This language has started to spread since 2012 ("V RPC prokommentirovali slova patriarha o 'predateljah v rjasah'" [ROC commented on the Patriarch's words on "betrayers in cassocks"], *Vzgljad* [4/23/2012]: https://vz.ru/news/2012/4/23/575723.html [accessed February 12, 2020]).

25. Pew Research Forum, "Orthodox Christianity in the 21st Century": https://www.pewforum.org/2017/11/08/orthodox-christianity-in-the-21st-century/. By the way, this figure is already ideological—it gives the impression that there is an Orthodox majority (for example, in Russia) in a situation where there are literally several percent of practicing believers.

26. Ria Novosti, "'Indeks very': Skol'ko na samom dele v Rossii pravoslavnyh" ["Index of faith": How many Orthodox are there really in Russia], *Ria Novosti* (8/23/2017): https://ria.ru/20170823/1500891796.html (accessed February 12, 2020).

27. Russian Public Opinion Research Center, "Orthodoxy and Baptism" (2019): https://wciom.com/index.php?id=61&uid=1697 (accessed February 12, 2020).

28. Religiosity in Russia in general is not impressive, even compared to other Central and Eastern European countries. See Pew Research Center, "Religious Belief and National Belonging in Central and Eastern Europe: National and Religious Identities Converge in a Region Once Dominated by Atheist Regimes" (2017): https://www.pewforum.org/2017/05/10/religious-belief-and-national-belonging-in-central-and-eastern-europe/ (accessed February 12, 2020).

CHAPTER

7

SALVATION AND SAME-SEX RELATIONS

AN ORTHODOX RESPONSE ON THE DECISION BY THE LUTHERAN CHURCH OF SWEDEN

Michael Hjälm

In 1998, the Lutheran Church in Sweden made the headlines in international press and in World Christianity. An exhibition of photographs were displayed in the Great Cathedral of Uppsala, center of Christianity in Sweden since the beginning of the second millennium. In the pictures, the disciples and Jesus Christ were presented as homosexuals, with the Last Supper turned into a gay event. The exhibition *Ecce Homo* ignited a rage against the Church of Sweden both domestically as well as internationally. Lutheran churches broke the communion with the Swedish Church, and the Pope of Rome canceled a meeting with the Lutheran archbishop. In the Orthodox world, the Coptic Church canceled the ongoing dialogue, and in 2005 the Russian Orthodox Church broke all international relations with the Lutheran Church in Sweden.

In the midst of all this, I was employed as the first theological secretary for the Eastern Orthodox and Oriental Orthodox Churches in the Christian Council of Sweden, January 1999. Parallel to the crisis with the *Ecce Homo* exhibition, we had the beginning of the Special Commission in the World Council of Churches where the Church of Sweden and EKD (the Evangelical Church in Germany) had been strong financial contributors. Belonging to the Serbian Orthodox Church, we also had the Church's involvement in the conflict of ex-Yugoslavia. As a much younger man at the time, I had to face issues that I could hardly imagine, and much less believe that I would face in reality. In this chaos, with the Lutheran Church of Sweden considered one of the most despicable Christian communities in the world by the Orthodox, and the Serbian Orthodox Church measured as one of the most loathsome churches in the eyes of liberal churches in the West, it seemed only natural to have a face-to-face encounter. That was actually what the Lutheran archbishop K. G. Hammar suggested in an evening conversation with me in one of the Catholic convents in Sweden.

The dialogue between the Lutheran Church of Sweden and the Serbian-Orthodox Church in Northern Europe officially started in 2002, and has now continued for more than ten years. However, same-sex relations were never a subject in the official dialogue.[1] In fact, we tried in every way to avoid the question, and yet we all knew tacitly that the issue of same-sex relations was *the* major stumbling block for the Church of Sweden in every kind of ecumenical relation post *Ecce Homo*.[2]

The reason why the Orthodox tacitly avoided the subject was due to our own inability to have a common vision and understanding on how to deal with the issue of same-sex relations and same-sex marriages. We could all agree that we should renounce same-sex marriage and same-sex relations, but why? Because it is unnatural, some would argue, or because it is written in the Bible, others would argue. Although, when we were sitting with the Lutherans on the other side of the table, we were quiet. Maybe we all wanted to state the obvious by tacitly saying to the other side that this is nothing to discuss: Either you turn or you will suffer the consequences.

The tacit tactic could well have been considered a diplomatic strategy if it had been conscious, but parallel to this, the pastoral problem on how to deal with our own homosexual members became an issue first in Helsinki, and then in Stockholm. In Helsinki, some of the Orthodox priests made an appeal for the support of homosexuals who claimed a Christian identity, including those who considered themselves Orthodox Christians. The appeal was not a support of same-sex marriages or even same-sex relations, just an appeal for supporting equal rights for homosexuals and heterosexuals. Parallel to the official dialogue, several initiatives both formal and less formal were taken by the Church of Sweden to gain support for their cause of supporting people with same-sex orientations.[3] The response by the Orthodox was weak, or even nonexistent in most cases. Even my own response was feeble and scant, but I nevertheless published two articles: One was on the interpretation of St. Paul,[4] and the other was on a public hearing just before the Church of Sweden took the official decision.[5] Both responses air the reluctance by the Orthodox Churches to engage in discussion on the issue. Besides these two responses, Father Misha Jaksic made a response in the same public hearing in 2004, and took the quest with some rigor and willingness to express an Orthodox view.[6] Taken together, this reveals that we did not have an official response on the issue by the Orthodox in Sweden, and the response by Orthodox officials was meager with only three attempts, only one of which could be considered serious.

Though behind the curtains we had a much deeper analysis, and my own preparations were concentrated on the issues of moral sin, salvation, and communion with God. My findings were at that stage somewhat in contradiction with Father Misha Jaksic, but more importantly at that precise moment in 2004, the Orthodox in Sweden were not equipped to discuss same-sex relations in a constructive way. Since then, with the establishment of Sankt Ignatios Theological Seminaries and Academy, we are braver and hope to be more prosperous in tackling difficult questions.[7] In this chapter, I will give the historical background to the position taken by the Lutheran Church in Sweden, and then give my view that never reached the public space.

The Historical Background of the Position Taken by the Lutheran Church in Sweden

Everything started in Sweden 1951 when the Lutheran bishops opposed criminalization of homosexuals.[8] Even though the bishops in their letter took a fierce stand against homosexuality, qualifying it as a sin and a disease that medical science should do everything to overcome, they opposed criminalization of homosexuals. Twenty years later the situation had developed further and the Lutheran bishops took a stand that was quite far-reaching, saying that same-sex relations are a reality that the Church must consider, and therefore they initiated an investigation to more fully explore the matter.[9] The investigation never came into effect, and it was not until 1995 that the Church of Sweden took a practical stand. The position of the Lutheran Church in 1995 was nevertheless still very cautious. The Theological Committee of the Church Assembly, including all bishops, decided that same-sex partnership, which was introduced by the Government in 1994, should not be considered morally wrong, and the Church should introduce a kind of blessing of same-sex couples.[10] This did not mean that the Church in any way was introducing same-sex marriage acts or even allowed an act of blessing in an official Church, but made the conclusion that same-sex relations also carry some kind of blessing.

A change took place in the Church of Sweden when the Church Assembly dealt with a petition in 1997 on allowing same-sex blessing in public churches, which moved the act of blessing from a pastoral concern to an official act in the Church of Sweden.[11] In 1999 the decision was taken that the act of blessing a same-sex couple allowed relatives to be present, but was still not considered a public act of the Church.[12] In 2005, blessing of same-sex couples became a public act of the Church, and finally in 2012 the act of marriage became one and the same, regardless of sexes, in the suggestion for a new church manual.[13]

Two things need to be added to this description. First, the Church of Sweden was until 2000 a state church, and the Church assembly was and still is a political body consisting of more or less the same political parties that we find in the Parliament. This means that the initiative to move same-sex blessing from a pastoral concern to a public act was taken by secular political parties, but the final decision to equalize same-sex marriage with heterosexual marriage was taken by the Church of Sweden after the separation from the state, and was confirmed by the Theological Committee. Therefore, it is fair to say that the decision reflects the contemporary Church of Sweden. Second, the transition was not without conflicts. The petition of 1997 was followed by a furious debate where other Christian communities reacted and individual advocates of homosexual rights were even exposed to death threats.[14]

The culmination of the debate came when the dean of the Uppsala Cathedral, Tuulikki Koivunen Bylund, decided to let the photographer Elisabeth Ohlson Wallin exhibit her photo collection *Ecco Homo*, which opened September 19, 1998, displaying the homosexuals as the new group of outcasts surrounding Jesus, reminding us of how Christ in the Gospels cared for the outcasts and unclean.[15] However, the exhibition was not just a question of how to describe the new outcasts, but Christ himself was depicted as a homosexual. This created an outcry especially among the free and the Orthodox churches. Many in the Church of Sweden condemned the exhibition. The bishop of Uppsala, Tord Harlin, stated that "in best case it is just bad theology, but in worst case it is blasphemy."[16] Nonetheless, the archbishop of the Church of Sweden, K. G. Hammar, approved the exhibition, even though this was after it had taken place.[17] This caused Pope John Paul II to cancel a meeting with the archbishop, and the meeting was postponed to May the year after.[18] The exhibition was also disposed in the parliament. The Christian Democrats reacted vehemently, and argued that it was a violation against their Christian belief.[19] Among others who reacted negatively was the previous prime minister, Carl Bildt, who said it was "an event [only] to provoke" and compared it with having an exhibition on Pol Pot. Others in the same political group as Carl Bildt were overtly positive, as for example Birgitta Ohlsson, who displayed one of the photographs in her office as minister for EU affairs.[20]

When the exhibition was moved to Norrköping, which is a stronghold of many Syriac Orthodox, the Syriac Orthodox community arranged a demonstration. The photographer Elisabeth Ohlson Wallin was threatened, and there were also those who threw stones at her.[21]

The event in Norrköping required a responsible stand on the issue of same-sex marriages, same-sex relations, and the exhibition *Ecce Homo*. I had separate meetings with the Orthodox Church leaders and met official representatives from different Christian communities. In the end, I could not find a mutual understanding among the Orthodox on how to act in this situation. The issue was therefore settled behind closed doors, and never reached the public. Today I regret this, looking back on the development of a continued or even increased hostility in regard to homosexuals and minority groups.

A Tentative Suggestion of a Response by the Orthodox Churches

The Supposed Evil Nature of Homosexuality

The immediate concern should have been to tackle the rage against homosexuals that thrived among the Orthodox and still flourishes both in Sweden and in many Orthodox countries. We have everything from bricks being thrown into protest marches to systematic violations of human rights by the authorities. For the most part, this concerns a kind of homophobia that is based in a more general fear of sexuality, which should be the object of an in-depth psychological or sociological study. To some extent, though, it does raise the concerns of a theological inquiry. First, we have the question of the supposedly evil nature of homosexuality. Secondly, there is the issue of salvation and homosexuality. Finally, we have the meaning of sexual differentiation per se.

Let us begin with the supposedly evil nature of homosexuality. In an attempt to contemplate the issue we have to consider the nature of what evil is. Dionysius the Areopagite in his reflection *On the Divine Names* makes the following comment:

> Evil qua evil makes no single essence or birth, but only, as far as it can, pollutes and destroys the subsistence of things existing. . . . For neither will the same by itself be both good and evil, nor the self-same power be of itself destruction and birth. . . . All things which are, in so far as they are, both are good, and from the Good; but, in so far as they are deprived of the Good, are neither good, nor do they exist. . . . So the fact that birth is born from destruction, is not a power of evil, but a presence of a lesser good, even as disease is a defect of order.[22]

What Dionysius is trying to articulate is the position we find among earlier and later Church Fathers: that evil cannot replace the good since it does not subsist in itself. In relation to the question of homosexual relations, this means that the good things that exist in the friendship and support that we can find among homosexual couples would in no way be replaced by something evil. Evil simply does not have that capacity. In fact evil in itself does not have any capacity. Human beings have a capacity to choose between good and evil, but to become evil per se, they have to replace what is good, which would exceed the nature of evil.

The illusion instead, and the temptation, is the belief that something good can be transformed into a malicious nature, as a kind of magic act. The good things a human being carries remain good regardless of different actions, attitudes, or sexual orientations. This is the meaning that Basil the Great attaches to Man as the image of God.[23] Whatever we do as humans, the image of God cannot be replaced by wickedness. Whether we are for or against same-sex relations, the human being as an image of God cannot be eradicated. Furthermore, the positive things contained in any human relation, such as friendship, support, trust, and mutual understanding, remain good, regardless if we involve homosexual orientations or not. Denying what is good by the existence of something potentially evil constitutes the original temptation that Adam and Eve experienced after they had eaten from the fruit of knowledge. This is the same temptation that Judas experienced after he had betrayed Christ, which opened the door to emptiness and darkness. In the same manner, acknowledging what is good despite the evil things that could be attached to it reveals the Gospel as the Apostle Peter perceived it after he betrayed Christ just as Judas had, but where he acknowledged that something good remained with him. Rage, hatred, enmity, and discrimination against homosexuals is an act of Judas, a denial of what God has given to us all, a denial of the love that the Father has for his divine Son, who is the pattern of all existence.

Homosexuality and Salvation

The second query regards the question of salvation. Could homosexual behavior or same-sex relations be an absolute stumbling block for salvation? This is not as easy to answer as the question on homosexual relations as ultimate evil. Even if good remains good in a homosexual relationship, it may still be an absolute stumbling block for salvation. Human beings remain an image of God, but this does not secure salvation for mankind, even if Gregory of Nyssa seems to make this affirmation.[24]

What constitutes salvation in the Eastern Orthodox tradition has been a debatable question, but if we begin in the doxological salutation in the prologue of the letter to the Ephesians we may have a beginning.[25]

> Blessed *be* the God and Father of our Lord Jesus Christ, who has blessed us with every spiritual blessing in the heavenly *places* in Christ, **4** just as He chose us in Him before the foundation of the world, that we should be holy and without blame before Him in love, **5** having predestined us to adoption as sons by Jesus Christ to Himself, according to the good pleasure of His will, **6** to the praise of the glory of His grace, by which He made us accepted in the Beloved.

In the letter to the Ephesians, salvation is closely connected to the Love of the Father to his divine Son, who in turn has adopted us to partake in this divine love. Salvation is then a question on how this divine adoption could be accomplished for the salvation of mankind. In Ephesians 3:17 it is clearly spelled out that we have to receive this love so "that Christ may dwell in your hearts through faith; that being rooted and grounded in love may be able to comprehend with all the saints what *is* the width and length and depth and height—to know the love of Christ which passes knowledge; that you may be filled with all the fullness of God."

Faith here is not faith in the existence of God or acknowledging the supremacy of the Lord. Instead, in the letter to the Ephesians, faith concerns the trust in the Lord that God really loves us so that receiving the love of Christ becomes possible through faith. It is not our love that fills us with the fullness of God, but the Love of Christ, which is the same love as God the Father has for his beloved Son. Salvation in the early Church, at least as it is interpreted by the early Church Fathers, does not come through our faith, but from the love of Christ that dwells in our hearts, when we receive it through faith. Love is what is left when we have fulfilled all our obligations, when all protocols have been signed, and all good deeds have been delivered. This is the Gospel that the Apostle Paul proclaims in his letters. Two examples can serve as an explanation to this. The first example is the letter to the Ephesians that tells us that we have to walk in love, which is exemplified by using marriage as an example, Eph 5:21, 22–33. The text is a mandatory reading in the Eastern Orthodox tradition for all marriages. The text is often misinterpreted as indicating the subordination of women, but it is quite the contrary.[26]

> **22** Wives, submit to your own husbands, as to the Lord. **23** For the husband is head of the wife, as also Christ is head of the church; and He is the Savior of the body. **24** Therefore, just as the church is subject to Christ, so *let* the wives *be* to their own husbands in everything. **25** Husbands, love your wives, just as Christ also loved the church and gave Himself for her, **26** that He might sanctify and cleanse her with the washing of water by the word, **27** that He might present her to Himself a glorious church, not having spot or wrinkle or any such thing, but that she should be holy and without blemish. **28** So husbands ought to love their own wives as their own bodies; he who loves his wife loves himself. **29** For no one ever hated his own flesh, but nourishes and cherishes it, just as the Lord *does* the church. **30** For we are members of His body, of His flesh and of His bones. **31** "For this reason a man shall leave his father and mother and be joined to his wife, and the two shall become one flesh." **32** This is a great mystery, but I speak concerning Christ and the church. **33** Nevertheless let each one of you in particular so love his own wife as himself, and let the wife *see* that she respects *her* husband.

The text begins with the clear commandment of equal subordination (Eph. 5:21) to make it very clear already from the beginning that this is not about the role of the women, and then comes the mystery of love revealed in the marriage. In order to understand the meaning of the text, we need to understand the allusion to Adam and Eve. Eve was disobedient and picked the fruit of knowledge and Adam received the fruit and devoured it for his own pleasure. The wife here is the obedient Eve who obeys the commandment of God and submits herself to her husband, according to the law. The husband is Adam who receives his wife's submission not for his own pleasure but out of love for his wife. This exemplifies the meaning of the Gospel. The law will oppress the wife, but if the law is received in love the law is fulfilled and submission is transformed into equality, where the husband loves his wife as he loves himself.[27]

The same content is delivered by the Apostle Paul in the letter to Philemon, as a second example of the meaning of the Gospel. He sends back Onesimus as a slave to Philemon, according to the law, but appeals to his Christian love, which transcends the law, and according to the tradition Philemon receives Onesimus as his equal, not because he must but because of love. In both of these examples the Apostle Paul teaches us that the Christian love does not omit the law, but transcends it and fulfills the law into something greater.[28]

One of the early Church Fathers, Ignatius of Antioch, summarizes the teaching of the early Church in one sentence: "All things together are good if you believe in/with love." It is the love of Christ that brings about the transformation of the world and brings all people together as one. Ignatius continues to explain the mystery of love and what he thinks differentiates the true Christians from the Judaizing Christians—a differentiation that did not do justice to the emerging Rabbinic Judaism, but that gives an explanation of the teaching of the early Church. Ignatius argues that it is not enough to fulfill the law out of obedience. The Gospel requires the conversion of the heart. The Torah is inscribed in the hearts of the Christians who not only obey God, but also know the paths of God and willingly out of love fulfill the law. Doing the law blindly without a converted heart resembles a slave, who obeys his lord because he must, but in Christ we are free, already redeemed through faith, and the walk in love, the Gospel, is the natural consequence of our faith in Christ.

From the perspective of Ignatius, and, I would add, the Apostle Paul, in the light of the letters by Ignatius, salvation is not a question of morality or the practical aspects of life. If so, we would all be doomed. Salvation instead is an ontological subject. It is not a question of imitating the love of Christ, or being obedient, these are just aspects of our faith in Christ. Salvation instead is the dwelling of the love of Christ in our hearts—i.e., in the very existence of what we are. In the same way that evil cannot substitute the good, the practical aspect of our moral and active life cannot substitute the ontological subsistence of creation inherent in the Love of the Father for his divine Son. The practical aspect of homosexuality can of course imply the denial of a relationship with God, but as long as this relationship is open, the practical aspect of homosexuality, whether it is a question of sexual orientation or sexual conduct, cannot replace and undo the Love of the Father for his beloved Son, which is the very foundation for our eternal and eschatological subsistence. Neither sexual orientation nor sexual desire will subsist in our eschatological existence.

Still there is a danger, and that is the illusion that our sexuality could be able to replace our spiritual and ontological existence. This seems to be the illusion of *ethnos* and *genos* where life eternal is defined from our earthly existence, but this is also the illusion when sexuality defines who we are, whether it is homosexual or heterosexual. The same illusion applies to us when we define the other based on his/her sexual orientation. In our earthly existence, our sexual orientations connect us to this vale of tears, to the soil we walk on, but it is something we have to let go of in the end of our days. Therefore, the grave danger for our salvation is not the sexual orientation that befits us, but whether we are capable to let go of this earthly soil in order to more fully embrace the Love of God the Father in Christ. To make homosexual orientation the ultimate obstacle for salvation would imply that our sexual orientations would equal the ontology of the divine and eternal Love of the Father, which would undo the economy of salvation.

The Sexual Differentiation from an Eastern Perspective

The last topic would then be the sexual differentiation itself. Genesis 1:26–27 reads as follows:

> Let Us make man in Our image, according to Our likeness; let them have dominion over the fish of the sea, over the birds of the air, and over the cattle, over all **[b]** the earth and over every creeping thing that creeps on the earth. So God created man in His *own* image; in the image of God He created him; male and female He created them.

This is the first of two mutually contradictory stories about creation. In the first story Adam and Eve are created last, as the crown of creation, while in the second story they are created prior to the multitude of creation. The second story of creation, which is probably older, is generally regarded among the fathers as less important, even though John Chrysostom, Basil of Seleucia, and Procopius of Gaza deal with the second story in length and aim toward a synthesis of the two.[29] Others, like Basil the Great, Gregory of Nyssa, and above all Maximus the Confessor, disregarded the second story entirely.

Common for Basil the Great, Gregory of Nyssa, and Maximus is their interpretation that humankind as communion is an image of God as communion—i.e., a revelation of the Trinity. The question then is whether the sexual differentiation is substantial for this image of God. Valerie A. Karras argues in an article that the fathers interpret the phrase "male and female he created them" in an inclusive way and not in a normative way. This may or may not be true for Basil the Great and Gregory of Nyssa, but the interpretation by Maximus the Confessor is different.[30]

In his interpretation of Genesis 1:26–27 he understands the differentiation of male and female in some sense as original for the image of God, which seems to be the foundation whereupon God restores humankind from disorder to the original harmony found in Paradise before the Fall. At the same time, in the economy of salvation the sexual differentiation not only restores but also transcends and surpasses its original harmony in Paradise. Male and female, following Maximus the Confessor, represents the mystery of the Holy Trinity. In the same way as the Father, the Son, and the Holy Spirit share the same nature and yet are different, male and female share the same nature but are yet different. This interpretation seems to be present already in the interpretation of Basil the Great and Gregory of Nyssa, though Maximus takes it one step further. Maximus describes salvation as a mediation between the creator and creation, accomplished in Christ, when God assumes flesh in the incarnation. He then moves further to explain why things stand as they do. The reason, Maximus argues, is that we have lost the memory of the divine, *agnoia*, because of the Fall. This leaves us confined to this vale of tears, where we long and yearn for what we only have fragment memories of. The loss of our "memory of the divine" makes us self-sufficient and self-righteous, *philautia*.[31]

As a result, this world seems sufficient to us and we see in it the goal of our journey. Through Jesus Christ, however, a series of mediations occurs between God and his creation. This world is again connected with the world to come, which will give bliss, peace, and rest. In Christ our words are fulfilled and in the liturgy we announce the end of all our yearning: to be like the Prince of Peace, to become more thoroughly human. In the restoration of our memory of the divine, however, in the *anamnesis*, Trinity appears to us as the perfect fellowship. This reflection, or icon, becomes clear in the Eucharist, as does the purpose of the difference between men and women.[32]

The first of the mediations, according to Maximus, occurs between men and women. He maintains emphatically that they are not of two different natures (otherwise there would have to be two Christs) but of one single, shared nature. Here it can be difficult to follow Maximus. As I understand him, the male and female are present in each one of us, but with the man the female element rests in the male and with the woman the male rests in the female. In this way a fundamental "us" is ever present within us.[33]

With the loss of our divine memory we also lose the memory of this "us." The man becomes self-sufficient and so does the woman. And according to Maximus, it does not end there: A tyranny is present between man and woman, where the woman is often the one to suffer most. This wrath shakes the very foundation of the fundamental "us," finding its outlet in our passions, as for example in sexuality, but also in oppression.[34]

In God's incarnation the shared principle of our human nature, the fundamental "us," is again recovered. In this earthly time we cannot retain our memory of "us" or of God but must continually remind ourselves of it in daily conversion, in daily anamnesis. Just as the people of Israel had to wander in the wilderness, as a symbol of this vale of tears, so we must remind ourselves that this desert can never give us rest. But just as manna fell from the skies, God's grace descends every day upon us, giving spiritual nourishment for our journey so that we can approach the Promised Land.[35]

Maximus understands the reconciliation between male and female as the final restoration of the Paradise lost, where Adam once more carries the imprint of Eve and Eve the imprint of Adam. In the relation between Christ and the Theotokos this is already fulfilled, but with an expectance to be fulfilled in everyone individually. In the virginity of the Theotokos the sexual differentiation is revealed as more profound than merely an act of procreation. The difference between male and female reveals the Trinity, which in turn is the life-giving fountain of all life. The sexual differentiation therefore seems to be a key element in the economy of salvation of humankind for Maximus, but in its eschatological fulfillment it seems to have nothing to do with procreative sexuality, which is part of this vale of tears, but nevertheless a necessary order for the multiplication of the human race.³⁶

With Maximus's approach to the differentiation of the sexes, neither heterosexual nor homosexual conduct has anything to do with eschatological fulfillment of male and female. Both conducts belong to this vale of tears, and will not be part of the fulfillment in the coming Kingdom. Instead, Maximus shares the perspective of Gregory of Nyssa in as much as both believe that the fleshly attitudes that are alien to the coming Kingdom will be substituted with what is appropriate to the human nature united with God. The sexual differentiation is appropriate for the unification in as much as they share the same nature but yet are different.

Conclusion and Pastoral Advices

Sexual orientations are not an ontological condition of the human nature. They do not define us as human beings, but they are part of our earthly existence. The desires that come with our sexual orientations can make our actions good or evil, but cannot substitute for our ontological existence as what we are, created in the image of God. Homosexual relations therefore carry both positive and negative elements as with any human relation. The first conclusion therefore comes as a positive affirmation of same-sex relations or as Cardinal Reinhard Marx, Roman Catholic archbishop of Munich, expressed it: "Take the case of two homosexuals who have been living together for thirty-five years and taking care of each other, even in the last phases of their lives. How can I say that this has no value?"³⁷ Certainly it has a value, and it is not just a matter of polite rhetoric, but an acceptance that sexual orientations can never replace the things that are intrinsically good in any relation between human beings.

In his address to the episcopal synod in Rome 2015, Cardinal Marx reaffirmed his position:

> We must make it clear that we do not only judge people according to their sexual orientation. . . . If a same-sex couple are faithful, care for one another and intend to stay together for life God won't say "All that doesn't interest me, I'm only interested in your sexual orientation."³⁸

We need as Orthodox to establish a firm pastoral care and interest for those who claim that they are homosexual—an interest that is not based on moral doctrines but on the Love and interest of Christ, an interest that does not replace the image of God with sexual orientation.

Secondly, salvation does not depend on our practical existence, but on the ontology of the indwelling of the love of Christ in what we essentially are as human beings. Faith in this perspective is the trust in the Lord that God loves us infinitely despite our liabilities and shortcomings. This trust is essential for our transformation into the likeness of God, which is rooted not in our actions but in the Love of God the Father through Christ in us. When we as Orthodox reduce our fellow human being to his or her sexual orientation, we not only deny the image of God, but also the indwelling of Christ in us. Through discrimination, rage, and intimidation, we jeopardize the trust in Christ that is more fundamental than our sexual desires and inclinations. To see Christ as primarily a homophobe neglects the fact that sexual orientations are just one aspect of this vale of tears, and in the end, homophobia would mean the final rejection of all humanity by Christ. Therefore, the second conclusion is that we have to allow homosexual members of our Church to remain as members of the Orthodox Church, as long as they are bound by their conscience and willingness to be in relation with Christ. I would even claim that the Eucharist is a necessity for them in order to be connected to their eschatological existence in Christ that goes beyond our sexual orientations, regardless if they are homosexual or heterosexual.

Finally, to follow the thinking of Maximus the Confessor, the economy of salvation is hidden in sexual differentiation. Marriage in an Eastern perspective is not just a matter of procreation, which the coronation clearly signifies, but as a sign of the communion that makes the indwelling of Christ active in our lives. Not as a separation of the sexes, but as an inclination toward communion. We are not created male and female, following Maximus, merely for multiplying our race, but Adam carried Eve within him as a continuous anamnesis of what he is and what God is: a communion transcending the borders of our earthly existence. Marriage begins in this vale of tears, but continues as a transformed existence toward communion with God. In marriage, the memory of the divine comes alive again in the midst of the Church, where the differentiation of male and female reminds us of Paradise where Adam and Eve constantly carried each other through the indwelling of God—an indwelling that will be present in everyone in the second coming of Christ. If we take away the sexual differentiation in marriage, marriage will be transformed into sexual orientation, and we would be back in the same dilemma as we have with the rage and discrimination we see against homosexuals. Therefore, as a third conclusion, we as Orthodox need to reaffirm sexual differentiation as constitutive for marriage, not through intimidation and hatred but through interest and care for the other. We certainly need more studies on the ontological aspect of marriage, but we also need to be careful not to mix the practical and the ontological aspects. Marriages are not defined by ecclesiastical courts, but in the mystery of Christ, revealed in the Church.

Notes

1. The author has been a permanent member of the dialogue since the beginning.

2. On a national level, relations are becoming more or less normalized again, but on an international level the Church of Sweden has problems with the Orthodox Churches, especially the Russian Orthodox Church, which still continues to ban all international relations with the Church of Sweden. The decision was taken December 27, 2005 and is available on the Department of External Affairs' Official website https://mospat.ru/archive/en/2005/12/28998/ (accessed November 21, 2016).

Within the Lutheran World Federation, the question has divided the churches, and on February 5, 2013, the Ethiopian Evangelical Church Mekane Yesus announced that it was severing its relationship with the Evangelical Lutheran Church of America and with the Church of Sweden, following their decision on same-sex marriage/partnership and ordination of same-sex ministers. "Lutheran Church in Ethiopia Severs Relationship with ELCA," *Evangelical Lutheran Church in America*, February 7, 2013, at http://www.elca.org/News-and-Events/7554 (accessed January 23, 2014). Since then efforts have been made to heal the breach.

3. The most important ecumenical initiative was taken by the Church of Sweden in its 2004 invitation to the various Christian churches in Sweden for a public hearing, published 2006 in English: *Love, Cohabitation and Marriage: Report from a Public Hearing September 6–9, 2004; The Theological Committee of the Church of Sweden*, translated by John Toy (Uppsala: Church of Sweden, 2006). The Orthodox contributions were given by Misha Jaksic and Michael Ellnemyr Hjälm. Misha Jaksic, "Marriage: Its Origin, Nature and Purpose," in *Love, Cohabitation and Marriage*, 210–14; Michael Ellnemyr, "The End of Suffering," in *Love, Cohabitation and Marriage*, 214–16.

4. Michael Ellnemyr, "Äktenskapet som grundperspektiv. En ortodox belysning av homosexualitet" [Marriage as a Foundational Perspective:

Reflections on Homosexuality], 141–49, in *Den hemlösa sexualiteten* (Libris: Örebro, 2001).

5. Michael Ellnmeyr, "The End of Suffering."

6. Misha Jaksic, "Marriage: Its Origin, Nature and Purpose."

7. The Sankt Ignatios foundation was founded by the Coptic Orthodox Church, the Syriac-Orthodox Church, the Serbian Orthodox Church, and the Romanian Orthodox Church in October 2012. Since then the foundation runs four seminaries in one college, and one academy.

8. *Ett brev i en folkets livsfråga. Till svenska kyrkans präster från dess biskopar* (Stockholm: Diakonistyrelsen, 1951).

9. The report from the investigation was published 1974. Holsten Fagerberg, ed., *De homosexuella och kyrkan* (Stockholm: Verbum, 1974).

10. The secretariat of the Council of Bishops issued a document for discussion as an appendix to its annual report for the first six months of 1995 (CsSkr 1995:3). Later the same year, the Council of Bishops issued a report on pastoral advices for blessing same-sex couples: *Pastorala råd angående förbön för dem som ingått partnerskap* [Pastoral advices on prayer over those who have engaged in [same-sex] partnership]. The pastoral advice was also part of the official reflection from the Liturgical Committee, 1997:7, *Välsignelseakt för homosexuella* [Blessing of homosexuals].

11. Paul Trossö made the petition to the Church Assembly in motion 1997:39 and asked the Church Board to decide on an order for the public blessing of same-sex couples. The Theological Committee then referred (Ln 1197:10) to its earlier statement (Ln 1995:18) where it had presented its general view on homosexual cohabitation, but which the Church Assembly had not dealt with. The Theological Committee had no doctrinal reservations against a public act.

12. The Council of Bishops amended its previous letter on pastoral advices 1999 with a new title: *Pastorala råd om förbön för dem som ingått registrerat partnerskap* [Pastoral advices on prayer over those who have engaged in [same-sex] registered partnership]. Relatives were allowed to be present but those present should be informed that it is not a public act of the Church, but falls under the pastoral responsibility of the individual priest.

13. Protocol of the Church Assembly 2005, September 27–30, October 25–28, §76; and protocol of the Church Board May 23–24, 2012, §60.

14. In 2004 all the major religious leaders except the Church of Sweden published an article with the headline: "'Homomarriage threatens the free churches.' Christian, Muslim, and Jewish religious leaders protest against the new legislation" (Dagens Nyheter, January 9, 2004).

15. Elisabeth Ohlson Wallin tells us her story in a radio interview with Martin Wicklin, August 20, 2015 (Sveriges Radio P1).

16. A more popular and tendentious story on the events around the exhibition can be found in Mikael Bergling and Fredrik Nejman, *Svenska skandaler. Fittstim, järnrör och doktorshattar. 117 avslöjanden som skakade Sverige* (Massolit Förlag, 2014).

17. Archbishop K. G. Hammar defended the exhibition *Ecce Homo*, while at the same time condemning the Mohammed caricatures on his website: www.svenskakyrkan/arkebiskopen (accessed November 16, 2006).

18. *Eskilstuna—Kuriren* May 7, 1999, "Påven sams med Hammar efter varmt möte i Rom."

19. *Dagens Nyheter*, February 5, 1999, "Ecce Homo orsakar träta i riksdagshuset."

20. Lina Kalmteg, *Svenska dagbladet,* June 16, 2010, "Nattvarden på Rosenbad"; and Gabriella Ahlström, *Ecce Homo—Berättelsen om en utställning* (Stockholm: Bonnier 1999).

21. Stina Klüft, *Aftonbladet*, 15 Mars, 1999, "Fotografen angreps med ruttna tomater."

22. Dionysios the Areopagite, *De Divinis Nominibus*, IV, 20 (Migne, vol. 4, col. 273).

23. St. Maximus the Confessor in *Librum de Divinis Nominibus Scholia* (Migne, vol. 4, col. 73); St. Athanasius the Great, *Against the Heathen*, Part I, §84; St. Basil the Great, *Hexaemeron*, Homily II, §4–5.

24. In his magnum opus, *On the Soul and Resurrection*, St. Gregory argues that the perfection of the Universe will take place in each human being individually. This implies that every human being will be the object of salvation.

25. In the seventeenth century, Patriarch Cyril Lucaris created a storm of opinions concerning salvation; see George P. Michaelides, "The Greek Orthodox Position on the Confession of Cyril Lucaris," in *Church History* 12, no. 2 (June 1943): 118–29.

26. See Turid Karlsen Seim, "A Superior Minority? The Problem of Men's Headship in Ephesians 5," in *Studia Theologica—Nordic Journal of Theology* 49, no. 1 (1999): 167–81.

27. See St. John Chrysostom, in *Eph. Cap. V. Hom. XX*, 62:135–47.

28. According to the mainstream tradition, Onesimus became bishop of Ephesus and is mentioned by St. Ignatius of Antioch in his letter to the Ephesians.

29. Basil of Seleucia, *Homily* 2, PG 85:41–48; John Chrysostom, *Genesis* PG 53:85D–130B; Procopius av Caesarea, PG 87:125–72.

30. Valerie A. Karras. "Patristic Views on the Ontology of Gender," in *Personhood: Orthodox Christianity and the Connections between Body, Mind, and Soul*, ed. John Chirban (Bergin and Garvey, 1996), 113–15.

31. Maximus the Confessor, *Epistulae* 2, PG 91, 397A.

32. Maximus the Confessor, *Ambiguum liber de variis difficibulus locis Sanctorum Dionysii Areopagitae et Gregorii Theologi* 41.

33. Maximus the Confessor, *Ambiguum liber de variis difficibulus locis Sanctorum Dionysii Areopagitae et Gregorii Theologi* 41; and *Quaestiones ad Thalassium* 48.

34. Maximus the Confessor, *Epistulae* 2, PG 91, 397A.

35. Maximus the Confessor, *Ambiguum liber de variis difficibulus locis Sanctorum Dionysii Areopagitae et Gregorii Theologi* 41, PG 91, 1325 B.C.

36. Maximus the Confessor, *Ambiguum liber de variis difficibulus locis Sanctorum Dionysii Areopagitae et Gregorii Theologi* 41, PG 91, 1309 A, 1325 B.C.; 42, PG 91, 1340 B.C.; *Quaestiones ad Thalassium* 21, 48.

37. "Divided bishops water down welcome to gays and the divorced," Cruxnow.com (accessed December 5, 2016).

38. http://ncronline.org/news/faith-parish/synods-purpose-underline-protection-importance-marriage-and-family-institution (accessed December 5, 2016).

CHAPTER

8

Homophobia in Orthodox Contexts

Sociopolitical Variables and Theological Strategies for Change

Andrii Krawchuk

Contrary to a monolithic image of Orthodox Christian reflection on homosexuality, theological positions elaborated in different sociopolitical contexts demonstrate significant diversity. After examining different Orthodox approaches in Egypt and the United States, we consider recent developments in the former USSR. The contextual variability of Orthodox responses to homosexuality indicates a capacity to recognize both the marginalizing, discriminatory nature of homophobic attitudes and the need for just alternatives. In this light, we propose three dialogical paths toward a more inclusive perspective and constructive change.

When Coptic patriarch Pope Shenouda III of Alexandria (1923–2012) addressed the subject of homosexuality in Egypt, he did so in a majority Muslim environment, where the persecuted Christian minority did not enjoy the protection of the state. The last thing the Coptic hierarch needed was to heighten the enmity that his community was already experiencing daily. Taken out of its context, Shenouda's categorical tract may appear extreme, even intolerant. But if one takes account of his complex sociopolitical situation, the effort of untangling his deepest convictions from the printed words is not at all straightforward. In contrast, Fr. Thomas Hopko (1939–2015), the eminent theologian and pastor of the Orthodox Church in America, worked in a pluralistic, democratic environment. Here, significant steps had been taken to protect the human rights of LGBTQ citizens, even as the struggle for full equality continued, and not without pushback. In his place and time, Fr. Hopko reflected courageously and in a sustained way on the need to balance fidelity to Orthodox tradition with sensitivity to human suffering and social justice.

In Putin's Russia on the eve of the Winter Olympics in Sochi (February 2014), legislators gained worldwide notoriety by introducing antigay laws that opened the door to acts of discrimination and physical abuse. The Russian Orthodox Church under Patriarch Kirill (Gundyaev) chose accommodation with the regime over prophetic critique. In neighboring Ukraine, where a popular uprising ousted the corrupt President Yanukovych and precipitated Russian land-grabs in Crimea and eastern Ukraine, an interreligious council supported democratization, but on the question of LGBTQ rights continued to march in lockstep with the former Soviet overlords. Despite a fundamental sociopolitical rift between Stalinist nostalgia in Russia and a faltering, yet determined quest for democratic values in Ukraine, the majority of Orthodox churches in both of the warring countries are surprisingly unanimous on one "traditional value." They have little to say about gay rights beyond theological condemnation and they remain silent on criminal acts of violence perpetrated against members of LGBTQ communities.[1] Heleen Zorgdrager of the Protestant Theological University in Amsterdam, who has visited and lectured in Ukraine for many years and who studies gender issues in relation to religious communities, has observed very perceptively:

> The churches foment aggression and violence towards sexual minorities and to women and men who do not conform to the assigned gender roles. They convey to gays and lesbians in their own religious communities the message that they are wrong, abnormal, and sinful. They have never publicly condemned violence committed against LGBT people. They increase the gap between the secular liberal part of society and the religiously-affiliated. They do not yet initiate a dialogue of equals, and reject those who are the topic of moral debate (gays, women who had an abortion, feminists) as full participants in the moral decision-making process.[2]

This troubling state of affairs merits serious critical scrutiny. First of all, it is troubling that the All-Ukrainian Council of Churches and Religious Organizations, which claims to represent over 90 percent of the religious organizations in the country, has opted in favor of discrimination over equal rights for members of LGBTQ communities. Second, if in many circumstances Orthodox ethical reflection has responded effectively to human rights issues, have Orthodox Churches resisted symphonic cooptation by oppressive regimes and their secular agendas of "traditional values?" And third, do Orthodox Churches in the post-Soviet space exercise prophetic, moral authority in defense of universal human rights? Such are the concerns that drove the present inquiry. They seek answers that cannot come from a priori theological or canonical conclusions. They require attentiveness to the lived moral experience, to the suffering and trauma of human beings, and to their hope for a spiritual vision that would embrace them in their humanity. Inasmuch as they go to the core of Christian identity, these ethical questions are also about the nature of the Church and its activity in the world.

Two Orthodox Approaches

For Coptic patriarch Pope Shenouda III, the issue of homosexuality was no mere canonical abstraction, but an urgent issue in his Church. When gays came to him requesting ordination to the priesthood and one of his bishops published a book in defense of homosexuality, he sounded the alarm and in 1993 published a lecture that laid down the law: Homosexuality is contrary to nature and condemned by scripture (Lev. 18:22, 20:13; Rom. 1:26–27; 1 Cor. 6:9; 1 Tim. 1:9–10).[3] He then weighed in with his own observations: Homosexuality contravenes health (the AIDS epidemic being a "self-evident" divine warning), manhood ("How can a person who is used as a woman be called a man?"), the good name of Christianity (other religions will not understand Christian spirituality if there is homosexuality in the Church and the Church is not clear whether it is wrong or right), and the sacrament of marriage. Throughout Shenouda's tract, homosexuality is treated as a sinful sexual activity. He views it in terms of what he calls "the action of sin," rather than as a type of relationship. As for any human rights concerns, he maintains that the Church can only recognize the right of homosexuals to be led to repentance.[4]

In this instance of Orthodox reflection on homosexuality, the focus is on sinful actions and the "sinners" who engage in them. The entire discourse is shaped by an a priori moral judgment with no room, or any perceived need, to appreciate homosexuality outside the limits of traditional normativity, or to consider its personal dimension in responsible, loving relationships. Homosexuals are set up as a class apart from the rest of humanity—marginalized, demonized, and stripped of their human rights. The patriarch in effect expressed religious convictions that persist in our time. Even as alternative Orthodox paths are sought and studied, it is important to take full account of such views. In order to be effective, the quest for change must understand the obstacles that stand in the way.

Fr. Thomas Hopko took a very different approach in his book *Christian Faith and Same-Sex Attraction*. His goal was to broaden the discussion by acknowledging same-sex attraction as not limited only to homosexuals, by examining how it relates to Christian faith and love, and by outlining practical guidelines for pastoral work. Based on his pastoral experience, Hopko demonstrated how Orthodox moral restrictions on sexual behavior apply equally to heterosexual and homosexual relationships. Looking outside of the usual normative judgments of fallen humanity and focusing instead on the goodness of creation, he formulated a number of ground-breaking insights, which may be summarized as follows:

> 1. *Homosexual love is a divine gift*: All human sexual activity in its diverse manifestations, heterosexual or homosexual, is "a God-given gift intended to be an expression of and a participation in humanity's communion with God, who is love."[5] As a pastor, Hopko affirms that "same-sex love, when properly experienced and purely expressed, is always God's sacred gift. Such love is a necessary, normal, and natural part of God's *essential goodwill* for humanity."[6]
> 2. *Godly love is written in hearts*: Beyond formal marriage ceremonies and blessings, something more profound is at work in the authentic union of two human beings. Even unmarried men and women may have "a truly divine union of sexual love in charity, eros, friendship, and affection," a union "truly of God because it is an expression of love that accords with God's law, which is "written in their hearts" (Rom. 2:12–16; 1 John 4:7–21).[7] Conversely, no legal or sacramental union is in itself a guarantee of godly love.[8]
> 3. *Loving desires between people of the same sex are normal*: "According to Orthodox Christianity, having loving desires for people of one's own sex is not at all sinful; it is perfectly natural, normal, and necessary."[9] It is only when such desires become lustful and self-centered that a moral problem arises. Still operating within an ethical

framework that condemns specific acts as inherently evil, Hopko affirms that same-sex desires are good.

4. *It is possible for homosexual acts to have authentic elements of godly love*: Hopko rejects the idea that such activities "are totally devoid of authentic elements of godly love. If such were the case, such actions would be completely demonic and totally destructive, which they obviously, and by God's grace and mercy, are not."[10] On logical grounds, Hopko calls into question a priori theological condemnations of homosexual acts.

5. *All are called to sanctity*: "The way of sanctity for heterosexuals and homosexuals alike includes the way in which they deal with the effects of ancestral and generational sin in their lives, as well as with all the sins that have been committed against them from their earliest days on earth, and even from before they were born."[11] This suggests a much broader Orthodox perspective. Rather than making sharp distinctions between particular classes of sinners and their sins, Hopko draws attention to the universal call to sanctity. All human beings are on the same ethical journey together.

Parting ways with the cumbersome legacy of normative judgments and condemnations, Hopko recovers from scripture and tradition the possibility of compassion. He reframes the discussion of homosexuality from the narrow image of an abhorrent aberration that serves to justify marginalization and discrimination, to a focus on persons who share the dignity, fallibility, and the eschatological hope of all humanity. Same-sex attraction is not reduced to a contravention of codes of conduct, but is understood in the larger setting of human sexuality in its diverse expressions. The shift here is away from the traditional discourse of condemnation and an exclusionary language of fallen humanity. Instead, the goodness of creation and salvific deification are affirmed as the operative and constructive guiding principles. Hopko's analogical approach identifies fundamental similarities between two types of human relationship and yields profound insights: The ideal of godly love applies equally to all human sexual relationships, and the betrayal of godly love is not limited only to one type of human relationship. His sensitive pastoral reflection humanizes the discussion, appreciates the suffering of Christians marginalized by fellow Christians, and rejects sanctimonious, holier-than-thou posturing.

These two elaborations give an indication of the range of Orthodox attitudes toward homosexuality. While the respective social and political contexts played a role, they did not determine the content of the response. Rather, each perspective was elaborated through a creative negotiation of tradition in conversation with practical, contextual concerns.

The Challenge of Religious Homophobia in Russia and Ukraine

In 2013, two decades after Russia had decriminalized homosexuality, its parliament passed anti–gay propaganda legislation, raising concerns that this was a return to state-sanctioned homophobia.[12] The reform not only banned perceived instances of "sexual propaganda." In the public space, it unleashed targeted campaigns of intimidation and persecution against members of sexual minorities. The documentary film *Hunted in Russia* records how vigilante groups like "Occupy Paedophilia" entrap unsuspecting gay victims, abduct and torment them, then post the humiliations on the internet.[13]

Behind the new policy were legislators like the author of the 2013 law, politician Vitaly Milonov, whose bombastic pronouncements presumed to make valid theological and historical claims. He considered homosexuality a "spiritual disease coming from some countries. . . . Do they really understand that this is sodomy? Do they really know the history—that all empires ended with this sin?"[14] Such crude reasoning revealed much about how Russian political history was being read at the highest levels in order to signal imminent threats to the state and about how, as in World War II, the Russian Orthodox Church was again being mobilized to provide unwavering support for sacred causes identified by the Kremlin.

The Church lost no time in embracing the new law. In the absence of sound theological reasoning, two features of that support stood out. The first was a kind of pop psychology purporting to advance a tenable diagnosis. In the words of Russian Orthodox pastor Fr. Sergei Rybko, "Even cattle don't engage in this. I just consider them spiritually and morally ill. Something is not right there [pointing to his head]."[15] The second was the unfounded assumption that there is a link between homosexuality and pedophilia. Again, Fr. Sergei Rybko voiced a principle that was assimilated from external sources, and that had no basis in Orthodox tradition: "These things are interconnected. Where gays are allowed, pedophilia will soon flourish. Permitted evil gives rise to more evil. Pedophiles, gays, and people like this are basically serving the Devil."[16]

Russia's new legislative and social environment soon had repercussions on the international stage. A month after the Sochi Olympics in February 2014, where Russia's antigay laws had attracted international protest, Russian military forces invaded and annexed Crimea, then in August invaded the Donbas region in eastern Ukraine. Although the motivations behind the current Russian-Ukrainian conflict have been the subject of scholarly analysis and a separate propaganda war, their connection to protests in Kyiv is undisputed. Citizens were enraged when President Victor Yanukovych failed to sign a promised trade deal with Europe and instead began to look toward Russia. Protesters at the central square in the capital (the Maidan, or Euromaidan) argued that the only acceptable path for Ukraine was with Europe. A trade deal was seen as the first step toward a deeper relationship with democratic states, and the alternative—subservience to Russia—was rejected as a regression to the Soviet order. Ukraine's religious communities were represented in the protests by clerics, who addressed the people and provided on-site spiritual services. In his speech to the protesters, Fr. Andrei Dudchenko of the Ukrainian Orthodox Church of the Moscow Patriarchate enumerated the core values of truth, justice, freedom, and the worth of every individual that were at the heart of Ukraine's aspirations.[17]

Yet in the preceding decade, Ukraine's interreligious body, the All-Ukrainian Council of Churches and Religious Organizations, had begun to carve out a significant exception to European human rights norms. In a discourse that affirmed "traditional values," they rejected gay rights and later added abortion and euthanasia to the mix.[18] Catholics on the Council, Roman and Eastern alike, did not waver from their "traditional" stance even after July 29, 2013, when Pope Francis famously responded to a question about homosexuality by asking, "Who am I to judge?" It was with a contrary, judgmental position that religious leaders joined Ukrainian citizens at the Euromaidan, supporting their call for integration with Europe and endorsing many Western values, but drawing the line on gay rights.[19] The pro-Russian religious opposition in Ukraine seized the opportunity to reinforce their polemics against Euro-integration with alarmist slogans of "Eurosodom" and "Gayropa."

Religious rivals in the Russia-Ukraine conflict thus became allies in opposing the European model of gay rights. Regardless of contrasting geopolitical orientations, pro-European and pro-Soviet, their shared "traditional values" remained intact. In the war of words over Ukraine's sovereignty and its future course, homophobia emerged as a powerful tool for mobilizing pro-Russian sentiments in Ukraine. Inserted into the religious discourse, it transcended political differences and co-opted unwitting allies among those who believed they were resisting Russian influence.[20] As a strategic ploy to orchestrate emotions and manipulate minds, it was a master stroke. But for the prospects of civil society and the emergence of a robust theology it constituted a real threat.

On February 24, 2022 Russia invaded Ukraine, and Orthodox Patriarch Kirill justified that military aggression. Without evidence, he alleged that people were being suppressed and exterminated in eastern Ukraine. The object of the alleged suppression was an imagined resistance in Donbas to an imagined imposition by force of gay pride parades.[21] The patriarch then wove his weaponized homophobia into an emphatic justification of Russia's war crimes and violation of international norms. He argued that states have the legitimate right to use force "coercing other countries, if they see a threat in them, to see that the threat is removed."[22] With preposterous claims and pseudo-theology, the patriarch aided and abetted Putin, and became complicit in the war crimes.[23]

Constructive Dialogical Proposals

We now propose three dialogical themes that may guide a constructive Orthodox theological reassessment of homosexuality. An epistemological strategy is needed to break through the impasse of conflicting truth claims and to overcome resistance to dialogue. An empathic dimension recovered from pastoral practice may ground ethical discourse in lived experience and unshackle it from juridical-canonical normativity. And an ecumenical dimension can heed interchurch voices and enable internal metanoia and reform: learning from the wisdom and experience of other Christian communities and applying new skills and knowledge to embrace the marginalized.

Breaking through Conflicting Truth Claims

The modern paradigm shift toward human rights, equality, and dignity encounters resistance and cognitive dissonance whenever it appears to defy "traditional values." All too often, the reflex is an entrenchment of exclusivist thinking and polarization. The very idea of dialogue becomes unbearable, traditional values are distorted and weaponized, and the notion of truth is compressed to justify one position over another. This pattern corresponds very closely to the definition of fundamentalism proposed by Rabbi Jonathan Sacks: "the attempt to impose a single truth on a plural world."[24]

Thomas Hopko makes a valuable contribution toward recovering the possibility of dialogue as an antidote to radical theological polarization. He distinguishes between the godly love connected with "the law of the Spirit of Life," and the self-love that submits to the "law of sin and death" and contravenes love of God and neighbor.[25] In the fallen world, Christianity itself is vulnerable to manipulation by people who espouse its values but consider themselves superior to others. Truths of the faith are thus distorted and subordinated to a delusion of supremacy that disconnects people from fellowship with others and with God:

> They do not allow themselves even to consider that they may, in fact, be mistaken about one or another, or even all, of their convictions. As such, they are never in dialogue. They never listen. They never converse. They are never at peace in themselves or with others. They are always in a crusade and a war that they must win at all costs. And it is exactly *they*, and not God, who must win it.[26]

In a conflict of theological interpretations, the opposition of godly and egoistic love, or of dialogue and monologue, is a powerful criterion for determining whose truth claims are consistent with authentic Christianity. It also reliably identifies the worst possible dialogue partner: one who has no interest in dialogue and who is no partner at all. When logical, reasoned argument only meets with seemingly logical, reasoned, self-righteous counterargument, no preponderance of evidence or coherent explanation will make any difference. The search for a meaningful breakthrough must seek other avenues.

A constructive strategy for dealing with conflicting truth claims would also include a debunking of myths, such as that of a causal link between homosexuality and pedophilia.[27] The equation of homosexuals with sex offenders, murderers, and thieves also needs to be challenged as unlawful and dangerous. Russia's 2013 law did not criminalize homosexuality but only its propaganda. But unregulated, the new situation quickly became a breeding-ground for a mob mentality. Some citizens concluded that they had a sacred right and authority to pronounce historical and theological "truths," and arbitrarily to deprive other citizens of fundamental rights. The resulting free-for-all was constructive neither for civil society, nor for sound theology.

An effective remedy would recognize that such deep-rooted, exclusivist convictions ignore the larger context. Ekaterina, a schoolteacher in Russia, offered a perceptive reading of the bigger picture that connected social attitudes with the prevailing economic challenges:

> Right now, it suits the state and the regime to organize this witch-hunt because our economic situation, our pensions, our salaries, our health care, and our education are all getting worse. *Understandably, people need someone to blame.* To stop people from focusing their anger on the authorities the regime is igniting and maintaining this conflict and hatred. They are making people fight amongst themselves.[28]

Behind the disturbing images of homophobia and distorted theology on the surface of social life in Russia, we may thus uncover a deeper truth: a socioeconomic crisis and deliberate scapegoating, orchestrated and fueled by the state. In this situation, homophobia is an instrument for advancing political interests, and it is propped up by a subservient, uncritical religious discourse.

The categorical turn of theology was evident in the Russian Orthodox Church's severance of ecumenical ties with the Episcopal Church of America (2003), the Lutheran Church of Sweden (2005), and the Evangelical Lutheran Church of Denmark (2012) over gay ordination and same-sex marriages. For Heleen Zorgdrager, the subsequent Russian Orthodox decision to cease recognizing baptisms performed by the latter two Churches elevated an ethical difference of opinion to a claim of absolute theological truth. Explaining their decisions, Russian Orthodox officials resorted to a "hands-tied" trope that dispenses with any need for sound reasoning: "We have no right to allow even a particle of agreement with their position, which we consider to be profoundly antichristian and blasphemous."[29]

Although the resulting social environment resists educational strategies and sensitivity toward LGBTQ communities, it may be possible to subject homophobia to critical analysis and critique in the public sphere. In the absence of political will, that will likely be an uphill struggle. Along with populist governments and traditional-values rhetoric, a formidable network of Western religious-right groups is also at work in Eastern Europe, inciting gender-based hatred and violence.[30] Nevertheless, the Russian Orthodox Church retains its voice, social responsibility, and the intellectual and ethical resources to take up the task. The Church is free to act on its own authority, without passively relying on external, political sources to tell it what the Orthodox tradition is. The Church is under no scriptural or traditional requirement to endorse every new state policy; or to judge an entire sector of society as if they were criminals; or to remain silent as innocent citizens are abused and killed; or to allow free rein to populist, homophobic fanatics in its ranks; or to subscribe to their improvisations of "traditional values."[31] Against such abuses, the Church *can* decide to uphold its authentic tradition as a dynamic, living reality.

Inasmuch as the ethical challenges of responsible, loving sexuality are faced equally by all human beings, Hopko makes the bold suggestion that homosexuals have a privileged appreciation of the true nature of moral evil in human life. Whether as a result of their experience of persecution or by virtue of their commitment to equal rights and dignity, homosexuals may possess a special insight into the spiritual conflict between good and evil:

> They, perhaps more than all others today, are blessed to bear witness to the truth that humanity's enemy is everywhere and always the same for everyone. Humanity's enemy is the self-love, self-will, self-affirmation, and self-delusion that dominate human beings and life in this corrupted and disordered world, which lies in the power of evil. . . . It is, ultimately, the "human gospel," the "gospel according to man" of those who worship "the god of this age" that they themselves have made, or that others have inflicted upon them in place of the true and living God who made them.[32]

Both as institution and as community, the Church has everything to gain from a sensitive approach that heeds the voices of the oppressed.

Drawing Theological Insight from Pastoral Ministry

Another resource for accessing empathy and integrating it into an inclusive theological vision is pastoral practice. Inspired by the parable of the Good Samaritan, which answers the question "Who is my neighbor?," the pastoral mandate is scriptural, and its principal guideline is compassion for all without discrimination. No "other," whether designated an enemy, or an outcast, or a sinner, is excluded from the pastoral reach of Christian charity. Again, critical discernment may help to determine whether a particular pastoral theology and practice is caring and compassionate, or whether it has assumed an exclusivist posture, reserving salvific ministry only for some and not for others. For Thomas Hopko, the responsibilities of Orthodox pastors in their spiritual conversations with homosexuals begin with a proper formation and a dialogical understanding of Christian spiritual counsel:

> For persons with same-sex attractions in our time, given all that is now occurring in our gravely disordered world, Orthodox Christian pastoral care requires extraordinary discernment, patience, compassion, and love. It calls for an extraordinary capacity to listen and hear, to see and understand, to say true things with love, and to suffer patiently, often in painful, prayerful, hopeful silence. It demands a willingness on the part of pastors, parents, counselors, and friends not simply to "go the extra mile" with their friends and relatives with same-sex attractions, but to carry on with them until the end, no matter what. Such pastoral care requires being constantly tested concerning one's own faith and love, one's refusal to condemn others, and one's readiness to give one's life so that others may live.[33]

In any context, including more "progressive" societies, Orthodox Christian pastoral work in relation to homosexuals faces formidable challenges—prevailing social stereotypes, internalized homophobia, discriminatory habits, scapegoating, and their cumulative traumatizing effects—all of which require special training and skills. The situation is all the more acute when the Church is confronted by social, political, and psychological impediments to its pastoral ministry and to the development of a strong, theological and spiritual reflection. In addition to training, effective pastoral care for Orthodox Christians with same-sex attractions requires a particular disposition and distinctive quality of pastors who are profoundly in tune with their Christian identity:

> Those exercising Christian pastoral care must love the people who come to them with this issue. They must identify with them. They must respect them. They must listen to them. They must put themselves in their place. They must feel the other's pain and suffering more than they do their own. They must advocate for them before God. They must be ready, if called, even to give their life for them.[34]

From decades of experience in the pastoral sphere, Hopko has identified a valuable starting point for a sensitive, caring approach by priests, who are prepared to do their work as counselors and not judges.[35]

Ecumenical Resources for a Critique of Gender Stereotypes

The recent studies of patristic trinitarian thought by Cambridge University professor Sarah Coakley are relevant to Orthodox discussions of sexuality and gender. An Anglican priest who rejects the social, or "relational," notions of the Trinity as too "tritheistic-tending" in favor of a more Western, "unity" model,[36] she advances an approach to gender that resonates with Thomas Hopko's empathic approach. Particularly noteworthy are her commitment to the thorough study and retrieval of the Fathers, her affirmation (following Gregory of Nyssa) of God's transcendence of gender categories and of the nonultimacy of human gender, and her Christian theology of gender as part of fallen creation living in the hope of redemption.[37] In addition, the following key elements have been noted in Coakley's "théologie totale" method of inquiry: opening up a radical attention to the "other";[38] "destabilizing settled presumptions" to move theologians beyond singular attempts at empathy;[39] attending to the gendered, socially located ways doctrine is constructed;[40] and attending to "social locations and worldly power—or powerlessness."[41] These elements converge with and reinforce Hopko's vision of a sensitive, socially just Orthodox approach that attends to the social and religious outcast, breaks through the slogans of pseudotheology, calls into question the gender bias often embedded in theological language, and stands up with courage in defense of the marginalized and oppressed.

Coakley finds in Gregory's description of the contemplative ascent of the soul an intriguing reflection relating to gender. In addition to his doctrinal works on the Trinity, Gregory elaborated a "trinitarian spirituality of human transformation." In its ascent to God, the mind enters a state of noetic darkness, and the physical senses are overtaken by the spiritual senses. The resulting "deep, receptive sensitivity" represents a symbolic gender reversal: "What has up to now been the spiritual quest of an ardent 'youth' going courting for Sophia becomes here conversely the 'more mature character of the bride, who actively seeks, yet is still more open to receive, the divine bridegroom.'"[42] Gregory's key mystical insights in connection with the Trinity are that "gender stereotypes must be reversed, undermined, and transcended" if the soul is to be united intimately with God, and that the language of sexuality and gender is no arbitrary rhetorical flourish, but is integral to the "epistemological deepening" that he describes.[43] These ideas have an enduring relevance to the goal of human transformation even today:

> Gregory's approach demonstrates how unwise it is to dislocate trinitarian debates from the matrix of human transformation that is the Trinity's very point of intersection with our lives. If Gregory is right, moreover, such transformation is unthinkable without profound, even alarming, shifts in our gender perceptions, shifts which have bearing as much on our thinking about God as on our understanding of ourselves.[44]

Coakley attends to the contemplative dimension of trinitarian theology and points toward a spirituality with transformative potential for persons and communities. Her account of the dialogical dimension of prayer as a matter of listening, of "being grasped, of the Spirit's simultaneous erasure of human idolatry and subtle reconstitution of human selfhood in God," evokes a spiritual healing that can open the way to alternative modes of authentic Christian personhood and community.[45]

Adrian Thatcher, an Anglican theologian at the University of Exeter, also sees the doctrine of the Trinity as having profound ethical relevance to Christian theological reflection on gender and human sexuality. Unlike Coakley, he applies a social perspective to formulate an inclusive, communitarian ethos: "The life of the Trinity is a communion or community where difference does not need to be overcome by elimination, domination, repression, or oppression, for each person is already 'in' the other, in the one Life that pours itself out in self-giving Love."[46] The harmonious dynamic of the trinitarian life sets a high standard for a just social order, beyond the impulses to segregate and discriminate: "There is no better way of imitating or embodying the divine Persons than by the equal and reciprocal treatment of human persons."[47]

Concluding Remarks

After examining two types of Orthodox approach to homosexuality, we considered the context of Russia and Ukraine, where same-sex opposition has been mobilized in political and religious discourses to advance a pro-Russian, anti-European agenda. The attachment of homophobic attitudes to cultural identity and "traditional values" poses serious challenges to the Orthodox Church in its efforts to educate minds and liberate hearts from sexist and demagogic aggression. We then explored three themes, rooted in Orthodox thought, that may inform a more robust appropriation of tradition and a more receptive Christian engagement with homosexual individuals and communities today. The common thread running through the three themes is that of a dialogue enabled by three elements: an inclusive approach to truth, an empathic approach to pastoral work, and an ecumenical approach to theology and gender. Dialogical engagement with the other can be the basis for an alternative ecclesial ethos, better equipped to respond to same-sex relationships than one that is enmeshed in patterns of isolation, aggression, the monopolization of truth, and the pursuit of power.

In Eastern Europe today, homophobia has become the standard currency of far right and ultranationalist agendas. In addition to fueling irrational fears over European integration, "traditional values" are coopted to mobilize opposition to international human rights instruments, such as the Istanbul Convention.[48] What is needed from the Orthodox Church is a liberating pedagogy that would awaken a new theological consciousness, enable social healing, and inspire constructive, civil debate. As the populist patterns of mob violence, hate-mongering, scapegoating, and political manipulation run their course, it is incumbent upon the Church to reclaim its authentic tradition from those who would hijack it, to hear the voices of the marginalized and curb those who seek only confrontation, and to take an unequivocal stand for civil rights and justice for all without discrimination. A significant first step would be to cease playing the innocent bystander and to embark on the path of Christ, who subverts "traditional values" through prophetic, counter-cultural outreach to the marginalized. This echoes a sentiment expressed in the open letter to Coptic Pope Tawadros, which proposed two further steps toward constructive change: Church leaders should seek education that can enable them to engage with alternative views on sexuality; and Church leadership should acknowledge its role in perpetuating prejudice and violence against members of the LGBTQI+ community and make amends. The document's signatories, straight and queer Copts, articulated their thoughts respectfully and in the hope that their call would be heard "with open minds and hearts so that we may all begin to heal."[49]

Notes

1. Since 2006, the All-Ukrainian Council of Churches and Religious Organizations issued a series of condemnations of same-sex relations. Andrii Krawchuk, "Constructing Interreligious Consensus in the Post-Soviet Space: The Ukrainian Council of Churches and Religious Organizations," in *Eastern Orthodox Encounters of Identity and Otherness: Values, Reflection, Dialogue*, ed. Andrii Krawchuk and Thomas Bremer (New York: Palgrave Macmillan, 2014), 286–87.

2. Heleen Zorgdrager, "Gender Issues in the Battle-Zone: The Narrative of 'Traditional Values' as Both Unifying and Confrontational" (draft paper presented at the BASEES Conference, University of Cambridge, U.K., April 2–4, 2016), 6.

3. His Holiness Pope Shenouda III, *The Ordination of Women and Homosexuality: Two Lectures* (London: Coptic Orthodox Publishers Association, 1993), 9–13.

4. Pope Shenouda III, *The Ordination of Women and Homosexuality*, 14–15. Shenouda's position that same-sex marriage has no basis in scripture or in Christian tradition is upheld by his successor, Pope Tawadros II. "'It's sin': Coptic Pope Tawadros II weighs in on same-sex marriage amid historic Australian visit," *SBS News* (August 30, 2017): https://www.sbs.com.au/news/it-s-sin-coptic-pope-tawadros-ii-weighs-in-on-same-sex-marriage-amid-historic-australian-visit/.

In November 2019, Pope Tawadros returned to the matter of homosexuality at a meeting of his Synodal Committee for Mental Health and Anti-Addiction. This elicited an open letter from Copts who took issue with the framing of homosexuality as a mental illness. "Open Statement against the Coptic Church's Position on the LGBTQI+ Community by Progressive Copts," *Orthodoxy in Dialogue* (January 16, 2020): https://orthodoxyindialogue.com/2020/01/16/open-statement-against-the-coptic-churchs-position-on-the-lgbtqi-community-by-progressive-copts/.

5. Thomas Hopko, *Christian Faith and Same-Sex Attraction* (Ben Lomond, Calif.: Conciliar Press, 2006), 21–22.

6. Hopko, *Christian Faith and Same-Sex Attraction*, 45.

7. Hopko, *Christian Faith and Same-Sex Attraction*, 26–27.

8. "Many men and women wed in Orthodox churches do not believe what is prayed and signified in the sacrament, nor struggle to actualize it in their daily lives." Hopko, *Christian Faith and Same-Sex Attraction*, 26. See also: "Sexual intercourse between faithfully committed men and women may be expressive of divine love, but it also may not be." Hopko, *Christian Faith and Same-Sex Attraction*, 44.

9. Hopko, *Christian Faith and Same-Sex Attraction*, 34.
10. Hopko, *Christian Faith and Same-Sex Attraction*, 25–26.
11. Hopko, *Christian Faith and Same-Sex Attraction*, 48.
12. There were earlier signs that such legislative reform was coming. Starting in 2009, Russia lobbied the United Nations Human Rights Council to recognize "traditional values" as a legitimate consideration in the formulation and implementation of human rights norms. The campaign succeeded three years later, when the Council adopted a resolution on "traditional values." Many considered it a threat to universal human values. Zorgdrager, "Gender Issues," 3.

Russia's revocation of antihomosexual legislation in 1993 under President Boris Yeltsin has been attributed to pressure connected with Russia's bid for a place in the Council of Europe. "Russia: Update on the Treatment of Homosexuals," Immigration and Refugee Board of Canada (February 29, 2000): refworld.org/docid/3ae6ad788c.html.

13. *Hunted in Russia,* Channel 4 documentary on homophobic violence, Director: Ben Steele, 2014. Disturbing content. www.youtube.com/watch?v=K-dDd4dtOFM.

14. *Being Gay in Russia*, CBC Documentary aired January 27, 2014, Correspondent: Nahlah Ayed. At 3:56 and 7:44. http://www.cbc.ca/news/thenational/being-gay-in-russia-1.2513518.

15. *Hunted in Russia,* at 13:57.
16. *Hunted in Russia,* at 14:41.
17. "Священик УПЦ (МП) зі сцени Євромайдану розповів про позицію митрополита Володимира та прочитав звернення до людей доброї волі," *Relihiia v Ukraini* (December 14, 2013): religion.in.ua/news/ukrainian_news/24288-svyashhenik-upc-mp-zi-sceni-yevromajdanu-rozpoviv-pro-poziciyu-mitropolita-volodimira-ta-prochitav-zvernennya-do-lyudej-dobroyi-voli.html.

18. On the Council's opposition to same-sex marriage and homosexuality, four documents were issued: (1) "Open Letter to the Parliament of Ukraine regarding Efforts to Legalize So-called Same-Sex Marriages" (November 24, 2006), in *The Ukrainian Council of Churches and Religious Organizations, 1996–2007: Collected Official Documents*, Doc. no. 304 (Kyiv: Sekretariat Vseukrains'koi Rady Tserkov i Relihiinykh Orhanizatsii, 2007), 503–5; (2) "Declaration of Opposition to the Phenomenon of Homosexuality and Efforts to Legalize So-Called Same-Sex Marriages" (May 15, 2007), in *The Ukrainian Council of Churches and Religious Organizations, 1996–2007*, Doc. no. 316, 514–16; (3) "Letter to President Viktor Yanukovych against Amoral Initiatives at the Parliamentary Assembly of the Council of Europe" (April 19, 2010): vrciro.org.ua; and (4) "Resolution of the Round Table on 'Religion-State Dialogue in the Context of the European System of Values,'" (December 20, 2010): vrciro.org.ua.

For the arguments against abortion and euthanasia, see: "Proposals for Amendments to the Constitution of Ukraine"; Appendix #2 to "Memorandum to President Viktor Yanukovych" (April 21, 2011): vrciro.org.ua; and "Letter to President János Áder of Hungary" (July 13, 2012): vrciro.org.ua.

19. Since the Maidan, pro-Europe religious leaders in Ukraine, especially Catholics, have again become more assertive and public in their critique of gay rights. See Zorgdrager, "Gender Issues."

20. Heleen Zorgdrager cites Ukrainian Greek Catholic Archbishop Major Shevchuk, who referred to "the illusion that Europeanness means liberation from the rules of morality and church presence in the public discourse," and she observes that it is something that could have been said by the Moscow patriarch. Zorgdrager, "Gender Issues," 5.

21. "In Donbas there is a fundamental rejection of the so-called values that are being put forward today by those who claim global authority. Today there is such a test of loyalty to that authority, a kind of entry pass into that 'happy' world of excessive consumption and of visible 'freedom.' Do you know what this test is? . . . —it's a gay pride parade. . . . Gay pride parades are designed to demonstrate that sin is one of the variations of human behavior. . . . We know how people resist these demands and how their resistance is suppressed by force. This means imposing by force a sin condemned by God's law, that is, imposing by force the denial of God and His truth." "Патриаршая проповедь в Неделю сыропустную после Литургии в Храме Христа Спасителя," *Russkaia Pravoslavnaia Tserkov* (марта 6, 2022): http://www.patriarchia.ru/db/text/5906442.html?fbclid=IwAR364NBBGQmorRmudkkzXlVaceABe6WQtuFJ-vq58lWF DEJXc9QiGKgRdwQ.

22. "Патриаршая проповедь в среду первой седмицы Великого поста после Литургии Преждеосвященных Даров в Храме Христа Спасителя," *Russkaia Pravoslavnaia Tserkov* (March 9, 2022): http://www.patriarchia.ru/db/text/5907484.html.

23. We discuss these developments and their implications in a forthcoming study.

24. Cited in Florin Buhuceanu, *Traditional Values, Religion and LGBT Rights in Eastern Europe*, European Forum of LGBT Christian Groups (October 22, 2014), 9: https://www.lgbtchristians.eu/funded-projects/spirit-of-human-rights/148-traditional-values-religion-and-lgbt-rights-in-eastern-europe.

25. Hopko, *Christian Faith and Same-Sex Attraction*, 16.

26. Hopko, *Christian Faith and Same-Sex Attraction*, 96–97.

27. Russian Orthodox priest Fr. Sergei Rybko sees gay rights not as a human rights issue but as a slippery slope toward a spiritual and social catastrophe: "With all these gay parades, gay clubs, and publications, they've started to plant the idea in young people's minds that all this is normal—that they are just a bit

different, that's all. Well, excuse me, in that case pedophiles and sex offenders are 'just different' too, murderers and thieves are 'just different.' So we should also give them freedom to do what they want." See *Hunted in Russia,* at: 13:57.

28. *Hunted in Russia,* at: 38:33. Emphasis mine.

29. Rob Moll, "Russian Orthodox Church Cuts Ties with Episcopal Church," *Christianity Today* (November 1, 2003): christianitytoday.com/ct/2003 /novemberweb-only/11-17-23.0.html and "Orthodoxy Disallows DK baptisms," *Politiken.DK* (September 10, 2012): politiken.dk/newsinenglish/ECE1758334/ orthodoxy-disallows-dk-baptisms/. Cited in Heleen Zorgdrager, "Homosexuality and Hypermasculinity in the Public Discourse of the Russian Orthodox Church: An Affect Theoretical Approach," *International Journal of Philosophy and Theology* 74, no. 3 (2013): 215–16.

30. The 2014 report of the European Forum of LGBT Christian Groups profiles several such groups, including the Family Research Council, the World Congress of Families, the Alliance Defending Freedom, and the European Center for Law and Justice. Buhuceanu, *Traditional Values, Religion and LGBT rights,* 26–31.

31. Just as the involvement of Western religious-right groups should not be underestimated, neither should the free agency of the Russian Orthodox Church, even in Putin's Russia. "In a 2009 agreement with Putin's ruling United Russia party, the country's top Orthodox official, Patriarch Kirill, won the right to review (and suggest changes to) any legislation being considered by the Duma. Since then, both Putin and Patriarch Kirill have stated explicitly and repeatedly that they believe in collaboration between church and state—a partnership that is helping to drive the government's campaign against homosexuality." Hannah Levintova, "How US Evangelicals Helped Create Russia's Anti-Gay Movement," *Mother Jones* (February 21, 2014): https://www.motherjones.com /politics/2014/02/world-congress-families-russia-gay-rights/.

32. Gal. 1:11; 2Cor. 4:4. Cited in Hopko, *Christian Faith and Same-Sex Attraction,* 124.

33. Hopko, *Christian Faith and Same-Sex Attraction,* 112.

34. Hopko, *Christian Faith and Same-Sex Attraction,* 117.

35. On this, see especially the section "Same-Sex Attraction and Pastoral Care," in Hopko, *Christian Faith and Same-Sex Attraction,* 117–22.

36. Sarah Coakley, "'Persons' in the 'Social' Doctrine of the Trinity: Current Analytic Discussion and 'Cappadocian' Theology," in her *Powers and Submissions. Spirituality, Philosophy and Gender* (London: Blackwell, 2002), 109–29.

37. Sarah Coakley, *God, Sexuality, and the Self: An Essay "On the Trinity,"* (Cambridge: Cambridge University Press, 2013), 53–54.

38. Coakley, *God, Sexuality, and the Self,* 43.

39. Coakley, *God, Sexuality, and the Self,* 48.

40. Coakley, *God, Sexuality, and the Self,* 59–60.

41. Coakley, *God, Sexuality, and the Self,* 59–60. Cited in Eileen R. Campbell-Reed, "Feminism and Fieldwork: Partners in the Work of Systematic Theology," *Perspectives in Religious Studies* 41, no. 4 (Winter 2014): 423. On power, see also Angela Yarber's insistence, to Coakley's notion of a totalizing theology that is personal and political, that it must also include "the voices of the sexually oppressed and marginalized." Angela Yarber, "Queering Iconography, Queering Trinity," *Perspectives in Religious Studies* 41, no. 4 (Winter 2014), 422.

42. Coakley, "Persons," 127.

43. Coakley, "Persons," 128.

44. Coakley, "Persons," 112.

45. Coakley, *God, Sexuality, and the Self,* 23. Cited in Molly T. Marshall, "Praying the Trinity: Sighing with God," *Perspectives in Religious Studies* 41, no. 4 (Winter 2014), 412. "Theologically and psychologically speaking . . . idolatry is often a defense against vulnerability." Campbell-Reed, "Feminism and Fieldwork," 426.

46. Adrian Thatcher, "Gender," in *Contemporary Theological Approaches to Sexuality*, ed. Lisa Isherwood and Dirk von der Horst (New York: Routledge, 2018), 34.

47. Thatcher, "Gender," 35.

48. The Council of Europe Convention on Preventing and Combating Violence against Women and Domestic Violence (Istanbul Convention, 2011) aims to prevent violence, protect victims, and end the impunity of perpetrators. Council of Europe, Treaty No. 210: https://www.coe.int/en/web/conventions/full-list/-/conventions/treaty/210. Its critics argue that the convention is an affront to traditional family values, that it promotes LGBT ideology, and that it is "a sinister attempt by Western Europeans to foist their overly-liberal policies on reluctant societies further east." Hamdi Firat Buyuk, et al., "Domestic Violence Treaty Falling Victim to Political Obtuseness," *Balkan Insight* (August 4, 2020): https://balkaninsight.com/2020/08/04/Istanbul-treaty-falling-victim-to-political-obtuseness/.

49. "Open Statement against the Coptic Church's Position on the LGBTQI+ Community."

CHAPTER

9

MEETING MICHELLE

PRACTICAL THEOLOGICAL REFLECTIONS ON THE PERSONHOOD OF A TRANSGENDER INMATE

Richard René

On June 19, 2017, the Liberal government of Canada passed Bill C-16, "An Act to amend the Canadian Human Rights Act and the Criminal Code."[1] The Bill amends the Canadian Human Rights Act by adding "gender identity or expression" as a prohibited ground of discrimination; in addition, it amends the Criminal Code by adding "gender identity or expression" to the definition of "identifiable group," making it a criminal offence to incite or promote hatred because of gender identity or gender expression.[2]

In light of the adoption of Bill C-16, the Correctional Service Canada (CSC) declared its commitment to "ensure a safe, inclusive and respectful environment for everyone, including staff, offenders, contractors, volunteers and visitors."[3] Accommodations for an offender's chosen gender identity or expression included a call to develop individualized protocols related to (among other things) frisk and strip searches, staff responses to voluntary nudity, and access to private and safe showers and/or toilets.[4]

However, despite CSC's clear-cut policies and statements committing to the support of incarcerated trans men and women,[5] at least one trans woman's actual experience in the correctional system has proven to be far from simple or easy. When Bill C-16 came into effect, the institution where I worked as the site-based chaplain[6] had just received an inmate who had been assigned a male sex at birth, but who now identified as a woman named "Michelle." The newly adopted legislation and the challenges it raised in managing Michelle in a male-only institution did not make for greater safety or inspire respect and inclusivity, but rather stirred up the latent cissexism, transphobia, and misogyny among many of the institutional staff.[7] In addition, Michelle challenged me, both in my role as a chaplain and as an Orthodox priest, to ask a basic question: How should I—or any Christian—engage, not just respectfully but *lovingly*, with others we view as different—whether that difference involves sex, gender, or some other aspect of their lives—while maintaining the integrity of our own traditional theological commitments?

In the essay that follows, I will suggest ways to answer this question. Having outlined Michelle's case and the pastoral challenges it presented me in the context of interfaith prison chaplaincy, I will engage with Orthodox personalist theologies of personhood, particularly that of Vladimir Lossky, as well as the anthropology of Maximus the Confessor, to articulate two principles of pastoral engagement with different others in a secular environment. The first calls Christians to participate with the Logos-Christ in "playing within" the fallen, contingent mode of human nature to draw others toward their preordained and eschatological essential nature (logos) in deified union with God. The second calls Christians to recognize the apophatic nature of the logos of human personhood, and exercise humility in the face of other persons. These principles challenge us to manifest apatheia out of a love that is equally disposed toward all others, regardless of difference.

Michelle is an offender in her mid-twenties who in her teens, when she still identified as a man, was convicted of rape and murder.[8] This offence, which resulted in a life sentence, is not incidental to our concerns; according to Michelle, she committed the crime to prove to her accomplices that she was a "real man." Thus, in her account, the crime was bound up with gender identity, and particularly, the cissexual stereotype of the aggressive male that she felt she had to live up to, or risk ostracization and even violence against herself. While one might question this as a form of rationalization or self-justification, Michelle would not be the first trans woman to struggle against the opposition of a society whose social norms value masculinity as superior to femininity, so that males who act in what is perceived as a "feminine" manner are ridiculed and denigrated.[9]

Michelle recalled identifying as a girl from the age of five. Her fondest memories of early childhood (in fact, the *only* pleasant memory she recounted of family life) involved a trip to the department store with her mother. Michelle kept demanding to try on a dress, and she recalled the joy she felt when her mother finally gave in, threw all her own clothes out of the cart, and went on a spree in the girls' clothing section.

Later memories around her gender identity and sexuality were less pleasant. She described how her father had sexually molested her while casting her in the role of a girl. Eventually, her mother, despite her own misgivings but under pressure from family friends, sent Michelle to a mental institution in an attempt to "correct" her dysphoria. This period marked the beginning of Michelle's dependence on a variety of psychotropic medications. Later, in her early teens, she ran away from home, and was taken into the care of the Ministry of Child and Family Services. She was placed in foster care, where her fundamentalist Christian "caregiver" decided that she was an abomination of Satan, tied her to a chair, and beat her with a Bible. Michelle's adherence to Satanism stems from this time, when she found comfort in Marilyn Manson albums.[10] Her logic was clear, if twisted and tragic: She would celebrate the fact that she was "God's mistake" by embracing the worship of God's enemy.

In her teens, Michelle became involved in criminal activities whose seriousness escalated, culminating in her most serious offence. While there is no direct evidence that Michelle's latent gender dysphoria was a criminogenic factor, this cannot be entirely discounted.[11] Certainly, Michelle's account suggests that her discomfort with her gender and her desire to prove her masculinity contributed to her motivation for what she did. Having been incarcerated at the federal level, she became the subject of frequent mental health and medical interventions as a result of emotional breakdowns, suicidal impulses, and suicide attempts—again, a tendency not unusual for the trans-person demographic.[12] Once she had come out as trans, Michelle experienced the same heightened level of vulnerability and exposure to violence that is prevalent among trans inmates generally.[13] Because CSC management viewed her as being unmanageable in a female institution, she was housed in male prisons, with all the attendant risks and potential harms to her physical and mental health.[14] As a result of her increased vulnerability, Michelle also spent more time in so-called "protective segregation" to keep her safe, which, as Edney points out, constitutes a "less than equal" level of punishment relative to other inmates, exacerbating Michelle's suicidal impulses and violent tendencies.[15]

At the time of the interview, the single bright spot in Michelle's existence was her engagement to another inmate in her last institution, who also self-identifies as a trans woman, and with whom she was seeking to be housed so that they might legally marry and consummate their relationship.[16] Michelle considers her fiancée to be the most significant relationship in a life that is otherwise devoid of family, friendship, or community supports. It should be noted also that neither Michelle nor her fiancé are seeking sex reassignment surgery, and are content to identify themselves as women in male bodies.

As one might expect, the arrival of a transgender rapist, murderer, and Satanist had a significant impact on the institutional staff. On a formal level, there were issues around pronoun usage. I corrected the management's inaccurate use of the term "female" rather than "woman" when referring to Michelle, as she clearly intended to identify her gender as a woman, while continuing to accept her birth-assigned sex.[17] In their own use of pronouns, the staff alternated between "they/them," "he/him," "she/her," and even "*it*."[18]

As I interacted with the correctional staff, I heard a variety of reactions to Michelle. Most of them simply did not know how to engage or interact with her. The new policy permits trans persons to be searched only by someone who identifies as the same gender, but in the absence of a woman officer, Michelle could not be searched at all.[19] As a result of this operational loophole, many staff felt that Michelle was using her chosen gender identity and expression for criminal ends. Others merely viewed her with disgust and loathing, as a "piece of garbage," the embodiment of evil and degeneracy.[20]

As the institutional chaplain, I was not immune to the challenge that Michelle posed. CSC policy is clear that a chaplain, though a QPOR (Qualified Professional Official Representative) of his or her own faith tradition, "is responsible to ensure the religious and spiritual needs of *all* inmates are met."[21] If the chaplain is unable to meet those needs directly, he or she is responsible for finding a faith community representative to do so. As can be imagined, Michelle's adherence to Satanism made this mandate very difficult, if not impossible, to fulfill. In accordance with my mandate as a chaplain, I made efforts to put her in contact with representatives of "the Church of Satan," but ironically, they had no interest in supporting incarcerated offenders. As a result, the accommodation of Michelle's spiritual needs fell to the discretion of the warden.[22] In practice, this meant that I was tasked with providing Michelle with incense, getting approval for her purchase of engagement rings for herself and her fiancée, and finding and issuing her pentagram pendant inscribed with a goat's head. . . .

As one can imagine, engaging in these activities presented significant ethical and spiritual difficulties for me. In my "Oath of Allegiance to the Holy Priesthood" I had explicitly promised to "uphold the teachings of truth . . . and to labor with every means available to return to the True Flock of Christ those who may have strayed from His path."[23] How could this be reconciled with helping someone pursue a path away from the "True Flock of Christ," ostensibly leading them into the bosom of God's enemy?

In addition, government policy prohibits those who serve trans inmates from refusing to use their preferred gender pronouns.[24] This alone presented me with challenges. I am an ordained leader of a Church where "alternative sexual and gender identities, whether publicly acknowledged and actualized or not, are broadly condemned as sinful, deviant, and unnatural."[25] Even relatively moderate hierarchical voices in the Orthodox Church, while counselling pastoral gentleness and patience toward trans persons, still view dysphoria as "confusion which can lead to delusion."[26] Given the virtually unanimous negative views of the Orthodox Church (of which I am a QPOR), how could I in good conscience follow CSC's commitment to accommodate Michelle's chosen gender identity and expression, including the use of her name and preferred gender pronouns? By "accommodating" her in this way, am I not feeding her confusion and adding to her delusion, condoning her "sinful, deviant, and unnatural" behaviors, not to mention helping her to follow (quite literally) a *satanic* spirituality?

In the end, I complied with CSC's requirements for accommodating alternative gender identities and expression, for two reasons. First, I wanted to keep serving inmates. If I did not follow CSC's policies, I risked losing my job, and that door would be closed. Moreover, if I refused to address Michelle using her preferred pronouns, I would have shut the door on the possibility of a pastoral relationship with her.

But my decision to comply with CSC's policies and Michelle's preferences was guided by more than utilitarian or expedient pastoral considerations. I was not being disingenuous for the sake of a "greater good," such as converting Michelle to Orthodoxy. I still call her "Michelle," even in this paper, because I fundamentally believe that there is something essentially *mysterious* about her personal identity. By "mysterious," I do not mean that she is enigmatic or puzzling. As I have suggested above, the features of Michelle's case can be rationally grasped in light of a wide variety of sociocultural, psychological, physiological, and spiritual factors. While the combination of these factors in her situation is certainly complex and unusual, it is ultimately not surprising, and does not constitute a "mystery" as I use the term. Rather, in speaking of mystery, I mean that in my encounters with Michelle, and as we developed a relationship, it became clear that she was somehow *hidden* not just from me and others, but from herself as well.[27] I came to the conclusion that *no one* could ultimately grasp the fullness of this person's identity; one could only experience her as she evolved and developed in the concrete context of her lived experience. As a result, while I wondered if Michelle's gender dysphoria might not ultimately be a product of mental illness and childhood abuse, I simply did not feel confident issuing the same definitive statements about her that I heard from others, whether from the institutional staff, or those Christians to whom I have related her story. In the end, my "gut" pastoral instinct was to give Michelle's self-expression the benefit of the doubt. Indeed, I contend that my hesitation and final stance with regard to Michelle is consonant with contemporary Orthodox theologies of the human person that draw on the insights of personalism.

As a broad philosophical movement, personalism emerged in the nineteenth and twentieth centuries as a response to systems of thought that subjugated individuals to abstract considerations of social or economic class, race or ethnicity, and/or religion, such as Marxism, communism, and other forms of nationalism, which ultimately resulted in genocides and mass abuses of human rights.[28] As Paul Ladouceur notes, Russian thinkers beginning in the 1800s adopted and developed personalist thought "to affirm the uniqueness and hence the absolute value of the human person, an extension of the theological understanding of the Divine Persons and of love as the basis of intra-Trinitarian relationships."[29] In particular, émigré theologian Vladimir Lossky defined the human person by drawing on fourth-century Trinitarian formulations, in which Father, Son, and Spirit share a single ousia, while being antinomically and radically personalized in three hypostases, whose personal distinctiveness derives from the differences manifested in their mutual, loving coinherence. By analogy, the human person

> signifies the irreducibility of man to his nature—"irreducibility" and not "something irreducible" or "something which makes man

irreducible to his nature" precisely because it cannot be a question here of "something" distinct from "another nature" but of *someone* who is distinct from his own nature, of someone who goes beyond his nature while still containing it, who makes it exist as human nature by this overstepping and yet does not exist in himself beyond the nature which he "enhypostasizes" and which he constantly exceeds.[30]

Building on Lossky's definition, Bryce E. Rich argues for "unique, new, authentically human actions that go beyond the properties that we all share."[31] Like the Trinity, in whose image and likeness we are made, human persons share a common human ousia, and therefore are homoousios with all other human beings; however, our uniqueness as hypostases derives from our mutual, self-emptying, loving relation with others, which is not subject to the dictates of our common nature. In this sense, Rich argues, personhood may be called a mystery in that it ultimately exceeds rational capacities to grasp its nature, because it is rooted in the apophatic reality of God in whose image and likeness it is made:

> While we may speak cataphatically about God, using analogies derived from that which we know from our experience of the world, we must also speak apophatically, denying that we can reduce the *Deus absconditus* who always exceeds our labels to any of the attributes we might wish to essentialize . . . the apophatic safeguard so central to Lossky's Trinitarian theology also carries over to any anthropology rooted in his work, recognizing our common human nature while affirming the freedom of each person in pursuit of a personal vocation that uniquely contributes to the whole of God's creation.[32]

Thus, Rich affirms with Elizabeth Behr-Sigel that the human person is as "mysterious, unique, unclassifiable, and free" as the apophatic Trinity.[33] As Metropolitan Kallistos Ware also puts it:

> We do not fully understand what are the limits of our human nature, what are the possibilities as yet latent within it. . . . My personhood stretches out of time into eternity, out of space into infinity. We need to be both subtle and humble in our approach to this human mystery, standing before it in awe, and fully prepared for surprises.[34]

The heart of personalist philosophy and Orthodox theologies of the human person is the distinction between person and *individual*. The latter is a countable, classifiable instance of human existence whose characteristics are "drawn from possibilities within the plenitude of our collective human nature."[35] Even "exotic" combinations of these characteristics, resulting in individuals that appear unique, are ultimately reducible to a common plenitude of human nature. Given enough people, it is possible for even the most unusual and rare instance of an individual to be duplicated and thus counted. By contrast, Rich argues, a person is *not* countable because like each of the divine Persons, it is absolutely unique:

> Just as the Father is not the Son or the Spirit, so also Paul is not Peter, and neither is Mary. Though these humans share a common nature and may even overlap in the characteristics expressed in their individuality, each is personally "always unique and incomparable" by virtue of not being the other.[36]

Rich applies these personalist insights to questions of gender identity and expression, arguing that essentialist understandings of gender deprive human beings of their capacity for free relations with others, and thus personhood, reducing them to mere individuals whose actions are determined by their natures, which are understood as fixed and incommensurate. By contrast, personalism "affirms a common nature shared by all human persons while also highlighting the freedom of each person that gestures beyond that nature through a variety of interpersonal relationships. These include relations between the various persons within the Body of Christ: the sacerdotal priesthood, spousal relationships, and familial structures."[37]

A personalist Orthodox theological anthropology offers helpful insights into my encounter with Michelle. According to personalism, she, just like *any* other person I encounter, is truly unique and therefore, absolutely "other" than me, though we share a common ousia of our human nature. Her life consists of a combination of human characteristics drawn from our shared nature, some of which overlap with mine. However, while her particular combination of characteristics represents her individuality, this is not what makes her a unique person. As a person made in the divine image, she is apophatic, fundamentally unknowable by rational means and therefore, a mystery to anyone who meets her. Her personhood only reveals itself in and through the web of her interpersonal relations, a web that is unique to her alone. Moreover, those relations, while unfolding within the matrix of her individual life, are not reducible to the dictates of her individuality, including her biology. In this way, personalism allows

Michelle to identify as a trans woman, apart from the "necessities" of her assigned biological sex.[38] As Philip Abrahamson puts it, "If the human person is free to love, and *not* reduced to notions of natural, biological or necessary sexual expressions, then space is opened up for lesbian, gay, bisexual, transgender, intersex and queer relationships."[39] In meeting Michelle as an "other" person, one can and should use her chosen gender pronouns and support her as a trans woman, simply out of respect for the apophatic mystery of her personhood in the image of God. Personalism is therefore helpful in accounting for my pastoral experience of Michelle's "hiddenness," and by extension, the "hiddenness" of any other person, that is, the mystery of their personhood.

There are limits to this approach, however—namely, its tendency to emphasize human personhood over nature. In the above-quoted definition, Lossky sees the human person as someone who "goes beyond his nature *while still containing it . . .* [and] *does not exist in himself beyond the nature which he 'enhypostasizes'* and which he constantly exceeds."[40] Lossky thus holds nature and person in antinomic tension, which is characteristic of his theology as a whole.[41] However, this antinomy appears to be asymmetrical, emphasizing person as the ultimate expression of human freedom and identity. While Lossky cannot be accused of demeaning nature, as other personalists might be,[42] his definition does not sufficiently address how a person "contains" their nature *while* going beyond it, or how they exist within their nature, *while* exceeding it. In the context of meeting Michelle pastorally, the question might be framed as follows: What roles do the various "natural" aspects of her life—psychology and physiology, social and cultural forces, criminogenic factors, religious and spiritual dimensions—play in forming her unique and free personhood? To answer this, we must "exceed" the limits of personalism and seek guidance from Maximus the Confessor.

This turn away from personalism to Maximus is far from unusual. Critics who accuse personalist theologians of denying or rejecting human nature have often invoked the Confessor's thought in their assertion of the inherent goodness of nature and its potential for communion with God.[43] Although these critiques are leveled particularly at the personalist theologies of John Zizioulas and Christos Yannaras rather than Lossky, Maximus does offer a constructive view of the role of nature in the formation of human personal identity. Paul Blowers in particular argues that Maximus takes a dialectical approach to human nature. On one hand, nature is "synonymous with common 'essence' (οὐσία), the utter stability of a single nature, together with its 'essential activity' (οὐσιώδης ἐνέργεια) and predisposition (ἕξις), as undergirded by the Logos who authors and orders the universe of created natures in their salutary diversity."[44] On this account, essential nature is "utterly 'personalized' by the indwelling Logos-Christ," so that "person" does not trump nature, "as though liberating it from nature's ontological oppression," but rather is "ontologically *simultaneous*."[45] Thus, Maximus corrects the personalist tendency to subordinate one to the other. On the other hand, the Confessor also speaks of nature negatively, particularly when discussing how it is lived out in the postlapsarian condition or circumstances "apart from indwelling grace, asserting itself as though it were independent of the Creator and groping for a mode by which to perpetuate itself."[46] Maximus's positive sense of nature is the persistent, stable principle (logos), the beginning (arche) and end (telos) of all created things in a deified mode of being (*tropos tês hyparxeôs*). By contrast, his pejorative sense is nature lived out in a "stunted" mode, subject to the consequences of the fall, including,

> the provisional constraints or "law" now imposed on humanity in the form of the irrational, passible side of human nature left to its own devices; the inexorable bouncing back-and-forth between pain and pleasure in human experience; and the relentless forward advance of sexually-generated procreation wherein life becomes a matter of biological survival rather than of flourishing according to humanity's authentic nature and origin (γένεσις).[47]

Human becoming is the "theodrama" that unfolds within this dialectic of nature.[48] The suspense of the drama consists in

> whether or how the all-resourceful Creator will eschatologically subjugate humanity's provisional "nature"—or rather, its provisional condition or mode [τρόπος] of nature—to the "nature" projected toward a supernatural, deified mode of being. Indeed, one of Maximus' theological preoccupations is to demonstrate how this contingent state of human nature nonetheless works to the Creator's ends.[49]

In his *Ambigua to John*, and specifically in *Ambiguum 71*, Maximus proposes that the Creator's "subjugation" of our provisional (mode of) nature can be viewed as a kind of game that God plays with us, drawing us toward our preordained and ultimate logos. Maximus draws out this intriguing view in a commentary on two lines from one of Gregory Nazianzen's *Poemata moralia* entitled, *Precepts for Virgins*:

> For the sublime Word plays in all kinds of forms, judging His world as He wishes, on this side and on that.[50]

Maximus offers four ways of interpreting these verses. First, he views "play" as Gregory's way of following the Apostle Paul, who uses "dissimilar similitudes"[51] to characterize the Incarnation as the foolishness and weakness of God (1 Cor. 1:25). Applying privations of human virtues to God in this way "[indicates] God's superlative possession of precisely their opposite as conceived in human terms."[52] In this sense,

> the "foolishness" and "weakness" of God, according to the holy apostle Paul, and the game of God, according to Gregory the wondrous and great teacher, signify the mystery of the divine Incarnation, since in a manner beyond being it transcends the whole order and arrangement of every nature, power, possession, and activity.[53]

God's play, however, is not just the Incarnation understood as "divine imprudence"[54]; it is (according to Maximus's second interpretation) the "visible realities" of creation surrounding human beings and constituting our life in history, which Maximus calls the "mean terms."[55] These "mean terms" have been providentially devised by God, who poises them between "the reality of those *future* things yet to be manifest for humanity, things God already ordained *originally* in his ineffable purpose and plan."[56] These original and future "things" are the logoi, the apophatic "rationales" for creaturely becoming and in the flux of the "mean terms," they remain "at rest," as stable and unchanging as Godself.[57] To convey this idea, Maximus uses the analogy of parents playing games with their children,

> indulgently taking part in childish games, such as playing with nuts and knucklebones with them, or showing them many-colored flowers and colorfully-dyed clothing to beguile their senses, thereby attracting their attention and filling them with amazement, for young children have no other kind of work or occupation. . . . Thus, perhaps the teacher [Gregory the Theologian] is saying that God, who is superior to all, by leading us through the nature of visible creations . . . after which he directs us to the contemplation of the more

spiritual principles within these things, and finally leads us by way of theology up to the more mystical knowledge of Himself, so far as this is possible.[58]

In the Logos's Incarnation, then, the unchanging God uses creation as a game to draw God's creatures toward the preordained and eschatological stability of their underlying divinely personalized principles, their logoi.

In his third interpretation, Maximus focuses on divine "play" as immanent in the mutability and contingency of creation:

> Or perhaps the mutability of the material objects which we hold in our hands, which shift things around and are themselves shifted around in various ways, having no solid foundation, save for the first intelligible principle [τοῦ πρώτου λόγου], in accordance with which they are carried along wisely and providentially, and carry us along with them . . . perhaps this, I say, was fittingly called God's "play" by the teacher, seeing that it is through these things that God leads us to what is really real and can never be shaken.[59]

Thus, the Logos, "divides himself indivisibly,"[60] relatively incarnating himself in the logoi of created things, and resourcefully "uses the 'chaos' in the 'flowing stream' of material creation to reorder and redeem his fragile creation."[61] While Tikhon Pino claims here that Maximus is not referring to "*fallen* realities as such,"[62] it is clear that Maximus views the chaos of the material world as stemming from human sin.[63] God therefore *does* use this fallen mode of nature, characterized by chaos, mutability, and contingency, to "lead us to what is really real and can never be shaken" in accordance with God's logos for us.

In his final interpretation of Gregory's verses, Maximus takes a more sober stance. Although he has affirmed the providential ways in which God's Incarnate Logos "plays along" with (and within, and through) fallen reality to draw human beings toward the stability of our underlying divine principles, he is clear that the "mean terms" of our history will pass away, transformed into another life. Thus, Maximus says, "This present life, when compared to the archetype of the divine and true life that is to come, is a child's toy, than which no other such toy could be more insubstantial."[64] It's important to note, however, that Maximus is not denigrating material nature per se; rather, he is speaking here about the "*prevailing sequence*" of our nature—that is, the historical condition of flux and change and decay to which our nature is subject and within which it must operate. In short, the provisional mode or *tropos* of our nature—and not nature itself—is the "child's toy" that will be set aside in the age to come in favor of a "mature," supernatural mode of being.[65]

We can now bring our reflections on Maximus to bear on Michelle's case. Before we do so, however, three caveats are in order. First, we should not force Maximus to speak to the question of gender dysphoria, a phenomenon that he did not address directly or indirectly, even if it may have been present in his time.[66] Second, we cannot impose on Maximus the sharp distinction we have come to make between sex and gender in the wake of feminism, though the patristic tradition did apply feminine and masculine characteristics allegorically to both males and females.[67] Nor can we claim beyond doubt that Maximus regards the sex/gender distinction as temporary, though he certainly believes that the *necessity* of sex and/or gender to defining our essential human identity is part of a fallen, provisional mode of nature that will dissolve in the age to come, even if sexual distinctives remain.[68]

Finally, Maximus was addressing Christians; therefore, we cannot impose those standards on Michelle. Indeed, she considers herself an "enemy" of Christianity as she understands it (and we have seen how her understanding was distorted by an abusive caregiver). Asking how Maximus might help us with Michelle, then, we must also ask how he might speak to someone who is unaware of (or unwilling to acknowledge) the providential work of the Logos and the deified mode of life to which he is calling her. Our response would do well to take into consideration Paul's salient questions: "What have I to do with judging outsiders? Is it not those inside the church whom you are to judge?" (1 Cor. 5:12)

With those qualifications in mind, we can draw two principles from Maximus's thought, as well as from our discussion of the contemporary personalist approach to the theology of the human person. As we have seen, Maximus affirms that God in the Logos-Christ works (or rather, plays) in the "mean terms" of our fallen, contingent mode of nature: first, through the Incarnation itself, understood as a form of "divine imprudence" through which God bears along with our fallen circumstances; second, in and through the visible realities of creation itself; and third, in and through the mutability and instability of the fallen world. Through these means, the Logos draws created beings—whether they are fully aware of it or not[69]—to their divine logoi, which have been preordained from eternity.

This divine providential strategy thus yields a first principle for responding to different others like Michelle. Just as the Logos plays in the midst our fallen *tropos*—which, in Michelle's case, is characterized by abuse, mental illness, and criminality—to reorient us toward a deified mode consonant with our essential and unique logoi, so too Christians meeting others are called to "play within" their contingent mode of nature in the hope of drawing them toward their true and essential nature in deified union with God. Concretely for me, this "playing within" took the form of using Michelle's chosen gender pronouns and respecting her as a trans woman. In so doing, I was not merely "humoring" her, as if I really believed that her chosen gender identity and expression were false and was simply biding my time until she became aware of her "mistake." Rather, while fully affirming that she is living in a fallen mode of nature characterized by the cycle of pain and pleasure and the tyranny of irrational passions, in giving her the benefit of the doubt, I allowed for the possibility that her ultimate identity, her essential nature, is *also* present in her life in a way that is hidden from me.

Is this "playing within" a tacit moral compromise, an implied endorsement of immorality? No more, I would contend, than Jesus's entrance into the houses of tax collectors and sinners, affirming the familial and loyal bonds of guest-friendship with them, without first requiring them to repent (see Luke 19:1–7). Likewise, Christians "playing within" the lives of those they view as different is simply a willingness to acknowledge that they are *guests* in those lives; it is a way of bearing along with provisional mode of human nature in all its fallenness, recognizing that their and our personhood—to the extent that it reflects the unfolding drama of the Incarnate Logos's ongoing playing within us all—is "yet to come." This no more requires us to compromise our own firmly held principles and moral integrity than entering the house of Zacchaeus (or other sinners) required Jesus to embrace and endorse their sinful behaviors.

This brings us to our second principle of meeting different others. As we have seen in our discussion of Lossky's personalism, the mystery of the human person is a unique complex of relations that has worked itself out within the "pool" of our shared human nature, while also exceeding the ontological limits of that nature. For Maximus, the mystery of personhood is our essential human nature already personalized by the indwelling Logos-Christ, who preordains it and works (or plays) within the "mean terms" of our contingent, fallen mode of existence to bring it to fruition in the eschaton, a fruition that will continue into eternity. In both views, the principle is evident: The person of Michelle—and indeed, *any* other person we meet—is an *apophatic* reality: that is, a mystery. While authentic human persons manifest their existence in the revealed mode of the Incarnation—that is, in self-emptying and perichoretic love for the other—the contours of anyone's personhood cannot be grasped by rational means, let alone labeled in simple moralistic or political terms. In the case of Michelle, neither "degenerate rapist-murderer and Satanist" nor even "trans woman"—nor *any* other label we might care to apply—are sufficient for me to summarize this *person* as I have met her. One could point out that due to her life circumstances and choices, she has not attained the personhood to which God calls her, but such a statement holds true for all human beings who fall short of the glory of God (Rom. 3:23). Why does one feel the need to point out Michelle's particular shortfalls, when all of us are struggling to become authentic persons, with more or less success?

This second principle—affirming the apophatic mystery of Michelle—calls us to suspend our attempts to grasp rationally at her personhood; in short, to suspend final judgements. We can certainly name (if we are asked to name) her physically, psychologically, and spiritually harmful behaviors, but we cannot name her *life*. Sadly, the inability to separate these two forms of naming is too often characteristic of the way we engage with different others. It has certainly been characteristic of the way Christians have responded to Michelle.[70] Instead of taking this easy path, however, Christians must strive to practice as a form of ascesis suspension of judgement over the lives of other persons. This requires an inner transformation. Indeed, for Maximus, "suspension of judgement" is a core marker of agape, which is "begotten of *apatheia*."[71] In his view, those who manifests apatheia (which Blowers renders as "engaged dispassion"[72]) show that they love all equally, as God does, regardless of their state:

> The one who is perfect in love and has reached the summit of detachment knows no distinction between one's own and another's, between faithful and unfaithful, between slave and freeman, or indeed between male and female. But having risen above the tyranny of the passions and looking to the one nature of men he regards all equally and is equally disposed toward all.[73]

The call to suspension of judgment when faced with the mystery of different others—the humility and openness to surprise that Met. Kallistos speaks of—is a challenge for Christians to strive for in their own lives, receiving and revealing the gift of divine love through the ways that tradition provides: ascetic praxis of virtues, contemplation, and *theologia* through participation in the sacramental mysteries of the Church. Only in this way can they truly attain the grace to suspend judgement on their neighbors, regardless of difference, and love them with a divine love that makes no distinctions and offers itself to all.

Notes

1. Government of Canada, "Government Bill (House of Commons) C-16 (42-1)—Royal Assent—An Act to Amend the Canadian Human Rights Act and the Criminal Code—Parliament of Canada" (accessed April 13, 2020): https://www.parl.ca/DocumentViewer/en/42-1/bill/C-16/royal-assent.

2. I will understand "gender identity or expression" to mean "a person's understanding of what their gender is and how they choose to express it," as (potentially) contrasted with their assigned sex at birth. Julian Walker, "Legislative Summary of Bill C-16: An Act to Amend the Canadian Human Rights Act and the Criminal Code," 1: https://lop.parl.ca/sites/PublicWebsite/default/en_CA/ResearchPublications/LegislativeSummaries/421C16E.

3. Correctional Service of Canada, Government of Canada, "Interim Policy Bulletin 584 Bill C-16 (Gender Identity or Expression)," x2017-12-13: https://www.csc-scc.gc.ca/lois-et-reglements/584-pb-en.shtml.

4. Correctional Service of Canada, "Interim Policy Bulletin."

5. I will follow Julia Serano and refer to my subject as a "trans woman," where "woman" refers to the lived and self-identified gender, while "trans" refers to her transition into that identity. Julia Serano, *Whipping Girl: A Transsexual Woman on Sexism and the Scapegoating of Femininity* (Emeryville, Calif.: Seal Press, 2007), 29.

6. A chaplain here is understood as "a Qualified Professional Official Representative (QPOR) of a religious or spiritual community who provides and/or facilitates religious/spiritual services and care in a secular or institutional context. . . . In the CSC context, a site-based Chaplain, while a QPOR of a specific tradition, is responsible to ensure the religious and spiritual needs of all inmates are met." Correctional Service of Canada, Government of Canada, "Chaplaincy Services" (October 6, 2014): https://www.csc-scc.gc.ca/acts-and-regulations/750-cd-eng.shtml. By contrast, a "tradition-specific" chaplain addresses the needs of a particular demographic (Muslim, Jewish, etc.).

7. I will follow Serano's definition of "cissexism" as the belief or assumption that the gender identities, expressions, and embodiments of cissexual people (those whose gender identity matches their sex assigned at birth) are more natural and

legitimate than those of trans people. She points out that "Trans women are so ridiculed and despised because we are uniquely positioned at the intersection of multiple binary gender-based forms of prejudice." Serano, *Whipping Girl*, 12.

8. Michelle's story is shared here with verbal permission and is based on an interview conducted in May 2019.

9. Serano, *Whipping Girl*, 14.

10. Manson is widely known as a high-profile member and honorary priest of the so-called "Church of Satan" founded by Anton LaVey.

11. See Kirsty A. Clark, Jaclyn M. White Hughto, and John E. Pachankis, "'What's the Right Thing to Do?' Correctional Healthcare Providers' Knowledge, Attitudes, and Experiences Caring for Transgender Inmates," *Social Science & Medicine* 193 (November 2017): 80. In addition, Jess Rodgers et al. argue that "the pathologised nature of trans subjectivity pushes trans people to the margins of society where they are more likely to become involved in crime." Jess Rodgers, Angela Dwyer, and Nicole Asquith, "Cisnormativity, Criminalisation, Vulnerability: Transgender People in Prisons," *Tasmanian Institute of Law Enforcement Studies*, Modern Spiritual Masters Series 13 (February 2017): 4.

12. Clark et al., "What's the Right Thing to Do?," 80.

13. Clark et al., "What's the Right Thing to Do?," 80–81. See also Richard Edney, "To Keep Me Safe from Harm—Transgender Prisoners and the Experience of Imprisonment," *Deakin Law Review* 9, no. 2 (2004): 328.

14. Rodgers et al., "Cisnormativity, Criminalisation, Vulnerability," 8. See also Edney, "To Keep Me Safe from Harm," 331.

15. Edney, "To Keep Me Safe from Harm," 333–34.

16. Same-sex marriage was legalized in Canada on July 20, 2005.

17. Edney notes that "traditional approaches of correctional administrators have failed to appreciate the distinction between sex and gender." Edney, "To Keep Me Safe from Harm," 337.

18. Rodgers et al. note that "'systemic misgendering' . . . including being misnamed and ridiculed by staff and prisoners—increases depression and anxiety." Rodgers et al., "Cisnormativity, Criminalisation, Vulnerability," 6.

19. Correctional Service of Canada, "Interim Policy Bulletin."

20. Given that the culture of correctional officers is male-dominated and masculinist, the disproportionate hostility I observed may be explained as defensive in nature. As Serano argues, "In a male-centered gender hierarchy, where it is assumed that men are better than women and masculinity is superior to femininity, there is no greater perceived threat than the existence of trans women, who despite being born male and inheriting male privilege 'choose' to be female instead." Serano, *Whipping Girl*, 15.

21. Correctional Service of Canada, "Chaplaincy Services." Emphasis mine.

22. Government of Canada, "Inmate Religious Accommodations" (September 23, 2016): https://www.csc-scc.gc.ca/politiques-et-lois/750-1-gl-eng.shtml.

23. Synod of Bishops of the Orthodox Church in America, "Guidelines for Petitioning for Ordination in the OCA" (Orthodox Church in America, 2013): http://orthodoxfaith.net/PDF/Forms/Ordination/Ordination-Packet.pdf.

24. Correctional Service of Canada, "Interim Policy Bulletin."

25. Brandon Gallaher and Gregory Tucker, "Eastern Orthodoxy & Sexual Diversity: Perspectives on Challenges from the Modern West" (British Council Bridging Voices Consortium of Exeter University & Fordham University, November 2019). For a classic example of statements regarding such identities, see the Russian Orthodox Church Department of External Church Relations' publication, "XII. Problems of Bioethics | The Russian Orthodox Church": https://mospat.ru/en/documents/social-concepts/xii/.

26. Bishop Alexander (Golitzin), "DOS 2018-0709A Pastoral Letter.pdf" (July 9, 2018).

27. A more precise definition of the term "mystery" follows below. At this stage, I am documenting my original intuitions within the context of my pastoral encounter with Michelle.

28. For a concise overview of personalism, see Paul Ladouceur, *Modern Orthodox Theology: "Behold, I Make All Things New"* (London: T&T Clark, 2017), 239–47. For a more in-depth overview, see Rufus Burrow, *Personalism: A Critical Introduction* (St. Louis, Mo: Chalice Press, 1999).

29. Ladouceur, *Modern Orthodox Theology*, 241.

30. Vladimir Lossky, *In the Image and Likeness of God*, ed. John H. Erickson and Thomas E. Bird (Crestwood, N.Y.: St. Vladimir's Seminary, 1974), 122.

31. Bryce E. Rich, "Beyond Male and Female: Gender Essentialism and Orthodoxy" (PhD diss., University of Chicago, 2017), 178. I am very grateful to Bryce for his assistance in understanding personalism.

32. Rich, "Beyond Male and Female," 170. In fact, Lossky's personalism has its roots in the theology of his teacher, Fr. Sergius Bulgakov, who asserts that "Humankind is transcendent to the world and in this sense is free of the world, is nonworld. It is not exhausted by any what, is not defined by any definition, but is, like God, an absolute not-what. It places outside itself and opposes to itself any worldly givenness as a certain what, while remaining free of it and transcendent to it. Moreover, humankind is transcendent to its own self in all of its empirical or psychological givenness, in every self-definition, which leaves the peace of its absoluteness unbroken and its depths not muddied." Sergiï Bulgakov, *Unfading Light: Contemplations and Speculations*, trans. T. Allan Smith, Twentieth Century Religious Thought (Grand Rapids, Mich.: Wm. B. Eerdmans Publishing Co, 2012), 286–87.

33. Quoted in Rich, "Beyond Male and Female," 168.
34. Met. Kallistos Ware, foreword to *The Wheel* 13/14 (Spring/Summer 2018): 6.
35. Rich, "Beyond Male and Female," 174.
36. Rich, "Beyond Male and Female," 174.
37. Rich, "Beyond Male and Female," 289.
38. Rich points out that the biological sciences, as well as feminist theorists like Judith Butler, have argued that even sex is the product of gender discourse. Rich, "Beyond Male and Female," 187.
39. Philip Abrahamson, "Trends in Eastern Orthodox Theological Anthropology: Towards a Theology of Sexuality," *Philosophy, Sociology, Psychology and History* 15, no. 2 (2016): 100.
40. Vladimir Lossky and John Meyendorff, "The Theological Notion of the Human Person," in *In the Image and Likeness of God*, ed. John H. Erickson and Thomas E. Bird (Crestwood, N.Y.: St Vladimir's Seminary Press, 1985), 120.
41. For an analysis of Lossky's antinomic theology, see Brandon Gallaher, "The 'Sophiological' Origins of Vladimir Lossky's Apophaticism," *Scottish Journal of Theology* 66, no. 3 (August 2013): 278–98.
42. Ladouceur offers an excellent summary of critiques of personalist theology, particular that of John Zizioulas and Christos Yannaras. He concludes that "The pendulum in Orthodox thought has perhaps swung too far in the direction of personhood defined largely or solely in a social and communitarian sense—communion or love—which appears to diminish or even deny dignity or merit to the individual human as such." Ladouceur, *Modern Orthodox Theology*, 253.
43. See Nicholas Loudovikos, "Hell and Heaven, Nature and Person. Chr. Yannaras, D. Stăniloae and Maximus the Confessor," *International Journal of Orthodox Theology* 5, no. 1 (2014): 25; Jean-Claude Larchet, *Personne et nature*, CERF edition (Paris: CERF, 2011), 236; and Paul M. Blowers, *Maximus the Confessor: Jesus Christ and the Transfiguration of the World* (Oxford: Oxford University Press, 2016), 155–56.
44. Blowers, *Maximus the Confessor*, 202–6.
45. Blowers, *Maximus*, 205. Blowers is here critiquing the personalism of John Zizioulas for subordinating nature to person. While Lossky's personalism cannot be said to denigrate nature to the same extent, he nevertheless does view created human nature as "profoundly tainted," and thus subordinate to person. Vladimir Lossky, "The Doctrine of Grace in the Orthodox Church," ed. and trans. Paul Ladouceur, *St. Vladimir's Theological Quarterly* 58, no. 1 (2014): 82–83.
46. Blowers, *Maximus the Confessor*, 204.
47. Blowers, *Maximus the Confessor*, 204.

48. See Hans Urs von Balthasar, *Cosmic Liturgy: The Universe According to Maximus the Confessor*, 3rd ed, Communio Books (San Francisco: Ignatius Press, 2003).

49. Blowers, *Maximus the Confessor*, 206.

50. Quoted in Maximus the Confessor, *On Difficulties in the Church Fathers: The Ambigua*, ed. and trans. Maximos Constas, Dumbarton Oaks Medieval Library 28–29 (Cambridge, Mass.: Harvard University Press, 2014), 1408C. Hereafter referred to as *Amb*.

51. This is a hermeneutical principle proposed by Pseudo-Dionysius the Areopagite, who said that ostensibly scriptural imagery or language referred to God paradoxically. Paul Blowers, "On the 'Play' of Divine Providence in Gregory Nazianzen and Maximus the Confessor," in *Re-Reading Gregory of Nazianzus: Essays on History, Theology, and Culture*, ed. Christopher A. Beeley, CUA Studies in Early Christianity (Washington, D.C: The Catholic University of America Press, 2012), 203.

52. Joshua Lollar, *To See into the Life of Things: The Contemplation of Nature in Maximus the Confessor and His Predecessors* (Turnhout: Brepols Publishers, 2013), 36. See also Blowers, "On the 'Play' of Divine Providence," 203.

53. *Amb*. 71, 1409C-1409D.

54. Blowers, "On the Play of Divine Providence," 205.

55. *Amb*. 71, 1412C.

56. Blowers, "On the Play of Divine Providence," 205.

57. *Amb*. 71, 1412B.

58. *Amb*. 1413B-1413C.

59. *Amb*. 71, 1416A-1416B.

60. *Amb*. 10, 1172C.

61. Blowers, "On the 'Play' of Divine Providence," 208–9.

62. Tikhon Pino, "Fr. John Whiteford: Response to 'Meeting Michelle' Part 1," *Fr. John Whiteford* blog (October 18, 2019): http://fatherjohn.blogspot.com/2019/10/response-to-meeting-michelle-part-1.html.

63. Blowers, "The 'Play' of Divine Providence," 209. See also *Amb* 8, 1104A: "It was thus that man plucked fruit . . . and so drew down on himself not simply the corruption and death of his body, but also . . . the instability and disorder of the material substance that surrounded him."

64. *Amb*. 71, 1416C.

65. Blowers, *Maximus the Confessor*, 206.

66. For an historical study of transgenderism in late antiquity, see Chiara O. Tommasi, "Cross-Dressing as Discourse and Symbol in Late Antique Religion and Literature," in *Transantiquity: Cross-Dressing and Transgender Dynamics in the Ancient World*, ed. Domitilla Campanile, Margherita Facella, and Filippo

Carlà-Uhink, Routledge Monographs in Classical Studies (New York, N.Y.: Routledge, 2017), 121–33.

67. Rich, "Beyond Male and Female," 104–6.

68. On the question of Maximus's view of gender/sex distinction, scholars have taken two positions. Von Balthasar and Louth, for example, hold that Maximus envisioned a total dissolution of sexual difference in the *eschaton*. See Hans Urs von Balthasar, *Cosmic Liturgy: The Universe According to Maximus the Confessor*, 3rd ed, Communio Books (San Francisco: Ignatius Press, 2003), 203, and Andrew Louth, *Maximus the Confessor*, 73. By contrast, Paul M. Blowers argues that Maximus did not countenance the dissolution of sexual difference per se, but only "the alienation between sexes, the legacy of pain and pleasure, and the drive for survival attending sexual procreation." Blowers, *Maximus the Confessor*, 221. In addition, Doru Costache contends that Maximus views gender and sexuality as problematic only to the extent that they are misused; in fact, the Confessor understands the enduring gender/sex distinction stands as an ongoing testimony of the capacity of both noncelibates and monastics to live "above gender" in dispassionate relationships. Doru Costache, "Living above Gender: Insights from Saint Maximus the Confessor," *Journal of Early Christian Studies* 21, no. 2 (2013): 261–90.

69. Blowers compares Maximus's view with that of Plotinus's: "Even if it is lost on the individual actors locked into the plot of the drama, there is a providence and benevolent necessity operative in the universal whole, which, though derivative of the generosity and goodness of the One, operates only through the Logos." Blowers, "On the 'Play' of Divine Providence," 212.

70. For example, Pino conflates the two when he asks, "Is Michael-Michelle a mystery, or are we allowed to have moral convictions about his state?" Pino, "Fr. John Whiteford: Response to 'Meeting Michelle' Part 1."

71. Maximus the Confessor, *Four Centuries on Charity*, 1.2. From *Maximus Confessor: Selected Writings*, ed. George C. Berthold (Mahwah, N.J.: Paulist Press, 1985).

72. Blowers, *Maximus the Confessor*, 278.

73. Maximus, *Four Centuries on Charity*, 2.30.

Part III: Thinking with Tradition

CHAPTER

10

A Desire for All Is the Desire for God

"Sexual Orientation" in Light of Gregory of Nyssa's Account of Gender, Desire, and the Soul's Ascent to God

Spyridoula Athanasopoulou-Kypriou

Preliminary Considerations: Homosexuality Debates and a Way through Contested Anthropologies

The topic of sexual orientation—that is, the sex of a person to whom someone is sexually attracted—has become such an emotive subject in contemporary theological discussion. Current homosexuality debates foster two extreme positions that oversimplify a much more complicated set of theological alternatives. On the one hand, there is the theological conservatism that is associated by its opponents with political conservatism, ecclesiastical authoritarianism, and repression, and, on the other, there is the theological liberalism that is associated with political liberalism, justice, and "promiscuous" libertinism. Both positions have been largely determined in relation to the way they respond to the recognition of LGBTQI rights in the political sphere.

Yet, despite their immense differences, both positions confine the mystery of the human persons created in the image and likeness of God to historically constructed categories—namely, "homosexuality," "heterosexuality," "bisexuality," "asexuality," etc.[1] An insidious view that identifies a human being as something—i.e., homosexual or heterosexual—has crept into theological discourse. Regardless of their different motives and ethical aspirations, both positions ascribe an identity to human persons and objectify them. The main purpose of objectification is to know somebody by defining *what they are* in terms of certain properties and qualities (age, color, nationality, weight, psychological state, sexual orientation, etc.). By identifying someone, the knower controls them. One can identify something in such a way that it can serve one's own needs or comply with one's own ideologies.[2] For example, one could identify women as tender and therefore more suitable for staying at home, bringing up one's children. One could identify people who are attracted to people of the same sex as promiscuous and thus as irredeemably sinful. When one objectifies someone, not only does one see them as commodities but one also imprisons them in one's own representation, annihilating the alterity of the other.

Besides admitting historically constructed categories and objectifying human beings, both positions assume a very narrow understanding of sexuality that limits it to sexual attraction and sexual intercourse.

If one were to liberate oneself from the constrains of historical and culturally constructed categories that have caused divisions and discriminations, and wished to resist objectifying others, one has first to assume an ontology of personhood that gives priority to "who" one is and not to "what" one is, and that defines the human person as a unique free being that surpasses their nature, rather than being determined by any biological necessity.[3] Second, one needs to adopt an eschatological perspective according to which we are no longer identified by our past but by our future.[4] Finally, one has to remain faithful to an ecclesial (that is, Christ-like) mode of being that is fully expressed, as I will demonstrate in what follows, in the ascetic life of the faithful.

Current homosexuality debates and theological discussions about sexuality need to be separated from culturally constructed understandings of the issue and categories that violate the freedom of human persons and insult the "image of God" in every human being—that is, that offend persons' uniqueness. The crucial question to be answered is whether there is a natural essence of homosexuality and/or heterosexuality. Critical theorists and other historians have traced the genealogies of these terms, showing that these categories are social constructions.[5] Similarly, can we argue for a natural essence of femininity and a natural essence of masculinity? Are human beings first understood as men and women who have then to fulfill socially imposed gender requirements?

Judith Butler's critical theory serves as the starting point of any contemporary discussion on the above questions of gender and sexuality. Her contribution to gender theory involves a radical critique of identity categories in which not only gender, but also sex, sexuality, and the body are conceived of as cultural products.[6] She reveals the ways in which sex and gender are produced within a binary framework that is conditioned by heterosexuality, rather than the other way round. Thus, it is not that sex and gender produce heterosexuality, but that heterosexuality produces sex and gender in a binary form.[7] For Butler, gender identifications are not something that are given in biology, or that form some sort of essential self. An important aspect of her critique of identity is that the categories through which embodied subjects come into being are never fully determining.[8] This allows for the possibility of resistance to gender identifications.[9] Summarizing Butler's arguments, the theologian Mary McClintock Fulkeston points out:

> As a dominant ordering of reality, compulsory heterosexuality regulates pleasure and bodies; it cuts up reality into two human identities and defines how they may legitimately experience. . . . [D]esire is channeled and defined by the sexes it connects; and those sexes are two—male and female. Any thinking about desire and human relations is locked into this grid; any subject which does not conform is disciplined.[10]

Within Orthodoxy, theological anthropology begins from the first three chapters of Genesis. Genesis 1:27 says, "So God created man [*anthropos*] in his own image, in the image of God he created him; male and female he created them." The Orthodox patristic scholar Verna Harrison points out that despite the androcentrism of the late antique Mediterranean world in which they lived, nearly all the Fathers conclude that men and women alike bear the divine image. Moreover, there is consensus among Orthodox theologians that being according to the divine image is intrinsic to our nature. It gives men and women the capacity to become like God or not. Intellect, freedom, and the capacity for virtue and communion with God are central properties of human nature that manifest the divine image and are shared by all human beings. Their nature thus makes all people, despite their peripheral properties, capable of likeness to God, communion with him, and eternal life in the age to come—that is, salvation.[11]

Yet, the ontological status of sex and gender along with its implications are a subject of lively debate. In other words, although there is agreement regarding the central properties of human nature, there is disagreement as far as the centrality and thus essentiality of sex and gender. Orthodox theologians like Paul Evdokimov and Fr. Thomas Hopko,[12] influenced by Russian religious philosophy, German romanticism, and even evangelical Protestantism, are more inclined to see masculinity and femininity as ontological components of the human being and male and female genders as created by God with separate, complementary charisms and roles.[13] But other Orthodox theologians draw upon the writings of the Church Fathers and review patristic teachings on gender, especially the teachings of Gregory of Nyssa (ca. 335–94) and Maximus the Confessor (ca. 580–662), and are skeptical of the claim that sexual differentiation in humans is part of God's original intention and will persist in the resurrection.[14]

Within Orthodoxy, current interest in the ontological status of sex and gender has been prompted by the challenging perspectives of feminist theology, the prospect of women's ordination, and very recently by homosexuals' plea for inclusion in the life of the Church. In the past thirty years there is a proliferation of conferences and academic writings on issues of gender and sexuality that all constitute direct or indirect responses to the rightful critiques that gender studies and liberation theologies have laid at the Orthodox Churches' door.[15] Admittedly, gender awareness has been introduced within Orthodoxy and the "lenses of the gender" have been rendered more visible than ever.

Current debates about anthropological issues revived theologians' interest in patristic thought and breathed new life into Eastern Orthodox tradition. Butler's thematization of gender fluidity and of subversive personal agency seem to echo older theistically oriented traditions.[16] The denaturalization of sex and gender is a theme shared with an older tradition of ascetical transformation.[17] Interestingly, Anglican and Roman Catholic feminist theologians like Sarah Coakley and Tina Beattie, as well as Orthodox theologians,[18] argue for the relevance of the Eastern Orthodox tradition to contemporary issues of gender and sexuality. It seems that many feminist theologians revisit the Eastern Orthodox tradition, particularly the works of Gregory of Nyssa and Maximus the Confessor, in order to find liberating resources. What these theologians try to do is to explore the different ways in which tradition might be interpreted in response to contemporary questions about sexuality.[19] Yet academic honesty requires subscribing to Harrison's observation that "while Gregory's ideas are often highly suggestive and of relevance to contemporary discussions, it is essential to understand him in his own historical and theological context and not to make a simple equation between his anthropology and philosophical or theological positions current in our time."[20]

Thus, in what follows I draw upon the writings of Gregory of Nyssa in order to present three aspects of his theological reflections on gender and sexuality that could be employed in current discussions about homosexuality and homosexuals' plea for inclusion in the life of the Church. Far from equating Gregory's teachings with current philosophical and queer theory positions and aspirations, I argue that Gregory's anthropology and his theory of gender, his understanding of desire along with his account of the soul's ascent to God, can be employed to achieve the following: first to challenge the assumption that sexuality is somehow exhausted in sexual intercourse, and second to overcome objectification and divisions and get past discrimination against LGBTQI people by stressing that everyone is in the image of God, and by reflecting on every human being's sexual orientation by the same theological standards—that is, of progressive nonattachment to worldly realities and of ascetical transformation of sexuality.

Gregory of Nyssa's Eschatologically Oriented Theory of Gender

Gregory's eschatologically oriented theory of gender, which is not captive to a culturally and historically defined sexual ideology, needs to be understood in the context of his profound apophatic sensibility about the divine essence and his doctrine of double creation that can be interpreted (and has been interpreted by the early generation of scholarship and Christian Orthodox patristic scholars[21]) as depriving sexual difference of any ontological significance.[22] In the seventh homily on the *Song of Songs*, Gregory understands the bridegroom's mother in the Canticle allegorically as God the Father and writes:

> Now no one who has given thought to the way we talk about God is going to be overprecise about the sense of the name—that "mother" is mentioned instead of "father," for he will gather the same meaning from either term. For the Divine is neither male nor female. (How, after all, could any such thing be conceived in the case of Deity, when

> this condition is not permanent even for us human beings, but when we all become one in Christ, we put off the signs of this difference along with the whole of the old humanity?) For this reason, every name we turn up is of the same adequacy for purposes of pointing to the unutterable Nature, since neither "male" nor "female" defiles the meaning of the inviolate Nature. Hence in the Gospel a father is said to give a marriage feast for a son, while the prophet addresses God, saying, "You have put a crown of precious stone on his head" and then asserts that the crown was put on the Bridegroom's head by his mother. So, there is one wedding feast and the Bride is one, and the crown is placed on the head of the Bridegroom by one agent. Hence it makes no difference whether God calls the Only Begotten "Son of God" or "Son of his love" (Col 1:13), as Paul has it, since whichever name is used it is one Power who escorts the Bridegroom to our marriage.[23]

In this passage, Gregory's apophatic sensibility about the divine essence along with his understanding of analogy and linguistic symbolism become apparent. Being neither male nor female, God can equally be called "father" and/or "mother." The genderless God is normative for humanity and not the other way round. So Orthodox Christianity does not understand the male (created) human being as the normative human.[24] Rather, in Christ, we put off the signs of sexual difference along with the whole of the old humanity. Gregory is not captive to sexual ideology, which allows him more linguistic freedom in terms of gendered analogies. In his *Homilies on the Song of Songs,* he seems interested in this "one wedding feast," in the only "marriage" that matters—that is, the human beings' spiritual union with God. That is why he represents the relationship between the soul and God, and between Christ and the Church, through nuptial imagery. But Gregory's "bride" is not a woman, for in Chapter 20 of his treatise *On Virginity,* when speaking of spiritual marriage, he clearly states that

> the argument applies equally to men and women, to move them towards such a marriage. "There is neither male nor female," the Apostle says; "Christ is all, and in all"; and so it is equally reasonable that he who is enamoured of wisdom should hold the Object of his passionate desire, Who is the True Wisdom; and that the soul which cleaves to the undying Bridegroom should have the fruition of her love for the true Wisdom, which is God. We have now sufficiently

revealed the nature of the spiritual union, and the Object of the pure and heavenly Love.[25]

Gregory's use of nuptial symbolism in his *Homilies on the Song of Songs* needs to be interpreted as a form of language that transcends the body's sexual particularity, for sexual difference is not permanent and has thus no ontological significance. When writing these homilies (391–94),[26] he had already written his treatise *On the Making of the Human Being* (378–79) where Gregory interpreted the creation stories in Gen. 1 and Gen. 2 in terms of a double creation. In Chapter 16 of this treatise, he makes a distinction between the first creation of spiritual beings in the image of God, and the creation of human beings, embodied and marked by sexual differentiation.[27] As Gregory explains:

> For as indeed a particular human being is enclosed by the size of his body, and the magnitude corresponding to the outward surface of the body is the measure of his subsistence, so, it seems to me, the whole plenitude of humanity was encompassed by the God of all through the power of foreknowledge, as if indeed in one body, and the text teaches this which says, "And God created the human being, according to the image of God he created him" [Gen 1:27a]. For the image is not in part of the nature, nor is the grace in a certain entity observed in it, but such power extends equally to all the [human] race. A sign of this is that mind is established in all alike; all have the power of rational thought and deliberation, and all the other things through which the divine nature is imaged in that which has been created according to it. The human being manifested at the first creation of the world and the one that will come into being at the consummation of all are alike, equally bearing in themselves the divine image. Because of this, the whole [of humankind] was named as one human being, since to the power of God nothing is either past or future, but what is expected is encompassed equally with what is present by the energy that rules all. So the whole nature, extending from the first to the last, is, as it were, one image of the Existing One; the distinction between male and female was fashioned last [Gen 1:27b], added to what was formed.[28]

Thus, according to the above excerpt, the first account of the human made in the image of God refers to a creation in which the human is a form of presexual, angelic being. As Gregory further explains in Chapter 17 of the same treatise, sexual embodiment is a feature of a secondary, material creation in which God's foreknowledge of the Fall makes sexuality contingent upon the coming of death into creation and does not refer to the image of God in the human. Therefore, at the resurrection we shall be restored to our original, presexual condition in the image of God. As Gregory puts it:

> but while looking upon the nature of man in its entirety and fullness by the exercise of His foreknowledge, and bestowing upon it a lot exalted and equal to the angels, since He saw beforehand by His all-seeing power the failure of their will to keep a direct course to what is good, and its consequent declension from the angelic life, in order that the multitude of human souls might not be cut short by its fall from that mode by which the angels were increased and multiplied,—for this reason, I say, He formed for our nature that contrivance for increase which befits those who had fallen into sin, implanting in mankind, instead of the angelic majesty of nature, that animal and irrational mode by which they now succeed one another.[29]

Valerie Karras draws upon the teachings of Gregory of Nyssa and various other Church Fathers and argues that God's creation of humanity follows a pattern of stages. (1) God decides to create humanity in His image, and after His likeness; (2) God creates humanity in His image, but adds gender, which is not part of God's image, due to His foreknowledge of humanity's Fall (and for procreative purposes); (3) humanity falls from grace, with the concomitant results of active human sexuality and the domination of man over woman; (4) Christ redeems humanity; and (5) in the resurrection God's design for humanity is completed and fulfilled: Humanity exists as God originally intended, without the distinction of sexual differentiation.[30] Eventually, human beings are affected by their biological (postlapsarian) nature and instincts, but are not restricted by their sexed body, for they are called to transcend biological necessity.

Thus, although Gregory envisioned the abolition of sexual division as a component of physical human nature in the eschaton, noetic gender—that is, gender understood as a concept of the mind—remains for him an important human characteristic but as a soteriological characteristic (that remains a concept in the symbolic order). Thus, he liberated gender(s) from the strictures of physical sexed body—that is, the garments of the skin—

calling us all to overcome gender stereotypes (pointing to their functioning as postlapsarian symbols), calling women to be "male" in terms of spiritual strength in this life and men to be "female" in terms of spiritual fecundity in the next. Thus, the best human traits (which are culturally attributed to both genders) are to be cultivated by all human beings irrespective of sex.[31] "In fact, the virtues of gender must be divorced from physical sex since otherwise they would become instincts, which—with the exception of the 'instinct' of erotic love for God—for Gregory cannot be virtuous since they do not emanate from acts of free will."[32]

The Education of Desire: Fleshly Passion and Passionate Desire for God

The previous section closed by highlighting the fact that, according to Gregory's eschatologically oriented theory of gender, regardless of their sexed bodies and/or gender, all human beings are free to cultivate the same traits and virtues and achieve spiritual fecundity. In this section, I focus on the importance of human sexuality and desire,[33] desire's malleable quality and its capacity to focus on blind impulses and things unnecessary and/or on good things, the true beauty—that is, God.

Thus, sexuality seems to refer to two things, one very specific and the other more general. Specifically, sexuality means sexual orientation: that is, the sex of a person to whom someone's sexually attracted.[34] In this sense, sexuality is bound to an individualized and physicalized desire, assuming that sexual enactment somehow exhausts it.[35] More broadly, sexuality is everything about someone's personhood and energy: the way they interact with others and the world. In this second understanding, sexuality is about everything that stimulates our excitement, creativity, and engagement with the world around us. In this sense, sexuality is linked to a broader understanding of desire(s). In this sense, desire is a very inclusive term (referring to a mode of being—that is, to longing itself). Thus, desire includes the desire to dominate, to subjugate, to consume, to own as well as to love, empathize, work for the common good, and so on.

In terms of the patristic tradition, desire is no less than that which continuously animates us to God, as Gregory of Nyssa also taught: It gives us the energy of the participation in the divine life. The faculty of desire (η επιθυμητική δύναμις) is placed in the soul to create a longing for God. Desire is given by God. In the fourth homily on the *Song of Songs*, Gregory says: "You see why you have a faculty of desire, in order, namely, that you may conceive an appetite for the *apple,* the delight of which takes many forms for those who have drawn near to it."[36] For Gregory, desire can be trained and is thus closely linked to free will and reason that play an important role in moderating desire in order to reach its proper goal, that is, passionate pursuit of the Beautiful and contemplation of the divine.[37] As Gregory puts it:

> When it has been trained and purified of all of them, appetite will be turned in its activity to what alone is to be longed for, desired, and loved, not by having completely quenched the impulses naturally innate in us for such things, but by transforming them for the immaterial participation in good things.[38]

It seems that desire is very much valued in the Eastern Orthodox tradition. Drawing upon the writings of Dionysius Areopagite and Maximus the Confessor, John Zizioulas argues that "God, the Other *par excellence,* as *eros* both moves outside himself and attracts to himself as *the ultimate destination* of their desire those whose desire he provokes." In terms of Zizioulas's understanding of desire, "desire cannot move beyond the Other, the desired one; the Other *is* the 'term' of desire. At the same time, the Other, who is the term of Desire, is also the *cause* of desire, as he moves himself towards us, even to the point of uniting with us (Incarnation)."[39] Therefore, desire is an ontological category belonging primarily to God, and only secondarily to humans as a token of their createdness "in the image."

Sarah Coakley points out that in God, desire signifies no lack—as it manifestly does in humans, reminding them of their created source.[40] Explaining the nature, role, and purpose of human desire, Gregory's sister, Macrina, says: "Again, if we were to define what desire is in itself, we shall call it a seeking for what one lacks, or a yearning for the enjoyment of some pleasure."[41] If desire belongs primarily to God and is thus ontologically basic, both sex and gender (which nowadays tends to connote the way embodied relations are carved up and culturally adjudicated) are to be set in right subjection to that desire.[42] Following in Sarah Coakley's footsteps, I think that the obsession with sex and gender and with the sex of a person to whom someone is sexually attracted resides in the lack of God as a final point of reference. According to a Christian understanding of desire, orientation, or attraction, the most important orientation is the orientation to God, toward divine desire. So, I suggest we should shift our attention from debating about the problem of homosexuality (or any other sexuality) to dealing with the more crucial questions of putting desire for God above all other desires, and of judging human desires only in that light.[43] But how can we identify the difference in these many desires that we have (most of which are toxic) in order to move from the corrupt to the sublime within them? How can we put desire for God above all other desires? By processes of education, self-knowledge, humility, prayer, and reliance on divine grace.[44] In short, we arrive at the realm of the ascetic life that involves the transformation of sexuality as the soul progresses in perfection.

Anagogic: Lifestyle and the Transformation of Sexuality

In his writings, Gregory of Nyssa elaborates at length on the stages of the soul's ascent to God—that is, on the soul's progress in perfection.[45] According to Gregory's threefold account of the stages of the soul's ascent to God, first we have the soul's initial withdrawal from wrong and erroneous ideas of God and then the soul becomes aware of the vanity of cosmic things and is guided through sense phenomena to the world of the invisible. Finally, after having been illuminated and purified and after having been transformed into something divine and sinless, the soul can enter within the secret chamber of the divine knowledge.[46]

By discussing the stages of the soul's ascent to God, Gregory actually presents his case for an anagogic lifestyle, a mode of living, an education of desires that will constantly draw a person toward God. In his treatise *On Virginity*, Gregory presents his vision of desire that does not require a disjunctive approach to marriage and celibacy.[47] It seems that the treatise "entertains the thought that the godly ordering of desire is what conjoins the ascetic aims of marriage and celibacy, at their best, and equally what judges both of them, at their worst."[48]

At the heart of Gregory's understanding of the anagogic lifestyle and the soul's progress in perfection lies his metaphor of the stream of desire and of its right direction, use, and even intensification in relation to God. In Chapter 7 of *On Virginity*, he writes:

> Imagine a stream flowing from a spring and dividing itself off into a number of accidental channels. As long as it proceeds so, it will be useless for any purpose of agriculture, the dissipation of its waters

making each particular current small and feeble, and therefore slow. But if one were to mass these wandering and widely dispersed rivulets again into one single channel, he would have a full and collected stream for the supplies which life demands. Just so the human mind (so it seems to me), as long as its current spreads itself in all directions over the pleasures of the sense, has no power that is worth the naming of making its way towards the Real Good; but once call it back and collect it upon itself, so that it may begin to move without scattering and wandering towards the activity which is congenital and natural to it, it will find no obstacle in mounting to higher things, and in grasping realities. We often see water contained in a pipe bursting upwards through this constraining force, which will not let it leak; and this, in spite of its natural gravitation: in the same way, the mind of man, enclosed in the compact channel of an habitual continence, and not having any side issues, will be raised by virtue of its natural powers of motion to an exalted love. In fact, its Maker ordained that it should always move, and to stop is impossible to it; when therefore it is prevented employing this power upon trifles, it cannot be but that it will speed toward the truth, all improper exits being closed.[49]

In Chapter 8 of the same treatise, the same illustration of the water and the spring is employed by Gregory in order to present his view of marriage: "While the pursuit of heavenly things should be a man's first care, yet if he can use the advantages of marriage with sobriety and moderation, he need not despise this way of serving the state."[50] So, marriage is not a sacrament outside ecclesial and ascetical life, for the goodness of marriage derives from that to which it refers—that is, the eschaton. Following Gregory's understanding of marriage, John Panteleimon Manoussakis stresses its relative value and says: "Given, though, that 'in the resurrection people will neither marry nor be given in marriage' [Mt. 22:30], marriage derives its goodness from its own dissolution and, strangely, it succeeds only to the extent that it fails."[51] In Chapter 13 of *On Virginity*, "without wishing to offend," Gregory speaks oddly of the spiritual generation and says:

> Truly a joyful mother is the virgin mother who by the operation of the Spirit conceives the deathless children, and who is called by the

Prophet barren because of her modesty only. This life, then, which is stronger than the power of death, is, to those who think, the preferable one. The physical bringing of children into the world—I speak without wishing to offend—is as much a starting-point of death as of life; because from the moment of birth the process of dying commences.[52]

The fact that Gregory praises virginity, spiritual marriage, and spiritual generation does not mean that sexual pleasure holds any intrinsic fear for him. Rather, his argument seems to be that we have to make a choice about what the final telos of our desire and sexual pleasure is.[53] Do we want to be "pleasure lover" or "God-lover?"[54] For Gregory, it is neither the body nor the sex that is the problem, but worldly interests and the freely chosen perverted passions.[55]

Karras examines *On Virginity* closely and shows that Gregory argues for a set of hierarchically ordered possibilities for erotic states of affairs—that is, for a hierarchy of lifestyles. More analytically, there is bad marriage, in which the external rules of fidelity may be kept but no spiritual unification of desire toward God occurs—no right channeling of eros/desire and no desire to bear the fruits of *leitourgia* (of service to others); bad celibacy, in which physical virginity may (or may not) be obeyed, but in which physical virginity is not leading to any transformation of the soul (there is no desire to bear the fruits of *leitourgia* and the virgin is still subject to false attachments); and then spiritually fruitful marriage and spiritually fruitful celibacy.[56] For Gregory, "since control of the higher spiritual passions and cultivation of virtue through active love are the most important elements in the spiritual life, the married person who can exercise proper control (channeling the water, to use Gregory's analogy) ranks significantly above the mere physical virgin. The highest level, however, is the true virgin who lives an eschatological existence in anticipation by combining control of the negative passions with nurture of the positive virtues, exemplified in active love for others."[57]

So, for Gregory, lifestyles are not hierarchically ordered on the basis of the type of people's sexual attraction or of their abstaining from any sexual intercourse. Rather, controlling toxic passions, like dominating others, transforming carnal passions into passionate desire for God, and actively loving others are the standards according to which we are all judged.

Concluding Remarks

The previous sections underlined three points in Gregory's teachings that can contribute to current discussions about human sexuality: First, by discussing the stages of the soul ascent to God, Gregory actually presents his case for an anagogic lifestyle according to which the ultimate goal of all the energy involved in sexuality is to intensify the desire for God. According to his threefold account of the stages of the soul's ascent to God, after having been illuminated and purified and after having been transformed into something divine and sinless, the soul (which is embodied and sexed) enters within the secret chamber of the divine knowledge, and here she "is entirely seized about by the divine darkness."[58] This final stage—which is the stage of unification with God through love—requires the soul's ultimate desire for God and is associated with the sacrament of Eucharist.

Second, Gregory reflects on marriage and celibacy alongside one another, using the same standards—that is, the goal of one's decision/praxis, the goal of *enkrateia*/ physical celibacy, the goal of marriage, etc. So sexual desire and physical attraction, be it for the opposite or the same sex (but in any case, for another soul) has to be reflected by the same exacting standards of progressive nonattachment and ascetical transformation. It seems that Gregory's appreciation of desire lies in the possibility of its transformation. Instead of craving after evil or desiring worldly things, the soul yearns for "that mystical kiss," for all the purified soul wants is to "bring her mouth to the fount of light"[59] that is God. In other words, fleshly desire of all kinds can be treated as a divine gift and can thus be transformed into passionate desire for God. Gregory hopes that the soul will love God "as much as the body has a bent for what is akin to it."[60] For Gregory, if one has not experienced the motions of the flesh, one can find it difficult to transform desire and turn it toward God.

The third point that can contribute to the current theological discussions about human sexuality is Gregory's eschatologically oriented theory of gender that is understood in the context of his apophatic sensibility about the divine essence. This "apophatic turn" has the capacity not only to undermine gender stereotypes, but to lead to a form of ever-changing modeling of desire for God. In terms of an eschatologically oriented gender theory, the denaturalization of sexual difference is invested with ontological validity. In other words, it is only within a Christocentric (ecclesial and sacramental) epistemological framework that the ontological claim "there is no sexual difference" is valid. The Christocentric and eschatologically oriented gender theory of Gregory subverts both gender essentialism and the culturally repressive web of sexual stereotypes.[61] Devoid of a meaningful horizon that is invested with ontological validity, human beings fail to achieve personal authenticity; everything is reduced to a physicalism that leads to despair and eventually brings death. So, in terms of Gregory's eschatological anthropology and his account of the soul's progress in perfection, the contemplative encounter with divine mystery will include the possibility of upsetting the "normal" vision of the sexes and gender altogether; but, as Coakley points out, it will also include an often-painful submission to other demanding tests of ascetic transformation—through fidelity to divine desire, and thence through fidelity to those whom we love in this world.[62]

Finally, arguing for both an eschatological anthropology and an ontology of personhood and against the objectification of the (O)ther, respecting the alterity of others and especially the Otherness of the divine, realizing that "God is Love" not only in the sense of God's self-disclosure as love in the person of Christ but also in the sense of God's loving before being, "doing the truth" instead of objectifying the others in order to know the truth, are crucial for our making of theology—that is to say, for our referring our speaking about God to communion with God. If we take the above into consideration, then certain practices would change: We would refuse labeling and objectifying others; the Church would struggle for inclusivity informed by love; and we would change our perspective when judging human relationships by focusing not on the sex of those who are in a relationship but on how they relate to each other, to the rest of the creation, and to God.

Notes

1. In the first book of his work *The History of Sexuality*, Michel Foucault traces the genealogy of the modern concept of sexuality. "Sexuality," he suggests, is by no means a fixed term that identifies an objective concept in the world. Rather, the notion of assigning an identity to an individual based on his or her sexual desire is a distinctively modern social construction. Before the nineteenth century there was no such thing as "sexuality" as such. Michel Foucault, *La volonté de savoir* (Paris: Editions Gallimard, 1976). On the constructed nature of sexualities, see also David M. Halperin, *One Hundred Years of Homosexuality: And Other Essays on Greek Love* (New York: Routledge, 1990).

2. According to feminist theory, (sexual) objectification determines the lives of women to the extent that they can think of themselves only as objects. Catharine MacKinnon, *Feminism Unmodified* (Cambridge, Mass.: Harvard University Press, 1987) and Andrea Dworkin, *Intercourse* (New York: The Free Press, 1987).

3. Since the mid-twentieth century, drawing upon patristic thought, Orthodox theologians have developed theological accounts of personhood. See Aristotle Papanikolaou, "Personhood and Its Exponents in Twentieth-Century Orthodox Theology," in *The Cambridge Companion to Orthodox Christian Theology*, ed. Mary B. Cunningham and Elizabeth Theokritoff (Cambridge: Cambridge University Press, 2008), 231–45. For an examination of some points of confluence between theological accounts of personhood and contemporary gender and queer theory, see Bryce E. Rich, "A Queer Personhood: Freedom from Essentialism," in *"For I Am Wonderfully Made": Texts on Eastern Orthodoxy and LGBT Inclusion*, ed. Misha Cherniak, et al. (Nieuwegein, Netherlands: European Forum of Lesbian, Gay, Bisexual and Transgender Christian Groups, 2016), 39–60.

4. Drawing upon the theology of St. Maximus the Confessor, and commenting on Maximus's observation that "the things of the future state are truth" (PG 4.137D), Metropolitan John Zizioulas of Pergamon argues for an eschatological ontology and elaborates on its ethical implications. As he puts it: "An eschatological ontology would lead to a non-judgmental attitude towards our fellow human being in ontological terms such as stereotypes and permanent characterizations. Every person is entitled to a new identity, to a future." John Zizioulas, "'The End Is Where We Start From': Reflections on Eschatological Ontology," in *Game Over? Reconsidering Eschatology*, ed. Christophe Chalamet, Andreas Dettwiler, Mariel Mazzocco, and Ghislain Waterlot (Berlin: Walter de Gruyter, 2017), 275.

5. See note 1 in this chapter.

6. Judith Butler, *Gender Trouble: Feminism and the Subversion of Identity* (New York: Routledge, 1990); Judith Butler, *Bodies That Matter: On the Discursive Limits of "Sex"* (London: Routledge, 1993).

7. Gill Jagger, *Judith Butler: Sexual Politics, Social Change and the Power of the Performative* (London: Routledge, 2008), 1.

8. Jagger, *Judith Butler*, 7.

9. In a severe critique of Butler's opposition to norms and normative ideas such as equality and dignity, and of her denial of any precultural agency, the feminist political philosopher Martha C. Nussbaum wonders where the ability to resist gender identification comes from if there is no structure in the personality that is not thoroughly culture's and power's creation. Martha C. Nussbaum, "The Professor of Parody," *The New Republic* (February 22, 1999): https://newrepublic.com/article/150687/professor-parody. Following Nussbaum's

criticism, the feminist theologian Sarah Coakley argues that although in Butler's analysis one detects a spiritual yearning for personal authenticity, Butler's theory of resistance is merely reinstating the conditions of sexual oppression against which Butler chafes. Sarah Coakley, "The Eschatological Body: Gender, Transformation and God," in *Powers and Submissions: Spirituality, Philosophy and Gender* (Oxford: Blackwell, 2002), 159.

10. Mary McClintock Fulkerson, "Gender—Being It or Doing It? The Church, Homosexuality, and the Politics of Identity," in *Que(e)rying Religion: A Critical Anthology*, ed. Gary David Comstock and Susan E. Henking (New York: Continuum, 1999), 188–201, 193.

11. Nonna Verna Harrison, "The Human Person as Image and Likeness of God," in *Cambridge Companion to Orthodox Christian Theology*, ed. Cunningham and Theokritoff, 80–81; and Nonna Verna Harrison, "Gregory of Nyssa on Human Unity and Diversity," *Studia Patristica* 41 (2006): 336.

12. Thomas Hopko, "On the Male Character of Christian Priesthood," *St. Vladimir's Theological Quarterly* 19, no. 3 (1975): 147–73; Paul Evdokimov, *Woman and the Salvation of the World: A Christian Anthropology on the Charisms of Woman*, trans. A. P. Gythiel (Crestwood, N.Y.: SVS Press, 1994).

13. Harrison, "The Human Person," 89; and Rich, "Queer Personhood," 48–49.

14. Harrison, "The Human Person," 89. See further Verna E. F. Harrison, "Male and Female in Cappadocian Theology," *Journal of Theological Studies* 41 (1990): 465–71; Valerie A. Karras, "Eschatology," in *The Cambridge Companion to Feminist Theology*, ed. S. F. Parsons (Cambridge: Cambridge University Press, 2002), 243–60; Valerie A. Karras, "Sex/Gender in Gregory of Nyssa's Eschatology: Irrelevant or Non-Existent?," *Studia Patristica* 41 (2006): 363–68; and Valerie A. Karras, "Orthodox Theologies of Women and Ordained Ministry," in *Thinking through Faith: New Perspectives from Orthodox Christian Scholars*, ed. A. Papanikolaou and E. Prodromou (Crestwood, N.Y.: SVS Press, 2008), 113–58.

15. The proceedings of two conferences, one in 1988 and the other in 2015, illustrate the development of Eastern Orthodox theological discourse concerning issues of gender, equality, and inclusion. Gennadios Limouris, ed., *The Place of Woman in the Orthodox Church and the Question of the Ordination of Women* (Katerini, Greece: Tertios Publications, 1992) [in Greek] and Petros Vassiliadis, Niki Papageorgiou, and Eleni Kasselouri-Hatzivassiliadi, eds., *Deaconesses: The Ordination of Women and Orthodox Theology* (Newcastle upon Tyne: Cambridge Scholars Publishing, 2017).

16. Coakley, "The Eschatological Body," 157.

17. Coakley, "The Eschatological Body," 159.

18. Karras, "Eschatology"; and Harrison, "Gregory of Nyssa on Human Unity and Diversity."

19. Tina Beattie, *New Catholic Feminism: Theology and Theory* (London: Routledge, 2006), 117.

20. Harrison, "Gregory of Nyssa on Human Unity and Diversity," 344.

21. Jean Daniélou, *Platonisme et théologie mystique: Doctrine spirituelle de Saint Grégoire de Nysse* (Aubier: Éditions Montaigne, 1944), 51–53, 56, 167–68; Harrison, "Male and Female," 467–68 and especially note 93; and Karras, "Sex/Gender," 363–68.

22. For a critical review of the scholarship concerning the ontological status of sex in Gregory of Nyssa's anthropology and the question of whether the resurrection body is degenitalized, see Raphael A. Cadenhead, *The Body and Desire: Gregory of Nyssa's Ascetical Theology* (Oakland: University of California Press, 2018), 96–98, 104; Morwenna Ludlow, *Gregory of Nyssa, Ancient and (Post)modern* (Oxford: Oxford University Press, 2007), 163–201; Warren J. Smith, "The Body of Paradise and the Body of the Resurrection: Gender and the Angelic Life in Gregory of Nyssa's 'De hominis opificio,'" *The Harvard Theological Review* 99, no. 2 (2006): 207–28. Although Gregory admits through his sister, Macrina, that we are unable to give a definitive answer to the question of whether human genitalia will be restored at the resurrection (Cadenhead, *Body and Desire*, 104), "the overall direction of his thought is clear: he regards gender as linked to sexuality and to the other passions, and as such it properly belongs to the problematic 'tunics of skin' that the Fall introduced. Gender, then, is something to be overcome." Hans Boersma, *Embodiment and Virtue in Gregory of Nyssa: An Anagogical Approach* (Oxford: Oxford University Press, 2013), 15.

23. Gregory of Nyssa, *Homilies on the Song of Songs*, trans. Richard A. Norris Jr. (Atlanta: Society of Biblical Literature, 2012), 225. For the Greek text, see "In Canticum canticorum," in *Gregorii Nysseni Opera*, vol. 6, ed. Hermannus Langerbeck (Leiden: Brill, 1952–).

24. Karras, "Eschatology," 252.

25. Gregory of Nyssa, "On Virginity," trans. William Moore, in *Nicene and Post-Nicene Fathers of the Christian Church*, Second Series, vol. 5 (Peabody, Mass.: Hendrickson, 1995), 343–71, 366. For the Greek text, see "De virginitate," in *Gregorii Nysseni Opera*, vol. 8, ed. J. P. Cavarnos, 247–343.

26. For the chronology of Gregory's oeuvre, see Cadenhead, *Body and Desire*, 163–78.

27. Andrew Louth, "The Body in Western Catholic Christianity," in *Religion and the Body,* ed. Sarah Coakley (Cambridge: Cambridge University Press, 1997), 115.

28. For the English translation of this passage of Gregory of Nyssa's *De hominis opificio*, PG 44, 185B-D, see Harrison, "Gregory of Nyssa on Human Unity and Diversity," 336. For the Greek text, see *De hominis opificio*, in *Patrologiae*

Cursus completus, Series Graecae, vol. XLIV, ed. J.P. Migne (Paris, 1857–1866) (hereinafter PG), 124–56.

29. Gregory, *De hominis opificio,* PG 44, 189C-D. English translation: *On the Making of Man,* trans. William Moore, in *Nicene and Post-Nicene Fathers of the Christian Church,* Second Series, vol. 5 (Peabody, Mass.: Hendrickson, 1995), 406.

30. Valerie Karras, "Patristic Views on the Ontology of Gender," in *Personhood: Orthodox Christianity and the Connection between Body, Mind, and Soul,* ed. John Chirban (London: Bergin & Garvey, 1996), 117.

31. Karras, "Sex/Gender," 367.

32. Karras, "Sex/Gender," 367.

33. The word "desire" translates a number of Greek words like *epithymia, eros, ephesis, pothos, pathos,* and *oreksis.*

34. Susannah Cornwall, *Theology and Sexuality* (London: SCM Press, 2013), 2.

35. Sarah Coakley, *The New Asceticism: Sexuality, Gender and the Quest for God* (London: Bloomsbury, 2015), 6.

36. Gregory, *Homilies on the Song of Songs,* 131.

37. For Gregory's theory of desire, see Cadenhead, *Body and Desire,* 62–70.

38. "In Regard to Those Fallen Asleep (De Mortuis, GNO 9)," in *One Path for All: Gregory of Nyssa on the Christian Life and Human Destiny,* trans. Rowan A. Greer (Cambridge: James Clarke & Co, 2015), 113. For the Greek text, see "De mortuis," in *Gregorii Nysseni Opera,* vol. 9, ed. Gunterus Heil, 28–68.

39. John Zizioulas, *Communion and Otherness: Further Studies in Personhood and the Church* (New York: T&T Clark, 2006), 50–51.

40. Sarah Coakley, *God, Sexuality, and the Self: An Essay "On the Trinity"* (Cambridge: Cambridge University Press, 2013), 10.

41. Gregory of Nyssa, *On the Soul and the Resurrection,* trans. Anna M. Silvas, in *Macrina the Younger, Philosopher of God* (Turnhout, Belgium: Brepols, 2008), 192. For the Greek text, see Gregory of Nyssa, "De anima et resurrectione," PG, 46:12–160.

42. Coakley, *God, Sexuality, and the Self,* 10.

43. Coakley, *God, Sexuality, and the Self,* 11.

44. For Gregory's account of the diachronic process of spiritual maturation, see Martin Laird, "Under Solomon's Tutelage: The Education of Desire in the 'Homilies of the Song of Songs,'" *Modern Theology* 18, no. 4 (October 2002): 507–25 and Cadenhead, *Body and Desire,* 123–37.

45. With the term "soul" (Greek ψυχή), Gregory assumes both the immaterial and the material natures of human beings. For him, there is a distinction between soul and body but the soul does not exist prior to the body. The soul is related to the whole body and along with it constitutes the human being that is

created in the image and likeness of God. In this respect, one can replace the word "soul" for the word "person" or "human being." For Gregory's understanding of the soul, see his "De anima et resurrectione."

46. Daniélou, *Platonisme et théologie mystique.*

47. Mark Hart, "Reconciliation of Body and Soul: Gregory of Nyssa's Deeper Theology of Marriage," *Theological Studies* 51 (1990): 450–78.

48. Coakley, *New Asceticism*, 30.

49. Gregory, "On Virginity," 352.

50. Gregory, "On Virginity," 353.

51. John Panteleimon Manoussakis, "Marriage and Sexuality in the Light of the Eschaton: A Dialogue between Orthodox and Reformed Theology," *Religions* 7, no. 7 (July 2016): 5, https://doi.org/10.3390/rel7070089.

52. Gregory, "On Virginity," 359.

53. Coakley, *New Asceticism,* 30.

54. Gregory, "On Virginity," 353.

55. John Behr, "The Rational Animal: A Rereading of Gregory of Nyssa's *De Hominis Opificio*," *Journal of Early Christian Studies* 7 (1999): 246.

56. Valerie Karras, "A Re-evaluation of Marriage, Celibacy, and Irony in Gregory of Nyssa's *On Virginity*," *Journal of Early Christian Studies* 13, no, 1 (2005): 120–21; and Coakley, *New Asceticism*, 50.

57. Karras, "A Re-evaluation of Marriage," 121.

58. Gregory, *Homilies on the Song of Songs*, 341.

59. Gregory, *Homilies on the Song of Songs*, 341.

60. Gregory, *Homilies on the Song of Songs*, 29.

61. Coakley, *God, Sexuality, and the Self*, 342.

62. Coakley, *God, Sexuality, and the Self*, 310.

CHAPTER

11

INTERSEX PEOPLE

NOT PHYSICAL MISTAKES BUT GOD'S IMAGE

Kateřina Kočandrle Bauer

Although intersex people—people born with a combination of male and female biological characteristics, such as chromosomes or genitals—represent around 1.7 percent of the population according to some researchers, they are largely "invisible," neglected, and a taboo.[1] Many of them feel that they were born as "physical mistakes"[2] because they are treated like it, both socially and medically. In the church context, they often hear that their bodies are the result of the fall. There have been attempts from medical, social, and cultural perspectives to attend to their problems,[3] but rarely has the church offered a theological response.[4]

As their bodies do not fit into the usual male or female categories, intersex people challenge traditional teaching from the book of Genesis regarding people being created in God's image as man and woman. Here I will argue that intersex people are also created according to God's image and likeness and that we need to approach the matter on such a basis. I will provide a theological interpretation of the biblical narrative of *imago Dei* that offers space for intersex people to find a fullness of humanity that is not based on binary opposition or the usual ontological hierarchy. I will also show that God's image in people is connected not only to a mythical story of the origins of the human race but also to the ultimate fulfilment of humanity. As John Behr reminds us, the end is the key to understanding the beginning.[5] I will therefore look at an alternative interpretation of God's image from an eschatological perspective. From the Orthodox worldview I will speak about the meaning of human lives from the perspective of deification as a dynamic process in which all human beings journey between *arche* and ultimate *telos*, where people live in the world, in history, and create relationships. I will focus on the significant issues that intersex people face in the process of the human and divine in their lives becoming a unity and in creating relationships with others. I will especially touch on the problems created by an ontological dualistic understanding of God's image in people, an understanding that threatens to lose the iconic nature of intersex people. Finally, I will show that through their lives, intersex people manifest a nondualistic concept of bodily existence and the importance of encountering the kind of otherness that makes relationships possible, and of accepting the other as mystery.

Between Androgyne and Angel

In the book of Genesis, two different stories describe in mythical language the creation of human beings (Gen 1:26–31; 2:5–25). A close look at these two stories reveals differing views concerning God's image in people. The first emphasizes the unity of God's image and only secondarily a bigendered image: "So God created humankind in his image, in the image of God he created them; male and female he created them" (Gen 1:27).[6] The second story describes the gradual creation of man and woman: "So the Lord caused a deep sleep to fall upon the man, and he slept; then he took one of his ribs and closed up its place with flesh. And the rib that the Lord God had taken from the man he made into a woman and brought her to the man" (Gen 2:21–22). This apparent discrepancy in the creation accounts shows that since the very beginning the question of God's image and its relationship to gender has been far from univocal. In the Christian tradition, the second story has prevailed, alongside an associated hierarchical understanding of man and woman in which the love between the two reflects a polarity characterized by rivalry rather than complementarity.

Leave aside this question of the polarity between man and woman, a favorite subject of feminist theologians,[7] I will focus on the first story, which has been much neglected through Christian history but which offers an alternative interpretation that will provide a more spacious arena for a discussion on intersex people and God's image in the human person. The first part of the first story emphasizes the unity of God's image in people, where gender has no significant role. It is a part of the story that has inspired the mystical tradition of the Church. The Jewish kabbala interprets the primordial person, Adam Kadmon (וּמְדָק םדָאָ), as androgynous, neither man nor woman.[8] We find a variation of this myth in the Protestant mystic Jacob Böhme (1575–1624), whose work in this area strongly influenced Russian religious thinkers and theologians and focuses on a mystical interpretation of the biblical story that presents an androgynous Adam.[9] The mythos was developed by Nikolai Berdayev (1874–1948),[10] who links the primordial heavenly androgynous person with the figure of Sophia, Holy Wisdom. Sophia is a divine element of the primordial person characterized by purity and virginity. The idea also influenced Orthodox theologians such as Sergei Bulgakov (1871–1944), who works with an androgynous image of God in people on the level of the soul rather than the spirit. Bulgakov identifies the feminine in the human soul with the Mother of God and the masculine with Jesus Christ: "All human hypostasis desires in the mind to give birth to divine logos and to love in the heart like his Mother."[11] Bulgakov's spiritual daughter Mother Maria Skobtsova (1891–1945) goes even further in her interpretation of the androgynous image of God in people. Like Bulgakov, she suggests that in one's most authentic being there always exists the Child-Mother dyad; that deep inside every human being is the bi-une[12] icon of the Mother of God with the Child.[13] Such an image is the starting point for an understanding of human solidarity with others. Through these archetypes, people orient themselves on the spiritual path, not only freely choosing their own cross, but also helping others with theirs.[14]

This forgotten interpretation of the creation of humankind as androgynous has a parallel in the New Testament, where Jesus offers an interpretation of people not on the basis of the beginning but on the eschatological fulfilment, where gender plays an equally insignificant role. In his discussion with the Sadducees in Matthew 22:23–33, Jesus is asked about marriage from the perspective of the Law of Moses. He answers: "For in the resurrection they neither marry nor are given in marriage, but are like angels in heaven" (Matt. 22:30). We find a similar emphasis in the patristic tradition—for example, in the Cappadocian fathers. According to Gregory of Nyssa (335–94), with respect to the ultimate fulfilment, gender is secondary.[15] In the modern period of Orthodox theology, the Orthodox theologian Elisabeth Behr-Sigel (1907–2005), drawing on the Cappadocian fathers, says that the uniqueness of every person cannot be expressed on the basis of gender, and sexual difference cannot be seen as a spiritual quality.[16]

These two interpretations of God's image in humankind—the androgynous image and the angelic perspective of eschatological fulfilment—help to break down interpretations based on polarity and hierarchy. The two images not only complement the second creation story in Genesis but can serve as a corrective to concepts linked only to gender and bodily existence and to fundamentalist concepts fixed on a single aspect of God's image in people. The androgynous concept brings otherness and openness into this teaching and introduces a more spacious and hence more complete image of a human being, integrating the "stranger" within the human self, which thus becomes the locus of an encounter with the other inside every individual, including intersex people. However, in focusing on the heavenly status of humankind, there is a danger of ignoring earthly bodily existence, which does need to be dealt with.

The Journey from *Eden* to *Eschaton*

In the Orthodox tradition, deification is not a status but a journey, from *arche* to *telos*. Based on the interpretation of the Church fathers, Orthodox tradition emphasizes the difference between God's image and God's likeness: "Then God said: 'Let us make humankind in our image, according to our likeness'" (Gen 1:26). The image is the given ontological state of humankind without any differences; the likeness is the dynamic element that humankind reaches in the process of deification.[17] This journey toward reaching God's likeness, the unity of the divine and the human, involves the human ability to create loving relationships, not just with God but also with others and with the whole creation, an ability that is not only abstract but also embodied. Here, the mythos of the androgynous and the angelic-eschatological states of humankind, although important concepts for deconstructing the hierarchical vision of God's image in people as man and women, do not say enough about the bodily existence of intersex people. In this context, three important issues need to be addressed. First, the rehabilitation of the body as part of God's image in people. Second, and conversely, the narrowing of the image of God to bodily existence alone. And third, the various forms of relationship that intersex people live in and in which they find fulfilment in love.

Intersex people face the problem of the taboo associated with their bodies. Some do not know they are intersex until they are adolescents; some are intentionally silent in public about the fact they are different in order not to be excluded from society, including from the life of the Church, sacramentally and otherwise. Behind this problem is the deep-rooted ontological dualism of mind and soul in the Christian discourse, and this needs to be overcome. Human bodily existence in general, and the intersex body in particular, has always been a misunderstood and underestimated part of God's image,[18] largely as a result of the voices within the Christian tradition that have deepened the polarized and hierarchical vision of cosmological reality in which God and creation are entirely separate; such a vision has dominated most theological anthropology. Neither cosmological dualism nor pantheism offers an integrated theological anthropology, as no real relationship of love between God and creation is possible in such approaches. Here the pan-en-theistic cosmological concepts can offer some help:[19] God is in everything, as Sergei Bulgakov says.[20] In Bulgakov's pan-en-theistic approach, because the world was created by God, it is imbued with something of the divine nature.[21] This positive belief in the goodness of creation is then reflected in a theological anthropology in which the body is an expression both of the fragility of our created state and of my inner self. Voices that rehabilitate bodily existence as part of God's image can be found as early as the patristic era. For Irenaeus of Lyon (150–202), humankind, both mind and body, is created according to God's image; the body, the temple of Holy Spirit, is also a part of human salvation.[22] It is not our bodily existence that separates us from God. As Olivier Clément (1921–2009) says, my body, each body, is not just a tool, it is the "I" in the relationship to others, the world and God.[23]

We should note that the problem with body/mind-spirit dualism is that in church circles it reduces the lives of intersex people to questions of sexuality and anatomical disorders. If we desire a proper theological understanding of human life as God's image, we must take human bodily existence seriously while not reducing God's image to mere corporeality, or, here, to flesh and sexuality. The Chalcedonian dogma provides a useful theological starting point for overcoming the body/mind-spirit dualism: Jesus Christ is the perfect union of divinity and humanity. At the time of the Council of Chalcedon, the theological extremes that either underplayed the humanity and bodily existence of Jesus Christ (Monophysitism) or insisted on a separation of his divinity and humanity (Nestorianism) were considered heretical. Vladimir Lossky reminds us, however, that the two natures mutually penetrate in Jesus Christ but are not combined as such.[24] Lossky uses the patristic term *perichoresis*[25] to express how two natures in one person dwell in each other without confusion.[26] Interpreting the theological anthropology of St. Maximus the Confessor,[27] Lars Thunberg

(1928–2007) relates the term *perichoresis* to the body/mind structure in human beings and in so doing helps to overcome the body/mind dichotomy.[28] The body as flesh does not express the wholeness of me as a person, but neither am I a bodiless angel in my earthly life. As a being created in God's image, I cannot be reduced to a single aspect of existence. Intersex people are their bodies, but as God's image they are nonetheless something more. In his inimitable poetic style, Olivier Clément reminds us that our body "reveals" but also "covers" our personality.[29]

The problematic issues outlined above affect the ability of intersex people to enter into loving relationships and find harmony and integration in their journey from *arche* to *telos*. They live their mutuality in all kinds of relationships, including marriage: from voluntary or involuntary single life, or homosexual, heterosexual, or bisexual relationships or marriages. The question of Church legalization of nontraditional relationships is beyond the scope of this paper. Here I focus on the problems intersex people must deal with if they are to live in a loving relationship.[30]

First, intersex people are sometimes involuntarily isolated from others and unable to enter a loving and fulfilling relationship because they are ashamed and feel they do not "fit in." They nonetheless retain the desire to be recognized and loved by others. Such social isolation can lead to psychological problems such as depression or anxiety. As both theological anthropology and Trinitarian theology emphasize the central role of loving relationships, the Church should play a supportive role without violating the privacy of intersex people. It should also be noted that friendship is a theologically and spiritually underestimated type of relationship and can play an important role.[31] The biblical emphasis on Christians being "friends of God"[32] encourages us to understand friendship as a theological model for the formation of relationships based on freedom and with no hierarchy. The Protestant theologian Jürgen Moltmann suggests that "'friend' is not an official category, or a title of sovereignty, or a function that is exercised only for a certain period of time."[33]

Secondly, as outlined above, our bodily existence is part God's image in us, but this does not mean that intersex people should be forced to fit into the binary model of male-female sex anatomy. An iconic vision of personhood implies an awareness that each of us is unique. Each body is different, just as each person is different. There are at least thirty congenital variations of sex anatomy in intersex people, which makes any kind of categorization meaningless. Sometimes the physical difference is clear from birth, sometimes from adolescence, sometimes not at all. Since the 1950s, genital surgery has been one of the options recommended to parents for their intersex children, but such drastic measures should never be imposed on them by anyone, the Church included. It is an approach that considers the other as a mere object to be manipulated, the fulfilment of narcissistic ideas about what the image of God should look like in other people.

Thirdly, making loving relationships can be difficult for intersex people if they are forced to accept fundamentalist notions of the image of God in the human person. Being forced to undergo corrective surgery and take hormones for the rest of their lives in order to become "normal" and have a "normal" married relationship is a form of violation. The situation is exacerbated when God's image in people is interpreted in terms of reproduction—"be fruitful and multiply"—which is not always possible for intersex people, nor indeed for heterosexual people. Here again we see a reduction of God's image in people and of the aim of deification. The Russian religious philosopher Vladimir Solovyov (1853–1900) describes such "love" as pathological:[34] The other becomes an object rather than the image of God. Olivier Clément suggests that this objectifying view of the other person causes a split between person and body.[35]

Finally, alongside reducing the relationship to a mere vehicle for reproduction comes the problem of involuntary sexual ascesis. Physical love should not be demonized. In a loving relationship, sexual relations are an important language of that relationship,[36] whether in relationships between intersex people or in a heterosexual marriage: Erotic desire needs to be directed within the relationship if relational harmony is to be protected.[37] Because of their anatomies, intersex people often find they need to challenge involuntary ascesis. In such a situation they should be free to decide how to connect their mind and their body in the process of deification, in which sexual love as one expression of love has a role to play, even if it means undergoing genital surgery or taking hormones. It is a question of human freedom. There is a difference between forcing someone to change their body to suit the concept of God's image and the human need to recognize the sexual aspect of love, not as an expression of pleasure alone but as an outworking of an encounter between two people who love each other.

The Church's role should always be to provide adequate pastoral care and to help intersex people accept and find themselves as people who are deserving of love and who bear a uniqueness that is part of God's image in them. They should also be allowed to share in church only what they want to share and should not be forced to expose their private lives if they do not want to.

Beyond Binary Oppositions

Intersex people challenge theological discourse in many ways, especially with respect to any insistence on the binary categories so deeply rooted in Western metaphysics and theological discourse. They live, in reality, what the postmodern theological and philosophical discourse calls the deconstruction of being and thinking on the basis of binary oppositions characterized by hierarchy and dualism. They deconstruct the metaphysical thinking that categorizes all reality, including the issue of gender, into opposing poles and where the category "in between" is completely overlooked. Intersex people help us to overcome such thinking and to consider ourselves and others as not being so simple to categorize or label. This reminds us of Martin Heidegger's awareness that Western metaphysics had forgotten the ontological distinction between being (*das Sein*) and beings (*das Seiende*).[38] If everything, including God and people, is considered as being (*das Sein*), human existence becomes static, objectified, and controlled.[39] But we cannot understand people as static, closed beings, but only on the basis of their existence, of being "here in the world," of being "always on the way" (*Da-sein*).[40] Intersex people, by their embodied existence, help us to understand our own existence and also the being of others as open, as on the way. Being on the way, as expressed poetically by Heidegger, means not just remembering the journey that has passed but being open to what lies ahead.

Such an understanding of the openness of existence is reflected in language; intersex people help us to deconstruct our language stereotypes. The French philosopher Jacques Derrida argues that Western language is marked and hierarchized by binary oppositions that have an effect on everything from our conception of the relationship between speech and writing to our understanding of difference on all levels of reality. The same is true of symbolic expressions used by the Church, particularly the dichotomic language of day/night, man/woman, father/mother, mind/body, which creates ontological hierarchies in which the first member of the pair is always linked with fullness of meaning and fullness of presence,[41] and in which the real existence of a person does not matter because it is trapped in an asymmetrical scheme. Here, intersex people again help us to understand that the dichotomic language that creates ontological asymmetry fails to express the complexity of the reality we live in. There are always intermediate aspects of created reality—not only darkness and light, but also shadows; not just day and night, but also twilight—which express the complexity and beauty of reality, or, in theological terms, the beauty of creation.

Intersex people also challenge our understanding of our existence beyond the binaries by reminding us that the openness of being that nourishes the intermediate and challenges our thinking and dichotomic language is characterized by a kind of ungraspability of the fullness of being and understanding. Derrida helps here by insisting that language has always allowed space for an absence of meaning and an absence of being; fullness of meaning and being is a false image we have in our minds, even with respect to God or other people.[42] Derrida's philosophy reminds us of the apophatic way of knowing God, which can also be related to ways of knowing people. Like God, people made according to God's image cannot be fully explained or grasped.[43] In order to remain truly other, the other person always transcends my imagination, and this is true of every human being. Nobody, therefore, should be forced to explain their existence, to bare themselves in front of others, in order to be understood. The other person should be respected as a different person; otherness should never be understood as sin or as a tool for manipulation.[44]

In sum, intersex people deconstruct standard Western metaphysics and challenge taboos and prejudices rooted in metaphysical concepts that are based on binary opposition. They are like an epistemological key through which we can realize that there is a richness to life beyond binary opposition and that human beings are not dead substances but real existences that are never the same and can never be measured or calculated. They show that dichotomic language can never fully represent the complexity of reality and that even gender cannot be interpreted according to fundamentalist notions of what is "normal."[45] Intersex people help us to realize that our being and understanding of our existence is always characterized both by the phenomenon "in between," which also enters into theological anthropology, and by the apophatic element, in which the other is always a mystery.

Notes

1. This essay is part of the work supported by Charles University Research Centre No. 204052. It is based on a chapter in a collective monograph. See Ivana Noble and Kateřina Kočandrle Bauer, "Teologický pohled na problematiku rodu [A theological view of the question of gender]," in *Kdo je člověk? Teologická antropologie ekumenicky* [Who is the Human Being? An Ecumenical Approach to Theological Anthropology], ed. Zdenko Širka (Prague: Karolinum, 2021).

2. See the interview with the Belgian model and intersex activist Hane Gaby Odiele, "My life as an intersex supermodel," *The Times* (April 22, 2017): https://www.thetimes.co.uk/article/my-life-as-an-intersex-supermodel-92f7d57xh.

3. See Katrina Karzakis, *Fixing Sex: Intersex, Medical Authority and Lived Experience* (Durham, N.C.: Duke University Press, 2008); Elizabeth Reis, *Bodies in Doubt: An American History of Intersex* (Baltimore, Md.: Johns Hopkins University Press, 2009), and others.

4. See the work on the theology of intersex people by Dr. Megan DeFranza: https://www.megandefranza.com/. See also her dissertation: Megan DeFranza, "Intersex and Imago: Sex, Gender, and Sexuality in Postmodern Theological Anthropology Theological Anthropology" (PhD diss., Marquette University, 2011).

5. See John Behr, "Standing in the Temple: The Liturgical, and Apocalyptic, Context of Theology" (conference paper, Contemplative Traditions. Theory & Practice: A Symposium in Honor of Professor Andrew Louth, Sigtuna, Sweden, December 15, 2019).

6. All Bible quotations are from the New Revised Standard Version (NRSV).

7. See, for example, Elisabeth Schüssler Fiorenza, *In Memory of Her: A Feminist Theological Reconstruction of Christian Origins* (London: SCM, 1983); Rosemary Radford Ruether and Eleanor McLaughlin, eds., *Women of Spirit: Female Leadership in the Jewish and Christian Traditions* (New York: Simon & Schuster, 1979); Lavinia Byrne, *Women before God* (London: SPCK, 1988).

8. See Judith Deutsch Kornblatt, "Solov'ev's Androgynous Sophia and the Jewish Kabbalah," *Slavic Review* 50, no. 3 (1991): 487–96.

9. See Jacob Böhme, *Cesta ke Kristu* [The journey toward Christ], trans. Martin Žemla (Prague: Vyšehrad, 2003), 194.

10. See Nikolai Berdyaev, "Studies Concerning Jacob Boehme: Etude II; The Teaching about Sophia and the Androgyne": http://www.berdyaev.com/berdiaev/berd_lib/1930_351.html.

11. See Sergei Bulgakov, "Ipostas' i ipostasnost'" [Hypostasis and hypostasy], in *Trudy o Troichnosti* (Moscow: O.G.I., 2001), 35.

12. Here, Mother Maria uses the Russian term *dvujedinoj*, usually translated into English as "biune." It means that God's image in people consists of two

inseparable images: God's Mother, and Her Son. See Mother Maria Skobtsova, *Essential Writings*, trans. Richard Pevear and Larissa Volokhonsky (Maryknoll, N.Y.: Orbis, 2003), 69.

13. See Mother Maria Skobtsova, "O podrazhanii bogomateri" [On the imitation of the Mother of God], in *Vospominanija, stat'i, ocherki I* (Paris: YMCA, 1992), 93–108, here 99.

14. See Skobtsova, "O podrazhanii bogomateri," 102.

15. See Gregory of Nyssa, *De anima et resurrectione*, in *PG*, 45.187–222.

16. See Elizabeth Behr-Sigel, *The Ordination of Women in the Orthodox Church* (Geneva: WCC Publications, 2000), 3.

17. See Andrew Louth, "Introduction to Genesis 1–11," in *Ancient Christian Commentary on Scripture, Old Testament I: Genesis 1–11*, ed. Andrew Louth (Downers Grove, Ill.: InterVarsity Press, 2001), 1.

18. There are many works on the theology of the body from the feminist theologians. See, for example, Lisa Isherwood and Elizabeth Stuart, *Introducing Body Theology* (Sheffield, U.K.: Sheffield Academic Press, 1998).

19. For more on the concepts of pan-en-theism, see James Copper, *Panentheism: The Other God of the Philosophers; From Plato to the Present* (Grand Rapids, Mich.: Academic, 2006).

20. For example, Sergei Bulgakov, *Ikona i ikonopochitanie: dogmaticheskij ocherk* [Icons and the Name of God] (Moscow: Iskusstvo, 1999), 262.

21. For more on the sophianic cosmology of Sergei Bulgakov, see Kateřina Bauerová, "The Mysticism of Pan-unity: Sophiology Revisited," in *Wrestling with the Mind of the Fathers*, Ivana Noble et al. (Yonkers, N.Y.: St. Vladimir's Seminary Press, 2015), 157–99.

22. See Irenaeus of Lyon, *Contra Haereses*, V, 6, 1, *PG* vol. 7, 1136–37.

23. See Olivier Clément, *Tělo pro smrt a pro slávu: malé uvedení do teopoetiky těla* (Velehrad: Refugium, 2004), 12. I work with the Czech translation of the French original, *Corps de mort et de gloire, petite introduction à une théopoétique du corps* (Paris: Desclée de Brouwer, 1995).

24. See Vladimir Lossky, *Mystical Theology*, 145–46.

25. In the Greek patristic tradition, the word *perichoresis* was used for the life within Holy Trinity, between the two natures of Christ and also among God and the creation. See Verna Harrison, "Perichoresis in the Greek Fathers," *St. Vladimir's Theological Quarterly* 35 (1991): 53–65.

26. For more on perichoresis in Christology, see Charles Twombly, *Perichoresis and Personhood: God, Christ, and Salvation in John of Damascus* (Eugene, Ore.: Pickwick Publications, 2016).

27. See Lars Thunberg, *Microcosm and Mediator: The Theological Anthropology of Maximus the Confessor* (Chicago, Ill.: Open Court Publishing Company, 1995) 101–4.

28. The Protestant theologian Jürgen Moltmann takes a similar approach. See Jürgen Moltmann, *God in Creation* (Minneapolis, Minn.: Fortress Press, 1993), 235.

29. See Clément, *Tělo pro smrt a pro slávu*, 12.

30. See the video of intersex experience in the family and the church by Lianne Simon and Megan DeFranza: https://www.youtube.com/watch?v=rrS8rXF1OqI.

31. See the passages in which Jesus introduces God as his friend—e.g., Luke 11:5–6. Jesus was himself surrounded by friends: John 11:11, 35–36; 15:15.

32. See John 15:15.

33. See Jürgen Moltmann, *The Living God and the Fullness of Life* (Louisville, Ky.: Westminster John Knox Press, 2015), 118.

34. See Vladimir Solovyov, "Smysl ljubvi" [The meaning of love], in *Sochinenija v dvuh tomah* (Moscow: Mysl', Vo. 7, 1988), 5–6, 8–9.

35. See Clement, *Tělo pro smrt a pro slávu*, 14.

36. See Clement, *Tělo pro smrt a pro slávu*, 83.

37. See Aristotle Papanikolaou, "Sex, Marriage and Theosis," *The Wheel* 13/14 (Spring/Summer, 2018): 91–97, here 94–97.

38. See Martin Heidegger, *Vom Wesen des Grundes* [On the Essence of Ground] (Klosterman, 1995).

39. See my book published in Czech: Kateřina Bauer, *Znovuobjevení symbolu u Louis-Marie Chauveta* [Rediscovering the symbol with Louis-Marie Chauvet] (Brno: CDK, 2010), 25–27.

40. See Martin Heidegger, *Sein und Zeit* [Being and Time] (Tubingen: Adler's Foreign Books Inc, 2006), 39–45.

41. See Jonathan Culler, *On Deconstruction: Theory and Criticism after Structuralism* (London: Routledge & Kegan Paul, 1983), 93.

42. For more, see Ivana Dolejšová, *Accounts of Hope: A Problem of Method in Postmodern Apologia* (Bern: Peter Lang, 2001), 36.

43. On apophatic anthropology, see André Scrima, *Apophatic Anthropology*, trans. Octavian Gabor (Piscataway, N.J.: Gorgias Press, 2016).

44. See Joy Ann McDougall, "A Trinitarian Grammar of Sin," in *The Theological Anthropology of David Kesley*, ed. Gene Outka (Grand Rapids, Mich.: Eerdmans, 2016), 107–26.

45. We are also reminded of the spiritual tradition of the fool for Christ. For more on this analogy, see Giacomo Sanfilippo, *Orthodoxy in Dialogue* (October 22, 2017): https://orthodoxyindialogue.com/2017/10/22/intersex-vs-transgender-addendum-to-greek-prayer-for-name-changes-by-giacomo-sanfilippo/.

CHAPTER

12

A Theology of Sex

Aristotle Papanikolaou

The Presuppositions

Perhaps my point is best illustrated through a story: During the fall 1999 semester, I taught at Holy Cross Greek Orthodox School of Theology in Brookline, Massachusetts, a course on ethics. We were discussing St. Maximus on virtues and how the development of virtues enables relations, and in so doing, makes space for the presencing of God. I then asked the students whether, if two people (I did not mention gender) were living together in friendship for fifty years and manifesting the virtues, this would be an example of communion and presencing of God? They all said yes. I then asked whether the fact that they had sex would negate the good resulting from their virtuous friendship: Half said it would, while the other half got the point that I will try to articulate in this short essay.

It is important, first, to clarify that the context to which I am speaking is the ecclesial one. Ecclesial ethics on sex and sexuality have been primarily about sex and the criteria for establishing a morally right sex act. Since my own intended audience is the Christian ecclesia, in the broadest sense, my focus is on the sex act, but insofar as I intend to focus on the dynamics of desire, issues related to sexuality are also in play. I do not engage, however, the wider academic and public discussion on sexuality. (If the Christian discussion perhaps has talked too much about sex, I think the broader discussion outside of, though not necessarily excluding Christian voices, has focused too little on sex, and my suspicion is that such a focus would be seen as some kind of concession to the seemingly puritanical impulses of religious discourse.) Whatever may be the case, we need to talk more about sex, both the act, but also, more importantly, the dynamics of desire surrounding the act.

I wanted to be clear about how the audience affects my argument, because even given the same presuppositions, there may be disagreement on my focus on the sex act. At this point, there may be some who would argue that to focus on the sex act is to concede too much to the ecclesial reduction of issues of sex and sexuality to the sex act. Marriage, itself, is more than simply sex and, moreover, Christians, perhaps, should expand their view on what erotic love looks like in order to include same-sex partnerships that involve homoerotic acts. To this point, I would argue that focusing on sex simultaneously does clarify the Christian understanding of love even if love cannot, obviously, be reduced to what can be said about the sex act. As the story above, however, demonstrates, the real issue is not the recognition of love between same-sex partners. There has never been a problem within Christian discourse of friendship—a form of love—between same-sex persons; in fact, there is more than ample evidence on the male side of how same-sex friendships in antiquity are actually more intimate than married relationships between a man and a women, with the latter being viewed in functional terms in relation to social goods.[1] The ecclesial issue has never been with *philia* but with *eros* among same-sex partners, and this is evident even today with some Christians supporting "spiritual friendship" as an option for those who openly acknowledge homoerotic desire.[2]

Given these stipulated presuppositions, my goal is to end my paper with a suggestion for a theology of sex grounded in a theological anthropology that itself affirms the human capacity for *theosis*—or union with God. I want to begin with a brief amplification of *theosis* as a learning how to love, especially drawing on the theology of virtue in Maximus the Confessor. I will then discuss marriage as an asceticism aimed at learning how to love—*theosis*. It is here that I will first attempt to elaborate what I mean by a theology of sex in light of *theosis*. I will then turn my attention to homoerotic relations, and I will argue that the Christian objection to homosexuality, writ large, amounts to an objection to same-sex sex. I will then argue that a Christian objection to same-sex sex chains itself to a deontological approach to sex that runs counter to the approach to sex grounded in *theosis*, and that is more consistent with an understanding of marriage as a sacrament—the presencing of God in and through material forms and practices.

A Theotic Ethics

Let me begin my argument with the claim that a theology of sex that would form the scaffolding for an ethics of sex must itself be grounded in the affirmation of *theosis*. I would make this claim to a broader Christian audience, attempting to demonstrate that a necessary implication of belief in the affirmation of the Incarnation is that humans are created to become gods. I would also expect it to be a given among Orthodox to believe in the possibility of *theosis*, even in this life, to a greater and lesser degree, as the possibility for *theosis* is not simply implied in the Incarnation itself—my primary criterion for a valid argument—but in scriptural, patristic, liturgical, and canonical texts.[3]

My next step is to draw from the very persuasive claim of Alasdair MacIntyre, who argued quite convincingly in *After Virtue* that what divided modern from premodern approaches is that premodern ethics was based on a three-fold structure "of untutored human-nature-as-it-happens-to-be, human-nature-as-it-could-be-if-it-realized-its-*telos*, and the precepts of rational ethics as the means for the transition from one to the other."[4] Modern ethics, he argues, eliminated the second element of this structure, which is "human-nature-as-it-could-be-if-it-realized-its-*telos*," and, as a result, is both incoherent and destined to fail insofar as it attempts to retain the precepts of premodern ethics while eliminating the teleological framework within which those precepts developed. If we accept MacIntyre's analysis, then we can affirm that the telos implied by the Incarnation is that of *theosis* and that the precepts "of rational ethics as the means for the transition from one to the other"—that is, from untutored human-nature-as-it-happens-to-be to human-nature-as-it-could-be-if-it-realized-its-telos—must somehow be related to *theosis*. In other words, deontological ethics even in the form of divine-command ethics is ruled out since the precepts of rational ethics cannot simply be for the sake of the precepts in and of themselves but must somehow contribute to the telos of human beings. Furthermore, natural law theory based on the strict divide between nature and grace would also be ruled out, but not a natural law theory that sees nature as graced.[5] To account for ethics in this way—that is, as precepts that facilitate the transition of human nature from one state to another—can only be done through a virtue ethics, because only the category of virtue can make sense of this—what might be called—existential transformation.

A Theotic Anthropology

The fact that language of virtue naturally flows from the Christian affirmation of *theosis* is not only implied in the theology of the Incarnation itself, but is also abundantly evident in the scriptural, patristic, liturgical, and canonical witness. Not only is the language of virtue the preferred language for expressing a theotic life, the dynamics of the soul involved in realization of such a life is explained through the language of virtue. This is especially clear in the seventh-century Christian thinker, Maximus the Confessor, who has one of the most, if not the most, developed understandings of a theotic dynamics of the soul.[6]

Maximus's own account of a theotic dynamics of the soul is based on a prior understanding not simply of *theosis* as the telos of human beings—not to mention the cosmos—but also an understanding of *theosis* in terms of the greatest commandment to love God with all of one's heart mind and soul and to love the neighbor as self. This movement toward a lived realization of the greatest commandment involves both the rational and affective parts of the soul—it has both a cognitive and affective dimension. There is a simultaneity in their operations, and the formation of the one affects that of the other. The two must be in sync and for this syncing to occur, both parts of the soul must be formed in the virtues.

Since *eros* is ultimately the fuel that propels and sustains the soul in union with God, Maximus gives a great deal of attention to the mechanics of love, or what I might call the learning to love, which ultimately means giving attention to the irascible and concupiscible/desiring dimensions of the human condition. The three greatest obstacles to love are fear, anger, and hatred, which themselves affect the capacity for temperance or the desiring part of the soul and the objects of desire, which, of course, affect our capacity for contemplation, or our ability to see objects in their truth as created by God. It is also quite interesting that Maximus uses *agape* in reference to the irascible part of the soul and exclusively in terms of our relation to the neighbor, and not in terms of the human relation to God, for which he uses the term *eros*. The point, which is almost Freudian, is that the cultivation of *agape*—which is the tempering of fear, anger, and hatred—leads to proper *eros* in relation to objects and to God and allows for contemplation. This means that at the root of an *eros* that objectifies is fear, anger, and hatred. This further means that asceticism is about finding a way to make clear those moments of the soul so as to temper their intensity and their ability to shape our *eros*, or to disentangle desire from fear, anger, and hatred.

A Theology of Marriage

Since the intended audience of this essay is ecclesial, and since much of ecclesial approach to sex has been understood within the context of marriage, including marriage as sacrament for Orthodox and Roman Catholics, it is necessary at this point to turn to a theology of marriage in light of a theotic anthropology that is implied by a theotic ethic. My argument will have to affirm that marriage is, indeed, a sacrament, since *theosis* and sacrament could be interpreted as almost synonymous, insofar as both affirm the realism of divine-human communion through material form. By doing so, I might alienate those Christians who reject sacramentality, and with that particular audience, the discussion on sex could not proceed without first resolving the debate on the ethical and anthropological implications of the common affirmation of the Incarnation. In short, a nonsacramental view of creation, including the human being, is simply not consistent with affirming a divine-human Jesus Christ. The sacramentality of the material world then would seem to appeal exclusively to Orthodox and Roman Catholic Christians, but there are those in the Protestant world, especially among Anglican, Lutheran, Reformed, and Methodist Christians, that would affirm the realism of *theosis* in some form.[7] It is to that particular ecclesial audience that what follows would be probable, if not necessarily convincing.

To identify marriage as sacrament is to recognize that the commitment between a man and a woman to live the rest of their lives together presences the life of God, and has the potential to increasingly presence the life of God. As Alexander Schmemann so beautifully put it, "the word sacrament was never restricted by its identification with our current seven sacraments. This word embraced the entire mystery of the salvation of the world and mankind (*sic*) by Christ and in essence the entire content of the Christian faith."[8] When thinking about sacrament, we think in terms of symbols. The symbols are not those material forms that simply point to something over there, but they make present that which is simultaneously something other. In relation to God, symbol, icon, and sacrament are where time and eternity converge. The ultimate icon of God is the human being, and in that sense, the human being is herself sacramental.[9] As we saw with

St. Maximus the Confessor, this sacramentality has something to do with the alignment of the various parts of the soul, or dimensions of the human condition. The sacramentality of the human beings, or even of all creation, is synonymous with the word *theosis*.

To identify marriage as sacrament, one cannot simply point to the marriage ceremony—this would not make sense. If sacrament means to presence iconically the life of God, then the sacramentality of marriage cannot be reduced to the ceremony. Marriage itself, much like created reality, is potentially sacramental, and the initial commitment consists of a presencing of God. The marriage ceremony, much like the Eucharist and Baptism, should be considered an event of this presencing; but, again—much like the Eucharist and Baptism—after the event, the ascetical struggle begins anew to return to that which has been given in Eucharist and Baptism.

In light of the human telos to be deified, and not in terms of deontological categories of obligation, marriage becomes an ascetical struggle to learn how to love through attention to the various parts of the soul or dimensions of the human condition, and any movement in love cannot be anything but a movement in God. If a married couple celebrates fifty years of marriage, adjectives used to describe such a love include "deep," "profound," or "authentic." Such a love may have endured difficulties, including possible betrayals, which need not obstruct and may have actually contributed to what might be recognized as "growth" in love, understood in terms of both *agape* and *eros*. For such a love to exist after fifty years, such virtues as honesty, patience, openness, truth-telling, self-control, empathy, compassion, and, most importantly, humility must have been operative over time, lending credibility to St. Maximus's claim that virtues can beget other virtues and that virtues constitute the building blocks of love. St. Dorotheos of Gaza analogizes the Christian life to building a house: "The roof is charity, which is the completion of virtue as the roof completes the house. After the roof comes the crowning of the dwelling place [i.e., railings around the flat roof]. . . . The crown is humility. For that is the crown and guardian of all virtues. As each virtue needs humility for its acquisition—and in that sense we said each stone is laid with the mortar of humility—so also the perfection of all the virtues is humility."[10] The marital relationship is this house that is built with materials of the virtues, which are formed through particular techniques and practices. The building of the house is the growth and deepening of love, all of which requires humility—that stance of recognizing more than oneself.

One of the reasons why marriage is an opportunity for manifestation of virtues is because marriage is also an opportunity for self-knowledge through attention to the various parts of the soul or dimensions of the human condition. The opportunity for self-knowledge surfaces as one calls the other out of oneself in mutual relationship. One of the vices that gets in the way of this mutual calling of the other is pride. St. Maximus defines pride as self-love (*philautia*), and, indeed, even a long-term commitment does not guarantee the tempering of selfishness. As a basic example, if one refuses to adjust a daily schedule in light of this long-term commitment, then pride obstructs the opportunity for learning how to love in this relationship. If, as a further example, one has been spoiled in family life and never had to do household chores, always had food waiting for him, laundry done, and so on, then his body may be habituated so as to physically resist—in the form of anger and frustration—entering a partnered situation where the other expects a sharing of these same responsibilities, or the virtue of justice to structure the relationship. That resistance could cause him to stubbornly insist on a situation familiar to him, or, it could lead to self-awareness that his life has been shaped—albeit with good intentions—in such a way that does not make it easy for his body to accept easily a shared home life. It could result in the question: "Why am I feeling such frustration?," which becomes an opportunity for self-knowledge. Such self-awareness—or cognitive attention—would constitute the first step toward overcoming his pride and engaging in the kind of shared life that might eventually lead to a different kind of embodied experience of such a shared home life. At the very least, a marital commitment makes possible a learning to love not possible if living a spoiled life of privilege.

Other vices also block love, and the three at the top of St. Maximus's list, as we saw, are fear, anger, and hatred. Again, St. Maximus:

> He knew well that this **fear** [of the Lord] is different from the fear which consists of being afraid of punishments for faults of which we are accused, since for one thing this (fear of punishment) disappears completely in the presence of love, as the great Evangelist John shows somewhere in words, "Love drives out fear." [1 Jn 4.18] (*Commentary on the Our Father*, Prologue)

> When you are insulted by someone or offended in any matter, then beware of **angry** thoughts, lest by distress they sever you from *agape*

and place you in the region of hatred. (*Four Centuries on Charity*, 1.29)

> The one who sees a trace of **hatred** in his own heart through any fault at all toward any man whoever he may be makes himself completely foreign to the love for God, because love for God in no way admits of hatred for human beings. (*Four Centuries on Charity*, 1.15)[11]

We can, at this point, combine St. Maximus's insights on pride and the affective trio of fear, anger, and hatred in a way not evident in St. Maximus, and with the help of basic psychoanalytical categories. If pride consists of the self-conscious inflation of the self, we know from psychoanalysis that our conscious sense of self masks unconscious emotions and desires that we simply do not want to confront. In this sense, pride could be a mask for self-loathing in the form of self-assertion. What then blocks love in marital relationships goes beyond selfish impulses, but probably has something to do with unconscious fears, anger, and hatred, formed in particular ways according to each person's unique history. In colloquial terms, we all have baggage, but that baggage lingers in the form of a particular affective architecture, which shapes how we see and interpret the world, including how people relate to us. If one, for example, has developed a fear of failure, then one could misconstrue an otherwise harmless statement as a form of criticism to which one would negatively overreact; in other words, one could easily project onto the harmless statement—and also the other who made it—all kinds of meanings that were never intended. Unconscious fear, anger, and hatred fuel the projection mechanism onto the other, obfuscating the truth of the self, other, and the situation—making growth in love difficult (but not impossible).

Many more specific, concrete examples could be given, but the basic point is this: Without attention (which is a form of contemplation and which Simone Weil says is the "rarest and purest form of gen*ero*sity"[12]), such misfirings between committed others in a marital relationship that emerge from unconscious fears, anger, or hatred could ultimately gain momentum and further fuel fear, anger, and hatred, and, thus, destroy the relationship; or, they could occasion, in a way not possible in another type of relationship, intense self-reflection through the practice of truth-telling (perhaps confession or therapy),[13] which could then lead to a self-knowledge that would enable the addressing of unconscious fears, anger, and hatred, which would then clear the way for love of the other and not projection onto the other. To engage in such intense self-reflection—or contemplation of the self—is to enter a space of vulnerability, which ironically can lead to a place of strength insofar as one is no longer shaped by fear, anger, or hatred; it can also increase one's capacity for empathy and compassion for the other. In the end, such self-reflection is a necessary (not simply sufficient) condition for loving as God loves, because love cannot exist in the midst of falsity as self-deception.

Sex and Marriage

After mapping arguments for a theotic ethics that then forms the basis for an ascetical understanding of the sacramentality of marriage, I now must consider the sex act within this particular horizon. If sacramentality means the presencing of God through the transformation of the material form, then there is nothing that is material that does not have sacramental potential—that is, that does not have the potential to be sacramental to a certain degree. It could very well be, as Dionysius the Areopagite has shown us, that some material forms have the capacity to image God to a greater degree than other forms; for example, a human being is more in the image than a rock.[14] A basic principle of the Incarnation is that all materiality is potentially sacramental, and this includes sexual desire.

If that is the case, then the sex act cannot simply be regulated by a rule that makes it "right" or "blessed" within the context of marriage, since the rule in and of itself would not explain the sacramental potential of the sex act within the context of marriage. If marriage is understood ascetically, and the ascetical has something to do with the syncing of the various parts of the soul, in the Maximian sense, then sexual desire as rooted in the concupiscible part of the soul is subject to a marital ascetic. Put another way, marriage is recognized as that ascetical structure that makes possible the performance of sexual desire in a way that facilitates growth in union with God—*theosis*. That sexual desire can lead to pure objectification of the other is easily demonstrated in a variety of forms of the performance of the sexual act, such as rape, prostitution, or consensual encounters where partners do not know each other's names. In these particular instances, what one sees is the presencing of the demonic rather than the divine.

The violence that accompanies sexual acts that render the other as a nonperson only magnifies that there can be a performance of the sexual act that moves toward the opposite end of the spectrum. To argue that only openness to the procreation of children moves in that direction would be in danger of reducing the sex act to a rule for the sake of the rule, which would not amplify the ascetical dimension of sexual encounters. It could be argued that the commitment to have sex only with openness to children is evidence of a kind of ascetical restraint, but restraint in and for itself is not always ascetically necessary; nor is it necessarily ascetical. And, as will be clear below, the fact that persons differ in terms of degree and intensity of sexual desire means that restraint of sexual desire could prove to be more spiritually damaging than helpful. St. Paul himself noticed this when declaring that "Now, to the unmarried and the widows I say: good for them if they also remain as I am; But, if they cannot remain continent, let them marry; for it is better to marry than to be afire" (1 Cor 7:8–9). Basic psychoanalysis would also confirm that unnecessary restraint of sexual desire only inflames the irascible dimension of the soul and can incite misdirected *eros*.[15] For those who discern, together, that they are able to restrict sex to those moments of openness to procreation, this discernment itself is part of the ascetical character of the sacramentality of marriage; however, for those who discern that it is not possible, given the attention to the degree and intensity of sexual desire in one or both of the partners, the restriction of openness to procreation functions as a kind of celibacy, which should not be forced.

To use language that has been common in Christian debates on sex, the ascetical understanding of the performance of the sex act has something to do with the becoming of a person.[16] Understanding sex in terms of the whole person places the emphasis more on the unitive potential of the sex act—that is, that sex itself is not simply about children but about progressively strengthening the unity of the couple and, in so doing, contributing to the becoming of each into personhood. Since there are those expressions of sex that depersonalize, it cannot be the case that marriage per se guarantees this personal and unitive capacity of the sex act. If the depersonalization capacity of sex is rooted in the way in which the various parts of the soul relate to each other, then even within marriage, this unitive and person-making capacity has something to do with an asceticism that is attentive to these dimensions of the soul. Put more concretely, if rape emerges from a particular configuration of the rational, irascible, and concupiscible/desiring part of the soul, then rape can occur even within marriage. For sex to realize its potential for unity and person-making, ascetical attention must be given to the soul's configuration.

The reconfiguration of the parts of the soul such that the potential for sex to be unitive and person-making is fulfilled cannot be reduced to a formula or a set of instructions. First, it must be clarified that sexual desire is a form of *eros*, and, for St. Maximus, the only pure form of *eros* is that which has been purified in such a way that God is the one and only "object" of such a desire. As he states, "The perfect soul is the one whose affective drive is wholly directed to God" (*Four-Hundred Centuries on Love*, 3.98).[17] In this state of union, the cognitive functions are saturated with the divine light, and all that remains is *eros*. If this is the case, that means that *eros* is the driving engine of nature and the fuel that propels one to the neighbor and to God. As Maximus states, "When in full ardor of its love (*eros*) for God the mind goes out of itself . . . through love the mind is ravished by divine knowledge and in going outside of creatures has a perception of divine transcendence" (*Four Hundred Centuries on Love* 1.10 and 1.12).[18] In relation to the neighbor, however, the word that Maximus uses is *agape*, which he also relegates to the irascible part of the soul to temper fear, anger, and hatred: "For the mind of the one who is continually with God even his concupiscence abounds beyond measure into a divine desire (*eros*) and whose entire irascible element is transformed into divine love (*agape*)" (*Four Hundred Centuries on Love* 2.48).[19] Maximus does not label our love for God as *agape*. The idea is that a purified *eros* toward God would translate into an *agape*ic stance toward the neighbor.

Until such union, *eros* is also directed toward finite objects. Such *eros* for Maximus is not bad in itself, especially since it is the means ultimately of moving toward God. It does mean that *eros* for created objects is intertwined with how we see them (contemplation) and with our irascible reaction to them (fear, hatred, and anger). Of course, for Maximus, *eros* can definitely go wrong, especially if there is an exclusive and excessive *eros* for created things, which is usually a signal that something is misaligned in both the irascible and rational dimensions of the soul. An irrational desire for created things would evoke negative emotions in the irascible part of the soul and further cloud the mind of contemplating truth of God in created realities, but this would imply a circular effect where such ignorance and negative temperament would further fuel one's irrational desire for created things.

Understanding pure *eros*, however, in terms of union with God also means that for Maximus, our desire for material things is never "pure" and, in that sense, is entangled in the circularity of the mis-seeing of the truth of created realities in God (contemplation) and an improper emotional stance in relation to such objects (irascible). It is important to recognize, however, that this improperly relating to created objects—or what one might call the objectification of the other—in terms of the configuration of the rational, irascible, and concupiscible dimensions of the soul occurs to a greater or lesser degree; sexual desire that results in rape does not manifest the same configuration as that which does not involve rape, even if all sexual desire in some sense is entangled in objectification—to treat the human being as an object of desire.

Attention to the dynamics of desire, especially as observed by Maximus, would lead to the conclusion that judging the sex act in terms of purity within marriage versus nonpurity outside of marriage—whether one conceptualizes such purity in terms of procreative, unitive, or person-making intentions—constitutes a deontological approach that simply cannot account for the phenomenology of sexual desire and incitement, again, on Maximus's own terms.[20] In other words, if the only pure desire is that experience in union with God, then all desire for created finite objects involves a form of "impurity" that is a form of objectification and, in that sense, is entangled in the irascible part of the soul—fear, anger, and hatred—to a greater or lesser degree, which then affects how we see—contemplatively—the other in front of us. If marriage is recognized as sacramental, it is because the Church has, in part, recognized such a long-term committed relationship as an ascetical form that would shape sexual desire in a way that facilitates movement—*eros*—toward God, *even while such desire simultaneously objectifies*. For marriage, however, to reconfigure the various parts of the soul in a way that propels it toward God, attention must be given to the various ways the human being experiences sexual desire, including fantasy and fetish. The goal is not nonobjectification, since that is impossible; the goal would be for objectification not to be definitive and not to preclude the growth in other virtues that is possible through the awareness and expression of sexual desire.

As a concrete example, there are those who experience foot fetishes, which means that sexual desire is incited at the presence of bare feet. This might be characterized as perverted or impure, but the fact remains that such an incitement of sexual desire is a reality, even as a causal explanation remains elusive. Some might command the fetishist not to be incited in this way, but one cannot command desire to either desire or not desire in a certain way. In marriage, it may be very difficult for a partner to express this dimension of their sexual desire, but—if a context is created where this is confessed, listened to without judgement, and integrated into the sexual life of the couple—even in the midst of this manifest objectification/fetishization, what is definitive is not objectification-as-demonization, but an ascetical movement in the virtues toward the personhood of the persons even without negating the objectification that results from the foot fetish. The movement toward *theosis* is not black or white, but always moving in the grey area of ambiguity, where progress occurs in the midst of sin, not when sin is eliminated. Grace does not necessarily cancel out sin; it simply does not allow it to become definitive.

Homoerotic Desire

What does this sacramental understanding of sex mean for homoerotic desire? First, it must be noted that the approach of this essay is one from establishing a theotic ethics, to a theotic anthropology, and then to a theotic understanding of desire as potentially sacramental. In other words, the starting point is crucial to the overall argument since it attempts to establish the presuppositions from which a consideration of desire must proceed, including homoerotic desire. If this particular starting point is rejected, then the discussion must be about the very presuppositions upon which to consider sexual desire. There are some who would argue that propositional statements in the form of Scripture, patristic texts, and canons are the basis on which to discuss the nature of desire. My argument is that the hermeneutical key for interpreting scriptural, patristic, canonical, and liturgical texts is the Incarnation and the theological anthropology implied by the affirmation of the Incarnation.

Second, given this starting point, I have argued that marriage as sacrament cannot mean simply the ceremony but the ascetical occasion for sacramentality or *theosis*. Friendships are also such an opportunity, and what distinguishes marriage from friendship is the sexual component, even if marriage can entail friendships, which are part of the structure of *theosis*. To clarify the ascetical structure of marriage, I have attempted to complexify the sexual act so as to de-deontologize it; the potential for holiness within marriage depends on attending to the messiness of sexual desire, for which there is no formula but ongoing discernment. The commitment to the ascetical structure of marriage that surrounds sexual desire has to do both with protecting from the dangers of erotic demonization and, more importantly, with the fact that *eros* itself is the vehicle for union with God. *Eros* without the ascetical structure of a long-term committed relationship can potentially demonize; within the ascetical structure, it has a chance to be an occasion for *theosis*, even if its performance is always complicated.

Third, since the Church's objection to homoerotic desire focuses on the sex act, my attempt to elucidate how marriage is sacramental and how that sacramentality involves attention to the messiness of sex provides the framework for discussing homoerotic desire. I begin by stating that homoerotic desire is a fact. Knowledge of why desire is experienced in this particular way is no more or less clear than why desire is experienced as heteroerotic. The only known "fact" is that there is simply a greater percentage of humans who experience erotic desire as heteroerotic. Although there has been much discussion in various forums, whatever the results of these discussion, it simply does not make sense to say that one chooses one's *eros*. Sexual *eros*—hetero and homo—is simply one that is noticed or recognized and not willed. In short, one does not choose to be gay or straight.

If this is the case, then in the ecclesial setting, or theologically, the question becomes how does one respond to or ascetically work on this *eros*. In the case of the awareness of heteroerotic desire, the Christian ascetical tradition—at its best—has suggested wrapping this heteroerotic desire in a discerningly ascetical structure so that such *eros* can be transformed to realize its sacramental potential. *Eros*, in short, as part of God's created reality is good, even as created *eros* it is inherently targeting created objects and, in so doing, entails a measure of objectification to greater or lesser degree. The important point here is that even in the midst of this objectification, an ascetical response to sexual desire in the form of the structure of a long-term committed relationship has the potential to shape *eros* to presence holiness—God. More strongly, sexual desire is such that it requires such an ascetical structure lest it lead to absolute objectification and, thus, demonization. In short, forced celibacy is spiritually dangerous.

The spiritual dynamics of homoerotic desire as sexual desire work no differently. It is, simply, sexual desire. As *eros*, it aims toward a created finite object even while such *eros* also points us to *eros* for God. As created finite *eros*, it contains a measure of objectification, but there is no reason to think that the structure of homoerotic desire is any different than heteroerotic desire such that even while objectifying, if shaped by a discerningly ascetical structure, it cannot also be an occasion for the experience of *theosis* through the virtues. There is ample anecdotal evidence that, in fact, such holiness-shaped *eros* is realized even in homoerotic relations. Forced celibacy has been acknowledged as spiritually dangerous, given the dynamics of sexual desire, albeit from a heterosexual perspective; if this is the case, it doesn't make sense that those who experience homoerotic desire are denied the opportunity to respond to this desire in an ascetically discerning way within the Church such that *eros* can become an occasion for *theosis* through the virtues.

If sexual desire is such that it can be shaped in such a way in which *eros* flows toward God rather than away—that is, facilitates the presencing of God in the form of love of God and love of neighbor—and if there are human beings who recognize that sexual desire is incited by the body, or even body parts, of someone who is of the same sex, that the object of sexual desire is a human being of the same sex, then that sexual desire can and must be shaped by the same kind of asceticism that is possible within a long-term committed heteroerotic relation, or what the Church for centuries has called a marriage. There is nothing in the nature of homoerotic desire that would not subject it to the same kind of ascetical discernment, especially given the potential for sexual desire in and of itself to demonize the other. And there's nothing in that form of homoerotic desire that indicates that an ascetical approach to such desire would not also lead to the reconfiguring of the soul that would allow for the presencing of God.[21] To simply label it a sin is not good enough, since all desire for finite things is implicated in sin. The issue is the ascetical architecture that surrounds this desire so as not to make sin definitive.

There is the argument, of course, that homoerotic desire should be subject to the asceticism of restraint, meaning forced celibacy. If, however, the Christian tradition has acknowledged—and this point really cannot be emphasized enough—that sexual desire is such that not all can be celibate, why is this applied only in relation to heteroerotic desire? If as a result of this acknowledgment, the Church recognized marriage as the ascetical architecture to shape sexual desire as that which contributes to *theosis* rather than militates against it, how is forced celibacy something that contributes to *theosis*, especially if desire in and of itself is entangled with the irascible dimensions of the soul, which includes fear, anger, and hatred? There are ample stories of those who experience homoerotic desire who testify that celibacy is simply impossible, resonating with the broader Christian affirmation that forced celibacy is simply not spiritually productive. Added to this is the sheer hypocrisy of the Church for centuries that both provided the prohibition and, simultaneously, the cover of its clergy and monastics for those experiencing homoerotic desire. If one were to approach sexual desire ascetically and, thus, sacramentally, there is nothing to indicate that the performance of homoerotic desire in and of itself is antitheotic, especially if homoeroticism, like heteroeroticism, is simply a particular form of eroticism, but the dynamics remain the same for all persons. If such an asceticism of erotic desire is productive of the virtues that reconfigure the parts of the soul to love God and love neighbor, then it is theotic.

Notes

1. In the Christian world, St. Augustine's *Confessions* comes to mind, but also the friendship between St. Basil the Great and St. Gregory the Theologian (Nazianzus). In pointing to the intimacy of the friendship that existed in late antiquity, I am not suggesting that these persons are gay—in the very modern sense of the word—or experienced homoerotic desire. I am only trying to indicate that the experience of love as friendship is present among well-known persons of late antiquity and was not considered morally problematic—in fact, it was celebrated. See John Panteleimon Manoussakis, "Friendship in Late Antiquity: The Case of Gregory Nazianzen and Basil the Great," in *Ancient and Medieval Concepts of Friendship*, ed. S. Stern-Gillet and Gary Gurtler, S.J. (Albany: State University of New York Press, 2014), 173–95. See also David Konstan, *In the Orbit of Love: Affection in Ancient Greece and Rome* (Oxford: Oxford University Press, 2018).

2. Wesley Hill, *Spiritual Friendship: Finding Love in the Church as a Celibate Gay Christian* (Grand Rapids, Mich.: Brazos Press, 2015).

3. One would be hard-pressed not to find the affirmation of *theosis* even with a cursory perusal of patristic text and of contemporary Orthodox theology. For a scholarly treatment, see Norman Russell, *The Doctrine of Deification in the Greek Patristic Tradition* (Oxford: Oxford University Press, 2004). For its centrality in framing debates in contemporary Orthodox theology, see Aristotle Papanikolaou, "Eastern Orthodox Theology," in *The Routledge Companion to Modern Christian Thought*, ed. Chad Meister and James Beilby (New York: Routledge, 2013), 538–48.

4. Alasdair MacIntyre, *After Virtue: A Study of Moral Theory* (Notre Dame, Ind.: University of Notre Dame Press, 1981), 53.

5. See Jean Porter, "The Natural Law and Innovative Forms of Marriage: A Reconsideration," *Journal of the Society of Christian Ethics* 30, no. 2 (2010): 79–97.

6. For a more developed discussion of what follows, see Aristotle Papanikolaou, "Theosis," in the *Oxford Handbook of Mystical Theology*, ed. Edward Howells and Mark A. McIntosh (Oxford: Oxford University Press, 2019).

7. Contrary to the typical contemporary Orthodox projection of the Christian West as having rejected *theosis*, ecumenical discussions of *theosis* are actually quite ubiquitous. As but one example, see the essays in Michael J. Christensen and Jeffery A. Wittung, eds., *Partakers of the Divine Nature: The History and Development of Deification in the Christian Traditions* (Grand Rapids, Mich.: Baker Academic, 2007).

8. Alexander Schmemann, *The Eucharist: Sacrament of the Kingdom* (Crestwood, N.Y.: St. Vladimir's Seminary Press, 2003), 217.

9. This point is more fully developed in Aristotle Papanikolaou, "Dignity: An Orthodox Perspective," in *Value and Vulnerability: An Interfaith Dialogue on Human Dignity*, ed. Matthew R. Petrusek and Jonathan Rothchild (Notre Dame, Ind.: University of Notre Dame Press, 2020).

10. Dorotheos of Gaza, *Discourses and Sayings*, trans. Eric P. Wheeler (Kalamazoo, Mich.: Cistercian Publications, 1977), 203. Earlier, Dorotheos identifies humility as the mortar of the house of the soul, "which is composed from the earth and lies under the feet of all. Any virtue existing without humility is no virtue at all" (203).

11. *Maximus the Confessor: Selected Writings*, translated by G. C. Berthold (New York: Paulist Press, 1985), 101, 38, 37.

12. From an April 13, 1942 letter to poet Joë Bousquet, published in their collected correspondence: Simone Weil and Joë Bousquet, *Correspondance* (Lausanne: Éditions l'Age d'Homme, 1982), 18. Italics mine.

13. See Aristotle Papanikolaou, "Liberating Eros: Confession and Desire," *The Journal of the Society of Christian Ethics* 26, no. 1 (Spring/Summer 2006): 115–36; and, "Honest to God: Confession and Desire," in *Thinking through Faith: New Perspectives from Orthodox Scholars*, ed. Aristotle Papanikolaou and Elizabeth Prodromou (Crestwood, N.Y.: St. Vladimir's Seminary Press, 2008), 219–46.

14. See Ashley Purpura, *God, Hierarchy, and Power: Orthodox Theologies of Authority from Byzantium* (New York: Fordham University Press, 2017). See also Papanikolaou, "Liberating Eros."

15. Sigmund Freud, *Three Contributions to the Theory of Sex* (IndieBooks, 2018).

16. For a good summary of the debate, see Todd A. Salzman and Michael G. Lawler, *The Sexual Person: Toward a Renewed Catholic Anthropology* (Washington, D.C.: Georgetown University Press, 2008).

17. Berthold, *Maximus the Confessor,* 75.

18. Berthold, *Maximus the Confessor,* 36–37.

19. Berthold, *Maximus the Confessor*, 53.

20. It should be noted here that Maximus does confine proper use of sexual desire exclusively to purposes of procreation: "First passion, as when we desire an object beyond reason, such as food outside the time or need, a woman outside the purpose of procreation or one not lawfully ours" (*Four Hundred Chapters on Love* 2.33; Berthold, 51). This would imply for Maximus that perfected desire would be one that would not be incited in any way whatsoever but simply be performed functionally for procreation. Even if granted this point, which is debatable, it does not contradict my effort to map Maximus's understanding of the interrelated dynamism of the various parts of the soul to a phenomenology of sexual desire that is discerning about how incitement and pleasure operate in a long-term relationship such that this desire can be ascetically shaped so as to facilitate love of neighbor and love of God and not the demonization of the other, which is possible through sexual desire.

21. It bears mentioning that the forms of same-sex sexual activity condemned by St. Paul and in the patristic corpus are rooted in exploitation of slaves, youths, prostitutes, and captured enemies. For more on this, see Bryce E. Rich's contribution to this volume. The performance of erotic desire, whether homoerotic or heterotic, in these particular relationships is clearly not ascetical and, thus, not theotic. What I am suggesting is not an anything-goes policy for personal satisfaction and fulfillment. The point is that when it comes to erotic desire, an ascetical structure needs to be discerned in order to activate its sacramental potential. Various kinds of relationships are discerned as clearly not theotic, including those that undiscerningly restrain sexual desire. What has been discerned as a proper ascetical structure is long-term committed relationships whose aim is progress in manifesting the virtues and, thus, growth in love.

CHAPTER

13

THE ANTINOMIC ESCHATOLOGICAL TRANSFIGURATION OF CHRISTIAN EROS AND SEXUALITY

Haralambos Ventis

For an honest discussion of Orthodoxy and sexuality to commence nowadays, a fresh critical groundwork must first be laid, sufficiently informed theologically and scientifically as befits reasoning Christians disdainful of tired platitudes and shallow forms of piety. For only then can the exchange be carried out in a responsible, more realistic context than the standardized legalist setting in which it has hitherto been framed. The required backdrop is still largely pending, if not entirely missing, for the obvious reason that to this day institutional Christendom has traditionally portrayed sexuality as a problematic aspect of human life that can only be tolerated in the confines of marriage, and even then solely for the purpose of procreation (notwithstanding the positive but neglected witness of theologians like Paul Evdokimov, Paul Florensky, and Sergei Bulgakov). Traditionally loaded with such a crudely utilitarian function, sexuality has been mainly dealt with as devoid of any intrinsic spiritual value, such as comprising a source of mutual fulfillment beyond offering mere pleasure. The sheer fact that erotic love has been largely reduced to a simplistic caricature of carnal hedonism both by Church leaders and the monastic tradition of the Church should ring a bell that the mindset at work behind this reductionism derives from legalism and not from Christ Himself. This is not the place to elaborate on the numerous poisonous inroads that legalist religiosity has been making in every walk of Church life since day one (more thickly and rapidly so, as the faith became increasingly codified as to encapsulate and manage every single aspect of human behavior). More modestly rather, our present purpose here is to suggest ways of disentangling sexuality from the guardianship of the legalistic attitude, with a view to challenging preconceived notions of gender and erotic love as lapsarian and not truly Christian in origin.

I submit that the appropriate context for exploring sexuality from a Christian perspective is that of eschatology.[1] This doubtless sounds problematic, for if anything eschatology implies, at best, an escape from history and physical materiality. At worst, even a cursory look at much of past Christian literature, especially of the ascetic genre, clearly indicates that eschatology has been appropriated by a morbid perspective, predominantly focused on a terrorizing foretelling of the end of the present world and the eternal condemnation of sinners. Not surprisingly, therefore, the extant eschatological record appears to be largely destitute of both theological creativity and a life-affirming Christian outlook on human affairs. In view then of its susceptibility to various strands of fundamentalist polemics, eschatology may reasonably be deemed inappropriate, if not pernicious, for informing current discussions of sexuality. For by definition, as an on-going narrative unfolding the existential consequences of God's enfleshment on earth, Christian theology must be very firmly rooted in history. Only thus can it pay heed to the agonies troubling humankind at every age as well as empathize with the downtrodden and the least of society, those who suffer injustices of every sort. For theology to retain its prophetic, healing flavor and to hope to make a difference in the world, it must find the courage to read the signs of the times and strive as much as it can to furnish fresh, viable answers to current problems and concerns.

Nevertheless, it is precisely on that score that eschatology must be factored into our theological perspective. Because, alongside the willingness to face historical challenges head on, to be able to exercise its prophetic ministry, the Christian Church must be ahead of society, not behind it (i.e., the opposite of what it has mostly done in its historical record, invoking as it does an ossified view of "tradition" usually turned into an idol). The only way that the Church and its theologians can obtain this forward-looking view is by lending an ear to the unpredictable workings of the Holy Spirit, whose role is to sanctify creation and everything in it precisely by refreshing history and human societies—in the process creating new and unprecedented forms of grace and biological realities, as He introduces the Eschaton in history (this line of reasoning assumes that creation may have been stalled by the Fall, but it is an unfinished, on-going project to be culminated in the end times). The Christian Eschaton inaugurates a challenging antinomy into the present, which can be very puzzling and, for this reason, quite liberating. It emancipates the mind from historical determinism and slavery to the past, inasmuch as God's Kingdom will not arrive courtesy of human effort or any "iron laws of history," thereby leaving the future open to unpredictability, change, and continuous reform. Essentially, the Eschaton is a temporal form of apophaticism. It will be remembered that the apophatic epistemological principle ensures that our experience of reality is not conceptually fettered or in any way reducible to its verbal articulation, assuming as it does an asymmetry between the world and the human cognizance of it. Likewise, the Eschaton interjects a corresponding asymmetry between the present and the future, albeit in this case the gap is radically enhanced by an insufferable antinomy, a galvanizing reversal of expectations. What does this eschatological paradox amount to? In contrast to protological narratives, which follow the linear type of causation we're all familiar with, the Eschaton poses an ontological prioritizing of the future (the promised Kingdom of God—i.e., creation in its conclusive form, as God ever intended it, had the Fall not intervened), from which flows a reverse causality rearranging past events under the Kingdom's lights. As an outcome of divine initiative (independently of historical evolution), this posthistorical vision of the Kingdom affords us a vantage normative yardstick by which to arraign any preceding historical milieu, even the most glorious, as at best incomplete and wanting—as inescapably falling far short of divine righteousness, inclusiveness, and catholicity. The Eschaton, as alluded to in the Gospels, promises startling *reversals* of what we have perennially thought of as natural and appropriate. It is the unfamiliar terrain where "the last shall be first and the first last,"[2] the transformed landscape where death, from a biological perspective the most natural thing in the world, is no more. The Christian Tradition is cumulative indeed (hence not dispensable, doctrinally speaking); by the same token, however, it is neither static nor complete as is so often sanguinely presumed: Rather, it is forward-looking, occasionally open to surprises and even ruptures from past modes of thinking regarding what lies ahead.

Eschatology, properly viewed, is thus not correlative with a dematerialization of creation, nor can it serve as a form of "religious escapism" diverting attention from time, history, and social affairs. Far from lending support to such hollow goals, it can actually kick-start critical theological reflection to a whole new level: As a merciless deconstructor of cultural triumphalism and historical determinism, eschatology looks at history as an unpredictable and inconclusive affair, maintaining that the best is yet to arrive—albeit not without terrible setbacks at every turn in history. In that capacity, eschatology is uniquely endowed to undermine theological complacency, conventional thought, and fixed perspectives on life that block social change. Above all, eschatology urges Christians to resist the temptation of glorifying (and, in effect, idolizing) the past, in recognition of the intrinsic imperfection of every historical era and human accomplishment. It nurtures constant alertness and readiness for the unfamiliar and the unpredictable, thereby training the mind to ceaselessly expand its frame of reference. Such expansion makes the human mind susceptible to the unbearably challenging *maximalism* of Orthodox Christian doctrine, with its puzzling notions of "Trinitarian monotheism" (the paradoxical notion that God is One and yet three Persons), of the "God-Man" (i.e., that Christ is neither God nor man alone), the Virgin Birth, and the Resurrection, to mention but a few: These are all unpalatable credos from the viewpoint of rigorous human logic, and clearly run counter to what nature, in addition to reason, permits. In view, then, of eschatology's tantalizing capacity to question harmless platitudes of all stripes, let us now attempt to see some of the ways in which it can shed some fresh theological light on sexuality.

Eschatology is a key concept for making sense of a troubling inconsistency encountered in the Gospels, succinctly alluded to in Christ's exhortation for people to marry in a single-flesh union on one hand (Mk. 10:8) and His (contrasting?) assertion that marriage is canceled in heaven, on the other (Mk. 12:25). This poses a serious problem for New Testament hermeneutics: Why is marriage viewed as a sacred institution, if it is not meant to survive in the Eschaton? Is it truly a holy union in the deepest possible spiritual sense? Or is it rather a mere convention, sanctified for as long as biological life drags on but essentially disposable upon the arrival of the anticipated "new heaven and earth"? And does this "impermanent," as it were, status of marriage also denote a negative stance on sexuality as a barely endured aspect of human life? Moreover, what are we supposed to make of the ostensibly contrasting lifestyles of marriage and monastic asceticism, if marriage is destined to perish after the Resurrection of the dead? When gauged by the yardstick of eschatology, aren't monastics a more privileged bunch of Christians versus their married brethren, who may have chosen a lesser mode of life out of "carnal" weakness?

These questions are intrinsically bound up with another major problem: Once it is accepted that "what is not assumed by Christ is not healed,"[3] in the memorable phrase of St. Gregory Nazianzus, doesn't a bleak, negative view of sexuality necessarily obtain from the fact that Christ had none of it, as Orthodox doctrine maintains? Christ is the par excellence eschatological human being, literally the new Adam; His body and mind must thus be deemed paradigmatic of the type of humanity implied in God's plan for the transfigured citizens of Heaven. If Christ is innocent of sexuality, shouldn't we be expected to follow in His steps (as Paul urges us to, anyway), in active anticipation of our eschatological transfiguration? And yet, the Church blesses marriage and has harshly condemned puritans who abstain from sex and the consumption of meat alike on grounds of uncleanliness. Are there ways out of this paradoxical deadlock, whose prolongation still troubles (poisons, actually) the lives of sincere Christians, who often find themselves unable to reconcile their human need for loving physical intercourse with a fundamentalist mandate for bodily purity and abstinence?

In this chapter, I submit that it would be a grievous theological error to consider the annulment of marriage in heaven as a termination of eros and sexuality per se. For, as created by God, sexuality cannot but entail a real spiritual dimension: It is a unique form of human fulfillment irreducible to bodily, self-serving pleasure, just as food amounts to more than physical nourishment or palate delight by serving as an occasion for convivial human fellowship. In light of this irreplaceable quality of physical intimacy to concurrently nourish body and soul, institutional Christendom must be reproved for leaving this major aspect of human life largely unappreciated, as it must also be for its long-standing grudging forbearance of sexuality as a barely tolerated indulgence for the purpose of procreation at best. Such a "sour" attitude against eroticism runs completely counter to the big-hearted, bold, and often unashamedly provocative approach to this sensitive issue exhibited in the Gospel narratives by Christ Himself. For one thing, Christ refrained from burdening the newlyweds of Cana with restricting "instructions" for their moments of intimacy, in contrast to what many self-appointed clergymen and "elders" are keen on doing. Just as scandalous for the sensibilities of puritanical Christians was his eagerness to provide guests at the said wedding with extra wine after they had already consumed so much of it, thus "wasting" a miracle to no useful purpose other than sheer (and questionable!) enjoyment. To be sure, sexuality has its well-known dark side and certain forms of it are flagrantly dehumanizing. To forestall being misunderstood, I should explain that sexuality, in the sense it is assumed in my paper, is not inclusive of any form of exploitation, forced or paid sex, promiscuity, or adultery. That said, it ought to become clear that theologically speaking, all forms of love, including the erotic kind, are not an incidental part of God's intentions for humankind. Far from it, love is endowed with an ontological status, if there is any gravity to the Scriptural verses that "God so loved the world, that he gave his only begotten Son" for its sake,[4] and that God is Himself love, as opposed to merely having love as one quality among others.[5]

Physical intimacy, to the extent that it is not self-serving but mutual and committed, is a *foretaste* of the intimate communion to be enjoyed with Christ and those sharing the Lord's banquet in His Kingdom, as is promised by the Gospel. Such posthistorical intimacy, while not sexual in character literally speaking, does restore human relatedness to a level of *uninterrupted* companionship originally intended by God but only rarely encountered in humankind's recorded existence. For within history, people are always faced with the grim prospect of separation and division from one another, as a result of the unhealed gap caused and perpetuated by the twin aspects of creation, space and time, which have been left *untransformed* as a result of the Fall. Bereft of divine grace (except to the minimum possible degree required for its endurance), space-time has left human relationships intrinsically fragile in an ontological sense involving much more than selfishness and aggression as causes for their breakup: Distance keeps people apart, both temporally and spatially, ceaselessly turning presence into absence, whose bitterest terminal upshot is death. Those closest to us inevitably cease to exist at some point in time, thereby leaving an irreplaceable void behind them if they are treasured as uniquely precious individuals. Thus because of space-time's inexorable impact on the bodily basis of relatedness, human beings are constantly prevented from forging uninterrupted bonds of communion with one another. Marriage is arguably the most effective way among other forms of fellowship for undoing the separation and division produced by the natural state of affairs in creation, since two people join one another in the (ideally) undivided union of one flesh, in a manner friendship alone cannot accomplish. As such, the institution is fine and good, and its spiritual value encompasses sexuality alongside companionship as a superb divine gift. Nevertheless, sexuality is to be transcended in the Eschaton, not because it is bad, but in order to be transformed and rid of its adverse aspects.

How so and why? First, in the sense that, from what we may gather from the Gospel narratives, eschatological fellowship, still as intimate and fulfilling as conjugal companionship, will be free from the exclusions involved in marriage. In the family, priority of love and resources is always given to its members, often at the expense of everyone else outside the circle of blood relations: By necessity the institution more or less discriminates against outsiders—hence Christ's exhortation to His disciples to even go as far as the extra length of hating one's biological parents should they stand as an impediment to an unconditional following of His commandments (here we can see how the blood of Christ shared inclusively at the Eucharist liberates us from the narrowness and necessity imposed by biological blood, which restricts us to the idolatrous loyalty to one's family, class, nation, and race). Second, in its current biological form, sexuality has its own serious downsides besides being a source of pleasure and communion: It is subject to grim limitations and impairments associated with barrenness, disease, compulsion, greedy lust and exploitation, rape, porn and prostitution (the commercialization of the human body), alongside other sorts of troubling disorders that ruin rather than foster loving relationships.

One major snag related to sexuality concerns the deprivation of human reproduction, in its standard biological manner, from freedom. This problem is not delimited to untreatable infertility or to the possibility of transmitting bad genes and hereditary diseases to offspring; it concerns rather a deeper issue associated with sexuality: the total dependence on it, if new life is to occur. The seedless birth of Christ, perhaps the event of freedom par excellence in the created order, is an indication of how God had intended procreation to occur progressively, had the Fall not interposed. Here, eschatology may once again serve as our guide for overcoming conventional, pious platitudes sold as "spirituality" and "traditional theology": God's plan for humankind and creation *unfolds gradually*, from *good to future perfection* as well as from simpler to more *diversified*, more *inclusive* forms of grace. Seen in this light, sexual reproduction is not in the least "bad," in and of itself. It was designed by God, and like everything else attributed to God, it is very good indeed. But our *entrapment* in it, following the annulment of God's long-term original plan for humankind, proved to be calamitous: First, because sexual reproduction isn't a viable option for everyone, regardless of one's sexual orientation—many straight people can't attain it or do so with difficulty; secondly, because as an exclusive mode of reproduction, sexuality ends up absolutizing gender polarity, a dichotomy surprisingly resisted by the majority of Church Fathers as a shortcoming attributed to the Fall.[6] Fascinatingly, there is a patristic consensus regarding a long-term prospect of gender transcendence, among other physical and cosmic dualities also meant to be overcome—a development destined to be consummated at the Eschaton, to an extent and manner unknown. Should this patristic vision hold any water, the interruption of this process as a result of humankind's Original Sin (the introverted breach of our communion with God) amounts to our historical confinement in a duality of sexes leading in turn to harsh exclusions of intersex and gay people as unwanted hybrids that lapsarian nature cannot accommodate or endure.

This is one case among several others attesting that in the botched human attempt for self-divinization known as Original Sin, we have found ourselves subjected to the natural limitations of a cruel universe that cares nothing for human beings as God's living icons: Its physical laws, while necessary for our existence, also work cumulatively to punish the hubris of human existence by obliterating it at every turn. What is precisely "natural" involves death at the very heart of it. In view, then, of this nonromantic awareness of nature as an enticing but ruthless battlefield (particularly as we know from Darwin onwards), glorifying what appears to be "natural," as some Eastern religions and conservative Christians are habitually keen on doing, is, from a theological perspective, completely misguided; for in doing so, we actually give theological sanction to a lapsarian state of affairs destined to be overcome in God's Kingdom. Worse still, this is the surest path for regression into paganism, whose classical version sees nature as an uncreated, self-sufficient sphere innocent of linear development and progress. Lamentably, our natural human longing for stock, prefabricated answers to ultimate questions out of fear of what is new and unknown often leads us Christians to forfeit our forward-looking, eschatological vision of reality, but in doing so, we unreflectively swap a horizon rich in unimaginable novelty for a sterile, idolatrous fixation with the past. This deeply interwoven inclination blinds us not only as to the continuous unfolding of God's plan for the arrival of the promised new world, but also as regards the evolving, cumulative nature of Christian Tradition as well—a tradition conveniently turned into a palatable caricature modeled after the agenda of the far right.

The past and the present must be assessed from the vantage point of the future, as St. Maximus the Confessor[7] and St. Isaac the Syrian[8] insisted; only thus can the Church perform its prophetic function and throw refreshing light on the world's problems. I humbly suggest that this is precisely

The Transfiguration of Christian Eros and Sexuality 273

how the question of same-sex unions must be theologically addressed—-i.e., from the lens of eschatology. But before broaching this pressing issue, permit me to make a brief detour.

At the time that these lines are written, billionaire tycoon Elon Musk has just announced a grand, ambitious, and detailed plan to send manned missions to Mars by the year 2024, some considerable time ahead of NASA. Feasibility aside, the project indicates a startling, admirable vision for the human race as an interplanetary species capable of visiting and eventually inhabiting other worlds. The very prospect of human colonies on the moon and Mars expands the notions of what it means to be human as nearly nothing else can. The radical transition from the geocentric to the Copernican worldview has irreversibly altered our view of the cosmos and our place in it: In an unimaginably vast universe filled with billions of galaxies, each teeming with billions of stars and orbiting planets, humankind cannot be readily seen as the apex of creation anymore—certainly not in any pre-Copernican sense as has been maintained by traditional monotheism, which is innocent of both heliocentrism and biological evolution. The continuing search for advanced extraterrestrial intelligence is an integral aspect of modern science, as are the prospects for the creation of strong artificial intelligence (AI), a silicon-based rival to our carbon-based species with potentially self-correcting and self-replicating abilities. *Speciesism* is a neologism concocted to account for the progressive dethronement of humankind from the medieval center stage as the sole, supreme sentient being in the known universe. Human subjects may still be viewed as made in the image and likeness of God but must henceforth be prepared to share that honorable title with other life forms, organic and inorganic alike. Concurrently, the recent discoveries of the true origins and age of our race create further problems of plausibility for the Christian narrative of our creation.

On the social sphere, Western societies, despite frequent setbacks, have long been set on a course of furthering civil and human rights following hard-fought battles, in effect showing more concern, sensitivity, compassion, and success in securing the freedoms and dignity of human persons than organized religion. Institutional Christendom has seldom been an ally to the champions of social and political freedom (except when being a minority), in large part because of the fear that a plurality of the idea of the Good[9] at best undermines the Churches' normative principles; at worst, because pluralism may well foster practices considered as sinful and contrary to the traditional teachings of Christianity. Small wonder, then, that many[10] Christian Churches have assumed a hardline stance toward the free, open society and liberal democracy, in essence implying that the only human right they are willing to accede to is that of worshipping God—not just any God, at that, but the true One preached from their respective pulpits. Further to that: It was only after a long series of bitter struggles, often involving costly personal stigma for those involved, that Western societies have finally discerned and accepted the reality, depth, sincerity, and yes, the sanctity of same-sex love as well as the genetic origins of sexual orientation as a given, ineradicable, and intrinsic aspect of human personality. Again, institutional Christendom, with some notable exceptions (particularly Anglicanism), has found this a bitter pill to swallow, for, like the Copernican and Darwinian revolutions, this recent insight has challenged religious complacency at its very core: While not hurting Christology or Trinitarian doctrine per se, the combined iconoclasm of these scientific milestones has thereafter largely undermined premodern notions regarding anthropology and cosmology. Although the message has yet to sink in collectively to Church leaders and congregations, it is no longer plausible from the side of any Christian body to publicly deny and assail heliocentrism and biological evolution, or to attribute homosexuality to lustful whim and choice. Perhaps more importantly, no responsible organized religion can claim that it has already and in advance, ahead of anyone else, voiced the complete, final truth about anything pertaining to the created order. If only grudgingly, it is finally acknowledged that empirical reality is always deeper and more complex than first meets the eye, and always features unexplored sides, often with crucial, unanticipated consequences for the integrity and overall quality of Christian witness to a world long estranged from static conceptions of life.

What the above points amount to is the lesson, still sorely missed by most Church leaders, that we live in a post-Christian world blaming monotheism of all stripes and sorts for the violence and tyranny of totalitarianism, secular as well as religious. Ours is now a culture collectively shaped by humanist values, the scientific revolution, and the blood-stained insight gained in the aftermath of the barbarism unleashed throughout the twentieth century—i.e., that *the infinity of human personhood cannot be squared*. In plainer terms, this last point suggests that human persons are intrinsically heterogeneous, radically indeterminate, irreducible beings, resistant to classification and narrow moral prisons more reminiscent of legalism than Christ—the One who turned the tables around and dared to violate the most sacred Law of the Sabbath out of sensitivity and respect for an ailing man's special needs. Nowadays, in our post-Christian world, nothing gives religion a black eye more than a rehashing of simplistic, legalist platitudes that merely replicate past ignorance and prejudices about the human condition. As novelist Milan Kundera so wisely indicated once,

> Man desires a world where good and evil can be clearly distinguished, for he has an innate and irrepressible desire to judge before he understands. Religions and ideologies are founded on this desire. They can cope with the novel only by translating its language of relativity and ambiguity into their own apodictic and dogmatic discourse. They require that someone be right. . . . This "either-or" encapsulates an inability to tolerate the essential relativity of things human, an inability to look squarely at the absence of a Supreme Judge. . . .
>
> The world of one single Truth and the relative, ambiguous world of the novel are molded of entirely different substances. Totalitarian Truth excludes relativity, doubt, questioning; it can never accommodate what I would call the spirit of the novel. . . . [Religions, ideologies, and books written in the service of ideologies] add nothing to the conquest of being. They discover no new segment of existence; they only confirm what has already been said . . . what everyone says (what everyone must say). . . . By discovering nothing, they fail to participate in the sequence of discoveries that for me constitutes the history of the novel.
>
> The novel's spirit [by contrast] is the spirit of complexity. Every novel says to the reader: "Things are not as simple as you think." That is the novel's eternal truth, but it grows steadily harder to hear amid the din of easy, quick answers that come faster than the question and block it off.[11]

To give credence to his claims, Kundera invoked the definitive absence of any "Supreme Judge" who can issue the perfect, flawless verdict from a heavenly Archimedean point. As Christians, however, we do in fact believe in the existence of a personal God who holds us accountable. Hence, the possibility of endorsing a programmatic, total relativism (which itself can prove unduly one-dimensional and sternly dogmatic) is neither feasible nor desirable for the Christian mindset. Nevertheless, there can also be no denying that our spirituality often relies on parochial stock premises contrived at a premodern time when not only the responses to various problems but the problems themselves had been different. Isn't it true that, for all its facile attempts to appear updated, Orthodoxy proclaims an ossified anthropology shaped by past ignorance and prejudice? Similarly, is it not true that the very notion of Tradition has been largely reduced to a petrified, tightly sealed doctrinal body used as a pretext for dismissing new questions and unprecedented challenges? In its struggle to remain true to the Byzantine worldview at any cost, the Eastern Church has opted to remain more Byzantine than truly Orthodox, if Orthodoxy signifies constant growth, self-critical development, and continuous expansion in space and time.

"The voice of reason or intellect," Sigmund Freud says in *The Future of an Illusion*, "is a soft one, but it does not rest till it gains a hearing. Finally, after a countless succession of rebuffs, it succeeds. This is one of the few points on which one may be optimistic about the future of humankind."[12] It has taken Western civilization a painfully slow time in terms of human cost to discern and acknowledge the human face of homosexuals as well as to weigh the bitter, life-long adversity that their sexual orientation constitutes. The rigidity with which much of institutional Christendom, and Orthodoxy above all, still refuse to side with the plight of our gay brethren raises serious doubts about the conscience and the divine inspiration of the Church's pronouncements on intricate social issues—these are usually set aside by recourse to shallow, tired platitudes and "end-of-discussion" verdicts, reminiscent of Islam's unwillingness and inability to explain why the consumption of pork is sinful, except by repeating that "it is sinful because it is sinful, period." That is most certainly not the way that the great ecclesiastical writers of the golden patristic era addressed contemporary challenges and problems; instead of pontificating, they argued reasonably and extensively, with reference to the best available knowledge of their time.

As an illustration of this timorous religious tendency to gloss over the sincerity of same-sex attraction, let us consider the standard reference to Genesis by "traditionalists," who cite it as a buttress of biblically sanctioned homophobia. Conservatives who assess homosexuality from a protological angle habitually invoke the genders of the original couple: God made them, so far as Scripture testifies, "male" and "female." From this premise they conclude that any attempt to compromise the binary stature of gender runs counter to God's intentions and can only be dubbed unnatural and therefore sinful. But that is to be stuck in a severely partial, superficial biblical hermeneutic, reminiscent of the limitations of Euclidian or, worse, a two-dimensional geometry versus its multidimensional variants. The related issue of race, still just as hotly debated as sexual orientation, can give us a clue as to the disastrous implications of a protological biblical approach applied to human nature and physiology. Assuming the biological reality of our Old Testament earliest ancestors is tantamount to agreeing that they belonged to a specific race, just as surely as they had a gender. What was their race, exactly? We have no idea, at least as far as the Bible is concerned, because none is mentioned in the biblical narrative. This is just as well, incidentally, for if Scripture mentioned any single race as the original one, all others would be readily dismissed (on theological justification to boot!) as somehow less real, less human, less worthy; in short, as a *regression* from the one true race created by God. The long, bitter, and on-going struggle over race still plaguing even advanced societies, apart from any scriptural or religious promotion of one single race against the rest, should give us enough pause and make us alert to the dangers surrounding the assessment of anthropological issues by a myopic reference to Scripture only.

Be that as it may, my point here is that, just as with regard to race God did not desist from creating a multiplicity of races over time that serve no obvious purpose other than adding to anthropological diversity, neither did He balk at furthering diversity by producing an inbred sexual orientation featuring same-sex attraction. Protologically speaking, this development seems useless, sort of like an evolutionary dead-end, because if anything it doesn't lead to procreation. Nevertheless, the said shortcoming must be seen against the aforementioned backdrop of the peculiar circumstances surrounding Christ's conception and birth, which points to what would've gradually replaced biological reproduction for all humankind, had the Fall not intervened—in all amounting to an eschatological transcendence of the biological mode of human procreation. To this must be further added the surprising patristic consensus already mentioned, that in the Eschaton, the notion of gender, while not altogether canceled, is somehow to be transcended in ways that we currently can't grasp, and that it was only thanks to the Fall that the human race was trapped in a gender polarity having no use for anything in between. Like much else concerning humankind's stature and being, the integral worth of gay men and women will be manifested in God's Kingdom, along with the full-fledged unfolding of our Creator's plan for us and the cosmos. This is but one among several crucial reasons why theological reasoning must begin from the End, as

Metropolitan of Pergamon John Zizioulas argued in an inspired paper.[13] Permit me to quote him briefly on the significance of the eschatological hermeneutic he is propounding:

> Between Plato and Paul there is a common mind as to the eternity of love, but there is also a fundamental difference in orientation. Plato looks for the ἀεί, the eternity of love, in what has always been the same, namely the world of Ideas, whereas Paul speaks of it in terms of *the future*. Plato approaches love *protologically* whereas Paul understands it *eschatologically*.[14] . . . The slogan "back to the Fathers," which appeared at a time when historicism was thriving, was received enthusiastically by Orthodox theologians who turned dogmatics essentially into history of dogma, loading it with quotations from patristic sources without any effort to interpret them in contemporary categories of thought. Any attempt at hermeneutics is usually met by "serious patristic scholarship" with an accusation of "anachronism" and "existential influence," as if the sayings of the Fathers or the historical facts could be conceived in themselves apart from their interpretation by us today. This leads to a conservatism that turns tradition into "passed," and, therefore, dead reality with no real appropriation by the human being in its present situation.
>
> All this happens without any appreciation of the hermeneutical character of tradition itself and its connection with eschatological thought. Already in the Old Testament prophesy was essentially an act of hermeneutics: the word of God and the actual events of history were placed in the light of their future meaning. The Holy Spirit inspired the prophets by revealing to them the "last things." . . . All this is based on the idea that the past always needs the future to verify and confirm it as true by renewing it so that it may become *existentially relevant* in each time and place. Placed in the context of the totality of history (we must bear in mind that the Judeo-Christian tradition operated with a view of history as a totality) this means that there will be an ultimate and final future which will "judge" and purify history as a whole, an eschaton preceded by apocalyptic in the sense of "judgment."
>
> The function of the Holy Spirit in the economy is to bring into history a prolepsis of the ultimate state so that historical existence may not be left without a guide to the truth.[15]

In the cited passage, Zizioulas champions an antinomic logic "which makes the future *cause* the past instead of being caused by it."[16] His argument is a long and intricate one, whose parameters and justification cannot be squeezed in our present paper. Suffice it to conclude our own thesis by suggesting that as soon as these counterintuitive eschatological intimations are seriously taken into account, institutional Christendom can begin seeing homosexuals in a different, vastly more positive light: namely, as a new biological human race struggling for its place in a fallen world that hates anything that strays from the natural order solidified by the Fall. Ironically, the maximalism of Orthodox theology, with its deep doctrinal antinomies already mentioned, is the only way we can make sense of the emergence of homoerotic sexual orientation, which is inbred, genetically formed, inalienable (from the cradle to grave), and an intrinsic part of human identity, affecting hundreds of millions of people worldwide. To ignore what we now know about sexual orientation in general, thanks to the advance of biology and the social sciences, is to remain fixed into a flawed anthropology—inevitably akin to perpetuating falsities about people who are unjustly condemned not because of character but for a genetic trait that they neither chose nor can change. I submit that nothing sets us apart from Christ more than this foul but still widespread attitude among Christians, which is making a mockery of the Lord's injunction to always prefer truth over pious myths based on uncritical prejudices that can't set us free.

Notes

1. For theologically sound and progressive takes by Orthodox Christian scholarship on eschatology, see the collective volume Εκκλησία και Εσχατολογία [*Church and Eschatology*], ed. and with a foreword by Pantelis Kalaitzidis (Volos: Mitropolis of Demetrias Publications/Εκδοτική Δημητριάδος, 2014). Also, Haralambos Ventis, Εσχατολογία και Ετερότητα [Eschatology and Otherness] (Athens: Polis Publications, 2019).

2. Mt. 20:16.

3. Gregory Nazianzus, PG 37.181.

4. Jn. 3:16.

5. 1 Jn. 4:7–21.

6. For references to patristic texts exhibiting the said consensus, see Stavros Yangazoglou, Κοινωνία θεώσεως: Η Σύνθεση Χριστολογίας και Πνευματολογίας στο Έργο του Αγίου Γρηγορίου του Παλαμά [Society of Deities: The Composition of Christology and Pneumatology in the Work of Saint Gregory of Palamas] (Athens: Domos Publications, 2001), 102.

7. Maximus the Confessor, *Schol. in eccl. Hier.* 3.3.2. (PG4, 137). For an excellent analysis of Maximian eschatology, see Metropolitan of Pergamon John D. Zizioulas, *Communion & Otherness*, ed. Paul McPartlan, with a foreword by Archbishop Rowan Williams (London: T&T Clark Press, 2006).

8. As St. Isaac indicates in his *Ascetic Writings*, "God examines future, not past events," in Greek, Ισαάκ του Σύρου, Ασκητικά, vol. Β3, Speeches ΙΒ'—ΜÁ, trans. Nestor Kavvadas (Athens: Thesvitis Publications, 2016), 153.

9. In the field of social and political philosophy, communitarians such as Charles Taylor, Michael Walzer, Michael J. Sandel, and Charles Larmore have expressed regret for the loss or retreat of commonly identified notions of the Good as defined by communities, not individuals. Alasdair McIntyre, another prominent communitarian, has also been ruefully vocal about the loss of eschatology, particularly of the Christian or at least the Aristotelian sort, which as he argues gave people some sort of general moral direction and a common scope in life. See especially his *After Virtue: A Study in Moral Theory* (South Bend, Ind.: University of Notre Dame Press, 1981), as well as its sequel, *Whose Justice? Which Rationality?* (South Bend, Ind.: University of Notre Dame Press, 1988). The notion of eschatology has been given a black eye as a bastion of nonfreedom, particularly due to its association with determinism and conformity to a rigid set of rules, as in its Marxist version. In this paper, I assume that Christian eschatology is neither deterministic nor narrow, but dynamic, open-ended, and inclusive. For a more elaborate, in-depth account of the liberating aspects of Christian eschatology, see my monograph: Ventis, *Εσχατολογία και Ετερότητα*.

10. I say "many" as opposed to "most" because several Protestant Churches in, for example, the US and Scandinavia have championed democracy and human rights for a long time now.

11. Milan Kundera, *The Art of the Novel*, trans. Linda Asher (New York: Harper & Row Publishers, 1993), 7, 14, 18.

12. Sigmund Freud, *The Future of an Illusion* [1927], in the *Standard Edition*, vol. 21, 53.

13. Metropolitan of Pergamon John Zizioulas, "'The End Is Where We Start From': Reflections on Eschatological Ontology" (paper read at the international conference on "Eschatology" organized by the Protestant Faculty of Theology, University of Geneva, 22–24 October, 2015).

14. Zizioulas, "The End," 9.

15. Zizioulas, "The End," 14–15.

16. Zizioulas, "The End," 19.

CHAPTER

14

SEX, LOVE, AND POLITICS

AN (UN)ORTHODOX THEOLOGICAL APPROACH

Davor Džalto

Sex: Gay and Gray

The topic of same-sex (sexual) relationships normally provokes a high level of excitement among tradition-appreciating religious communities. The world of Orthodox Christianity is not an exception in this respect. In terms of the level of excitement and emotional outbursts this topic provokes, the only real competition same-sex relationships have is the question of national identity and national politics. This alone confirms the aptness of the topic and the need for its deeper exploration from a theological perspective.

However, there are also other reasons why this topic deserves a closer attention. As the "Open Letter from the European Forum of LGBT Christian Groups to the Holy and Great Council of the Orthodox Church" (2016) states, LGBT people are not necessarily outside the Church—many of them belong to the Church.[1] The letter also appeals to the Council to do everything possible in order to stop violence against sexual and gender "others." In many countries where Orthodoxy is the dominant and traditional faith, the violence is often very real, appearing behind the mask of fighting for "Orthodoxy," "tradition," or "traditional (national) values." Therefore, the topic of nonheterosexual (including same-sex) sexualities and sexual activities in the context of Orthodoxy is not an alien or an abstract subject, relevant only for small circles of specialists, but something that affects church life on a daily basis.

One can start by asking a simple and somewhat naïve question: What is problematic about same-sex sexual relationships from an (Orthodox)

Christian perspective? Traditionally, one can point to biblical texts that seem to be very clear in their condemnation of same-sex (especially male) sexual relationships.[2] These passages are very well known and include the narratives from the book of Genesis, Judges, and Leviticus, as well as from the New Testament books, such as the Epistles to Romans, First Corinthians, or First Timothy.[3]

Of course, there have been many attempts to "soften" the character of these passages in order to offer interpretations that would show biblical text as somehow more "gay friendly" (or at least less antigay) than it has been traditionally understood. Such interpretations do not usually sound very convincing and, at best, they barely scratch the surface of the issue.[4]

Should we, then, conclude that same-sex sexual relationships are simply *sinful* and unacceptable from an (Orthodox) Christian perspective? Should we take their condemnation, so clearly expressed in the biblical text, as a sufficient evidence for simply dismissing sexual intercourse between people of the same sex, as something that cannot be reconciled with Christian anthropology and something so obviously *wrong* that it does not even require a serious theological exploration? On the other hand, is it not clear that good old (heterosexual) marriage, procreation, and (happy) family life are blessed by the Church, and that practicing these *proper* ways of conducting one's private (sex-related) affairs leads also to a *healthy* nation (a kind of extended family), where all members of both the *small* and the *large* family (tribe or nation) are supposed to live in harmony with God, one another, and the rest of the world?

Despite the overwhelming evidence of a very strong "antigay" position in the Judeo-Christian tradition, things do not appear to me to be that simple. One reason for that is the apparent lack of *good* and more elaborate Orthodox Christian theologies of sex and sexuality. However, only if one makes an effort to understand the issue of human sexuality, and the meaning of sexual intercourse from the point of view of Orthodox Christian theology, can one hope to give a more meaningful account on the issue of same-sex relationships. This is the reason why I will first explore the broader issue of human sexuality and sexual intercourse before addressing the specific issue of homosexuality. This exploration, in order to shed light on theological approaches to sex, sexuality, sexual intercourse, and their religious and political implications, will look into the broader historical, cultural, and religious context in which many Judeo-Christian ideas and practices appeared.

Sex and Sexuality: *Ceci n'est pas une pipe*

As soon as one looks at the place and meaning of the (human) sexual intercourse in the context of the Judeo-Christian tradition, one realizes that it occupies a strange and rather ambivalent place. Already at the beginning of the Old Testament, human sexuality (expressed through the male/female duality) appears connected with the story of the Fall, and the evil that came as a result of the Fall.[5]

The very last sentence of the second chapter of Genesis informs us that man and woman "were both naked . . . and were not ashamed" (Genesis 2:25). This would change as soon as they ate from the Tree of Knowledge of good and evil, as their eyes "were opened, and they knew they were naked" (Genesis 3:7). This means that the immediate consequence of the original sin has something to do with both *knowledge* (or rather the *kind* of knowing) and sexuality (linked with shame and reproductive organs). The Fall is marked by the realization of human "nakedness" and the emergence of shame in respect to the reproductive organs. This recognition of nakedness and shame manifests itself as the need for covering the penis and the vulva with "fig leaves" (Genesis 3:7),[6] and hiding from "the face of God" (Genesis 3:8–11).[7]

The punishment for the original sin is also related to sex and procreation; God informs the woman: "I will greatly multiply your sorrow and your conception; in pain you shall bring forth children; your desire shall be for your husband and he shall rule over you" (Genesis 3:16). Sex, pregnancy, procreation, and the "rule" (in which one can easily see a potential for domination) appear all at once, as the immediate results of the changed mode of existence and the human inability to *acquire* (or sustain?) the way of knowing that would reflect (in an iconic way?) the way God *knows*. The change could also be described as the human choice of instrumental (objectified) knowledge over *wisdom* (symbolized by the Tree of Life).[8] This also reflects a broader issue of female sexuality being perceived as much more complex but also much more dangerous than male sexuality.[9] Sexual desire, sexual intercourse, conception, and procreation can thus be interpreted as the very signs of the Fall.[10] The taboo of sex becomes intrinsically linked with guilt and shame, but also with passion and suffering.

Another aspect of the taboo of sex, reproductive organs, and childbirth (procreation) can be seen in the concept of "uncleanliness" that applies both to women and men. The issue of uncleanliness is discussed at length in Leviticus, which specifies that the flow of menstrual blood and sperm make human bodies unclean, and so does sex with a woman during her monthly period.[11]

However, in spite of the presence of the taboo of sex, the Old Testament tradition (at least post–First Temple tradition) generally takes a positive stance toward procreation and holds procreation to be the primary purpose of marriage and even sexuality as a whole.[12] Having many children was perceived as a sign of God's favor (in the fallen state, of course). It seems that, given the negative connotations of the reproductive organs and the liquids associated with them, procreation appears as something that, paradoxically, redeems the sinfulness and uncleanliness of sexual intercourse.

Sex, Blood, and the Tomb of the Womb

The taboo of sex is, of course, not something that is only present in the biblical tradition. A look at other ancient traditions can be illuminating, both in regard to the similarities and differences of these traditions. Sexuality and sexual intercourse are associated with fertility, procreation, and the proliferation of life—even in the realm of the gods. Most important female deities across the Mediterranean were associated with procreation and fertility functions. Moreover, it seems that in the earliest recorded memory of humanity it was the fertile female deity that was perceived as having ontic and mystical precedence over other gods. Nammu, Ishtar (Inanna), Cybele, Gaea (Gaia), Demeter, Mater Matuta, and Vesta all have the attributes/functions of the "Great Mother" (*Magna Mater*) who gives birth, out of whose womb the entire (earthly) life springs.[13] Even the Greek Chaos ("opening" or "gap"—therefore, maybe, also "womb"), in spite of having a masculine form, can be related to the "virgin mother goddess."[14] On the other hand, supreme male deities (e.g., Zeus, Jupiter) often appear as administrators, those who have the political/managerial power, but not the mystical, life-giving potential immanent to the parthenogenetic function of the Mother deities.[15]

In addition to the motif of virginity, there is also the motif of incestuous relationships sometimes attributed to Great Mothers. Those relationships can also involve human sacrifices, at least on a symbolic level. Thus, in the cult of Ishtar, her sexual intercourse with King Damuzi/Tammuz who (typically) appears both as her son and her lover, and the ritualistic death (sacrifice) of the king, secures nature's rebirth and fertility.[16] At the same time, we can see here the motif of the "sacred marriage," the ceremony that has a cosmic significance—since it secures fertility and life. "Sacred marriage" is also reenacted in religious rituals, giving sexual intercourse a religious-mystical meaning.[17] We find similar features in the story of Cybele and her son-lover Attis, or with Isis and Osiris.[18]

In some cases, the identification of the Great Mother with the Earth, and thus with the entirety of nature, is even more literal. For the Okanagan North American people, the soil is the mother's flesh, plants her hair, stones her bones, and wind is her breath.[19]

All these images make the incestuous associations all the more explicit; it is not only that the womb functions as the generator of life (with or without male impregnation)—at the end of one's life journey, one returns to the womb of the Mother (Earth) through funerary rituals.

This means that the womb of the Great Mother functions as a trope. The womb is, at the same time, the origin of life and its grave. Life ends in the womb of the Mother (Earth) just as it springs out of it. But even in the act of giving life (at birth), the womb is not without its ambivalent meaning, as childbirth happens "at a point when one is truly on the threshold between life and death."[20] Childbirth, as well as motherhood, thus also become a metaphor for crisis, punishment, and death. Hence, the symbolism of blood as both a life-giving principle and a symbol of death.

Blood coming from the mother's womb can be the unclean (menstrual) blood, but it can also be a flow of blood caused by aborted children, thus being related to death. Here we can see another tropetic function of the womb and sexual intercourse (and, consequently, procreation): The issue of blood makes the body of a woman "unclean" precisely because it is related to the blood sacrifice, and more specifically, human blood sacrifice. Stillborn (or aborted) children represent such sacrifices in blood. However, the very menstrual blood already has an ingredient of death in it (since everybody born "of flesh" has death as his or her "natural" *telos*). Childbirth justifies sexual intercourse and yet, it is also a death-bearing phenomenon, an "unclean" event. The pollution of childbirth is removed only by blood sacrifices (performed normally by men).[21] In the end, the Mother (Earth) eats her children, assembling them again in the depths of her womb.

The vagina is, thus, a taboo as it is the (sacred) "door" out and into the mother's womb, into the cradle and the grave. Hence, there is an incestuous aspect to the (major) female deities; those born out of the (nature's) womb, have to return to it, they must both exit and (re)enter the mother's vagina at least once during their presence on this planet. In actual reality, this entering and exiting through the (mystical) vagina, as the doorway to the (mystical) womb of the mother, was often practiced more than once, through the symbolic reenactment of the religious-mystical incest. We find one instance of this in the already mentioned "sacred marriage" rituals or in the so-called "sacred prostitution," in which having sexual intercourse with, for instance, a priestess of the Great Mother could have signified a mystical union with the Goddess herself.[22] Orgasm would thus stand for the *realization* of the "mystical" union of "this world," which does not escape its boundaries, even though it reaches its edges.

Liberation from the Tomb (of the Mother)

Given the ancient polytheistic context, as well as the Old Testament tradition (especially in the Second Temple period, and in post-Temple Judaism), where sexual intercourse, childbirth, and procreation, in spite of their uncleanliness, have nevertheless a positive dimension, one cannot but notice the radicalism of Christianity vis-à-vis the questions of sex, procreation, and the established social roles (including family ones). The New Testament texts, together with much of the later Church tradition, often contrast (biological) family, sex, and procreation to the Kingdom of God and its existential logic.

Christ explains that "there are those who choose to live like eunuchs for the sake of the kingdom of heaven" (Matthew 19:12). In the Gospel of Luke the message is even more explicit:

> The people of this age marry and are given in marriage. But those who are considered worthy of taking part in the age to come and in the resurrection from the dead will neither marry nor be given in marriage, and they can no longer die; for they are like the angels. They are God's children, since they are children of the resurrection. (Luke 20:34–36)

We are also informed that "At the resurrection people will neither marry nor be given in marriage; they will be like the angels in heaven" (Matthew 22:30; see also Mark 12:25), which is reflected in Paul's message "It is good for them to stay unmarried, as I do" (1 Corinthians 7:7–11).

The change of perspective is clear here: The eschatological reality, with its new mode of existence, gains the upper hand over history, biology, and the social and political realities. The coming Kingdom of God becomes the criterion of truth, not ethical or legal norms, not even biological or physical laws. Viewed from this perspective, the relationships that belong to "this world," which means the world of necessity, must *die* to be *born* in new reality, which is based on freedom.

This also applies to very fundamental social institutions, such as the family. Christ is explicit:

> If anyone comes to me and does not hate father and mother, wife and children, brothers and sisters—yes, even their own life—such a person cannot be my disciple. (Luke 14:26)

> From now on there will be five in one family divided against each other, three against two and two against three. They will be divided, father against son and son against father, mother against daughter and daughter against mother, mother-in-law against daughter-in-law and daughter-in-law against mother-in-law. (Luke 12:52–53)

What Jesus was preaching for others, he applied to himself—having been informed, according to the Gospel of Mark, that his mother and brothers were outside looking for him, he replied: "'Who are my mother and my brothers?' he asked. Then he looked at those seated in a circle around him and said, 'Here are my mother and my brothers! Whoever does God's will is my brother and sister and mother'" (Mark 3:33–35).

Of course, the presence of these explicit messages about the changed meaning of interhuman relationships does not mean that Christian tradition would not embrace and justify (often in a remarkably Old Testament manner) procreation and (heterosexual) sexual intercourse that leads to procreation, just as Christians would also develop theologies that justify and sanctify the existence of a variety of sociopolitical institutions. All of this, in my view, has primarily to do with blurred eschatological expectations and the compromises that the Christian community has been making with "this world" since the very early period, as well as with our (all-too) human weaknesses.[23]

Once we acknowledge the radicalism of *authentic* Christianity vis-à-vis family, sexual intercourse, and procreation, we should try to provide a more solid theological explanation for this radicalism. We can still ask what is so problematic about sexual intercourse, procreation, and with them related social institutions? They seem to be somehow linked with the very core of the Christian doctrine—the appearance of Christ and the promise of the future Kingdom of God (which is not of "this world").

A short answer would be that sexual intercourse and procreation are problematic and cannot easily "fit" into the broader fabric of Christian anthropology and ontology because the problem of sex (and procreation) is intrinsically linked with the problem of human freedom. And the issue of freedom is the cornerstone of the "good news" about the Incarnation and the coming Kingdom of God. Now comes the longer answer.

What Christ's Kingdom brings, from an Orthodox point of view, is a new mode of existence, the existence that is not based on the necessities of "this world." In the language of the New Testament, "this world" can be understood as precisely indicating the sphere of necessity, both physical-biological and sociopolitical. This is why "flesh and blood" (of "this world") will not "inherit the Kingdom of God."[24] "Flesh and blood" in this context can be identified with what John Zizioulas calls "hypostasis of biological existence,"[25] which means a pregiven, natural existence. Nature, biology, and blood (and their continuation through blood-ties) will not inherit the Kingdom of God. That is why baptism is necessary as a "new birth," the birth from "above," and not from mother's womb. This birth from "above" is the birth in (and from) the *Spirit*,[26] and the "food" and "drink" that feed this new hypostasis (while still on earth, in history) is the bloodless sacrifice (of bread and wine) that becomes the new *flesh* and *blood* of a new, free existence, whose very *realness* is manifested to us (in history) through the aspects of the world that we can experience in their immediate, concrete and "real" (historical) presence—the bread and the wine. In view of both the New Testament text and the later tradition of Triadology, the "Spirit" here stands for the Holy Spirit. Important to note is that the noun "spirit" is feminine in Hebrew (and neuter in Greek), which allows for an interpretation of the (Holy) Spirit as the "Heavenly Mother" (as opposed to the "Mother Earth").[27] The Spirit can also be identified with freedom—the Spirit stands for a new "birth" in and out of freedom, not a birth out of the necessities of nature (biology), or the power of social and legal norms.[28] The Spirit also signifies Wisdom (Sophia), the life-giving wisdom, which humans can acquire, that replaces death (of the fallen existence) and the knowledge (of "this world," which turns out to be false knowledge, the knowledge of death).

John Zizioulas's distinction between the "individual" and "personal" mode of existence is also useful in this context. The "personal" mode of existence implies an "opening up" of one's being, it is a different logic of existence, in which one's own unique identity is not identified with who one *is*, in one's (physical, biological, factual) *essence*, but rather with a loving relationship with other(s). "Love" in Zizioulas's words "is identified with ontological freedom."[29]

On the other hand, individual existence, which is attached to our "hypostasis of biological existence," is marked by a different logic. The biological existence suffers, in Zizioulas's view, from

> two "passions" which destroy precisely that towards which the human hypostasis is thrusting, namely the person. The first "passion" is what we may call "ontological necessity." Constitutionally the hypostasis is inevitably tied to the natural instinct, to an impulse which is "necessary" and not subject to the control of freedom. Thus the person as a being "subsists" not as freedom but as necessity.... The second "passion" is a natural consequence of the first. At its earliest stage it may be called the "passion" of individualism, of the separation of the hypostases. Finally, however, it is identified with the last and greatest passion of man, with the disintegration of the hypostasis, which is death.[30]

The result is that the human being, as natural existence, in its individual hypostasis, is "intrinsically a tragic figure."[31] Sexual intercourse, which aspires to reach a communion with another individual, is also *tragic* in this sense, and appears as an ontic "failure." It is a manifestation of the existence destined to die—in the womb of the Mother (Earth-Nature); its attempt to reach a communion necessarily fails because it necessarily leads to a separation and alienation between individual beings. Pregnancy, as a possible outcome of sexual intercourse, also becomes a sign of individualized existence, which enables nature (and the necessity attached to it) to dominate over personhood. In childbirth, just as in the ancient Mother Earth myths, the species survives, not personal identities. Procreation thus appears as a symbol of failure, one's inability to reach a personal existence.

Nikolai Berdyaev, although starting from somewhat different premises, reaches similar conclusions. Sexual difference and sexual intercourse appear as a sign of the incompleteness of the human being. The initial, "androgynous" state of human existence becomes affected by the Fall,[32] which is where the "gap" or the incompleteness in the human being comes from. Sexual desire is an urge for the fulfillment of the gap; sex is "the seal of the Fall of man, an imprint which marks the loss of the integrality of human nature."[33] But this also means, following Berdyaev, that sex is "one of the sources of human slavery and one of the most profound of such sources, which are bound with the very possibility of the continuance of the human race."[34]

However, questioning the meaning of sexual intercourse does not imply a denial of sexuality or sexual (male/female) identity. On the contrary, according to Berdyaev, precisely in the act of sexual intercourse, sexuality and sexual energy lose their meaning and their personal potential. Sexual intercourse stands for "alienation of sexual energy," turning it into a "particular function."[35] That is why virginity (e.g., in monasticism) is the personification of the fullness of sexuality, prevention of its alienation and disintegration.[36] To abstain from sexual intercourse is, for Berdyaev, not a negation of sexuality but its affirmation; it is the affirmation of the androgynous identity of the human being, which is the image of God.[37] Attempts to restore the completeness of human identity through sexual intercourse is the source of human slavery to the necessities of nature; the restoration of the human androgynous nature comes with Christ's Incarnation.[38] This means that virginity in "this world" becomes the icon of the virginity characterizing the Wisdom of God, the "Heavenly Mother" (i.e., Holy Spirit) who keeps the integrity of all creation, bringing it into the fullness of being (life). This Heavenly Wisdom then impregnates (without sexual intercourse and without taking away her virginity) the Theotokos, the earthly image of the Heavenly Wisdom.

From this, it would proceed that marriage, understood as a union of love between a man and a woman, has only one purpose—the multiplication of love. Attempts to reach a union through sexual intercourse turn out to always be an illusion, an impossible task that gives testimony to our mortality and the disintegration of our (biological, historical) being. Sexual intercourse is an affirmation of individuality and, consequently, of necessity. Sexual energy, following Berdyaev, should be invested in a creative act, which allows for its transformation from a necessary (biological) force into an expression of freedom (the work of the Spirit). Thus, birth giving (in/from "this world") and creation (spiritual "birth") appear as two opposite, and mutually conflicting activities.[39] Giving birth is attached to necessity and death, creation is attached to freedom, Spirit, and life. From this perspective, marriage and procreation appear as opposing concepts. The *ontic roots*, so to say, of sexual intercourse and procreation are in death and disintegration—i.e., the womb of Mother Earth–Nature—as their final destination. They are a symbol of the triumph of necessity over freedom, nature over personhood, biology over a particular and irreplaceable (personal) identity.

One can clearly see at this point why Christian justifications of heterosexual sexual relationships (as opposed to the homosexual ones) based on the procreation argument are fundamentally confused. Procreation stands for a failure of personhood, a triumph of disintegration, and a death-bearing principle.[40] This is also the reason why procreation in itself can never be a goal for Christians. However, this is also the reason why Christian apologists who criticize homosexuality with the argument that homosexuality is "unnatural" or that such intercourses "cannot lead to procreation" simply miss the point. The problem of homosexuality, just as of heterosexuality, is the problem of human freedom and necessity, individuality and love, not the problem of ethics or natural laws, let alone our biological reproduction. What Orthodox Christian anthropology proposes is a change of the mode of our existence—through *theosis*—that does not come as a result of sexual intercourse, no matter how "normal" or "perverted" it may appear.

Politics of Sex

There is, however, one more reason why Christianity takes a cautious and even critical stance toward sexual intercourse and procreation. The individual mode of existence, which is manifested and affirmed in the act of sexual intercourse, has another important aspect that Christianity confronts and questions—the political one. There is a political, power dimension to sex. Sexual intercourse and procreation are not only about the necessity of biological/individual presence, but also about the necessity attached to power.

Paul Veyne successfully shows how the ethics of sexual intercourse in ancient Rome was essentially a public (political) matter. Sexual intercourse (hetero- or homosexual) was understood as being primarily about domination and a (symbolic) conquest (over the other party), which translates into active vs. passive roles in sexual intercourse.[41] That is why the sphere of sex and the sphere of the political turn out to be so closely related. Building on Veyne's interpretation of the ancient Roman view of sex (at least prior to the Antonine dynasty), one can say that at the bottom of the quest for power (viewed from a male perspective), whether it be manifested in bed or in the political arena, is the desire to (symbolically at least) dominate, and to affirm one's individual self through that domination. This affirmation of one's self (active/dominant position) was closely related to one's social standing and the power one had (or aspired to have) in the sociopolitical realm. That means, as Veyne explains, that sex (oral, anal, or vaginal) with those of a lower social ranking (in the master-slave tension for instance) were considered acceptable as long as the one in the dominant position (i.e., of a higher social status) assumed the active position, and the one of the lower rank assumed a passive/subordinate position.[42] Sex and sexual roles are thus symbolic, and appear as functional/instrumental to politics. Taking the active position in sexual intercourse becomes thus a statement about power dynamics, a visible manifestation of power (or a desired self-image, a fantasy of one's power in its actual absence).[43] This, however, also means that the one who is convinced of *his* (mostly his) power, the one on "top" (of the pyramid of power), can afford to refrain from having sexual intercourse (as there is nothing to "concur" any longer), becoming thus some kind of a *fallen image* of (heavenly) virginity, the virginity of "this world."[44]

If we try to translate this perspective into the "individual" vs. "person" language, one could claim that it is this insecurity of our individual existence, the fear of death (as its ultimate destiny), which is driving one's individual self. A powerful expression of this drive is the sexual desire and orgasm. One's "self," however, is never simply a biological datum but also a socially informed construct. The hypertrophy of individuality (ego) is there to cover up for nothingness and death that function as the foundation of our individual being in history. In contrast to that, following the existential logic of Christianity, those who aspire to the greatest power turn out to be the *weakest*. The greatest courage is required to overcome one's individuality, which means one's fear for one's own individual existence manifested as the need for the affirmation of one's self and domination over others. One's hope that one's identity will be solidified by that self-affirmation and domination, and will survive through procreation (which, in addition to biological, has also sociopolitical implications—in securing the perpetuation of social classes, for instance), turns out to be illusionary. What from a natural, social, or biological perspective seems most "real," and the only way to secure one's individual existence (i.e., self-affirmation, domination, procreation) is a dangerous illusion from a Christian perspective. To ground one's identity and existence in one's self or one's pregiven nature, is to sacrifice one's real person(hood). That is why domination, the desire to impose and affirm one's individual self, whether that be in sexual intercourse, through procreation, or in the political sphere more narrowly taken, is a sign of weakness, and a manifestation of the logic of "this world."

The desire for power and domination is incompatible with freedom. Power (real or imaginary) corrupts, but it does not only corrupt in the sense that it morally distorts—it corrupts in the very basic sense that those in power become slaves, they become nothing more than jokers, puppets that need to conform to the circumstances that define them as those who have the power (or aspire to acquire it) and compel them to act according to how others (or an entire political system) expect them to act.[45] In the end, slaves and concubines become the masters of their masters. All they need to learn is how to manipulate or control the master's passions, fantasies, and egotism. To their disappointment, those on *top* (masters) discover that there is nothing there. The *all-potence* thus turns into *all-impotence*, which needs to be perpetuated.

This was well understood, for instance, by Marcus Aurelius. However, his solution was a Stoic one—one should accept one's role (even though it is apparently a ridiculous one) as a necessity and try to fulfill one's duty as much as one can, as the ultimate ethical ideal.

This is what separates Aurelius from Christ. Faced with the last and greatest temptation in the wilderness, Christ refuses to submit to it.[46] Power is rejected in the name of freedom. What appears as power—one's slavery in the name of self-affirmation, political influence, natural or social laws—is rejected in the name of one's freedom and love as the real (metaphysical) powers that (from the perspective of "this world") appear as slavery (see Matthew 9:35). This is why the Christian approach is the approach of love and service, not of power and domination. The self-emptying (kenotic) love and serving others out of love becomes the Christian path to liberation. Loving, and serving others out of love, liberates us from the constraints of the position of power (and submission to it) and of the necessities of individual existence.[47] To the necessities and the power structures of this world, individual-egotistical and biological impulses that only appear as bringing "possibilities" and "freedoms" when affirmed, Christianity contrasts love—love, as a means of opening up one's being for a kenotic and ecstatic embrace of the other. In this sense, love transcends sex, renders it insubstantial, even grotesque. Sexual intercourse objectifies, turns persons into objects of desire, a thing to conquer, and use in order to satisfy the urges of the individualized being, to allow it to dominate (and to submit to that domination). Its compelling character turns out to be an obstacle to perfect love, which animates, turning objects into personal beings.

Only from this perspective one can understand why Christianity has traditionally been skeptical about homosexual sexual intercourse. This skepticism comes out of a more general skepticism regarding sexual (including heterosexual) intercourse as a means of affirmation of one's individual existence, and therefore a manifestation of one's slavery in and to "this world." Christianity proposes a new existence in which all the necessities attached to our death-bearing existence (in history) will be overcome, in which love transcends all the necessities, including the necessities of our biological hypostasis manifested in sexual intercourse.

However, historical Christianity has been making many compromises with the "world," sometimes without a legitimate excuse, and sometimes for the purpose of the salvation of the world, and taking into account our (all-too) human weaknesses. Such compromises include the acceptance of (heterosexual) sexual intercourse, not as the "perfect" way of practicing one's sexuality and iconicity to God, but as something exhibiting the features of an existential failure (which, nevertheless, can lead to the appearance of a new biological hypostasis, with another opportunity for a personal relationship). It would be, therefore, difficult to find an excuse not to show a similar tolerance, a similar "oikonomic" conciliatory attitude, when it comes to the same-sex relationship (even though, in their traditional form, they cannot lead to the birth of a new human being).

This does not mean that either hetero- or homosexual intercourse should be promoted as a means of salvation; they should be understood as yet another manifestation of our individualized existence in history, our existential fears, our urge to dominate over other individuals or objects in this world, or to submit to domination in this world (at a symbolic-fantasy level at least). Thus, heterosexual, same-sex (sexual) relationships manifest themselves as yet another incapacity (among many!) that comes out of fear, insecurity, and misdirected sexuality, that we live with, trying to overcome the boundaries of our individual selves and affirm, through the affirmation of freedom and love, our likeness to God.[48]

The situation in this regard is similar to the one we find in another realm of our lives—in the necessity to consume food. Christianity and the Church *tolerate* eating other living beings, including animals. This, however, does not mean that eating meat is considered "good" in principle. On the contrary, it is a tragedy, it means killing other living beings to satisfy our (selfish, individual) needs. However, it is accepted as part of our tragic and in many ways paradoxical existence in "this world." Those who aspire to maximize the iconic potentials of their lives (through a monastic life for instance) normally also refrain from eating meat, or anything else above the absolute minimum to sustain their lives.

Eating a steak, thus, does not reflect the eschatological mode of existence, does not reflect love; quite the contrary—in itself, it stands for the objectification of another living being (e.g., the body of a cow), to which we relate instrumentally, for the benefit and pleasure of our individualized being, and not through love. However, under certain circumstances, the same meat can turn into an instrument of salvation, if we use the steak to feed the hungry or share it in love with other people. Nevertheless, the meat of other living beings that we eat remains an artifact of "this world," something that is rooted in the logic of necessity and death, rather than in the logic of freedom. This dynamic is often very complex in real life situations. One can, so to speak, enjoy eating a juicy steak, and—without being a hypocrite—still advocate for vegetarianism, as something more perfect, something one should aspire for (even if one is still too weak to practice it him/herself). In a similar way, sexual relationships demonstrate their compelling (biological-instinctual, individual, and instrumental) character, even though they can eventually lead two individuals toward *free love*. The point is, thus, not to *resist* sex, or render it "bad," but to outgrow it, to get to the point where one is free from its compelling character.

There are important lessons here, of a more general character, that we can learn from Orthodox theology. We should refrain from the glorification of our weaknesses, from turning weaknesses and incapacities (especially if they are our own) into virtues or principles. Because we are weak and we submit to the urges of our individual existence (and this includes theologians), that does not mean that we should construct theologies to justify our weaknesses, or that we should not try to overcome the boundaries of our individual self and affirm, through the affirmation of freedom and love, our likeness to God. One can acknowledge that one position, principle, value, or action is just and meaningful while, at the same time, acknowledging one's inability to live up to it, just as one can, without ending up in a hypocrisy, be in favor of vegetarianism and believe that to be the only meaningful diet, and yet not be strong enough to practice is, not all the time at least.

Another lesson is that there are no simple solutions in existential questions, there is no easy way out, everything needs to be lived through in order to acquire existentially relevant knowledge. We must try to get to the transformative experience of love, not by ignoring the issues (including our own weaknesses) or pretending that they are not there, but by transforming those very weaknesses into freedom. We should, as it were, speak the truth, even if we are unable to live up to it, rather than create narratives that will make us "look good" in our or somebody else's eyes. This is the ascetic dimension of an (academic) theological enterprise.

If we think of the Kingdom of God from this perspective, then the Resurrection of Christ, and the promise of the universal resurrection, manifest themselves as the triumph over biological death, but also over the *womb of the* (earthly) *Mother*. Christ's birth, which lacks the incestuous symbolism characteristic of ordinary births, and His Resurrection can be interpreted as an act of overcoming the womb of the Mother (Earth), both as the grave and the source of (compelling) life. The new life is not blood-related or blood-dependent. Hence the lack of blood sacrifices, and the vigilance toward sex and procreation.

Notes

1. Mikhail Cherniak (On behalf of the Orthodox Working Group of the European Forum of LGBT Christian Groups), "Open Letter to the Holy and Great Council of the Orthodox Church," European Forum of Lesbian, Gay, Bisexual and Transgender Christian Groups: http://www.euroforumlgbtchristians.eu/index.php/en/media-press/press-releases/223-open-letter-to-the-holy-and-great-council-of-the-orthodox-church (accessed June 16, 2019).

2. The concept of "same-sex relationship" is used in this text to imply sexual intercourse between people of the same sex. As such, it is equivalent to what is sometimes called "sexual behavior" as opposed to "sexual orientation," "sexual attraction," or other types of same-sex relationships of an erotic nature. In order not to (dramatically) exceed the envisioned length for this paper, under the rubric

of "same-sex (sexual) relationships" I will focus on male same-sex relationships, but I believe that the conclusions, to a large extent, generalize.

3. See Genesis 19:4–7; Judges 19:22–23; Leviticus 18:22–23; Leviticus 20:13; Rom. 1:27; 1 Cor. 6:9–10; 1 Tim. 1:9–10.

4. For a brief summary of these positions, see Volodymyr Bureha, "Attitudes to Homosexuality in Christianity," in *"For I Am Wonderfully Made": Texts on Eastern Orthodoxy and LGBT Inclusion*, ed. Misha Cherniak, et al. (Nieuwegein, Netherlands: European Forum of Lesbian, Gay, Bisexual and Transgender Christian Groups, 2016), 149–54 (and the literature quoted therein). A remarkably different (and very insightful) approach, which seeks to offer a *communitarian*, personalistic, and *iconic* understanding of male-female (sexual) relationships and, consequently, offer an explanation for a traditionally negative attitude toward homosexuality (based on the relevant biblical texts) can be found in Stanley J. Grenz, "Homosexuality and the Christian Sex Ethic," in *Christian Perspectives on Gender, Sexuality and Community*, ed. Maxine Hancock (Vancouver, Canada: Regent College Publishing, 2003), 127–50.

5. For the purposes of this analysis, I approach the story from Genesis 1 primarily as a story about the origin of the world. However, the story can be read, following Margaret Barker, as a symbolic depiction of the temple creation (which I find much more convincing). See Margaret Barker, *Creation: A Biblical Vision for the Environment* (London: T&T Clark, 2010), 38–49 (compare also to the temple symbolism in Ephrem the Syrian, *Hymns on Paradise*, Hymn III). One, of course, does not need to contrast these approaches; the symbolism of the story can be read as conveying a set of multiple meanings at the same time, all of them, this way or the other, related to the First Temple worship.

6. One possible interpretation, which goes back to the patristic era, is that without the Fall (that is, without the "false knowledge" as a *false* way of existing-knowing), there would not have been sexual intercourse and procreation—i.e., reproductive organs would not have even been there, or would have performed a different (nonreproductive) function. See Ephrem the Syrian, *Hymns on Paradise* (Hymn VII, 8, the state of virginity is restored in the eschaton—the paradise regained, see Hymn VII, 5, 6); Maximus the Confessor, *Questions and Doubts* (QD I, 3), and *Ambigua* 41.

7. Using, on multiple occasions in the biblical text, the verb "to know" (someone) to describe sexual intercourse, is, therefore, consistent with the story of the Fall. It may be related (as explained later on in the paper) with a particular—instrumental—way of knowing/relating to the world, and, ultimately, to the issue of power.

8. See Margaret Barker, *The Great Angel: A Study of Israel's Second God* (Louisville, Ky.: Westminster John Knox Press, 1992), 55–62.

9. In addition to the above-mentioned consequences of the Fall, the new biological (and therefore sex-related) dimension of human existence in history is implied in God's words that man will return to the Earth, out which man was taken (Genesis 3:19), as well as in the mentioning of the "garments of skin" (Genesis 3:21) that can be understood as our biological bodies that became capable of biological procreation and thus also of biological death. "Garments of skin" replaced "the robe of glory." See Ephrem the Syrian, *Hymns on Paradise*.

10. The line from the Old Testament that is often used to affirm the thesis that (biological) procreation, supposedly, characterized human existence from the very beginning, even in the Garden of Eden, is taken from Genesis 1:28. It is commonly translated as "increase and multiply" (or "be fruitful and increase in number"). However, it seems that we deal here with a wordplay, characteristic of the biblical discourse, which carries a very different meaning. As Barker explains: "Adam, *while he was still wearing the robe of glory and everything it represented*, was told 'be fruitful and multiply, and fill the earth'—the usual translation—which should also be read in the temple context: Adam was to fill the earth with glory. Since the Hebrew words for 'be fruitful,' *parah*, and 'be beautiful/glorified,' *pa'ar*, are similar, and 'multiply,' *rabah*, can also mean 'be great,' the wordplay . . . showed the original Adam created to be beautiful and great, and to fill the earth with glory." Barker, *Creation*, 204.

11. See Leviticus 15:16–20; Jonathan Klawans, *Impurity and Sin in Ancient Judaism* (Oxford: Oxford University Press, 2000).

12. In the words of Elaine Pagels: "For centuries—indeed, for over a millennium—Jews had taught that the purpose of marriage, and therefore of sexuality, was procreation. . . . To ensure the stability and survival of the nation, Jewish teachers apparently assumed that sexual activity should be committed to the primary purpose of procreation. Prostitution, homosexuality, abortion, and infanticide, practices both legal and tolerated among certain of their pagan neighbors, contradicted Jewish custom and law." Elaine Pagels, *Adam, Eve, and the Serpent* (New York: Vintage Books, 1989), 11.

13. These "Great Mothers" often appear as *virgins*, those who give birth without the participation of a male deity, without sexual intercourse. See Margaret Rigoglioso, *Virgin Mother Goddesses of Antiquity* (New York: Palgrave Macmillan, 2010), 1.

14. "Chaos, whose name literally means 'Opening' or 'Gap,' was the void, the abyss, the infinite space and darkness, unformed matter. Caldwell (in Hesiod 1987, 35) notes that the etymology of the verb to which Chaos's name is related, *chaskô* ('open, yawn, gape'), 'may suggest a womb [that] opens to bring forth life.' I would therefore argue that despite the fact that in Greek *chaos* is a Masculine noun, in the divine entity of Chaos, the first state of the universe, we have an intimation of a specifically female goddess of the void. Chaos, a 'cosmic womb'

continued to reproduce parthenogenetically bearing the male Erebus (Darkness) and his sister, Nyx (Black Night)." Rigoglioso, *Virgin Mother Goddesses*, 16.

15. Stephanie Lynn Budin proposes a different thesis in regard to the Middle Eastern cosmogonies, claiming that "male sexuality is the dominant force for fertility in ANE [Ancient Near Eastern] mythology—it is associated with baseline creation, either of reality itself of or the natural phenomena constituting the world." Stephanie Lynn Budin, "Fertility and Gender in the Ancient Near East," in *Sex in Antiquity*, ed. Mark Masterson et. al (London: Routledge, 2015), 32. One way to reconcile these positions is to postulate that the invasion of the Middle Eastern region by the "Indo-Europeans" during the Bronze age brought the gods who were more associated "with the sky rather than the earth . . . fatherhood rather than loving motherhood." See David Leeming, *The Oxford Companion to World Mythology* (Oxford: Oxford University Press, 2009), 157. Both of these narratives might have continued to influence later mythologies to various degrees.

16. See Leeming, *Companion*, 195–97.

17. See Stephanie Lynn Budin, *The Myth of Sacred Prostitution in Antiquity* (Cambridge: Cambridge University Press, 2008), 17, 22.

18. As Lynn E. Roller notes, Attis in Phrygia was the title of a Meter/Matar priest, not a god's name. However, given the character of the later myth of Cybele and Attis, the function of the Attis priest could have been the one of the main (male) actor in the "sacred wedding" ceremony. See Lynn E. Roller, *In Search of God the Mother: The Cult of Anatolian Cybele* (Berkeley: University of California Press, 1999), 178.

19. See Leeming, *Companion*, 156.

20. Claudia D. Bergmann, *Childbirth as a Metaphor for Crisis* (Berlin: Walter de Gruyter, 2008), 100.

21. "Among the Israelites, the pollution of childbirth, and also of menstruation, typified pollution in general. . . . The Greeks were not comparably concerned about menstrual blood, but here too the pollution of childbirth appears to have been a paradigm for ritual pollution. . . . Here too the pollution of childbirth could be removed only by sacrifice. . . . Around the world, ordinarily only adult males (fathers, real and metaphorical) may perform sacrifice. Where women do so it is as virgins or in some other specifically nonchildbearing role." Nancy Jay, "Sacrifice as Remedy for Having Been Born of Woman," in *Women, Gender, Religion: A Reader*, ed. Elizabeth A. Castelli, Rosamond C. Rodman (London: Palgrave Macmillan, 2001), 175. She also notes that "Both birth and killing are acts of power, but sacrificial ideology commonly construes childbirth as the quintessence of vulnerability, passivity, and powerless suffering." Jay, "Sacrifice," 182.

22. See Roller, *God the Mother*, 155n32; Budin, *The Myth of Sacred Prostitution*.

23. To some extent, this was probably necessary. It is not surprising that the blade, so to speak, of the Christian "sword" (see Matthew 10:34) gets blunter over time in its attempts to transform the world. This is also not necessarily something bad, as long as the blunt blade does not become the principle, replacing the sharpness. The compromises with "this world," and the famous Orthodox principle of *oikonomia*, when practiced out of love, sympathy, and compassion (and not out of ignorance, laziness, corruption, or disbelief), safeguard the Church and Christian faith from becoming an abstract dogma, or a fundamentalist principle, leading to the rejection of the world, turning the Church into an exclusivist cult, which de-churches itself by the lack of concern, love, and compassion for the entirety of creation.

24. "I declare to you, brothers and sisters, that flesh and blood cannot inherit the kingdom of God, nor does the perishable inherit the imperishable." 1 Corinthians 15:50.

25. John Zizioulas, *Being as Communion* (Crestwood: SVS Press, 1985), 49–53.

26. "Jesus replied, 'Very truly I tell you, no one can see the kingdom of God unless they are born again.' 'How can someone be born when they are old?' Nicodemus asked. 'Surely they cannot enter a second time into their mother's womb to be born!' Jesus answered, 'Very truly I tell you, no one can enter the kingdom of God unless they are born of water and the Spirit. Flesh gives birth to flesh, but the Spirit gives birth to spirit. You should not be surprised at my saying, 'You must be born again.'" John 3:3–7.

27. See Margaret Barker, *The Mother of the Lord* (London: Bloomsbury, 2012).

28. See Nicolas Berdyaev, *The Realm of Spirit and the Realm of Caesar* (London: Victor Gollancz, 1952).

29. Zizioulas, *Being*, 46.

30. Zizioulas, *Being*, 50, 51.

31. Zizioulas, *Being*, 52.

32. "But the world-differentiation into male and female can never finally wipe out the basic genuine bisexuality, the androgynous quality in man—the image and likeness of God in him. In truth neither man nor woman is the image and likeness of God but only the androgyne—the youth-maiden, the integral bisexual man. The differentiation into male and female is a result of the cosmic fall of Adam." Nicolas Berdyaev, *The Meaning of the Creative Act* (San Rafael, Calif.: Semantron Press, 2009), 184.

33. Nikolai Berdyaev, *Slavery and Freedom* (New York: Charles Scribner's Sons, 1944), 223.

34. Berdyaev, *Slavery*, 224.

35. "The fractional function of the sexual act is a loss of integral sex-energy: it alienates this energy from the integral being of man. . . . The opposite of chastity, dissipation, is an extreme degree of the fractionalization of sex-energy, alienating it from man's integral nature; it is a loss of integrity. And in the sexual act there is necessarily an element of dissipation, for it is a fractionalization of sex-energy and its alienation from the integral life of body and spirit, making sex into a particular function." Berdyaev, *The Meaning*, 182–83.

36. A phenomenon that many people with a strong sex drive are also often (honestly) attracted to the Church and, particularly, to monasticism, has been noticed. It is not as paradoxical as it may seem, given this dynamic. Serbian psychotherapist and Orthodox philosopher Vladeta Jerotić spoke of the connection between strong eros-drive as a precondition for becoming a *saint*—taking into account that this sex/erotic drive is sublimated. From this perspective, the strong sex/erotic drive seeks its transformation into freedom as a relationship of love, by which the deification is acquired.

37. "Virginity is not a denial, a minimizing or even the absence of sex; virginity is a positive sex-energy. . . . For, in the true sex-life, one may give one's whole self but one cannot give a part—one cannot cut oneself in pieces." Berdyaev, *The Meaning*, 183.

38. Following Boehme, Berdyaev writes: "'Christ on the Cross liberated our virginal image from both man and woman and in Divine love encrimsoned it with his heavenly blood.' Christ restored the androgynous image of man and returned the Virgin-Sophia to him. . . . Jesus again united in himself the male and female into one androgynous image and became 'man-virgin.'" Berdyaev, *The Meaning*, 187.

39. "The sex-urge is creative energy in man. In it there is a superfluity of energy which demands outlet into the world, into an object. . . . He who begets the most creates the least. Begetting takes away energy from creativity." Berdyaev, *The Meaning*, 200.

40. Even though the possibility of love among family members is not denied—it has a potential to *redeem* the existential failure, changing the *growth in death* into the *growth in love*.

41. See Paul Veyne, "La famille et l'amour sous le Haut-Empire romain," in *Annales: Économies, Sociétés, Civilisations* 33, no. 1 (January–February 1978), 35–63; quoted here after Pol Ven, *Porodica u rimskom carstvu* (Loznica: Karpos, 2012), 60.

42. Ven, *Porodica*, 57–66.

43. The same, just in reverse, can be said about having a passive role in sexual intercourse—it can be an image of submission (reflecting the power dynamic outside of sexual intercourse), but it can also be a fantasy about one's submission to

power as a prospect of one's seizing the control (through seduction and submission, for instance) over the active/intruding force, or by becoming "one with it" (e.g., in the fantasy of one's *power* and *strength*, which overwhelms the passive actor, becoming the source of excitement). Related to this are also the traditional (mostly *male*) interpretations of female orgasm as something *mystical*, which enables a mystical union (with *nature*, for instance, or at least one's "own nature" from which one has been alienated) and an ecstatic "getting out" of one's individual "self" (as opposed to male orgasm as something more self-centered, providing individual pleasure, but contained within one's pre-given "self"). Following this logic, the structure of the female fantasy implies the presence of the *other* in a substantive sense, while the *other* in male's sexuality appears as instrumental to the affirmation of the male's ego, as an "instrument" which provides the fantasy framework in within which the (symbolic) domination can happen.

44. This also means that refraining from sex, marriage, or procreation can also be out of egotistic reasons, in which case it lacks the iconicity of the eschatological.

45. When those in power (having almost absolute political power, for instance) choose to try to exercise their freedom, while being in power, the result is—*madness*. An iconic case in this respect are the Roman emperors who tried to abandon their slavery (to the system that codified their power, codifying thus also the *proper* way of doing things), without abandoning power itself.

46. See Matthew 4:8–10.

47. See Matthew 20:25–28.

48. Moralistic solutions do not work here. Attempts—so common in (secularized) Protestant countries—to regulate sex in an administrative-like manner, to categorize and prescribe who should do what, when, and how, in order to render sexual intercourse and the whole issue of sex and sexuality "acceptable," "OK," or "decent," are, at best, tragicomic. Behind the attempts to make sex-related issues "safe" for everyone, eliminating any potentially "dangerous" aspects of sexuality and sexual intercourse, is a manifestation of sad, late-modern, hyperindividualistic obsessive rationality, all the more bizarre when dressed up in theological robes. All those moralistic theologies manage to do is to remove the pleasure from sex. The pleasure of having sex is thus ruined, and nothing ("spiritual") is gained.

CHAPTER

15

From Adam to Christ

From Male and Female to Being Human

John Behr

Be my witnesses (*martyres*)! I too am a witness, says the Lord God, and the servant whom I have chosen[1]

We often theologize with already formed categories—what it is to be human and what it is to be God—and then seek to bring these together in the incarnation, to understand how in Christ divinity and humanity have become united, so that as God became man we now might become gods. The thrust of the conciliar definitions and the theological reflection that accompanies them, however, work the other way round: The one Lord Jesus Christ—the crucified and risen one, as proclaimed by the apostles in accordance with Scripture unveiled and encountered in the breaking of the bread—defines for us what it is to be God and what it is to be human, together and simultaneously, without confusion, change, division, or separation, in one *prosōpon*—one "face"—and one *hypostasis*—one concrete being. He alone is fully divine and fully human, in one: He shows us what it is to be God in the way that he dies as a human being, voluntarily laying down his life, as one over whom death has no claim, so that it is by his death that he tramples down death and gives life to those in the tombs.

It is therefore to the one Lord Jesus Christ that we must look to understand not only what it is to be God but also what it is to be human. As Nicholas Cabasilas put it, at the end of the Byzantine era:

> It was for the new human being that human nature was created at the beginning, and for him mind and desire were prepared.... It was not the old Adam who was the model for the new, but the new Adam for the old.... Because of its nature, the old Adam might be considered the archetype to those who see him first, but for him who has everything before his eyes, the older is the imitation of the second.... To sum it up: the Savior first and alone showed to us the true human being, who is perfect on account of both character and life and in all other respects.²

Christ is the first true human being: He is "the image of the invisible God" (Col. 1:15), *in* whose image we were created. Adam was but "a type of the one to come" (Rom. 5:14), as are we who have come into the world in Adam: a preliminary sketch, the starting point from which we are called to grow into "the measure of the stature of the fullness of Christ" (Eph. 4:13).

One of the most striking examples bearing witness to this, and what it involves, is St. Ignatius of Antioch, on his way to Rome, beseeching the Christians there not to impede his coming martyrdom:

> It is better for me to die in Christ Jesus than to be king over the ends of the earth. I seek him who died for our sake. I desire him who rose for us. Birth-pangs are upon me. Suffer me, my brethren; hinder me not from living, do not wish me to die.... Suffer me to receive the pure light; when I shall have arrived there, I shall be a human being [ἐκεῖ παραγενόμενος ἄνθρωπος ἔσομαι]. Suffer me to follow the example of the passion of my God.³

Our usual understanding of the fundamental categories of life and death, birth and being human, are emphatically reversed. Ignatius is not yet born, not yet living, not yet human; only by his martyrdom, in imitation of Christ, will he be born into life as a human being.

In this light, we can now see a new dimension in the opening verses of Scripture: Having spoken everything else into existence—"Let there be"... and it was and it was good—God announces his own particular project: "Let us make a human being in our image after our likeness" (Gen. 1:26). God does not speak his project into existence with an imperative, but rather uses a subjective: His particular purpose, the only thing upon which he deliberates, is a project, initiated by God, but completed by Christ voluntarily going to the cross. Upon the cross, in the Gospel of John (which deliberately alludes in its opening verse to the opening verse of Genesis: "In the beginning"), he says "It is finished" or "It is perfected," with Pilate having said a few verses earlier, "Behold the human being" (John 19:30, 5).[4] Scripture thus opens with God setting the stage and announcing his project, and concludes with the fulfilment of this project, such that, as the Byzantine hymn for Holy Saturday, when the body of Christ lies in the tomb, says:

> Moses the great mystically prefigured this present day, saying: 'And God blessed the seventh day.' For this is the blessed Sabbath, this is the day of rest, on which the only-begotten Son of God rested from all his works, through the economy of death he kept the Sabbath in the flesh, and returning again through the resurrection he has granted us eternal life, for he alone is good and loves humankind [lit: loves ἄνθρωπος].[5]

It is by giving his own "let it be" that St. Ignatius in turn, following Christ, is born into life as human being. If, as said above, Christ shows us what it is to be God in the way he dies as a human being, he simultaneously shows us what it is to be human in the same way, in one *prosōpon* and one *hypostasis*. Moreover, and even more strikingly, for the only work that is said to be *God's own work*—making a human being in his image—*we are the ones who say "let it be"!*

This is a very different way of understanding the work of God than we habitually assume. We are more likely to think in terms of God's creative work as having been completed at the beginning, as an initial perfection from which we then fell, requiring God to respond by sending his Son to restore fallen humanity. So much is this the case that from medieval times we regularly ask the question whether Christ would have become incarnate had human beings not fallen. Put crudely, we tend to think in terms of a Plan A, which we then messed up, followed by Plan B. But, equally bluntly: *Christ is not Plan B!* From the beginning of the proclamation of the Gospel, as we saw above, Adam is spoken of as "a type of the one to come" (Rom. 5:14)—an initial sketch of the fullness that is first manifest and realized in Christ alone.

It should be recognized that we, of course, speak of a newborn baby as a human being. Yet if by a human being we mean, as we often do, someone who can walk or talk, the baby cannot (yet) do these things. This is, it is important to note, not due to any "imperfection" in the newborn: An infant with perfectly formed limbs and tongue needs to exercise these organs to develop them—a development that includes occasions of falling down, getting bruised, or misspeaking. And if we define what it is to be human by what Christ shows us, in the love he displays by laying down his life, then it requires more than simple physical growth: It requires a life of *askēsis* in learning virtue, of taking up the cross, culminating in our actual death, to become human.

The Apostle also puts the contrast between Adam and Christ in terms of the difference between the breath of life that animated the first Adam and the life-giving Spirit (1 Cor. 15:44–48, see Gen. 2:7). Irenaeus of Lyons, building upon this comparison, sketches out the overarching economy of the work of God in this way:

> *Just as*, at the beginning of our formation in Adam, the breath of life from God, having been united to the handiwork, animated [*animavit*] the human being and showed him to be a rational being, *so also*, at the end, the Word of the Father and the Spirit of God, having become united with the ancient substance of the formation of Adam, rendered the human being living [*viventem*] and perfect, bearing the perfect Father, *in order that, just as* in the animated we all die, *so also* in the spiritual we may all be vivified. For never at any time did Adam escape the Hands of God, to whom the Father speaking, said, "Let us make the human being in our image, after our likeness" [Gen. 1:26]. And for this reason at the end, "not by the will of the flesh, nor by the will of man" [John 1:13], but by the good pleasure of the Father, his Hands perfected a living human being [*vivum perfecerunt hominem*], in order that Adam might become in the image and likeness of God.[6]

It is at the end, not from the beginning, that we are perfected as a living human being, vivified by the Spirit, so that just as Adam was a "type of the one to come," so also the breath that animated Adam at the beginning is but a sketch of the life that he is called to live in Christ. This is, moreover, a process in which the Hands of God are continually working, forming us to be in the stature of Christ. "The human being is earth that suffers"[7]—suffering as we are molded by the Hands of God, as clay in the hands of the potter, into his image, a process that continues throughout our lives, culminating in our death and resurrection, at which point one can even say that we are "created," finally made into that which God has planned from the beginning: "When you take away their breath they die and return to their dust; when you send forth your Spirit, they will be created [κτισθήσονται] and you renew the face of the ground" (Ps. 103/4: 29–30).

The decisive step in this direction, from Adam to Christ, occurs when we voluntarily embrace the cross and our own death in Christ through the sacrament of baptism. But it is important to note how the Apostle changes tense from the past to the future: "If we have been united with him in a death like his, we shall certainly be united with him in a resurrection like his" (Rom. 6:5). Our sacramental death in baptism is once for all, and in the past; but until we are actually dead in the ground, the resurrection lies in the future, and so we must "consider ourselves dead to sin and alive to God in Christ Jesus" (Rom. 6:11). Until that point, we are, as it were, stuck in the first-person singular, only able to say, "I am dying to myself to live to God," with all the inevitable paradoxes that flow from that ambiguity. When, on the other hand, I am actually dead, placed in the ground to become earth, then I stop working and God can finally be the Creator.

By following this line of thinking, Ignatius and Irenaeus, and then the later Fathers following in their footsteps, can see our "fall" into apostasy, sin, and death, as inscribed within the single economy of God that starts from Christ and culminates in Christ, the Alpha and the Omega of all things. The whole economy, from the beginning to the end, turns upon and is shaped by the Passion of Christ (for it is only in the light of the cross that the Scriptures are opened or unveiled, so that we can read the narrative of the arc that leads from Adam to Christ).[8] His death destroys death, not by obliterating it, but by turning it inside out, "changing the use of death" as Maximus put it, such that instead of being the end, it becomes in fact the beginning.[9]

In other words: We come into existence "in Adam," animated by a breath of life, a breath that is inherently transitory and will expire. From the beginning of our existence we do all that we can do to hold on to our breath of life; but no matter how well we live or whatever we do, the breath will expire. In times long past, Irenaeus points out, it was only *said*—not *shown*—that Adam was created in the image, and as such he easily lost his likeness to Christ by trying to snatch immortal life (see *Haer.* 5.16.2). But now Christ, as *the* image of God, has shown us the life of God, and has done so not simply by destroying death (we still die, after all), but rather destroying "him who has the power of death," so that he might "deliver all those who through fear of death were subject to lifelong bondage" (Heb. 2:14–15). It is the fear of death that drives us to try to hold on to our breath of life and gives rise to all the passions that flow from this egoism, ensnaring ourselves ever further in our mortality. If we try to preserve our life, as Christ points out as the basic law of life, we will without doubt lose it (Matt. 16:25, etc.). But if, on the other hand, we lose our life, he continues, by laying it down for his sake, we will gain it: We will begin to live a life that cannot be touched by death because we have entered into it through death.

According to Irenaeus, the breath and the Spirit cannot coexist (*Haer.* 5.12). This is not because one is a "natural" life and needs to be removed before a "supernatural" life can begin. It is rather because the breath, when used in a Christ-like manner, by dying to itself opens out to the life of the Spirit. We come into existence "in Adam," thrown into the world, with no free choice about the matter—*No one asked me if I want to be born!* as Kirilov protested in Dostoyevsky's *The Possessed*. We come into existence, moreover, animated by a breath of life that is inherently transient and finite, which will expire: We are as good as dead from the beginning. Necessity and mortality characterize our existence "in Adam." Motivated by the fear of death, we try to hold on to our breath, entrenching ourselves ever more firmly in that mortality and the passions to which it gives rise. But if, in faith and love, we are ready to use our breath to lose our lives in a Christ-like manner, for the kingdom and our neighbors, then we are born into a life that cannot be touched by death, the immortal life of the Spirit, and as such are born into life as human beings as Christ has shown that to be. Through Christ's having "changed the use of death" we are able to change the ground of our existence from necessity and mortality to freedom and self-sacrificial love—the very uncreated being and life of God himself.

Rather than seeing ourselves as already human (and always having been so, needing only to be redeemed from the apostasy into which we have fallen), we are instead called to view all things in the light of Christ, such that there is one single creative-salvific economy of God, leading us from the sketch to the reality, from a breath to the Spirit, from Adam to Christ, by sharing in the death of Christ, to be "a living human being," "the glory of God" (*Haer.* 4.20.7). If we are yet to become human, what are the implications for understanding ourselves as male and female?

Marriage Is Martyrdom

If God's project is to create living human beings in his image and likeness, what he in fact does is to create males and females. When we look at the structure of Gen. 1:27, we see that being "in the image" and being "male and female" are put in parallel with one another:

> [27] So God created the human being in his own image,
> in the image of God he created him;
> male and female he created them.
> [28] And God blessed them, and God said to them, "Be fruitful and multiply, and fill the earth and subdue it."

In the poem that is the first chapter of Genesis, two things are left unexplained: being "in the image" and being "male and female." Although we tend to link "male and female" to the blessing to "be fruitful and multiply," this same blessing is bestowed upon the other animals (Gen. 1:22), yet they are not said to be created as male and female (only later, in Gen. 6:19, are they described this way). Regarding the term "image," it is often said that the purpose of Gen. 1:27–28 is to "democratize" the status of being "in the image"—something that in the ancient Near East was held to be the prerogative of the king—so that it now belongs instead to all human beings to have "dominion" over the earth. This again, however, is not said in the scriptural text, here or elsewhere. Reading the text in the light of Christ, as we have above, we may well make a distinction between *the* image, who is Christ (Col. 1:15), and human beings who are made *in* the image. However, the verse also suggestively places being in the image in parallel with being male and female. I do not mean to suggest that there is anything in God corresponding to male and female. Rather, I would suggest, that if God's project is to make human beings in his image, as we have seen above, and his way of initiating this project is to make males and females, then our existence as sexed and sexual beings turns out to be the horizon in which we learn to become human.

It is important to note that when the Apostle asserts that Christ is "the image of the invisible God," it is in the context of hymning the one who makes peace by "the blood of his cross" (Col. 1:15–20). It is, as we have seen above, in laying down his life that Christ shows us what it is to be God and what it is to be human. Our existence as male and female is in fact the horizon in which we (or at least most of us) learn, through the power of erotic attraction, to lay down our lives for another: Through the erotic drive deeply implanted in us by God, we are drawn out of ourselves, to "die" to ourselves and live our lives in virtue of another. As Dionysius the Areopagite puts it: "The divine eros brings ecstasy, so that the lover belongs not to self but to the beloved."[10] *Eros* is perhaps the only force capable of overcoming the fear of *thanatos*. Marriage, then, is ultimately about martyrdom, and in marriage males and females are, quite literally, "humanized"!

Given the preponderance of monastics among those counted as saints by the Church, it is not surprising that there is a great tendency to think that sanctification consists in approximating the monastic life, whether literally (as is often advocated) or spiritually (the "interior monasticism" of Paul Evdokimov). It is sometimes claimed that from the fourth century, monasticism replaced the martyrdom of earlier centuries as the form of sanctity known by the Church. But this needs to be nuanced, or restated: It was by understanding itself as martyrdom that monasticism continued the martyrdom of the early Church. St. Anthony is depicted by St. Athanasius as having gone out into the desert to live out a life of martyrdom: The contest with the wild beasts in the arena is continued in the desert in the battle with the demons depicted as wild beasts. It is martyrdom that is the paradigmatic form of holiness known by the Church—a martyrdom that is continued in the monastic tradition, but also within marriage: The couple are crowned in the marriage ceremony not because they are "king and queen for the day," but because they are entering upon the path of martyrdom. Marriage, just as much as monasticism, continues the fundamental Christian vocation of martyrdom, and does not need to be (and should not be) approximated to monasticism. This recognition also gives greater clarity to the place of the single, nonmonastic person. It is not that marriage and monasticism are the only two "legitimate" forms of Christian life: Martyrdom is *the* form of Christian life and is lived either through marriage or through monasticism or in the single state. The cross is one and the same for all.

Children, although a blessing (and an increased opportunity for martyrdom!), are not the goal of marriage. It is noteworthy that when Christ reaffirms what was from the beginning—that we were created male and female to become one flesh—nothing is said about procreation (Matt. 19:4–6). Similarly, when the Apostle affirms that because of the temptation to sexual immorality—because we have been created as sexual beings—each man should have a wife and each woman a husband, and that their bodies are not their own but each other's, and that each should give themselves to each other, again nothing is said about procreation (1 Cor. 7:2–4). This is such a difficult calling that, virtually from the beginning, Moses allowed divorce "because of your hardness of heart" (Matt. 19:8), and Paul also "concedes" the possibility of separating, but only by mutual agreement for a short period of time, for the sake of prayer (1 Cor. 7:5–6), insisting that they come back together again lest they be tempted by Satan. Only with Augustine does Paul's concession come to be understood as a concession to come back together again, with the further specification that it be for the sake of procreation. Although the blessing of children is clearly implied in the scriptural understanding of marriage, it is only with Clement of Alexandria that the purpose of marriage comes to be subsumed under a procreative finality: Neither the Lord nor the Apostle mentions this when either speaks of the purpose of existence as male and female.

Marriage, then, is not—or not primarily—about or defined by procreation, legitimizing sexual activity, or providing a "safe space" for its exercise. Neither is it about preserving "traditional values" or the "nuclear family." It subverts and sublimates these intentions, providing a horizon for achieving the fullness of the stature of being human that Christ has shown by the way of the cross. Sexuality embodies the erotic drive toward transcendence, transforming those who love with the martyrish love shown by Christ into another state, neither male nor female but human, through martyrdom and in Christ.

Male and Female in Adam

If males and females, men and women, become human through martyrdom—for only a man or woman can say "let it be" and so become human—then males and females do not in fact beget human beings, but only procreate more males and females, each of whom are called to the fullness of being human. But this means that procreation (and sexual activity more generally) is inherently *in Adam*, not *in Christ: One cannot procreate "in Christ."*

This point (though rarely stated so bluntly) is immediately apparent when one considers that a man and woman, no matter how holy or dispassionate in their sexual intercourse, *cannot* procreate an infant who would be, as it were, already baptized at birth. Baptism is a conscious voluntary movement from Adam to Christ; it requires a statement of intent, "let it be" (leaving aside the question of infant baptism, for the point remains). That procreation is not "in Christ" is not due to fallenness, sinfulness, or passion, as it would be in a "Plan-A/Plan-B" model, where it might be claimed that sexual procreation is only the result of the fall and that before the fall we had another, nonsexual manner, mode of procreation. No, it is simply a different category: Procreation is in Adam, birth into life is a passage from Adam to Christ; procreation continues the race of Adam, begetting sons and daughters of Adam, all of whom will die, while baptism is the filling up of the body of Christ with martyrs, living human beings. It is this distinction that Gregory of Nyssa and Maximus allude to when they suggest that perhaps there was another mode known to God for the genesis of human beings besides procreation as males and females; the problem with procreation is not so much the impassioned embrace of husband and wife, but the involuntary coming into existence of the one thus begotten, in contrast to the voluntary birth into life of the one taking up the cross.

This point, moreover, frees human sexuality from the almost unbearable burden put upon it by a "Plan-A/Plan-B" model, in which sexual activity is taken to be only for the sake of procreation and is to be undertaken only in an as angelic-like (or "monastic") manner as possible. No! Procreation is certainly a blessing of marriage and an increased opportunity for martyrdom, but the erotic drive of our existence as males and females is that which leads us, as we have seen, toward the self-sacrifice that culminates in our becoming human. Eros is, of course, equally capable of driving us toward behavior that is no more than animal. Our experience of eros, at least in this life, is not a black-and-white matter, but always "grey." It is never experienced as "pure" self-giving, but is always bound up with passion, selfish pleasure, and power; we must struggle with these passions to learn martyrish love. Just as we take a decisive, once-for-all, step in baptism, dying with Christ so as to live in him, but until our actual death we remain in the paradox of the first-person singular, so too driven outside ourselves in love for another and ultimately for Christ, we are enmeshed, our erotic drive, in passion until the grave. Even for the aged Anthony, after decades in the desert, the one passion that remained was *porneia*.[11]

Neither Male nor Female in Christ

Through sexual attraction and desire, then, most males and females are called to overcome themselves, and so become human in Christ. But it is not that in doing so we cease being males and females; rather, it is that we both become human. To adapt the image first used by Origen: An iron knife is known by its particular properties (cold, hard, sharp), but when placed in the fire, while remaining the iron it is, it is no longer known by those properties but only by the properties of fire (hot, fluid, burning). So too an iron knife and a bronze knife, when placed in the fire, become indistinguishable while remaining the matter they are. Likewise, males and females are called to enter into Christ through their death (anticipated sacramentally in baptism) and, entering into the consuming fire that is God through taking up the cross, while remaining the males and females they are, they become indistinguishably human in Christ, in whom there is neither male nor female. As Maximus puts it, the distinction between males and females is overcome, through the most dispassionate virtue, by both finding their common logos as truly human in Christ, the Logos.[12] It is not that they stop being male or female, or that they become somehow androgynous or asexual; the one thing said in Genesis to be "not good" is to be "only human" (Gen. 2:18, οὐ καλὸν εἶναι ἄνθρωπον μόνον, usually translated "for man to be alone," though see Maximus, *Ambig.* 41). It is rather that the difference between male and female no longer "registers," as it were, for both are and are seen to be truly human in Christ.

Through our existence as sexed and sexual beings, then, our existence as sexed and sexual beings is transcended, though not abandoned. The erotic drive of males and females can lead to a transcendence in which it is sublimated in a divine Christ-like manner, in which both become human. Sexuality and the sexual drive have a positive role to play in this economy of God, driving us toward an ecstatic existence in which we no longer live for ourselves, just as it is by using our mortal breath of life in a particular Christ-like manner that we enter upon a manner of living that is no longer that of a mortal breath but that of the immortal Spirit, immortal because entered into through death. Once again, we are, in the present, in the grey area of the paradoxical situation between our baptismal death to existence in Adam and our actual death to be raised in Christ. Yet even while in this grey area, to the extent that we identify ourselves by our sexuality, male or female (or, as is said today, anywhere on the spectrum in between), we are in Adam, not in Christ, merely iron or bronze, no longer transfigured by the divine fire.

"Sing O Barren One!"

Bringing into focus our birth through death into life, as living human beings, also opens out for us the vision of the Church as the Virgin Mother, who "in every place, because of that love which she cherishes toward God, sends forth, throughout all time, a multitude of martyrs to the Father" (Irenaeus, *Haer.* 4.33.9). The basis for this understanding is the verse in Isaiah that follows the hymn of the Suffering Servant (Isa. 52:13–53:12), the passage that, more than any other, provided the imagery and vocabulary for understanding the Passion of Christ:

> Sing, O Barren One, who did not bear; break forth into singing and cry aloud, you who have not been in travail! For the children of the desolate one will be more than the children of her that is married, says the LORD. (Isa. 54:1)

As a result of the Passion—for it is into the death of Christ that sons and daughters of Adam are baptized—the Barren One gives birth to many living children of the living God. Citing this verse, the Apostle speaks of her as "the Jerusalem above" and "our Mother" (Gal. 4:26) and Christians thereafter refer to her as simply "the Virgin Mother." Citing this verse from Isaiah, regarding the birth of the Son known by the name "Wonderful Counsellor, Mighty God" (Isa. 8:3 and 9:6), Irenaeus describes how, in his birth from the Virgin, "the Pure One opens purely that pure Womb which regenerates human beings unto God and which he himself made pure" (*Haer.* 4.33.11). The Church, embodied on earth in specific local communities, is not simply identified with these local communities, but is the heavenly womb in which we are born through death into life, entering as males and females but emerging as living human beings. Baptism is not simply a rite of entrance, which, having been undergone, we leave behind to enjoy the rights of membership, but a sacramental enactment of our death in Christ and a commitment to continuing living by taking up the cross, anticipating the moment that we too die with Christ to rise with him. The Eucharist, likewise, is not merely the reception of spiritual nourishment or a celebration of thanksgiving, but also an anticipatory participation of our death of Christ. When Christ asks, "Are you able to drink the cup that I drink or to be baptized with the baptism with which I am baptized" (Mark 10:38), he is not simply speaking about approaching the chalice on a Sunday morning—or rather he is, if we were to properly understand what is meant by partaking of the chalice. Likewise, the Psalm verse sung before communion at feasts of the Virgin, "I will receive the cup of salvation and call upon the name of the Lord" (Ps. 115:4/116:13), is a call to martyrdom, to birth in the Virgin. This Eucharistic anticipation of our participation in the paschal offering of Christ is completed in our martyrish death in witness to Christ—as seen, for instance, in St. Ignatius praying that he, as wheat, might be ground by the teeth of the wild beasts to become the "pure bread of Christ" (*Rom.* 4), and when Polycarp's body, consigned to the flames, appeared to be bread.[13] Our own death is the paschal mystery for each of us, a passage that we must all undergo, and that we anticipate in the sacraments, the *mysteria*, of baptism and Eucharist. It is, moreover, a "mystery" or "sacrament" in which each person is the priest, in the image of Christ, as the one who offers and is offered.[14]

The context or womb for our birth in Christ is the Church, not understood merely as local community coming together in particular structure and the celebration of various rites, but as our Mother, the heavenly Jerusalem: It is this that the local community images and the two cannot be conflated. And the primary reality of this ecclesial birth is the taking up of the cross to live the life of Christ. Baptism is our sacramental, once-for-all death to Adam and birth in Christ, but it is a sacramental realization of what will be physically realized in our actual death. Receiving the Eucharist is our participation in the body and blood of Christ to become his body through our own sharing in his passion. Baptism and Eucharist are thus not simply sacramental acts of grace dispensed by the bishop in a church merely understood as a gathering of human beings; they are grounded in our actual death, which—when conformed to the Passion of Christ—is our birth through the Church as mother.

Thus when we speak about elements of culture being "baptized" in the Church, this does not mean simply giving these elements, such as marriage, a religious tint or veneer, but rather transforming them radically, through death as birth into life. That we habitually do not do so, however, can be seen in many ways, especially in our unthinking adoption of patterns of speech from out contemporary culture. For instance, we today often speak about "the sanctity of life," without realizing that this is in fact a pagan notion! For something to be sanctified, it must be set apart, sacrificed; to take anything as sacred in its own nature is paganism. As we have seen earlier, we do not come to life apart from through death and resurrection. Likewise, Christian marriage is not simply the natural (pagan) institution given a religious tint, demarcating a "safe space" for sexuality, "sanctifying" the nuclear family, and preserving our "traditional values"; it is the way of martyrdom, leading to life and true humanity.

Within the space between our sacramental death in baptism (and thereafter in the Eucharist) and our actual death and resurrection in Christ, we are in a paradoxical and grey condition, in which we are learning to die to ourselves, but are doing so by the mortal breath that has not yet expired, and as still male or female but not yet human. As Christians, we continue to live in this world between Adam and Christ. That this condition is grey, not black or white, means that our life is constantly marked by repentance, turning ever again to Christ with a renewed mind and a renewed effort. This being so, we have learned to live with a certain ambiguity. For instance, although we are made male and female to become one flesh, with the injunction that "What God has joined together, let not man put asunder" (Matt. 19:6), Christ gives an exception—"apart from *porneia*" (Matt. 19:9)—though only in the Gospel of Matthew (another exception). The Orthodox tradition thereafter does not "annul" a marriage that does not work out in order to allow one of the partners to enter into (another, but now a supposedly first or single) marriage, but instead recognizes the reality of our "grey" existence—that things don't always work out, despite best intentions—and blesses a *second* marriage, though the form of the service is different, often spoken of as having a "penitential" character. This practice occurs in a variety of circumstances that, on one level, should not arise: a second marriage of lay people; a second marriage of a priest; the marriage of monastics who have left their profession. In such cases, the Church has found a way of accommodation through repentance, accepting at the chalice those who take this route. As noted above, the economy of God that leads from Adam to Christ embraces our apostasy into sin and death, turning it inside out, through the cross and our repentance, into the means of our being made human in Christ. Where sin is, grace abounds, the Apostle reminds us, adding that this doesn't mean we should remain in our sin (Rom. 5:20–6:2). Rather as we strive after virtue, we will always find that the depths of our brokenness are greater than we ever knew before, so that the transforming power of God can refashion the hidden depths of our being, while the depths of our recognition of our sinfulness are, in turn, the reverse side of the height to which we have come to know God.

All Christians are thus called, repeatedly and insistently, to repentance: One can only approach the chalice as a repentant sinner, not as a "right." There is an almost overwhelming tendency to regard the approach to the chalice as being a matter of being "worthy." This can even turn the sacrament of repentance into that which makes us "worthy" to do so! But this is not the case: The only qualification to approach the chalice is to be a repentant sinner, the chief among sinners. Being a heterosexual married couple confers no "right" to approach the chalice; marriage, as explored above, is not a legitimization of permitted sexual activity (with procreative intent), but a road to the martyrdom expected of all. Our sexuality, our existence as sexual and sexed beings, is always, as noted earlier, "grey"— always immersed in the struggle with the temptation to *porneia*—for Anthony the Great just as much as for married couples. We learn, through striving after virtue and repentance, to discern the difference between an impassioned eros seeking selfish pleasure and power, and an eros—the same erotic drive—aiming at transcendence through self-offering to become human. Yet even in this grey area, it bears repeating, to the extent that we identify ourselves in terms of sexuality, we remain in Adam and not in Christ.

What it is to be human, and the role of existence as male and female, are indeed the burning issues of our epoch. Although it does not approach these issues through the language of modern science, theology can however speak to them by considering carefully the scriptural framework of God's own purpose, to make living human beings in his image. There are many issues that this essay has not addressed. Its aim has been to explore carefully various dimensions involved in the framing and accomplishment of God's project. Most important in this has been the role of death, as birth into life, and the Church as the Virgin Mother in whom we are born as living human beings, martyrs. We are not, as male and female, that to which we are called, and the Church is not a bastion of "traditional values," as we might think of them and expect her to be. The arc of the economy, the work, of God, the movement from Adam to Christ, from male and female, through the womb of our Virgin Mother, to becoming human, is instead an always surprising call to radical divine-human transcendence, to birth into life as "the glory of God."

Notes

1. Opening quote from Isaiah 43:10 LXX. This chapter was initially published as an article in *The Wheel* 13/14 (Spring/Summer 2018): 19–32; it is reprinted here in a lightly revised version with kind permission of the journal. It has also been republished in G. Thomas and E. Narinskaya, eds., *Women and Ordination in the Orthodox Church: Explorations in Theology and Practice* (Eugene, Oreg.: Cascade Books, 2020), 3–20.

2. Nicholas Cabasilas, *Life in Christ* 6.91–94, trans. C. J. De Catanzaro (Crestwood, N.Y.: St. Vladimir's Seminary Press, 1974) (6.12—English translation modified); ed. and French trans. M.-H. Congourdeau, SC 355, 361 (Paris: Cerf, 1989, 1990).

3. Ignatius, *Letter to the Romans* 6, in Ignatius of Antioch, *Letters*, ed. and trans. Alistair Stewart, PPS (Crestwood, N.Y.: St. Vladimir's Seminary Press, 2013).

4. John 19:30, 5. For a full discussion, see John Behr, *John the Theologian and His Paschal Gospel: A Prologue to Theology* (Oxford: Oxford University Press, 2019), 195–217.

5. Doxastikon at the Praises for Holy Saturday Matins, in *The Lenten Triodion*, trans. Mother Mary and Kallistos Ware (South Canaan, Pa.: St. Tikhon's Seminary Press, 1999), 652–53 (English translation modified); original Greek text in Τριώδιον Κατανυκτικόν (Rome, 1879), 374.

6. Irenaeus of Lyons, *Against the Heresies* (hereafter *Haer.*), 5.1.3, in *The Ante-Nicene Fathers*, vol. 1, ed. A. Roberts, J. Donaldson and A. Cleveland Cox (New York: Christian Literature Publishing Co., 1885, and reprinted many times thereafter) (English translation modified and emphasis added); original text: *Haer.* 1–3, ed. A. Rousseau and L. Doutreleau (Paris: Cerf, 1979, 1982, 1974), SC 263–64, 293–94, 210–11; *Haer.* 4, ed. A. Rousseau, B. Hemmerdinger, L. Doutreleau and C. Mercier (Paris: Cerf, 1965), SC 100; *Haer.* 5, ed. A. Rousseau, L. Doutreleau, and C. Mercier (Paris: Cerf, 1969), SC 152–53.

7. *Letter of Barnabas* 6.9, in *The Apostolic Fathers*, vol. 2, ed. and trans. K. Lake, Loeb Classical Library (Cambridge, Mass.: Harvard University Press, 1985).

8. See Irenaeus, *Haer.* 4.26.1.

9. Maximus, *Ad Thalassium* 61; Maximus, *On Difficulties in Sacred Scripture: The Responses to Thalassios*, FC 136, trans. Maximus Constas (Washington, D.C.: CUA Press, 2018); original text: *Ad Thalassium* 61, ed. Carl Laga and Carlos Steel, in *Maximi Confessoris Quaestiones ad Thalassium*, CCSG 7, 22 (Turnhout: Brepols. 1980), 90.

10. Dionysius the Areopagite, *On the Divine Names*, 4.13, trans. Paul Rorem, Classics of Western Spirituality (Mahwah, N.J.: Paulist Press, 1987); original text in *Corpus Dionysiacum* I, ed. B. R. Suchla, Patristische Texte und Studien 33 (Berlin: De Gruyter, 1990).

11. Anthony, Saying 11, in *The Sayings of the Desert Fathers*, trans. B. Ward (Kalamazoo Mich.: Cistercian Publications, 1975), 3.

12. Maximus, Ambiguum 41; Maximus the Confessor, *On Difficulties in the Church Fathers: The Ambigua*, trans. Nicholas Constas, 2 vols. (Cambridge Mass.: Harvard University Press, 2014), vol. 2, 102–21; original text: *Ambiguum 41*.

13. *Martyrdom of Polycarp*, in *The Apostolic Fathers*, vol. 1, ed. and trans. Bart Ehrman, Loeb Classical Library (Cambridge, Mass.: Harvard University Press, 2014), 15.

14. See the prayer of the priest before the great entrance in the Liturgy of St. John Chrysostom, addressing Christ: "You are the one who offers and is offered." *The Divine Liturgy of Our Father among the Saints John Chrysostom: Slavonic-English Parallel Text*, trans. Ephrem Lash (Chipping Norton: Greek Orthodox Archdiocese of Thyateira and Great Britain, 2011), 37.

Contributors

Thomas Arentzen is a reader in church history and works as a researcher in Greek philology at Uppsala University and as a senior lecturer in Eastern Christian studies at Sankt Ignatios College, Stockholm School of Theology. He specializes in Byzantine literature and ecocriticism. Publications include *The Virgin in Song: Mary and the Poetry of Romanos the Melodist* (2017) and *Byzantine Tree Life: Christianity and the Arboreal Imagination* (2021), coauthored with Virginia Burrus and Glenn Peers.

Spyridoula Athanasopoulou-Kypriou holds a PhD in systematic theology from the University of Manchester. She is a research and teaching associate at the International Hellenic University, lecturing on Christian Orthodox feminist hermeneutics, and a trained psychotherapist. Her latest book is entitled *Here and Now: Essays on Philosophical Theology Concerning Gaze, Sexuality, Desire and Other Issues* [in Greek] (2020).

Kateřina Kočandrle Bauer, Th.D., is a senior researcher and lecturer in the Ecumenical Institute of the Protestant Theological Faculty of Charles University in Prague. She teaches systematic theology and Christian spirituality. She has written widely on Russian religious philosophy and anthropology within Orthodox theology, including the coauthored monographs The Ways of Orthodox Theology in the West (2015) and Wrestling with the Mind of the Fathers (2015).

John Behr is the Regius Professor of Humanity at the University of Aberdeen, previously having been at St. Vladimir's Seminary, New York, where he also served as dean. His recent publications include an edition and translation of Origen's *On First Principles* and a study of the Gospel of John.

Davor Džalto is a professor of religion and democracy in the Department of Eastern Christian Studies at University College Stockholm. His research interests cover the fields of theology, social and political philosophy, and the theory and history of art. He is the author of numerous books, including *Anarchy and the Kingdom of God*, *Art as Tautology*, and *The Human Work of Art*.

Susan Ashbrook Harvey is the Willard Prescott and Annie McClelland Smith Professor of Religion and History at Brown University. Among other publications, she is the author of *Scenting Salvation: Ancient Christianity and the Olfactory Imagination* (2006) and *Song and Memory: Biblical Women in Syriac Tradition* (2010), and coeditor with Margaret Mullett of *Knowing Bodies, Passionate Souls: Sense Perception in Byzantium* (2017).

Michael Hjälm is the dean of Sankt Ignatios College, Stockholm School of Theology. His field of studies is critical ecclesiology, where he makes use of a critical approach toward the practical aspects of the Church, developing theories for improving praxis. His most recent publication identifies the connection between the popular nationalist movements and the Russian Orthodox position on nationalism.

Pantelis Kalaitzidis is the director of the Volos Academy for Theological Studies, a research center in Greece dealing with contemporary issues for Eastern Orthodoxy. He is a member of the Executive Committee of the European Academy of Religion (Bologna), and the chair (with Aristotle Papanikolaou) of the Political Theology group of the International Orthodox Theological Association (IOTA).

Andrii Krawchuk is professor emeritus and past president of the University of Sudbury, Canada. Author of *Christian Social Ethics in Ukraine* (1997) and coeditor of *Eastern Orthodox Encounters of Identity and Otherness* (2014) and *Churches in the Ukrainian Crisis* (2016), he is studying religious responses to the Maidan and the war in Ukraine.

Aristotle Papanikolaou is professor of theology, the Archbishop Demetrios Chair of Orthodox Theology and Culture, and the cofounding director of the Orthodox Christian Studies Center at Fordham University. He is also a senior fellow at the Emory University Center for the Study of Law and Religion. His publications include *Being with God: Trinity, Apophaticism, and Divine-Human Communion* and *The Mystical as Political: Democracy and Non-Radical Orthodoxy*.

Ashley M. Purpura is an associate professor of religious studies in the School of Interdisciplinary Studies at Purdue University. She publishes on gender and Orthodoxy, and is the author of *God, Hierarchy, and Power: Orthodox Theologies of Authority from Byzantium* (2018).

Richard René is a PhD candidate at the University of St. Michael's College, University of Toronto. He serves in the Archdiocese of Canada of the Orthodox Church in America (OCA). He is the Regional Chaplain, Pacific Region for Correctional Service Canada (CSC) and the director of St. Silas Orthodox Prison Mission.

Bryce E. Rich holds a PhD in theology from the University of Chicago. He has participated in six conferences on Orthodoxy and sexuality in Finland, Norway, and England. His first monograph, *Gender Essentialism and Orthodoxy: Beyond Male and Female*, is forthcoming from Fordham University Press.

Ekaterini Tsalampouni is currently associate professor at the Faculty of Theology of Aristotle University of Thessaloniki. She teaches New Testament exegesis and theology. Her research focuses on the sociohistorical background of the New Testament, exegesis and theology of the Gospels and Pauline letters, ecological hermeneutics, and early Christianity.

Dmitry Uzlaner is a research fellow at the Moscow School of Social and Economic Sciences. He has coauthored the book *The Moralist International: Russia in the Global Culture Wars* (with Kristina Stoeckl, forthcoming on Fordham University Press) and coedited the volume *Contemporary Russian Conservatism: Problems, Paradoxes, and Perspectives* (with Mikhail Suslov, 2019).

Haralambos Ventis is an assistant professor of the philosophy of religion in the Department of Social Theology and Religious Studies at the Faculty of Theology of the National and Kapodistrian University of Athens, Greece. He is the translator of Christos Yannaras's early work *Heidegger* *and the Areopagite: On the Absence and Ignorance of God* (2005), as well as the author of *The Reductive Veil: Post-Kantian Non-Representationalism versus Apophatic Realism* (2005) and *Eschatology and Otherness* (2019).

Gayle Woloschak is a professor of radiation oncology and associate dean of the Graduate School at Northwestern University. She has a PhD in biomedical sciences from the University of Toledo as well as a DM in in Eastern Christian studies from Pittsburgh Theological Seminary. Her interests are in evolution, molecular biology, and nanotechnology.

INDEX

1 Corinthians, 52–53, 83, 86, 89–90, 141n77, 174, 202, 204, 256, 282, 286, 300n24, 306, 311
1 John, 175
1 Kingdoms, 61n15
1 Peter, 48
1 Samuel, 61n15
1 Timothy, 52–53, 86, 89, 174, 282
2 Peter, 85

Abrahamson, Philip, 200
Adam, 159–162, 165, 167, 236–237, 298n10, 300n32, 304–308, 311–312, 316–317
adelphopoiesis, 28, 42n26
After Virtue (MacIntyre), 249
Agadjanian, Alexander, 145
aggressive liberalism: Orthodox identity and, 146; Russian Orthodox Church and, 149n2; sexual diversity and, 144
akribeia, 137n36
Alexius I Komnenos, 119–120
alteritism, 81–82
Ambiguum 71 (Maximus the Confessor), 201–202
Ambrose of Milan, 121
Ambrosius, Metropolitan, 109
Amoun of Nitria, 26–27
anal penetration, 7–8, 49–51, 53, 292
androgynos, 50, 62nn18–20
androgyny, 236–238, 300n32
anger, 129, 250–251, 253–255, 257–258
anthropology, 4, 58, 79–80, 193, 199, 217, 219, 229, 239–240, 248, 250–251
Antony, Saint, 25, 55
apostasy, 145, 307–308, 316

Apostolic Tradition, The (Hippolytus), 112
Armenopoulos, 113
arsenokoitēs, 52–54, 57
Artemidoros of Daldis, 61n16
asceticism, 25, 31, 33, 36, 126, 216, 218–219, 225–226, 228–229, 248, 250–252, 255–262, 264n21, 268
Athanasopoulou-Kypriou, Spyridoula, 4
Attis, 285, 299n18
Augustine, 32, 262n1, 311
Aurelius, Marcus, 293

Bailey, Derrick Sherwin, 84–85
baptism, 307, 312, 315; of Adam, 34; asceticism and, 252; of children born into civil marriage, 106; of Christ, 33; *Corpus Areopagiticum* and, 121; death and, 313–314; Eucharist and, 123; as new birth, 288; nude, 30, 34; schism and, 181
Barker, Margaret, 298n10
Basil of Caesarea, 31–32
Basil of Moscow, 7
Basil of Seleucia, 164
Basil the Great, 113, 115, 164, 262n1
Bauman, Zygmunt, 126
Beattie, Tina, 218
Behr, John, 235
Behr-Sigel, Elizabeth, 198, 237
Berdyaev, Nikolai, 58, 237, 289–290, 301nn35,38–39
Bildt, Carl, 158
binary oppositions, 242–243
bisexuality, 46, 49, 55, 59, 110, 200, 215
blood, 285–286, 299n21

Blowers, Paul, 200, 206, 211n63, 212n69, 510n42
body: commercialization of, 271; as cultural product, 217; Eucharist and, 315; in Gregory of Nyssa, 233n45; intersex people and, 239–241; menstruation and, 285; nude, 7; relationality and, 24–28; rhetorics of, 29–37; sexual desire and, 261; sexual differentiation and, 221–223
Böhme, Jacob, 237
Boswell, John, 28, 42n26, 82
Boumis, Panayiotis I., 114, 122
Brinkschröder, Michael, 12
Brooten, Bernadette, 94n11
brother-making, 28
"brother-making," 8–9, xi
Budin, Stephanie Lynn, 299n15
Bulgakov, Sergei, 58, 208n20, 239, 265
Burrus, Virginia, 29
Butler, Judith, 1, 217–218, 230n9, 231n9
Bylund, Tuulikki Koivunen, 157

Cabasilas, Nicholas, 303–304
Canadian Human Rights Act, 192–193
celibacy, 1, 6, 92, 225, 227–228, 260–261, 286
Chalcedonian dogma, 239
Chaos, 284, 298n14
Cherniak, Misha, 12
Christian Faith and Same-Sex Attraction (Hopko), 5, 175–176
Chrysostom, John, 25, 164
civil unions, 107–120
Clément, Olivier, 239, 241
Clement of Alexandria, 62n18
Coakley, Sarah, 184–185, 218, 224, 229, 231n9
Colossians, Epistle to, 220, 304, 309
communion, 3, 55, 112, 117, 119, 121–123, 125, 156, 164, 167, 185, 210n42, 217, 229, 270–272, 289, 315
communitarianism, 185, 210n42, 280n9, 297n4
Community (ecumenical organization), 12
concubinage, 111–120
continuism, 81
Corpus Areopagiticum, 121
Costache, Doru, 212n68
Council of Nicaea, 6
creation, 68, 85, 87–88, 163–164, 176, 198, 203–204, 221–222, 236–239, 251–252, 266–267, 270–271, 276–277, 300n23
criminalization, 156–157, 177, 180–181
critical theory, 217
Cybele, 285, 299n18
Cyprian, 121

deities, female, 284–286
Demetrios Chomatinos, 113
Denmark, 181
Derrida, Jacques, 242–243
desire, 29–37, 54–55, 223–225, 259–262
Deuteronomy, Book of, 85
Diagnostic and Statistical Manual of Mental Disorders (DSM), 73
Dionysius the Areopagite, 159, 255
divorce, 119, 311
dokimasia, 51
domination, 291–293
"don't ask don't tell," 66–67
Dorotheos of Gaza, 252
Dostoevsky, Fyodor, 308
Dudchenko, Andrei, 178
Džalto, Davor, 4

Ecce Homo (exhibition), 154–158
Egypt, 172–173
embodiment, 23–24, 222
environment, in homosexuality, 72–73
Epanagoge, 118
ephebophile, 54, 64n44
Ephesians, Epistle to, 4, 160–161, 304
Ephrem the Syrian, 297n6
eschatology, 132, 219–223, 235, 237–238, 266–268, 270–271, 278, 280n9, 287
Eschaton, 266–267, 272
ethics, theotic, 249
Eucharist, 117–119, 121–124, 228, 252, 271, 315
Euchologion, xi
eunuchism, 6–7
Evdokimov, Michel, 129–130
Evdokimov, Paul, 5, 58, 218, 265, 310
Eve, 159, 161–162, 165, 167
evil, homosexuality as, 158–160, 174–175
evolution, 73–76, 273
Exabiblos (Armenopoulos), 113
Ezekiel, Book of, 85

faith, salvation and, 160–161
Fall of Man, 164, 222, 232n22, 266–267, 270–272, 277, 279, 283, 289–290, 297nn6–7, 298n9, 300n32
family, 287
family couples, 26
fear, 253
feminism, 146–147, 230n2, 236
fetishes, 258–259
Florensky, Pavel, 128, 265
Ford, David, 65n52
fornication, 55, 107, 111–116
Foucault, Michel, 11, 47–48, 60nn2–3, 229n1

Four Hundred Centuries on Love (Maximus the Confessor), 257, 264n20
Francis, Pope, 178
Freedom of Morality, The (Yannaras), 122–123
Freud, Sigmund, 276
"friendship union," xi
Future of an Illusion, The (Freud), 276

Galatians, Epistle to, 314
Gallaher, Brandon, 13
gender: Adam and, 311–312; Christ and, 313–314; creation and, 236; as lapsarian, 266; noetic, 222–223
gender differentiation, 163–168
gender identity: in Canadian Human Rights Act, 192–193
gender inversion, 47–48
gender stereotypes, 184–185
gender subordination, 57
gender theory, in Gregory of Nyssa, 219–223
geneseōs enallagē, 52
Genesis, Book of, 48, 84–85, 98n59, 163–164, 217, 235–236, 238, 276–277, 282–283, 297n5, 298nn9–10, 304, 306, 309, 313
genetics, in homosexuality, 67–72
Gerassimenko, Olga, 12
Great Mothers, 284–285, 298n13
Gregory of Nazianzus, 31–32, 202, 262n1, 269
Gregory of Nyssa, 44n66, 160, 164, 166, 170n24, 184–185, 218–228, 232n22, 233n45, 237
Gundyaev, Kirill, 173, 179, 190n31

Halperin, David, 48, 62n21
Hammar, K. G., 155, 157
Harlin, Tord, 157
Harrison, Verna, 65n52, 217
hatred, 28, 111, 168, 181, 192, 250–251, 253–255, 257–258
Hebrews, Book of, 308
Heidegger, Martin, 3, 242
Hippolytus, 112
History of Sexuality, The (Foucault), 47
Hjälm, Michael, 9, 13
Holiness Code, 49, 53, 85
Homilies on the Song of Songs (Gregory of Nyssa), 220–221, 223–224
homoerotic desire, 259–262
homophobia: challenge of, in Russia and Ukraine, 177–179; Christ and, 167; dialogical proposals on, 179–185; as fear of sexuality, 158; in Orthodox contexts, 172–186; Russian Orthodox Church and, 150n10

homosexuality: Bible and, 81–84; biblical evidence of, 84–91; criminalization of, 156–157, 177, 180–181; debates, 215–219; as divine gift, 175; environment and, 72–73; as evil, 158–160, 174–175; evolution and, 73–75; genetics and, 67–72; as genocide, 110–111; as normal, 175–176; salvation and, 160–163; as term, 59n1
Hooker, Evelyn, 73
Hopko, Thomas, 5, 172–173, 175–176, 180, 183–184, 218
Hovorun, Cyril, 13

Ieremias, Metropolitan, 110
Ignatius of Antioch, 116–117, 121, 162, 170n28, 304
incest, 284–286, 296
individual, person *vs.*, 198–199
intersex people: binary oppositions and, 242–243; body and, 240–241; defined, 235; taboo and, 238–239; theological discourse and, 242
Irenaeus of Lyon, 239, 306, 308
Isaac the Syrian, 272
Isaiah, Book of, 314
Isis, 285
Islam, 172, 276

Jaksic, Misha, 156
Jay, Nancy, 299n21
Jerotić, Vladeta, 301n36
Jesus Christ: baptism of, 33; gender and, 313–314; as image of God, 309–310; marriage and, 269; mediations and, 164–165; on relationships, 287; salvation and, love of, 161–163, 167
Jillions, John, 125
John, Gospel of, 38, 300n26, 304–305
John of Damascus, 23, 121
John of Edessa, 27
John Paul II, Pope, 157
John the Faster, 53
Josephus, 48
Judas, 159–160
Jude, Book of, 48, 85
Judges, Book of, 48, 282
Justin the Martyr, 121
Justinian, 52, 113
Justinian's Novels, 7

Kalaitzidis, Pantelis, 13
Karras, Valerie A., 164, 222, 227
kinaidos, 50–51, 62nn18,21
Koliofoutis, Athanasios, 127, 140n73

Kosmas, Metropolitan, 110
Krueger, Derek, 26, 29, 37
Kundera, Milan, 275

Ladouceur, Paul, 197, 210n42
Laiou, Angeliki E., 112–114, 136n29
Larmore, Charles, 280n9
Leo VI, Pope, 113, 118–119
Leviticus, Book of, 49, 52–53, 84, 90, 174, 282
liberalism. *See* aggressive liberalism
Loader, William, 83–84, 97n40
Logos, 202–203
Lossky, Vladimir, 10, 193, 198, 200, 205, 209n32, 239
Louth, Andrew, 13
love: freedom and, 289, 293–294; as lapsarian, 266; marriage and, 161–162, 290–291; in medieval thought, 7; theotic anthropology and, 250–251
Lucaris, Cyril, 170n25
Luke, Gospel of, 36–37, 85, 205, 286–287
Lutheran Church, 153–158, 168n2, 181
Lysias, 63n23

Maccabees, 85
MacIntyre, Alasdair, 249, 280n9
Makrides, Vasilios, 56
malakos, 50, 53
Manoussakis, John Panteleimon, 226
Marcus Antonius Polemon of Laodicea, 62n19
Mark, Gospel of, 268, 286–287, 315
marriage: civil, 105–107, 111–120; civil unions and, 107–120; gay, 11, 125–126, 273; love and, 161–162, 290–291; as martyrdom, 309–311; as sacrament, 121–128; sex and, 248, 255–259; spiritual, 220–221, 226–227; theology of, 251–255; unmarried, 286; virtue and, 252–253
Marx, Reinhard, 166
Marxism, 280n9
Mary of Egypt, 29–31
Matthew, Gospel of, 6, 10, 85, 226, 237, 286, 293, 300n23, 310–311, 316
Maximus the Confessor, 10, 164–167, 193, 200–206, 212nn68–69, 218, 224, 230n4, 239, 247, 250, 253–254, 257–258, 264n20, 272, 313
Menéndez-Antuña, Louis, 81
menstruation, 285, 299n21
Meyendorff, John, 117–119, 123
microprolactinoma, 69–70
Milonov, Vitaly, 177–179
Milošević, Nenad S., 116–117, 128, 141n77
Moltmann, Jürgen, 240

monasteries, 25
monasticism, 25–28, 30, 32, 34, 36–38, 75, 121, 290, 301n36, 310, 312
Monophysitism, 239
Moschos, John, 37–38
mother deities, 284–285
Musk, Elon, 273
mysteries, 121

nationalism, 197
Nestorianism, 239
Nikodemos the Hagiorite, 113, 122
Nikolaos, Metropolitan, 110–111
Nikolopoulos, Panos, 120
noetic gender, 222–223
Nomocanon (Photius), 114, 120
nudity, 30, 34, 42n34
Nussbaum, Martha C., 230n9
Nygren, Anders, 3

Obergefell v. Hodges, 125
Ohlsson, Birgitta, 158
oikonomia, 129, 137n36
Okanagan people, 285
On the Divine Names (Dionysius the Areopagite), 159
On the Making of the Human Being (Gregory of Nyssa), 221
On the Soul and Resurrection (Gregory of Nyssa), 170n24
On Virginity (Gregory of Nyssa), 220–221, 225–227
Oneirokritika (Artemidoros of Daldis), 61n16
orgasm, 286, 292, 302n43
Origen, 44n66
Original Sin, 272
Orthodox Rainbow Society, 12
Osiris, 285
Overton window, 144–145

Pantazopoulos, Nikolaos, 114, 120
Papadopoulos, Konstantinos, 112
Papanikolaou, Aristotle, 13
Papathomas, Grigorios, 138n49
passions, 54–55
pastoral ministry, 182–184
Paul, 52–53, 82, 86–89, 91, 116, 155, 161–162, 202, 264n21, 269, 278, 286
Paul of Qentos, 27
pederasty, 51, 63nn23,32, 86
pedophile, 54, 64n44
pedophilia, 177–178, 180
peer couples, 26–27
perichoresis, 239–240

Index

person, individual *vs.*, 198–199
personalism, 197, 199–200, 205–206, 208n20
personhood, 274–275
Peter, 159–160
Petersen, William, 53
Phaedrus, 63n23
Philemon, 162
Philo, 48, 62n20
Photius, 113–114, 118, 120
Pino, Tikhon, 203, 212n70
Plato, 31, 278
pleiotropic genes, 69, 77n14
Plotinus, 212n69
Poemata moralia (Gregory Nazianzen), 202
Possessed, The (Dostoyevsky), 308
postmodern thought, 1–2
Precepts for Virgins (Gregory Nazianzen), 202
Procopius of Gaza, 164
Prodigal Son, 37
prostitution, 25, 50, 52–53, 56, 85–86, 89–90, 113, 116, 141n77, 255, 286, 298n12
Protestantism, 9
Psalms, Book of, 307, 315
Pseudo-Dionysius the Areopagite, 121, 126, 140n71, 211n51, 224
Purpura, Ashley, 13
Putin, Vladimir, 190n31

queer theory, 46, 48

rape, 49, 52, 56, 59n1, 255–258, 271
Rapp, Claudia, 26, 28, 42n26
Reformation, 9
relationality, 3, 6, 23–28, 31, 33, 38
reproduction, 3, 57–58, 73–76, 264n20, 271–272, 284–286, 288–289
rhetorics of body, 29–37
Rich, Bryce E., 198–199, 264n21
Ricoeur, Paul, 92, 96n29
rigorism, 56, 58
Roller, Lynn E., 299n18
Romanos the Methodist, 33–35
Romans, Epistle to, 52, 64n36, 82–83, 85–91, 99nn67,77, 174–175, 206, 282, 304–305, 307, 315–316
Rozanov, Vasily V., 2
Rudder (Nikodemos the Hagiorite), 113, 122
Russian Orthodox Church, 144, 149n1, 168n2, 173, 177–179, 181
Rybko, Sergei, 177–178, 189n27

Sacks, Jonathan, 180
salvation: faith and, 160–161; homosexuality and, 160–163; likeness to God and, 217; love of Christ and, 161–163, 167; marriage and, 161–162
same-sex eroticism: as term, 59n1
Sandel, Michael J., 280n9
Sanfilippo, Giacomo, 128
Saul, 49
Schemann, Alexander, 251
Scroggs, Robin, 82–83
Sedgwick, Eve Kosofsky, 48, 55
self-knowledge, 253–255
self-love, 253
Serano, Julia, 207nn5,7, 208n20
Seraphim, Metropolitan, 109–110
sex: blood and, 285–286; Fall of Man and, 283; lesbian, 8; marriage and, 248, 255–259; in medieval thought, 7; in Orthodox perspective, 2–5; politics of, 291–296; in postmodern thought, 1–2; as taboo, 283–286; violence and, 256
sexual differentiation, 163–168
sexual diversity: aggressive liberalism and, 144; opposition to, sources of, 145; Orthodox identity and, 146, 148; as threat, 146–147; undecidedness around, 147–148; us *vs.* them mentality and, 146, 149
sexual orientation, 47–48
sexuality(ies): desire and, 223; exploitation and, 269–270; in Foucault, 229n1; gender inversion and, 47–48; rise of, 47–55; as sexual orientation, 223
Shenouda III of Alexandria, 172–174, 187n4
Sinful Woman, 35–36
Sirach, Book of, 85
Skobtsova, Maria, 237, 244n12
slaves, 52, 293
Sodom and Gomorrah, 48–49, 84, 96nn33–34,37
sodomy, 47, 54, 57
Solomon, 52
Solovyov, Vladimir, 2, 58, 241
Song of Songs, 44n66
Song of Songs, 219–220
Sophia, 237
speciesism, 273
stereotypes, gender, 184–185
submission, 108, 161–162, 229, 294, 301n43
Sweden, 154–158, 168n2, 181
Symeon the Fool, 32
Symeon the New Theologian, 36–37
Symposium (Plato), 31

Taylor, Charles, 280n9
Tertullian, 27

Testimony of Naphtali, 97n47
Thatcher, Adrian, 185
Theodore of Mopsuestia, 121
Theodoret of Cyrrhos, 27
Theodosius the Great, 52
theosis, 15, 55, 59, 248–249, 251–252, 255, 259, 261, 262n3
theotic anthropology, 250–251
theotic ethics, 249
Thermos, Vasileios, 5, 129
"third way," 25
Thunberg, Lars, 239–240
transgender individuals: childhood experiences of, 193–194; personhood and, 192–207
Triadology, 288
tribas, 50–51
Trinitarian monotheism, 268
Trinity, 38, 164–165, 184–185, 198
Trossö, Paul, 169n11
Tucker, Gregory, 13, 93n3

Ukraine, 173–174, 177–179, 189nn19,21
Ukrainian Orthodox Church, 178
Uzlaner, Dmitry, 9

Veyne, Paul, 291–292
Victorianism, 2
virginity, 1, 29, 165, 226–227, 237, 284, 290, 292, 301n37

Wallin, Elisabeth Ohlson, 157–158
Walzer, Michael, 280n9
Ware, Kallistos, 3, 127–128, 198, 206–207
Weil, Simone, 254
Williams, Craig A., 61n17, 63n23
Winkler, John J., 62n21
Wisdom of Solomon, 52, 84–85
Woloschak, Gayle, 3
womb, 285–286
women, 88, 163–166, 284–286

Yannaras, Christos, 3, 5, 122–123, 140n68, 200, 210n42
Yanukovych, Victor, 178
Yeltsin, Boris, 188n12

Zizioulas, John, 200, 210n42, 224, 230n4, 278–279, 288–289
Zorgdrager, Heleen, 173, 181
Zosimas, 29

ORTHODOX CHRISTIANITY AND CONTEMPORARY THOUGHT

SERIES EDITORS
Ashley M. Purpura and Aristotle Papanikolaou

Sarah Riccardi-Swartz, *Between Heaven and Russia: Religious Conversion and Political Apostasy in Appalachia*

Davor Džalto, *Anarchy and the Kingdom of God: From Eschatology to Orthodox Political Theology and Back*

Christina M. Gschwandtner, *Welcoming Finitude: Toward a Phenomenology of Orthodox Liturgy*

Pia Sophia Chaudhari, *Dynamis of Healing: Patristic Theology and the Psyche*

Brian A. Butcher, *Liturgical Theology after Schmemann: An Orthodox Reading of Paul Ricoeur.* Foreword by Andrew Louth.

Ashley M. Purpura, *God, Hierarchy, and Power: Orthodox Theologies of Authority from Byzantium*

George E. Demacopoulos, *Colonizing Christianity: Greek and Latin Religious Identity in the Era of the Fourth Crusade*

Thomas Arentzen, Ashley M. Purpura, and Aristotle Papanikolaou (eds.), *Orthodox Tradition and Human Sexuality*

Aristotle Papanikolaou and George E. Demacopoulos (eds.), *Fundamentalism or Tradition: Christianity after Secularism*

George E. Demacopoulos and Aristotle Papanikolaou (eds.), *Christianity, Democracy, and the Shadow of Constantine*

George E. Demacopoulos and Aristotle Papanikolaou (eds.), *Orthodox Constructions of the West*

Aristotle Papanikolaou and George E. Demacopoulos (eds.), *Orthodox Readings of Augustine* [available 2020]

John Chryssavgis and Bruce V. Foltz (eds.), *Toward an Ecology of Transfiguration: Orthodox Christian Perspectives on Environment, Nature, and Creation*. Foreword by Bill McKibben. Prefatory Letter by Ecumenical Patriarch Bartholomew.

Lucian N. Leustean (ed.), *Orthodox Christianity and Nationalism in Nineteenth-Century Southeastern Europe*

John Chryssavgis (ed.), *Dialogue of Love: Breaking the Silence of Centuries*. Contributions by Brian E. Daley, S.J., and Georges Florovsky.

Georgia Frank, Susan R. Holman, and Andrew S. Jacobs (eds.), *The Garb of Being: Embodiment and the Pursuit of Holiness in Late Ancient Christianity*

Ecumenical Patriarch Bartholomew, *In the World, Yet Not of the World: Social and Global Initiatives of Ecumenical Patriarch Bartholomew*. Edited by John Chryssavgis. Foreword by Jose Manuel Barroso.

Ecumenical Patriarch Bartholomew, *Speaking the Truth in Love: Theological and Spiritual Exhortations of Ecumenical Patriarch Bartholomew*. Edited by John Chryssavgis. Foreword by Dr. Rowan Williams, Archbishop of Canterbury.

Ecumenical Patriarch Bartholomew, *On Earth as in Heaven: Ecological Vision and Initiatives of Ecumenical Patriarch Bartholomew*. Edited by John Chryssavgis. Foreword by His Royal Highness, the Duke of Edinburgh.

www.ingramcontent.com/pod-product-compliance
Lightning Source LLC
Chambersburg PA
CBHW032026290426
44110CB00012B/687